D0919862

STUDIES IN INTERNATIONAL POLITICAL ECONOMY
Stephen D. Krasner, Editor
Ernst B. Haas, Consulting Editor

Ruling the Waves

RULING THE WAVES

The Political Economy of International Shipping

Alan W. Cafruny

Library
Lakeland College

UNIVERSITY OF CALIFORNIA PRESS
Berkeley · Los Angeles · London

University of California Press
Berkeley and Los Angeles, California

University of California Press, Ltd.
London, England

© 1987 by
The Regents of the University of California

Library of Congress Cataloging-in-Publication Data
Cafruny, Alan W.
  Ruling the waves.
  (Studies in international political economy)
  Bibliography: p.
  Includes index.
  1. Merchant marine.   2. Shipping.   3. Shipping
conferences.   4. Maritime law.   I. Title.   II. Series.
HE735.C34 1987   387.5'1   86-30889
ISBN 0-520-05968-9 (alk. paper)

Printed in the United States of America

1   2   3   4   5   6   7   8   9

387.51
C 129r

For my son, Daniel

Many the wonders but nothing walks stranger than man.
He crosses the sea in the winter's storm,
making his path through the roaring waves.

Sophocles

He who commands the sea commands the trade routes of the
world. He who commands the trade routes, commands the
trade. He who commands the trade, commands the riches of
the world, and hence the world itself.

Sir Walter Raleigh

CONTENTS

LIST OF TABLES AND FIGURES

Tables

Figures

ACKNOWLEDGMENTS

In writing this book I have benefited greatly from the help of colleagues and family. Peter Katzenstein provided encouragement and scholarly perspective throughout the course of my research and writing. I owe him a large debt. Susan Strange's interpretation of America's role in the world economy has influenced my treatment of the topic of international shipping, and her comments and criticisms have been very helpful. Robert Keohane generously offered valuable insights. Mark Zacher read the manuscript twice, and I was fortunate to benefit from his considerable knowledge of the shipping industry and regimes in general. Stephen Krasner, as series editor, offered astute comments and criticism and helped me to sharpen the theoretical framework of the book. My father, Edward J. Cafruny, carefully read and commented on an early draft of the manuscript. Individually and collectively these people have influenced the course of my work, but none bears the responsibility for my interpretations or conclusions.

I would also like to thank numerous shipping executives, politicians, government and trade union officials, and journalists on both sides of the Atlantic for giving me the opportunity to hear their views on a complex and fascinating industry. Finally, Naomi Schneider, Mary Renaud, and Jane-Ellen Long of the University of California Press worked very hard on various aspects of this book, for which I am grateful.

Research for this book was supported, in part, by a fellowship from the Institute for the Study of World Politics, the University of Virginia Summer Grants, and a research grant from the White Burkett Miller Center of the University of Virginia. Portions of this book were published in *International Organization* 39 (Winter 1985).

LIST OF ABBREVIATIONS

ASEAN	Association of Southeast Asian Nations
BDI	Bundesverband der deutschen Industrie (Association of Federal German Industry)
CAACE	Comité des Associations d'Armateurs des Communautés Européennes (Committee of National Shipowners of the EC)
CASL	Confederation of American Shipping Lines
CASO	Council of American Flag Ship Operators
CBI	Confederation of British Industry
CCAF	Comité Central des Armateurs de France
CENSA	Council of European and Japanese National Shipowners Associations
CGM	Compagnie Générale Maritime
c.i.f.	Cost, insurance, freight; exporter indication of a quoted price that includes the cost of shipping cargo to its ultimate destination and the cost of insurance
CSG	Consultative Shipping Group, the intergovernmental grouping of Western European countries and Japan
dwt	One unit of measurement of ship size; refers to weight in long tons of cargo, fuel, stores, etc. that the ship can carry at maximum load level
EC	European Community
ECLA	Economic Commission for Latin America
EEC	European Economic Community
ELMA	Empresa Lineas Maritimas Argentinas
ESC	European Shippers Council
EUSC	Effective United States control (of flags of convenience)

FACS	Federation of American Controlled Shipping
FMB	*See* FMC
FMC	Federal Maritime Commission (succeeded Federal Maritime Board, FMB, in 1961)
f.o.b.	Free on board; exporter indication of a quoted price that includes only the cost of loading a shipment on a vessel designated by the importer
FOC	Flag of convenience
GATT	General Agreement on Tariffs and Trade
GCBS	General Council of British Shipping
grt	One unit of measurement of ship size; refers to cubic capacity, rather than weight; 100 cubic feet of permanently enclosed space equals one gross ton
ILC	International Law Commission
IMCO	Intergovernmental Maritime Consultative Organization (changed to International Maritime Organization, IMO, in 1982)
IMO	*See* IMCO
INSA	International Shipowners Association (shipping firms of the Eastern bloc states, Cuba, and India)
LAFTA	Latin America Free Trade Area
LDCs	Less developed countries
MARAD	U.S. Maritime Administration (located in the Department of Transportation)
MNC	Multinational corporation
MTC	*See* OECD
NATO	North Atlantic Treaty Organization
NIEO	New International Economic Order
NIMO	New International Maritime Order
OECD	Organization for Economic Cooperation and Development (Maritime Transport Committee, MTC, is responsible for OECD shipping affairs)
OEEC	Organization for European Economic Cooperation (changed to Organization for Economic Cooperation and Development, OECD, in 1961)
OPEC	Organization of Petroleum Exporting Countries
TSCL	Trans-Siberian Container Link

UMA	*See* UMCC
UMCC	United Maritime Consultative Council
UNCTAD	United Nations Conference on Trade and Development
VDR	Verband deutscher Reeder (German Shipowners Association)

INTRODUCTION

As a basic infrastructure of international trade, shipping is a key source of power in world politics. The industry is an independent producer of wealth, an important lever of national economic development, and a crucial element of military power. Although conflicts over shipping have repeatedly reflected general crises in world politics, shipping is a relatively neglected area of study in international relations.

This book describes the rise and fall of a succession of shipping regimes, beginning with the freedom-of-the-seas regime organized by the Netherlands and defended by Hugo Grotius. It presents a detailed analysis of the post–World War II system of international shipping and offers an explanation for major changes that have taken place as a result of challenges to the system. These challenges began in the 1960s, expanded in the 1970s, and continue into the present decade. The book is based on the assumption, prevalent in recent literature on international relations, that conflict in international regimes is an expression of the crisis resulting from the erosion of American hegemony over the international political economy.

My use of the term *political economy* in this study has specific implications for the analysis of shipping. It is possible, and often useful, to divide the study of shipping into economic and political components, using *economics* and *politics* to depict separate, albeit interacting, spheres of reality. From this perspective the *politics* of shipping refers to the intrusion of state power into shipping markets; merchant shipping is characterized as an instrument of national security and self-determination.[1] Developments in

---

1. Neo-mercantilist conceptions of shipping are advanced most forcefully by Third World spokesmen. The classic formulation can be found in L. M. S. Rajwar et al., *Shipping and Developing Countries* (New York: Carnegie Endowment for International Peace, 1971). Stephen Krasner distinguishes between economic and political motivations behind the Third World's

shipping are explained in terms of state objectives. The state is considered to be an autonomous actor, constrained primarily by the international distribution of power. The strength of this perspective lies in its treatment of politics as central to change and conflict in shipping. However, in emphasizing the role of formal institutions and the bargains struck between actors, it does not pay sufficient attention to the informal but no less significant structures of power inherent to the marketplace or to "issues" that seldom reach the bargaining table and cannot be resolved within existing political and economic structures.

Shipping *economics* refers to the operations of the global marketplace for the transportation of commodities. It seeks to explain events in terms of the constraints imposed by the market on shipowners, shippers, and governments. Technological innovation serves as an especially powerful engine of change, because it affects the competitiveness of various shipping firms and competing modes of transportation. Knowledge of shipping markets is essential for the analysis of international shipping because the marketplace does greatly influence the behavior of all relevant actors.

Yet the study of shipping reveals that the separation of economics and politics is analytical, and not real. Economics and politics are not self-contained arenas of social reality. The existence of a market for shipping services presupposes national and international power structures. At times it reinforces these structures; at other times it undermines them. Technological progress unfolds according to a logic that is incremental and scientific, but it also reflects power relations among people and states. Market forces are sometimes overwhelmed by the use of power, yet the market also sharply delimits the actions of states. The market is a creation of politics, but it also resists governmental attempts to arrest its destabilizing impact on international relations.

Shipping is a dynamic and highly conflictual system of international relations. It is currently experiencing structural change arising from internal or regime-specific factors and also from more general shifts in the international division of labor. Thus shipping is ultimately part of a deeper cri-

---

drive for a New International Economic Order. He argues that "control" rather than wealth is the primary objective, although control implies a degree of wealth; see "Transforming International Regimes: What the Third World Wants and Why," *International Studies Quarterly* 25 (March 1981); and also Krasner, *Structural Conflict: The Third World Against Global Liberalism* (Berkeley and Los Angeles: University of California Press, 1985).

sis of the postwar order, involving conflict between North and South, East and West, and among Europe, America, and Japan. As the chairman of the Council of European and Japanese National Shipowners Associations (CENSA) recently warned, revealing the great tensions that have arisen between Europe and America over shipping, "I hope . . . our American friends will reject . . . go it alone policies on the important issue of shipping which represents an essential feature of the Western Alliance; if they do not, it will be a serious blow to the very fabric of that Alliance."[2]

The maritime industries are notoriously sensitive to the cyclical fluctuations of world trade, the effects of which are rapidly transmitted to shipping and shipbuilding, with devastating results. The generalized crisis of shipping which this book addresses developed independently of the cyclical tendencies of international trade. Yet the crisis has been deepened by the protracted slump in freight markets following the oil crisis of 1973–74, from which shipping has not recovered. A global shipping economist for the Chase Manhattan Bank has succinctly described the pressing problems confronting shipowners, bankers, governments, and workers:

Indeed, across the whole spectrum of the shipping market—with the possible exception of pure car carriers, but most assuredly including the liner trades— ocean transportation is being provided today not merely at less than its full cost, but at freight rates which barely cover fuel and labour expenses alone. The amount of capital invested in cargo-carrying ships is at least twice what it was 10 years ago and market interest rates are virtually double what they were in 1973; yet vessel earnings, after payment of direct running costs, add up to billions of dollars less per year than they did in 1973.[3]

At the end of 1983, approximately one-fifth of world shipping tonnage was idle, representing more than 150 million deadweight tons. Shipbuilding output plunged from a peak of 34 million gross registered tons (grt) in 1975 to 9 million grt in 1980, recovering only to 12 million tons in 1984. At various times throughout the past decade Japanese shipyards have had a capacity in excess of global demand.[4]

The proliferation of protectionist measures in shipping recalls the maritime nationalism of the 1930s. But the current crisis of shipping is much

2. Quoted in *Fairplay International Shipping Weekly* 276 (16 July 1981), p. 5.
3. Peter Douglas, "Let's Focus on Freight Rates!" *Seatrade* (February 1984), p. 112.
4. UNCTAD, *Review of Maritime Transport, 1984* (Geneva: United Nations, 1985); OECD, Maritime Transport Committee, *Maritime Transport, 1984* (Paris: OECD, 1985).

more serious. Today's crisis is generalized, rather than being limited to the great powers. Brazil and South Korea are among the world's leading ship-building nations, and many Third World countries are developing sizable merchant fleets. Moreover, in contrast to the experience of the 1930s, during the 1970s and early 1980s shipping tonnage was not reduced in proportion to the slowdown in the expansion of world trade or the tre-mendously increased productive capacity of vessels. During the 1930s, shipping did experience overcapacity. However, the imbalance between supply and demand during the interwar years was relatively mild by today's standards, especially when it is recalled that in absolute terms international trade declined dramatically during the Great Depression. Today, both gov-ernments and the steel industry are subsidizing shipbuilding, artificially in-creasing the demand for ships. Shipping firms, in turn, are receiving mas-sive government support, further exacerbating the crisis of overcapacity in shipping. Ironically, the surplus capacity in ocean transportation may con-tribute to the expansion of world trade, since it has resulted in a decline in the cost of transportation.[5]

Do prevailing theories of international relations adequately explain events in shipping? At the outset, I considered that the theory of hege-monic stability was the one most likely to apply. The theory of hegemonic stability, though not unassailable, provides a plausible explanation for basic changes in the history of international relations.[6] It posits that liberal leaders preside over open trading orders, with help from their friends. When hegemony declines, periods of economic nationalism and war en-sue. The theory also provides a persuasive general explanation for basic trends in the history of shipping: the Grotian doctrine of freedom of the seas expressed the interest of ascendant Dutch commerce; the Navigation Acts spearheaded Britain's mercantilist challenge to Dutch hegemony; and

5. According to the International Trade Commission, freight rates as a percentage of value declined by 25 percent between 1977 and 1983. This decline accounted for 27 per-cent of the real growth of United States imports. See the *Journal of Commerce*, 12 October 1983, p. 5.

6. See esp. Charles P. Kindleberger, *The World in Depression, 1929—1939* (Berkeley and Los Angeles: University of California Press, 1973); Stephen Krasner, "State Power and the Structure of International Trade," *World Politics* 28 (April 1976); Robert Gilpin, *U.S. Power and the Multinational Corporation* (New York: Basic Books, 1975). For a critique of the the-ory, see Timothy J. McKeown, "Hegemonic Stability Theory and Nineteenth Century Tariff Levels in Europe," *International Organization* 37 (Winter 1983).

the repeal of the Navigation Acts helped to lay the foundation of a new era of free trade under British leadership.

Despite the uniquely transnational character of this industry in which, perhaps more than any other, sovereignty is held at bay, shipping vividly exemplifies the national economic rivalries inherent in international relations. I have concluded that there is a strong correlation between growing maritime conflict and the political processes anticipated by the general theory of hegemonic stability. However, my interpretation of the theory differs from standard accounts in two ways. First, most studies have hypothesized a connection between hegemonic ascendancy and free trade. My analysis concludes that although this hypothesis is correct with reference to historical shipping regimes, in the twentieth century hegemony is related to stability, but not necessarily to free trade. Laissez-faire in shipping died during the 1880s, as the industry became cartelized. Moreover, there is no consensus among economists on the definition of *free trade* in shipping. Since the mid-1960s there has been no straightforward tendency toward closure. Indeed, in response to American pressure, in important respects the industry is becoming more competitive.

Second, most students of hegemonic stability have emphasized the relationship between the loss of American power and the growth of international economic conflict, assuming that there is a demonstrable trend toward international pluralism and that cooperation within pluralist systems is problematic. This study, however, makes a fundamental distinction between the "politics of hegemony" and the "politics of power." Hegemonic leadership includes, inter alia, a measure of restraint and accommodation on the part of the leader. The politics of hegemony reduce and temper the impact of America's internal politics on the regime. However, in the politics of power America's still-preponderant position means that international regimes are directly influenced by what happens in Washington. The forceful projection of American interests produces great conflict among advanced industrial states.

The theory of hegemonic stability challenges the observer to show connections between the data and the structure of international power. In particular, it places a spotlight on the relationship between international regime change and the degree and nature of American power. Although I have tried to show how basic changes in the shipping industry have been closely related to power shifts, I hasten to add that the structure of power has not, in the strict sense, *determined* the *nature* of the regime. The legacy of the past—conceived as the accumulation of ideas and institutions, both national and international—has operated as a powerful constraint on policymakers and shipowners. After World War II, the United States inherited a massive complex of rules, procedures, and traditions, largely reflecting Britain's imprint, that had developed over the past century. The whole shipping regime could hardly have been swept aside and replaced by a *tabula rasa,* regardless of the extent of American power. To paraphrase Marx, changes in power relations give birth to new regimes, but each new regime displays birthmarks acquired during the passage from the womb of an older regime. This is perhaps most evident in the system of liner conferences or cartels, which continues to prove highly resilient. The system is not an American design, nor has it been particularly congenial to American ideas or interests. Nevertheless, it is a system to which the United States has had to adapt and onto which American power has had to be grafted.

The theory of hegemonic stability does account for basic trends in shipping. However, the theory is an extremely blunt instrument. Use of power structure as the sole independent variable would greatly limit the explanatory and empirical scope of this study.[7] An emphasis on the political processes of declining hegemony suggests that domestic structures must be included as an important determinant of change in shipping. The interplay of domestic and international structures produces specific outcomes in shipping. The extent to which domestic structures influence the nature of the regime increases as American hegemony wanes and the regime becomes more anarchical.

Comparison of differential rates and patterns of change in the two basic sectors of shipping reveals disparate outcomes that are useful in the evaluation of alternative theories. *Bulk shipping* transports raw materials, including oil (liquid bulk) and dry bulk. *Liner shipping* carries manufactured goods and some other products, such as fruits, that require packaging. Po-

---

7. As Kenneth Waltz, a leading proponent of structural explanations, observes, "Is structure . . . an empty concept? Pretty much so, and because it is it gains in elegance and power. Structure is certainly no good on detail. Structural concepts, although they lack detailed content, help to explain some big, important, and enduring patterns" (*Theory of International Politics* [Reading, Mass.: Addison-Wesley, 1979], p. 70).

litical outcomes in these sectors diverge. In bulk shipping, on the one hand, the postwar regime established under the auspices of the United States has remained stable, despite challenges. This stability reflects the continuing predominance of the American state and corporations. In liner shipping, on the other hand, the United States originally accepted a regime favorable to Western Europe. Although this regime ran counter to American interests, narrowly conceived, it was tolerated because it helped to foster systemic stability. As U.S. hegemony has eroded, the United States has passively accepted and at times participated in the assault on this sector of the postwar regime, provoking serious conflict within the Western Alliance.

Of course, the descriptive account of shipping presented in this study is guided by theoretical concerns. The shipping industry is extremely complex, and generalizations about it are hazardous. The selection and presentation of evidence is itself an interpretive task. This will be particularly evident not only to shipping economists but also to the international civil servants in Geneva who address a range of shipping questions of direct relevance to less developed countries (LDCs). The concept of hegemony has led me, unlike many observers, to focus on the policies and actions of the United States as the central factors in the political economy of the regime. In my view the prevailing emphasis on developments within the United Nations Conference on Trade and Development (UNCTAD) and the challenge emanating from the Third World overstates the salience of North-South conflict and neglects the significance of rivalry among advanced industrial states, and especially between Europe and America. I view Atlantic shipping rivalry as the primary axis of global shipping conflict.

To be sure, America has been bedeviled by maritime backwardness for over a century. The history of shipping relations since 1945 reflects America's attempt to come to terms with an industry traditionally dominated by the maritime powers of Western Europe. Nevertheless, in contrast to most analysts, I argue that America's power, not its weakness, in international shipping is the most significant element in explaining the instability in shipping that has been growing since the mid-1960s. This power has been obscured at various times by the legal fiction of flags of convenience (FOCs), by the inability to develop a consistent U.S. maritime policy, and by the willingness to make concessions to trading partners. The lack of policy coherence and the resulting instability in some sectors of international shipping are, however, manifestations of American power. They are also symptoms of hegemonic decline, or of the inability to devise multilateral solutions to conflict that promote stability without harming the competitive position of the United States economy. In recent years a number of scholars taking various theoretical perspectives have pointed to the ways in which United States actions and policies have fomented international economic instability.[8] This analysis of international shipping is consistent with such interpretations.

In Chapter 1, I present a definition of *regime* and discuss the implications of the concept for the study of international relations. A regime may be defined in terms of the practices of the leading states which, in turn, inspire principles and norms. The concept of regime aids in rigorous description of the dependent variable of this study: change in international shipping. A postwar or Atlantic regime for shipping was established as one element of America's reconstitution of the international political economy. The principles and practices of this regime are now subject to challenge by all parties, including the United States.

In the second part of Chapter 1, I present an interpretation of the theory of hegemonic stability and suggest how the theory might be applied to shipping. The distinction between *power* and *hegemony* is crucial to the theory and necessary for an appreciation of the central role played by American power and interest in the postwar period. The theory of hegemonic stability is commonly assumed to be a systemic or international-level approach to international relations, as distinguished from a reductionist or domestic-level approach. However, the theory contains implicit assumptions concerning the role of domestic politics in the making of foreign economic policy, so that the analysis of domestic structures is necessary for the comprehensive explanation and description of change in the regime.

Chapter 2 reviews the history of shipping in modern international relations. Historically, control over merchant shipping has been a necessary condition for economic and military success. Shipping policies can best be

8. These interpretations have focused on international monetary policy, but they have emphasized the relationship between monetary policy and trade, viewing monetary policy as the main element of U.S. foreign economic policy. See esp. David P. Calleo, *The Imperious Economy* (Cambridge, Mass.: Harvard University Press, 1982); Riccardo Parboni, *The Dollar and Its Rivals: Recession, Inflation, and International Finance* (London: New Left Books / Verso, 1981); and Giovanni Arrighi, "A Crisis of Hegemony," in Samir Amin et al., *Dynamics of Global Crisis* (New York: Monthly Review Press, 1982).

described as derivatives of broader commercial and security policies. Shipping has conformed to general patterns of economic and political relations and to the needs of states and firms to trade and to conduct war. Within these broad limits, developments in shipping have played an important role, significantly modifying general patterns of world politics. The history of shipping confirms the utility of the concept of regime. Mercantilist and freedom-of-the-seas regimes have corresponded to cycles of hegemonic ascendancy and decline. The Atlantic regime represented the partially successful reestablishment of a maritime order out of the chaos of the interwar years. The history of shipping demonstrates close relationships between technological innovation and domestic and international conflict.

Part II describes the establishment of a relatively stable postwar regime guided by the principle of privatization and identifies the main contradictions that developed within it. The regime is described in terms of its two major components: Chapter 3 details the compromise reached between Europe and America in the organization of the liner sector; Chapter 4 describes the creation of an American-dominated raw materials network, in which bulk shipping played an important role. Flags of convenience were established and defended by the United States government and raw-materials multinationals, and they served to underwrite American predominance in this sector.

Part III describes the growth of international conflict in shipping beginning in the mid-1960s. Chapters 5 through 7 deal with the liner sector. Here conflict has been sharpest and the Third World challenge has been strongest, producing tangible results in the form of legal and institutional changes embodied in the movement from privatization to regulation. Such changes reflect the partial accommodation of Third World demands. Chapter 5 describes the erosion of the postwar compromise, detailing the conflicts of interest that developed, and Chapter 6 assesses the nature of the Soviet-bloc and Third World challenges to the regime. It concludes that Soviet maritime policy is relatively insignificant in terms of regime change; it produces global tensions primarily because it accentuates conflict among Western states. The Third World challenge is much more significant, despite the fact that only a handful of Third World countries have achieved even limited gains, largely because of opportunities created by divisions between America and Europe. Chapter 7 analyzes the formation of United States liner shipping policy, emphasizing the relationship between domestic politics and the changes in America's global role. Despite ideological and legal differences, America and the Third World have been unwitting collaborators in the demise of the postwar regime in this sector.

Chapter 8 evaluates Europe's attempt to fashion a political response to the political challenges posed by the Third World and the United States and the commercial challenge of Soviet and Soviet-bloc merchant fleets. Through European Community policy, individual states have sought to reduce instability, reverse the decline of shipping tonnage, and, in some cases, profit from the establishment of a more nationalistic regime. American power, however, has precluded European attempts to defend the status quo. Divisions among the major maritime powers—France, Britain, and West Germany—have further impeded the development of EC policy.

Chapter 9 examines the future of international liner shipping. It argues that the significance of Third World progress should not be overestimated, despite the passage of UNCTAD's Code of Conduct for Liner Conferences. The role of the European Community in global shipping is largely defensive, whereas Japan, although a key actor in the regime, continues to avoid playing a prominent role in international shipping politics. The U.S. Shipping Act of 1984 signaled America's determination to increase its influence over the regime. Change and instability in liner shipping are likely to continue, not only because of deep cleavages over which regime will be appropriate, but also because change in the regime serves important United States interests. Yet this instability also betokens a loss of American hegemony. In liner shipping, industrial weakness discourages the United States from pursuing multilateral solutions. At the same time, the United States is sufficiently powerful that it can implement parochial policies, restructuring the international regime in accordance with narrowly defined national interests.

Chapter 10 discusses the Third World's recent efforts to abolish the flag of convenience, the key institution in the bulk sector, where change has been minimal. Concessions to the Third World have not been made and are unlikely in the future. The relative stability of this sector reflects America's continuing investment in the status quo.

PART ONE

Global Shipping Regimes: Theory and History

1

The Crisis of Hegemonic Decline

It would be difficult to exaggerate the significance of merchant shipping in the evolution of international relations. Historically, questions of merchant shipping have preoccupied government officials; maritime policies have been at the center of mercantilism, imperialism, and war. Since the time of Grotius, the legal foundations of international order have been closely related to the needs of international shipping. The study of shipping reveals that the distinction between trade policy and foreign policy is an artificial one.

Merchant shipping is, by definition, an international business. This distinguishes it from most other areas of economic activity. The cosmopolitan features of the *Torrey Canyon*, an oil tanker that sank off the British coast in 1967, illustrate the great mobility of labor and capital in shipping. The *Torrey Canyon* was owned in Bermuda but registered in Liberia. She was under long-term lease to the Union Oil Company of California but had been subleased to British Petroleum to transport oil from Kuwait to Britain. The ship was built in the United States but significantly modified in a Japanese shipyard. Insurance was bought from Lloyds of London. The captain and crew were Italian.[1] The entrepreneurial character of shipping is respected even by the Soviet Union, whose shipping firms compete vigorously in international freight markets. During the late 1970s the president of Morflot America, a subsidiary of Sovinflot, the Soviet's "multinational" shipping ministry, was a graduate of the United States Merchant Marine Academy who had previously served as the president of Grace Lines and as executive vice president of Seatrain Lines.[2]

Yet the international character of shipping has not caused a withering away of the state. Despite the major investments of private capital and the free-enterprise ethos, the state has always maintained a strong presence in shipping. The nature of this presence has varied in different historical periods and among states. The apparent contradiction between business internationalism and state intervention can be resolved through the proposition that the unique vulnerability experienced by shipowners in international markets and their inability to retreat behind protective national walls have demanded the active involvement of the state in the affairs of the shipping industry. Internationalism and nationalism in shipping are mutually reinforcing tendencies.

International Shipping Regimes

Since 1880 the international shipping industry has been dominated by transnationally organized cartels. Today, in the bulk sector, multinational firms control raw-materials markets; control of cargoes enables these firms to dominate, albeit not control totally, the transportation of raw materials. In the liner sector, shipping conferences hold sway, although their power has weakened somewhat in recent years. In both sectors, however, the behavior of firms is conditioned by state power; the political economy of shipping cannot be reduced to the analysis of oligopolistic competition. The concept of regime is adopted in this study because it provides a framework for describing the intrusion of states into markets as they attempt to pursue strategies that resolve international conflicts and simultaneously enhance national economic and political interests. Today, virtually all commercial activity in shipping is viewed by one or more states as political.

1. Samuel A. Lawrence, *International Sea Transport: The Years Ahead* (Lexington, Mass.: D. C. Heath, 1972), pp. 19–20.
2. Herbert E. Meyer, "The Communist Internationale Has a Capitalist Accent," *Fortune* 45 (February 1977), pp. 134–39.

Government officials and shipowners often use the term *regime* to refer to their understanding of the nexus between international politics and markets. The concept of regime also helps to identify and compare periods in the historical development of shipping. In recent years, this concept has been applied to the study of various areas or sectors of the world political economy, including monetary relations, trade, control of various commodities, and North-South relations. *Regimes* can be defined as "sets of explicit or implicit principles, norms, rules, and decision-making procedures around which actor expectations converge."[3] There is little scholarly agreement concerning the scope and significance of regimes. Some have conceived of regimes as operating in a restricted area of world politics, pertaining only to those activities occurring outside the sphere of economic and political power. Traditional approaches (both realist and Marxist) view regimes as reflections of the balance of power within the international system in general or within particular functional areas governed by regimes. Some have argued that international regimes can be studied as social and politicoeconomic structures having a relatively high degree of autonomy from the overall distribution of power. Even for these analysts, however, power is a crucial element in regimes. Regimes, therefore, are worth studying not because they challenge "power politics as usual" but because they operate within its sphere. The study of regimes thus identifies the limits of purely contractual, as opposed to power-oriented, behavior in international relations.[4]

3. Stephen D. Krasner, "Structural Causes and Regime Consequences: Regimes as Intervening Variables," in Krasner, ed., *International Regimes, International Organization* (special issue) 36 (Spring 1982), p. 186.

4. For various approaches to the concept of regime, see Krasner, ed., *International Regimes*. See also Robert O. Keohane and Joseph S. Nye, *Power and Interdependence: World Politics in Transition* (Boston: Little, Brown, 1977); Oran Young, "International Regimes: Problems of Concept Formation," *World Politics* 32 (April 1980); and Ernst Haas, "Why Collaborate? Issue Linkage and International Regimes," *World Politics* 32 (April 1980). Finlayson and Zacher contend that "scholars study regimes because they are interested in trends and behavior that diverge from what is presumed to exist in the 'traditional' interstate system. Given this, it is desirable to equate regimes with regulatory systems in which 'interdependence norms' are prominent, and to analyze the strength or autonomy of regimes in terms of the importance of interdependence norms" (Jock A. Finlayson and Mark W. Zacher, "The GATT and the Regulation of Trade Barriers: Regime Dynamics and Functions," *International Organization* 35 [Autumn 1981], p. 565). However, most approaches have been closer to a structuralist or realist position, in which regimes reflect the international distribution of power. Yet Krasner asks, "If regimes alter not just calculations of interest and the weight of power but also the interests and capabilities that underlie these calculations and

Use of the concept of regime in this study does not imply a normative preference for elements of order that can be identified or celebrated in an otherwise anarchical international society. The identification of order or stability in a regime, be it international or national, can be used to lend ideological support to existing power structures. Order and stability are not always desirable goals and must be evaluated in terms of consequences for particular states, classes, and individuals.[5] This study employs the concept of regime as a neutral or descriptive aid; it directs analysts to focus on long-term patterns of development rather than on discrete historical episodes.[6] Used in this fashion, it can provide a common focus for scholarship from varying theoretical perspectives. It implies neither legitimacy nor that regimes are nonpolitical, and hence desirable. On the contrary, this study shows that the structure of international shipping, including even quite technical business practices, is closely tied to particular national interests and the pursuit of power.

International shipping regimes are systems of belief that legitimize certain practices and proscribe others. Stephen Krasner has defined regimes in terms of principles, norms, rules, and decision-making procedures:

> Principles are beliefs in fact, causation, and rectitude. Norms are standards of behavior defined in terms of rights and obligations. Rules are specific prescriptions or proscriptions for action. Decision-making procedures are prevailing practices for making and implementing collective choice.[7]

International regimes, like domestic ones, contain normative assumptions that justify legal and customary practices. Some scholars view norms and principles as primarily philosophical; others consider them as ideological justifications of the status quo.

The determination of regime change, as opposed to changes within a regime, depends on the theoretical orientation and analytical purposes of

---

weights, have not principles, norms, rules, and decision-making procedures become confounded with more conventional variables?" ("Regimes and the Limits of Realism," in Krasner, ed., *International Regimes*, pp. 509–10).

5. Mark Kesselman, "Order or Movement? The Literature of Political Development as Ideology," *World Politics* 26 (October 1973). For a related argument, see Susan Strange, "Cave! Hic Dragones," in Krasner, ed., *International Regimes*.

6. See Robert O. Keohane, "The Theory of Hegemonic Stability and Changes in International Economic Regimes, 1967–1977," in Ole Holsti, Randolph Siverson, and Alexander L. George, eds., *Change in the International System* (Boulder: Westview, 1980), p. 134.

7. Krasner, "Structural Causes and Regime Consequences," p. 186.

the observer: all observers agree that the French Revolution destroyed the old regime, but there is less agreement on whether or to what extent the Nazi seizure of power involved regime change. Liberal theorists of democracy argue that it did; Marxist scholars might argue that it did not. Krasner has claimed that norms and principles provide the "basic defining characteristics of a regime."[8] The abandonment or transformation of principles and norms signifies change of the regime itself. Changes in rules and decision-making procedures, however, involve internal changes in the regime. When practice increasingly diverges from principles and norms, then the regime is weakening.

Although this information is often useful, it is not always applicable. In national and international regimes, practice seldom, if ever, reflects stated principles. In international shipping, for example, the norm that there should be a "genuine link" between the ownership of a vessel and its flag of registry has been accepted by most states and people. Yet today, over one-third of world tonnage in the bulk trades sails under flags of convenience. Historically, few regimes have been considered legitimate by all governments in the international system. And where principles and norms have been perceived as legitimate, they have seldom, if ever, coincided fully with practice. Thus, although changes in principles and norms may be necessary features of regime change, they are not infallible indicators. A careful examination of actual practices is an essential element of the analysis of regime change.

A New International Regime for Shipping?

Historically, change in the international distribution of power has coincided with change in international shipping regimes. Germany's pre–World War I challenge to British maritime power, involving merchant shipping as well as naval rivalry, spelled the end of the relative stability of the freedom-of-the-seas regime. World War II brought to an end a long period of shipping conflict that the Great War failed to resolve. In place of the shipping nationalism of the interwar years, a more cooperative Bretton Woods or Atlantic order emerged, dominated by the United States and Europe and providing opportunities for Japanese shipping and shipbuilding to expand.

8. Ibid., p. 187.

During the 1960s the principles and practices of this regime gradually began to erode. The analytical problems in understanding present shipping politics are indeed formidable. In the absence of war between great powers over the essential features of the international political economy, structural changes are nevertheless occurring. Previously, war periodically swept aside the particular ideas and interests associated with shipping regimes; today, in contrast, the ambiguities of the new order are pronounced. Since there is no sharp break with the past, the distinguishing features of the new regime do not reveal themselves with great clarity. Change is uneven, and unlikely alliances are being formed.

For the purpose of political and economic analysis, it is useful to describe the international shipping regime in terms of its two principal sectors, the bulk sector and the liner sector. The logic of this division becomes evident both in the examination of widely divergent commercial practices and in the analysis of the politics of each sector of the regime. However, it is also useful to describe the regime in terms of its basic constituents: *jurisdiction, technical standards, control of negative externalities, freight rates, market shares,* and *industry promotion.* Of course, national policies and international regulation in one area often affect other areas; in practice the constituent elements overlap. Nevertheless, for the purpose of simplification the constituent elements may be defined as follows.

1. *Jurisdiction,* the law of the sea, is a fundamental issue in shipping. However, at the present time the issue is largely "invisible"; in contrast to disputes involving exploitation of ocean resources, the policy of territorial exclusion is seldom applied to maritime commerce. In the modern era, economic nationalism tends to be expressed not in the exclusion of shipping but, rather, in various direct or indirect policies to protect national flag fleets.

2. *Technical standards* refer to the classification of ships by type and size, for purposes of regulation and insurance. Standards are set by private societies such as the American Bureau of Shipping, Lloyds, and Det-NorskeVeritas.

3. *Control of negative externalities* refers to international regulation of safety and pollution. Such regulation is carried out under the authority of the International Maritime Organization (IMO) as well as national governments.

4. *Freight rates* in shipping are determined by the operation of the inter-

national freight market. However, the market is oligopolistic and is also heavily influenced by national policies. The international regime influences rates by affecting the competitive environment (introducing distortions). States alter the balance of power between shippers and shipowners and regulate the commercial environment by creating, preventing, or controlling oligopolies.

5. *Market shares* refer to the proportion of cargo carried by national flag fleets. The international regime influences market shares primarily by making rules governing access to cargo and vessels. Flag discrimination and cargo reservation protect national flag vessels.

6. *Industry promotion* refers to the mixture of costs imposed and benefits bestowed on national maritime industries. Promotion usually takes the form of subsidies, tax depreciation allowances, and other direct and indirect aids to the maritime industries.

Although the law of the sea encompasses all issues of international shipping and defines, in the broadest sense, the nature of the regime, in the modern era categories 4, 5, and 6 comprise the substantive shipping issues. These issues have been neglected in much shipping literature, yet they generate the basic conflicts among firms and nations. Therefore, this book focuses on categories 4–6; issues falling in categories 1–3 will be examined only when they become issues of "high" international political economy.

The definition of regime change is often quite problematic. The assertion that basic changes have taken place depends, in part, on the theoretical orientation of the observer, as well as on the interpretation of a mass of complex information. Since World War II, the international shipping industry has undergone numerous changes, some quantitative, some qualitative. These changes can be described in terms of legal innovation, institutional development, and the introduction of new ideas and principles. I argue that it is possible to identify a relatively distinct postwar regime, operating from the end of World War II to the mid-1960s, and a new or incipient successor. I base my argument on a definition of regime change that specifies that basic changes occur in both principles and practices. Others might plausibly contend, based on different interpretations, that international shipping has passed through more than two basic phases during the postwar era or, in other words, that changes I deem quantitative are in fact qualitative. For example, the passage of the U.S. Shipping Act of

1984 does seem to prefigure major international changes. This legislation could be said to introduce new developments that are sufficiently radical to merit the label "regime change." I will seek to show, however, that the passage of this legislation is the culmination of trends that began to emerge in the 1960s. Nevertheless, it is to be hoped that the identification of only two regimes does not do unnecessary violence to the complexities of shipping and the evolutionary as well as revolutionary character of change in the industry.

Principles: From Privatization to Regulation

Viewing regimes as sets of principles and practices serves as a method of organizing the descriptive analysis of change in a complex sector such as shipping and also facilitates comparative and historical analysis. The constitutive principle of the postwar regime was *privatization*. Shipping firms, operating largely outside the realm of government intervention, were the key actors in the regime. "Free enterprise" was justified on the grounds that it allowed a true international division of labor in transportation by promoting greater efficiency and thereby lowering the cost of transportation.

The principle of privatization, articulated by spokesmen on both sides of the Atlantic, was reflected in the nature and purpose of international organizations as they related to shipping. Although Atlantic relations were sometimes stormy, the West was united in opposition to the creation of meaningful international organizations that would have jurisdiction over maritime affairs, including business arrangements, safety at sea, pollution, and labor markets. Hence, the role of international organizations was sharply circumscribed during the negotiations over the Intergovernmental Maritime Consultative Organization (IMCO) in the late 1940s. The Western powers refused to permit the establishment of an organization under United Nations auspices that would consider "economic" (meaning political and economic) questions in international shipping. As a result, IMCO was set up as a small, consultative organization limited by its charter to the examination of technical questions.[9] The *Code of Liberalization of Current*

9. On the workings of IMCO, renamed the International Maritime Organization (IMO) in 1982, see Harvey Silverstein, *Superships and Nation States—The Transnational Policies of IMCO* (Boulder: Westview, 1978); and David J. Padwa, "The Curriculum of IMCO," *International Organization* 14 (Autumn 1960).

Invisible Operations, written by the Organization for European Economic Cooperation (OEEC) in 1951, encouraged member states to bring about competition in shipping, and especially to allow free access to vessels and cargoes.[10]

Although the principle of privatization seemed generally to correspond to the concern for promoting an open international economy, the postwar shipping regime was not "liberal" in the classical sense of the term. The private reign of shipowners, most of whom were organized in cartels, greatly restricted the workings of the marketplace. Shipowners from the traditional maritime nations appealed to the doctrine of comparative advantage, contending that the incursions of Third World firms into shipping would require substantial subsidies and that the inefficient allocation of resources would inhibit economic growth. They argued that the domination of the liner trades by shipping cartels was a result of the unrestricted workings of the marketplace. In the bulk trades, shipowners using flags of convenience argued that such flags extended the international division of labor by taking advantage of global sources of cheap labor and thereby further decreasing the real cost of transportation.

The principle of privatization and the economic arguments advanced in its name did not escape challenge. But various states or blocs of states were either too weak to mount an effective challenge or else were willing to accept the principle because it promoted other goals. In the liner trades, both the Third World and some voices in the United States were opposed to privatization, on pragmatic as well as philosophical grounds. Freedom for shipping cartels effectively secured the continuing domination of European liner shipping. However, until the mid-1960s the Third World was too weak and disorganized to attempt to disturb the status quo in any serious way. The United States acquiesced to privatization in the liner sector because change would have been highly disruptive to Atlantic integration, although it did reserve the right to implement limited protectionist measures unilaterally. Moreover, American support for flags of convenience could be expressed in terms of privatization, a matter of great importance.

The principle of privatization was not satisfactory to all states, nor was it universally followed as a guide to behavior. Nevertheless, it served as

10. Henry C. Aubrey, *Atlantic Economic Cooperation: The Case of the OECD* (New York: Council on Foreign Relations, 1967), p. 67. The general principles were extended to the Code of Liberalization of the OECD. See *Code of Liberalization of Current Invisible Operations* (Paris: OECD, 1961), Annex A, note 1.

the organizing principle of the postwar regime. The New International Maritime Order (NIMO) is more difficult to categorize, for two reasons. First, the postwar regime represented a somewhat uneasy modus vivendi among the four major shipping blocs: the Eastern bloc; Western Europe and Japan; the Third World; the United States as a bloc. These blocs, which can be defined in terms of distinctive and contending maritime philosophies, have now broken apart, and no single maritime philosophy seems capable of winning universal acceptance. Second, the dominant actor, the United States, is a highly opportunistic shipping power. It is capable of imposing its preferences on the regime, but it lacks a clear vision of an appropriate new order.

The constitutive principle of the new order is *regulation*. This principle is endorsed in both the Third World and the United States, although for very different reasons. For the Third World, regulation is the natural by-product of a mercantilist solution to the problem of general economic backwardness: state intervention is both a goal in itself and a means to promote a more equitable international division of labor. For the United States, in contrast, regulation is favored in order to break up monopolies and promote marketplace values. Regulation of shipping is, therefore, related to the deregulatory thrust of American domestic and international politics in the 1980s. Shipping is an industry in which the tendency toward monopoly is especially pronounced; it is necessary to regulate in order to produce competition. The Third World seeks to regulate shipping on behalf of consumers as well as the merchant fleet. However, the interest of consumers may contradict the view of shipping as an end in itself.

The UNCTAD Code of Conduct for Liner Conferences

In the mid-1960s serious challenges were issued to the postwar regime on the levels both of principle and of practice. The immediate cause of dissatisfaction was the desire of Third World elites to reform the international shipping industry in accordance with their general developmental strategies. In 1964 the United Nations Conference on Trade and Development (UNCTAD) was established to promote the political and economic aspirations of less developed countries (LDCs). Third World leaders and intellectuals such as Raul Prebisch argued that the structure of shipping, dominated by the West, perpetuated unequal terms of trade. The Group of 77, the coalition of LDCs within UNCTAD, elaborated a shipping program to complement strategies for economic development in trade, finance, and the extraction of natural resources. In 1965 a permanent committee on shipping was established under the directorship of Wladyslaw Malinowski. Shipping thus emerged as an important element in the political and economic programs elaborated by LDCs to achieve a greater measure of control over domestic and international economic activities.

The efforts of the UNCTAD secretariat and the Group of 77 amount to a strategy for a New International Maritime Order. The logic of this order leads to a qualitative change in the nature of government intervention in shipping and to a comparable shift in the nature and role of international organizations as elements within international shipping. Hence the NIMO represents, like the Navigation Acts, "an experiment in social engineering."[11] Statist or neo-mercantilist conceptions of the national interest replace the free market. Although these conceptions have their origins in the aspirations of governments and shipowners in the North, the general principles have been enunciated most systematically and with greatest urgency by the Third World.

Initially, UNCTAD's shipping program focused on the structure of liner shipping. Despite the Third World's heavy involvement in raw-materials trades, spokesmen for LDCs attacked liner conferences for imposing excessively high levels of freight rates, denying Third World lines admission to liner conferences, and excluding them from consultation about issues that affect basic trading strategies and policies.[12] The UNCTAD Code of Conduct for Liner Conferences, passed in 1974 and ratified in 1983 (but not by the United States), allocates 80 percent of cargoes to the vessels of exporting and importing nations. More recently, the UNCTAD secretariat has broadened its program to include the bulk trades. The Third World has sought the abolition of flags of convenience as a condition of Third World fleet development in this sector.[13]

The United States refuses to endorse the UNCTAD Code of Conduct, arguing that its protectionist intent violates both America's stated commit-

11. Lawrence A. Harper, *The English Navigation Laws: A Seventeenth Century Experiment in Social Engineering* (New York: Columbia University Press, 1939).

12. UNCTAD, *Establishment or Expansion of Merchant Marines in Developing Countries*, TC/26/Supp. 1 (Geneva: United Nations, 1967).

13. UNCTAD, *Merchant Fleet Development*, TD/222 (Geneva: United Nations, 1979).

ment to free trade and American commercial interests. Moreover, the United States continues to defend the principle of privatization as it applies to flags of convenience. Nevertheless, during the mid-1960s the U.S. government also began to challenge important elements of the postwar regime. During the 1960s and 1970s opposition to shipping conferences gained ground in the United States: many observers contended that such conferences as then constituted were harmful to American exports and to the development of American liner shipping. The U.S. Shipping Act of 1984 represented the culmination of two decades of legislative efforts to reform liner conferences. The act embodies a very different vision of liner shipping from either privatization or the UNCTAD Code of Conduct, for it seeks to enhance the role of the marketplace. Underlying both the Third World's Code of Conduct for Liner Conferences and the U.S. Shipping Act of 1984, however, is the principle that unregulated shipping conferences are no longer legitimate. Ultimately, the establishment of this principle completes the decline of Europe as the central power in world shipping.

Practices: Changing the Balance of Power
Between Shipping Firms and Shippers

Table 1 indicates the nature of the transition from the postwar regime to the new order. The movement from private regulation or self-regulation to state regulation is evident in each of the substantive constituents of shipping described above and is most pronounced in the liner sector. As both the foregoing discussion and Table 1 indicate, it is not possible to identify a straightforward tendency toward closure or neo-mercantilism. The UNCTAD Code of Conduct embodies the statist proclivities of the Third World, and government intervention in shipping has generally increased; yet a generalized protectionist or bloc-organized regime is unacceptable to the United States, the ultimate arbiter of the regime.

Freight Rates

In the postwar regime, decisions concerning freight rates were made by individual firms. In practice, this meant that rates would be determined by oligopolies: in bulk trades, multinationals would strongly influence rates; in liner trades, shipping conferences or cartels would negotiate rate increases internally. Shippers had little choice but to accept the going rate.

Table 1.   Characteristics of the Postwar Regime and Its Successor

	Postwar (Atlantic) Regime	The New Order (circa 1970)
Organizing Principle	*Privatization*	*Regulation*
	(Self-regulation) Shipping firms are the key actors in the regime.	Power shared between shipping firms and consumers of shipping services (shippers).
Key Practices		
Freight Rates	Conference or oligopolistic decision-making.	National and international regulation of conference decision-making affecting freight rates.
Market Shares	Formally free access to vessels and cargoes. Conferences allocate shares. Conferences possess strong powers to ensure shipper loyalty.	States influence/redistribute market shares through decree (UNCTAD Code of Conduct; national legislation) or through regulation of conference practices (U.S.).
Industry Promotion	Few subsidies or other direct and indirect government aids to the maritime industries.	Substantial government support for maritime industries.

Although independent shipowners acting as outsiders provided some competition, the powers enjoyed by conferences to bind shippers through various "loyalty" contracts ensured that the role played by outsiders would be limited. The transition from privatization to regulation has been greatest in the liner sector. Although conferences continue to set rates, both international (UNCTAD Code) and national laws establish guidelines for freight rates. Even more important, the regulation of conference practices, especially by the United States, provides shippers with stronger countervailing powers.

Market Shares

Before the mid-1960s, conferences regulated market shares through internal allocation of sailings and cargoes. States played only a limited role in determining national shares of cargoes. Power within the conferences was held by the leading firms, most of which were of Western European origin. In practice, this meant that new shipping lines were discouraged from entering trades. Under the new regime, the power of conferences to allocate market shares is restricted by the state in two ways. First, states acting either unilaterally or under the terms of the UNCTAD Code of Conduct implement cargo-sharing legislation, dividing cargoes among the fleets of the trade-generating nations. Second, by regulating conference practices the United States government makes it possible for shippers to select non-conference vessels without fear of commercial retaliation. In the bulk trades, private shipping companies continue to influence market shares. Proposals for cargo-sharing in the bulk trades have not generally been implemented. Recent studies indicate that the large, extractive multinationals are statistically somewhat less important than they were during the 1950s and 1960s as actors in bulk trades, although, given the severity of overtonnaging in recent years, this has had little practical effect on rates (which are below cost) or market shares.

Industry Promotion

As was noted in the Introduction, laissez-faire in shipping died in the nineteenth century. Since that time, all governments have possessed numerous means of promoting national flag merchant fleets. The postwar regime, although by no means classically liberal, was substantially freer than the heavily nationalistic interwar regime, as governments generally resisted the temptation to manipulate the competitive environment for national benefit. Prior to the mid-1960s, governments generally respected the OEEC and the Organization for Economic Cooperation and Development (OECD) Codes and limited the use of subsidies, cargo-reservation schemes, and discriminatory fiscal measures. Notably, the United States was the most significant violator of such proscriptions. Since the mid-1960s, however, most governments have increased promotional efforts substantially.

The 1960s ushered in a period of great change in international shipping. The principles and practices of the postwar regime were overthrown, although no successor regime has become firmly implanted, and conflict in shipping continues to grow. Although great changes have taken place, significant continuities can also be identified. Change and conflict have been greatest in the liner sector. In the bulk trades, despite a great deal of Third

World opposition, flags of convenience continue to flourish and under-write an essentially privatized system.

Explaining Regime Change: Hegemony, Power, and International Shipping

The theory of hegemonic stability is the focus of vigorous scholarly de-bate, yet no definition of the term *hegemony* is generally accepted. At one extreme, scholars follow the Chinese, using *hegemony* to describe the impe-rialist policies of a great power. At the opposite extreme, *hegemony* de-scribes benevolence and the provision of "collective goods." The term gen-erally means dominant power, and evidence adduced for hegemony is often quantitative. In this study I draw a sharp distinction between *power* and *hegemony*. This distinction is given little prominence either in formal models of the theory or in case studies, but it is very important in the analysis of current international conflict.[14]

Hegemony and Power

A system based on the exercise of power alone is unfettered and uncon-cerned with stability. A hegemonic system, however, is one in which the leading actor accepts restraints, orienting policies toward the achievement of systemic stability. The leader practices self-restraint in order to maximize self-interest, granting concessions in order to maintain equilibrium. It can thereby appropriate the lion's share of the gross world product with the cooperation or acquiescence of would-be rivals. This definition reconciles

14. Charles Kindleberger stresses the "burdens" of American hegemony; see *The World in Depression, 1929–1939* (Berkeley and Los Angeles: University of California Press, 1973), esp. pp. 28, 307. See also David P. Calleo, "Systems of International Economic Organization," in Calleo, *Money and the Coming World Order* (New York: New York University Press, 1976), p. 33. Calleo, adopting important elements of the French critique, emphasizes American domination, especially in his work *The Imperious Economy* (Cambridge, Mass.: Harvard Uni-versity Press, 1982). Kindleberger acknowledges that "it is often difficult to distinguish domi-nance from leadership in international economic relations" ("Dominance and Leadership in the International Economy: Exploitation, Public Goods, and Free Rides," *International Studies Quarterly* 25 [June 1981], p. 242). Calleo in turn recognizes systemic benefits of American hegemony; see, for example, Calleo, "American Foreign Policy and American Eu-ropean Studies: An Imperial Bias?" in Wolfram Hanreider, ed., *The United States and Western Europe* (Cambridge, Mass.: Winthrop, 1974).

two opposite approaches to hegemony: as "leadership" in the public-choice tradition, and as "domination" in power politics. Antonio Gramsci encompasses both these perspectives in this comment:

> The fact of hegemony presupposes that account be taken of the interests and the tendencies of the groups over which hegemony is to be exercised, and that a certain compromise equilibrium should be formed—in other words, that the leading group should make sacrifices of an economic-corporate kind. But there is no doubt that such sacrifices and such compromise cannot touch the essential; for though hegemony is ethical-political, it must also be based on the decisive function exercised by the leading group in the decisive nucleus of economic activity.[15]

Recent research has variously sought to establish a correlation between hegemony and stability or between hegemony and free trade. The definition of hegemony I adopt strongly suggests that stability or equilibrium, and not free trade, is the appropriate correlate. A hegemonic system undoubtedly implies a degree of free trade, for the international economy itself or the "free world" portion of it becomes the leader's bloc. However, the scope of free trade must necessarily be limited: given the inevitability of uneven development, restraints on free trade must be tolerated in order to prevent weaker states from defecting from the coalition. The postwar international economic system, for example, was based on a mixture of openness and discrimination against the United States. Under conditions of hegemonic decline the system should also reveal a mixture of openness and closure as states jockey for position without regard to a basic organizing principle; the former leader eschews its concessionary functions and seeks to exploit both power and comparative advantage sector by sector.

15. Antonio Gramsci, *Selections from the Prison Notebooks* (London: Lawrence and Wishart, 1971), p. 161. It should be emphasized that although formal models and empirical studies have generally not distinguished between power and hegemony (implicit in Gramsci's definition), explications of the theory have certainly done so. Bergsten, Keohane, and Nye use the phrase "hegemonic equilibrium" and note that "the systemic orientation natural to hegemonic power, which identifies its interests with those of the system it manages, is challenged by a more nationalistic perspective" (C. Fred Bergsten, Robert O. Keohane, and Joseph S. Nye, "International Economics and International Politics: A Framework for Analysis," *International Organization* 24 [Winter 1975], p. 16). Stephen Krasner notes the tendency for the former hegemonic leader to pursue short-term "consumption goals" at the expense of "investment" objectives; see Krasner's "American Policy and Global Economic Stability," in William P. Avery and David P. Rapkin, eds., *America in a Changing World Political Economy* (New York: Longman, 1982).

The difference between a hegemonic and a non-hegemonic system is not the degree of openness, but that in a hegemonic system the principles and rules of various regimes or sectors facilitate a compromise equilibrium.[16]

The hallmark of hegemonic power is the ability to design foreign and domestic policies that will achieve long-range objectives. The leader must maintain the integrity of the system, renounce the temptation to pursue short-term gains, and help to solve the problems of trading partners. However, as many have noted, hegemonic systems seem to contain an internal contradiction.[17] Policies and regimes that promote systemic goals undermine the leader's position. As Europe and Japan gained strength during the 1960s, American hegemony began to erode. The American attempt to supply generalized benefits (for example, stable money, open markets, military aid) began to weaken the domestic economy and provoke domestic opposition.

Contradictions between domestic and international economic policy objectives thus became increasingly acute. Yet the decline of hegemonic power is not necessarily revealed in the loss of power in specific regimes. On the contrary, power resources not tapped by the hegemonic leader may be brought to bear as its hegemony erodes. Observations of increases or decreases in relative power within a single regime or sector cannot constitute reliable evidence of hegemonic decline. The erosion of hegemony can be proved only by showing a relationship between the policies of the (former) leader and growing systemic instability.

16. John Ruggie terms this mixture of openness and protectionism "embedded liberalism"; see "International Regimes, Transactions, and Change: Embedded Liberalism in the Post-War Economic Order," in Krasner, ed., *International Regimes*. John Conybeare has shown that the pure theory of international trade does not support the contention that a major hegemonic leader such as the United States should rationally seek to establish an open system; see "Public Goods, Prisoner's Dilemmas, and the International Political Economy," *International Studies Quarterly* 28 (March 1984). But the theory of hegemonic stability is not based on the pure theory of international trade; it was, rather, developed in explicit opposition to it. A generally open international economy was (and remains) rational for the United States, which, after World War II, possessed a virtual monopoly on credit, technology, and raw materials, and which sought cheap labor, expanded markets, and a higher rate of return on investment abroad. These factors are problems for the pure theory of international trade, whose logic does suggest, however, the considerable power an open regime confers on major hegemonic powers; for them the cost of closure for the national economy (but not for large banks and multinationals) is relatively low.

17. See esp. Robert Gilpin, *U.S. Power and the Multinational Corporation* (New York: Basic Books, 1975); and Krasner, "Regimes and the Limits of Realism," p. 508.

Many regimes, then, will exhibit an inverse relationship between the decline of hegemony and the projection of power, a relationship that is more evident today than during the interwar period. The decline of British hegemony coincided with a precipitous loss of British power. The interwar system is accurately described as plural, involving a rough balance of power despite Britain's pretensions during the 1920s. This system has provided a rich vein of evidence for those interested in the problem of cooperation among roughly equal actors. However, America's hegemonic decline has resulted in an international structure of power qualitatively different from that of the interwar period. America remains an "extraordinary power," albeit a non-hegemonic one.[18] A fundamental asymmetry exists between the United States and its major economic rivals. This asymmetry, which is increasing under conditions of global recession and economic instability, has major implications for regime change.

One method of applying the theory of hegemonic stability is to define *hegemony* operationally in specific regimes or sectors; as United States hegemony within a particular regime erodes, the regime might be expected to become unstable.[19] This type of analysis suggests a definition of *hegemony* as "dominant power" or "preponderant power" as indicated by possession of resources that are important to the regime or sector. The advantage of this approach is precision: the decline of hegemony can be quantified. But because it uses the terms *hegemony* and *power* interchangeably, it cannot account for a greater projection of power by a declining hegemonic force. Moreover, to define power in terms of resources limits the explanatory and predictive scope of the theory.

This approach, in Robert Keohane's terms, uses a "basic force model" in which power is defined in terms of tangible resources. Tangible resources, however, do not reliably indicate power. For example, in Keohane's analysis of international monetary instability, America's loss of monetary reserves is

18. The phrase and evidence, especially in the monetary sphere, appear in Susan Strange, "Still an Extraordinary Power: America's Role in the Global Monetary System," in Ray Lombra and Bill Witte, eds., *The Political Economy of International and Domestic Monetary Relations* (Ames: Iowa State University Press, 1982).

19. See the following works by Robert O. Keohane: "The Theory of Hegemonic Stability" and "Hegemonic Leadership and U.S. Foreign Economic Policy," in Avery and Rapkin, eds., *America in a Changing World Political Economy;* and *After Hegemony: Cooperation and Discord in the World Political Economy* (Princeton, N.J.: Princeton University Press, 1984), esp. pp. 197–202.

assumed to indicate a significant loss of United States power in the regime. Yet Keohane's explanation for instability has little to do with loss of power as indicated by resources. He argues that the United States had the ability to change the rules of the game (in 1971) and "also had the political power to do so."[20] The "basic force model" does not predict or help to conceptualize America's considerable (if not increased) exploitation of power in international monetary affairs since 1971.

Although most observers have accepted the proposition that American hegemony has declined, a few have drawn attention to significant continuities in the projection of American power. From the vantage point of the mid-1980s, the decline of American power seems neither as precipitous nor as inexorable as it did a decade ago. Bruce Russett, for example, has pointed to "significant continuity in the ability of the United States to get what it wants."[21] Russett calls for more sophisticated measurements of hegemony, while concluding that U.S. hegemony has not in fact vanished. My conception of power is similar to Russett's in that it focuses on outcomes rather than on the power base or tangible resources available to various states. However, although the analysis of outcomes in shipping certainly demonstrates the impressive ability of the United States to "get what it wants," the distinction I draw between hegemony and power provides an alternative to Russett's plea for better measurement. A nation may be extremely powerful in the sense that it can impose its will on other nations without necessarily being hegemonic. Hegemony should be conceived of not as the ability of a state to "get what it wants" in the short term but, rather, as the ability of a hegemonic power to underwrite the cohesion and expansion of a system in which it is the prime long-term beneficiary.

In this analysis, the distinction between structural or overall power and regime- or sector-specific power is useful. Great care must be taken, however, to show the penetration of power from one regime or sector into another. The significance of developments within a regime must be evaluated in terms of impact on a state's overall foreign policy. For example, events in

20. Keohane, "The Theory of Hegemonic Stability," p. 151. Peter Cowhey and Edward Long similarly propose that "the strongest version of the hegemony hypothesis would predict a tight linkage between the decline of American power in the [automobile] sector . . . and regime change"; see their article "Testing Theories of Regime Change: Hegemonic Decline or Surplus Capacity?" *International Organization* 37 (Spring 1983), p. 171.

21. Bruce Russett, "The Mysterious Case of Vanishing Hegemony, Or, Is Mark Twain Really Dead?" *International Organization* 39 (Spring 1985), p. 222.

the trade regime, which is the basic empirical referent in most studies of hegemonic stability, are closely linked to international monetary affairs. Conclusions about the significance of an event in trade such as a protectionist or free-trade trend are of limited value unless viewed in the monetary context of, for example, competitive depreciation or manipulation of the key currency to achieve domestic objectives without regard for international consequences. Today there is a clear trend toward greater state exploitation of the relationship between maritime and general foreign economic policy. This proposition is true not only of the Third World and the Eastern bloc, where it is openly articulated, but also of the OECD and even of traditionally liberal maritime countries.[22]

The approach to power in this book is based on a "force activation model," including an evaluation of opportunity costs and the structural positions of the actors. In its regime-specific dimension, maritime power refers primarily to the performance of national shipping firms. This includes the size and technological sophistication of the national flag fleet and its influence in international shipping cartels. The best indicators of power are carrying capacity and ability to compete in international freight markets (including cross-trading, i.e., carriage of cargo between countries by a third party) without subsidies or government cargo reservation. Maritime power, however, ultimately derives from the domination effect, or national power in its totality, which includes the direct and indirect participa-

---

22. "It is important to appreciate the close connection between political and economic aims in German expansion before the war, since the German mercantile marine was an instrument well-suited for the furtherance of German objects. German shipping was, in fact, the spearhead of German aggression. It was used to force a way into markets to which access would have otherwise been difficult, and so pave the way for German penetration" (United Kingdom, Departmental Committee on Shipping and Shipbuilding, *First Report* [Booth Committee Report], Cmnd. 9092 [London: HMSO, 1918], p. 100). My analysis implies a conception of state-society relations that, indebted to Marxism and realism, is at odds with assumptions that various regimes or sectors contain their own political logic. As Perroux observed: "The elements of the domination effect—bargaining power, size, nature of activity— are therefore transposable to the total aggregate that is the national economy. The aggregate effect is all the more striking because the bargaining power of the State and of the groups within it, the size of the State and that of the groups and firms, the proportion of strategic activities to the whole, instead of neutralizing or contradicting each other, work in the same direction to engender an asymmetric or irreversible influence over other national economies, that is, other aggregate systems" (François Perroux, "An Outline of the Theory of the Dominant Economy," in George Modelski, ed., *Transnational Corporations and World Order: Readings in International Political Economy* [San Francisco: W. H. Freeman, 1979], p. 144).

tion of nationally owned firms in world trade. Maritime power thus also includes financial resources and shipbuilding capacity (including the ability to sponsor ship production elsewhere and to earn the foreign exchange to purchase ships). The structural and regime-specific levels of power cannot be separated, as was recognized in the Convention of the Intergovernmental Maritime Consultative Organization. Its governing council included the eight largest shipping nations (in tonnage) and the eight largest trading nations. Because maritime power involves both these levels, it follows that maritime policies (and power) must be evaluated not only in terms of shipping tonnage under the national flag and its surrogates but also in terms of degree of influence over international freight markets and general conditions of world trade. American maritime power is indicated not by the relative size of its merchant fleet, which varies over time, but, rather, by the overall strength of the American political economy.

International and Domestic Structures

International and domestic-level explanations are often presumed to be analytically distinctive or even contradictory approaches to the study of international relations. An international or systemic explanation generally views change as a function of the interaction among units. Realists emphasize changes in the distribution of power;[23] Marxists seek to relate changes in the distribution of power to the combined but uneven development of national capitals.[24] For the realist tradition and some interpretations of Marxism the nature of particular domestic structures is a secondary concern; national economics and politics are conditioned largely by international processes, although domestic structures may account for lags in the correspondence of foreign policies to international or systemic change. On methodological grounds it has been argued that although domestic structures are, in principle, part of a complete theory of regimes, the inclusion of domestic structures as an explanatory variable would violate the canon of parsimony.[25] A purely domestic analysis, in contrast, seeks to re-

23. See esp. Kenneth Waltz, *Theory of International Politics* (Reading, Mass.: Addison-Wesley, 1979).

24. V. I. Lenin, *Imperialism—The Highest Stage of Capitalism: A Popular Outline* (New York: International Publishers, 1939).

25. Keohane, "The Theory of Hegemonic Stability," p. 135.

duce foreign policy behavior to variables operating within the units of the system. A regime is the product of national policy, which is determined largely by domestic politics. In practice, however, domestic- and international-level explanations are not contradictory, but complementary. An understanding of both systemic and internal forces is necessary for a comprehensive explanation of regime change. Katzenstein, for example, has suggested that

> a selective focus on either the primacy of foreign policy and the internalization of international effects or on the primacy of domestic politics and the externalization of domestic conditions is mistaken. Such a selective emphasis overlooks the fact that the main purpose of all strategies of foreign economic policy is to make domestic politics compatible with the international economy.[26]

Although hegemonic stability is generally assumed to belong to the category of systemic theory, it is preferable to combine the analysis of domestic and international structures. An emphasis on the interplay of these variables is necessary for at least three reasons. First, my interpretation of hegemonic stability rejects a simple openness-closure scheme in which hegemony is associated with openness or free trade and the erosion of hegemony produces a system of protectionist blocs and states. The post–World War II hegemonic system was characterized, above all, by a relative stability or equilibrium; national economies were integrated or "knitted together" not on the basis of free trade but on the basis of mutual accommodation and adjustment. This suggests that regimes must be evaluated in terms of their compatibility with the domestic structures of various states.

Second, the theory of hegemonic stability as I have interpreted it implies important assumptions concerning the relationship between domestic structures and international regimes. Analyzing domestic structures is a necessary step in assessing the validity and utility of the theory. During periods of hegemony, international considerations such as the need for national adjustment, provision of "collective goods," and a long-range focus should prevail over domestic considerations such as demands of particular interest groups in the foreign policy of the hegemonic power. In the case of middle powers, regimes must accommodate at least some of the interests and requirements of the domestic political economy. In the case of the he-

---

26. Peter J. Katzenstein, "Introduction: Domestic Structures and International Forces," in Katzenstein, ed., *Between Power and Plenty: Foreign Economic Policies of Advanced Industrial States* (Madison: University of Wisconsin Press, 1978), p. 4.

gemonic power, domestic forces opposing the regime must be suppressed or bought off. However, as Katzenstein has argued, in the past, "the relative weight of domestic structures in the shaping of foreign economic policy increased in periods of hegemonic decline."[27] This is especially true of the domestic structure of the hegemonic power. Bereft of leadership, states become less willing and able to pursue regime-oriented policies that preserve the integrity of the system. Anarchical or centrifugal tendencies are unleashed.

Finally, the empirical claim concerning the extraordinary and post-hegemonic nature of American power suggests that the domestic politics of the United States maritime sector should intrude much more directly into the international politics of various regimes and sectors. Regimes should bear the sharp imprint of American domestic politics; the study of international economic regimes becomes the study of the global effects of American foreign economic policy.

The United States and the traditional shipping powers of Western Europe are now pursuing quite different maritime policies. Policy conflicts reflect the divergences in the maritime structures that have evolved since the nineteenth century. These structures were determined by the sequence of national entry into international trade, and they reflect national interests at a given stage of development. During hegemonic periods regimes represent a modus vivendi under the patronage of the hegemonic power. International and domestic structures are more or less synchronized. Under conditions of hegemonic decline, however, the role of domestic structures looms larger in the regime, generating conflict. The stronger the power, the greater the impact of its domestic structure on the international regime.

The international structure thus may explain the existence of a *relatively* open (but not necessarily liberal) regime, but it cannot explain or predict how various states respond to the decline of hegemony. The analysis of domestic structures draws attention to explanatory variables within societies that condition differences in national shipping policies and form the basis of present international shipping conflicts. Once the international context is taken into account, the analysis of domestic structures provides a deeper, more comprehensive explanation that accounts for a wider range of data relevant to the analysis of the regime.

The theory of hegemonic stability predicts that international shipping

27. Ibid., p. 11.

should grow increasingly unstable as American hegemony erodes during the 1960s and 1970s. It seeks to explain conflict in terms of a growing rivalry between the United States and its major trading partners. The empirical claim concerning the overwhelming power of the United States and the assumption that power can be translated readily from one regime to another suggest that outcomes in international shipping should reflect American interests, although these interests are conceived more narrowly than previously. The scope and direction of change, if not the rhetoric, should conform to an American agenda. As hegemony erodes, the domestic structures of states become more important in determining the nature of the regime. The domestic structure of the United States, the strongest power, can be expected to have a major influence on international shipping developments.

In areas of the postwar system such as bulk shipping, where the United States did not grant concessions to its trading partners, it can be expected to attempt to maintain the status quo. However, in areas such as liner shipping, where the United States made compromises, it might be expected to prefer change, either through benign neglect in the face of challenges from other forces or by participating in demands for change. A hegemonic power prefers stability and is willing to pay for it, but the strongest power in a non-hegemonic world, plagued by uncertainty about the future and no longer confident of its ability to restore stability, has much to gain from an anarchical environment.

After World War II, the United States confronted a system of shipping that was skewed toward the interests of Western Europe. It modified the system but did not destroy it. In the bulk sector, the United States government and multinational firms established dominance through the creation of flags of convenience, which expressed America's determination to control the global transport of raw materials. In this sector flags of convenience buttressed a competitive shipping policy aimed at the traditional maritime nations, and the United States continues to uphold stability, despite challenges from the Third World. In liner shipping, however, the sector in which manufactured goods are carried, the United States originally accepted practices that involved costs for domestic interests but furthered systemic goals of global economic integration and equilibrium. Provision of "side payments" in this sector illustrates the concessionary nature of hegemonic power. But these concessions proved increasingly onerous for the

United States because they exacerbated balance-of-payments problems. Since the mid-1960s, United States firms and the government have accepted and, indirectly, fomented instability in the liner trades. The Third World agitation in liner shipping, which coincided with changes in American policy, has caused many observers to view UNCTAD as the primary source of change. However, the Third World challenge has gained ground because of opportunities created by the revisionist nature of United States policy and by the ensuing maritime conflict between the United States and Europe.

2

International Maritime Relations: Mercantilism, Freedom, Imperialism

Shipping occupies a central place in the history of international relations. The historical importance of shipping lies in its dual role as creator and guarantor of national trade and as military auxiliary. Historically, issues involving merchant shipping have been at the center of mercantilism, imperialism, and war. The flag follows trade; but the reverse statement is equally valid, as is suggested in the statement attributed to Walter Raleigh, the English pirate, merchant, and navigator: "He who commands the sea commands the trade routes of the world. He who commands the trade routes, commands the trade. He who commands the trade, commands the riches of the world, and hence the world itself."[1]

Shipping is a small industry, but its effect on relations among nations is disproportionately large. In his classic account of Allied shipping organization during World War I, Arthur Salter estimated the pre–World War I value of world merchant shipping to be 300 million pounds, "less than the capi-

---

1. Quoted in Eivinn Berg, "United States/Norway—Partners or Opponents in International Shipping?" *Norwegian Shipping News* 32 (10 December 1976), p. 4.

tal invested in two English railway companies."[2] In 1981 the gross world revenue for merchant shipping was $120 billion, representing 6.6 percent of the value of world seaborne trade.[3] In 1980, the earnings of the United States flag merchant fleet were $7.7 billion, which accounted for 0.003 percent of the gross national product.[4] The shipping industries of the OECD nations employed approximately 385,000 workers in 1983.[5] However, the qualitative significance of shipping to some OECD nations is great: income from merchant shipping has historically accounted for 10 to 20 percent of the foreign exchange earnings of many European countries. Today, 95 percent of world trade is seaborne. Total world carriage of goods by rail equals only one-fifth of the ton-miles of merchant vessels.[6]

The study of shipping highlights the economic bases of modern international warfare. Before the nineteenth century, the organization of shipping was often the underlying cause of global war, and sometimes it served as the immediate or proximate cause. For example, the first Anglo-Dutch war was sparked by the issue of whether Dutch ships should salute English naval vessels in English territorial waters.[7] Beneath this symbolic issue lay the fundamental conflict between the Netherlands and England over control of international shipping. The Navigation Acts were, perhaps, the foreign-policy instrument most important in enabling Britain to gain control over its domestic economy and organize an imperial division of labor. According to Judith Blow Williams, between 1650 and 1750 "the primary objective of England was the preservation of British shipping."[8] Issues of

2. J. A. Salter, *Allied Shipping Control: An Experiment in International Administration* (Oxford: Clarendon Press, 1921), p. 7.

3. UNCTAD, *Review of Maritime Transport, 1982* (Geneva: United Nations, 1983), pp. 39–40.

4. U.S. Bureau of the Census, *Statistical Abstract of the United States, 1981* (Washington, D.C.: G.P.O., 1982), tables 1135, 1136. These figures do not include U.S.-owned vessels registered under foreign flags.

5. OECD, Maritime Transport Committee, *Maritime Transport, 1982* (Paris: OECD, 1983), table 21a, p. 157.

6. Thorsten Rinman and Rigmer Linden, *Shipping: How It Works* (Gothenburg, Sweden: Rinman and Linden, 1979), p. 15.

7. Ralph Davis, *English Merchant Shipping and Anglo-Dutch Rivalry in the Seventeenth Century* (London: HMSO, 1975), p. 32.

8. Judith Blow Williams, *British Commercial Policy and Trade Expansion, 1750–1850* (Oxford: Clarendon Press, 1972), p. 27. On the development of English shipping, see also Ralph Davis, *The Rise of the English Shipping Industry in the Seventeenth and Eighteenth Centuries* (London: Macmillan, 1962); C. E. Fayle, *A Short History of the World's Shipping Industry*

merchant shipping figured prominently in the development of the Anglo-German political and commercial rivalry that culminated in World War I.

During the mercantilist period, international rivalry focused on the control and exploitation of colonial territories. Consequently, in an era defined by the lack of cross-trading (carriage of cargo between countries by a third party), control of shipping played a decisive role in the division and redivision of the world economy among a small group of great powers. Indeed, the Navigation Acts served as the legal foundation of mercantilism, and their abolition signified the beginning of the laissez-faire era. During the nineteenth and twentieth centuries the importance of shipping has been partially concealed by the commanding position of the hegemonic powers—first Britain, then the United States—on the seas. Germany's immediate challenge to Britain was primarily Continental, both for reasons of geography and because of Britain's formidable maritime power. Similarly, the Soviet challenge to the United States is primarily land-based, although it does contain an important maritime dimension. Moreover, America's maritime supremacy has been exercised in hegemonic terms, through alliances and the establishment of an internal maritime division of labor within a U.S.-led bloc. Although the erosion of American hegemony has important consequences for international shipping, there is no corresponding maritime challenge from a rising power.

Ever since the rise of Dutch commerce in the sixteenth and seventeenth centuries, waves of hegemonic rise and decline can be discerned in the history of international maritime relations. Before about 1880, the organization of shipping oscillated between periods of openness when the hegemonic power favored free trade, and closure, the strategy of the rising power. Each successive regime facilitated the expansion of the international division of labor and the national development of the hegemonic power. However, the simple model of openness-closure does not adequately describe the main trends in international shipping since 1880. In the context of monopoly and the new type of generalized state intervention that arose

(London: Allen and Unwin, 1933); Edgar Gold, *Maritime Transport: The Evolution of International Marine Policy and Shipping Law* (Lexington, Mass.: D. C. Heath, 1981), esp. chapter 3; Carlo Cipolla, *Guns, Sails, and Empires* (New York: Pantheon, 1965); W. O. Stevens and A. Westcott, *A History of Seapower* (New York: Doubleday, 1944); J. E. Otterson, *Foreign Trade and Shipping* (New York: McGraw-Hill, 1945); and J. A. Williamson, *The Ocean in English History* (Oxford: Clarendon Press, 1941).

during this period, *free trade* in shipping became an ideologically loaded term; it has been adopted by status-quo maritime powers who exercise oligopolistic power in international freight markets.

Grotius and Freedom of the Seas

Developments in shipbuilding technique and navigation were instrumental in shifting the locus of power and wealth from the Mediterranean to the Atlantic during the late Middle Ages. In the fifteenth century these developments redirected Europe's expansionist impulses from overland routes converging on the Middle East to the maritime crossing of the Atlantic and, eventually, to circumnavigation of the globe. Early developments gave rise to quasi-regimes reflecting the ambitions of Portugal and Spain, the leading powers. These regimes were not accepted by all nations, and neither country was able to enforce them universally. The papal bull of 1493 dividing the non-European world into Portuguese and Spanish spheres had a maritime counterpart: the oceans themselves were divided along a line 370 miles west of the Cape Verde Islands, with Portugal allotted the Brazilian coast.[9] The prevailing doctrine of *mare clausum* or "closed seas" represented the extreme form of mercantilism. Although violation of the principle was punishable by death, it was not generally recognized; in practical terms it did not apply to either France or England.[10]

In 1580 Spain conquered Portugal and thus held legal claim to Central and South America. However, Spain's international position cannot be considered to have been hegemonic. Lacking an industrial or commercial basis, Spanish power essentially rested on the plunder of bullion from the Americas. In Europe, Spain was challenged by Arabs and continually harassed by rebellions in the Netherlands and Italy. On the seas, English, Dutch, and French privateers raided Spanish merchants with impunity. Spain's hold on the Netherlands was broken in the late sixteenth century. The independence of the Netherlands was established in 1609, following the negotiation of a twelve-year truce with Spain. The truce was won as a result of a series of wars of national liberation against the Spaniards.[11] En-

---

9. Stevens and Westcott, *History of Seapower,* p. 84; Gold, *Maritime Transport,* p. 35.

10. Gold, *Maritime Transport,* p. 35.

11. J. R. Jones, *Britain and Europe in the Seventeenth Century* (New York: W. W. Norton, 1963), esp. chapter 3.

gland's defeat of the Spanish Armada in 1588 destroyed Spanish seapower. Ironically, it established a political environment in which Dutch trade and shipping would flourish briefly, threatening England's economic and political development.

After the defeat of the Spanish Armada and its wars of national liberation with Spain, the Netherlands enjoyed a short-lived international ascendancy until it was humbled by a series of wars with England in the mid-seventeenth century. Although to use the term *hegemony* may be to overstate Dutch power, the half-century of Dutch supremacy did lead to the establishment of a new and qualitatively different type of international system. Dutch power rested not only on military prowess but also on industrial strength and commercial superiority, especially in banking, shipping, and shipbuilding. Under Dutch leadership, the range of world trade was extended from luxury goods to everyday items.[12]

The Netherlands consolidated power primarily through the use of merchant shipping. Hemmed in by the militarily stronger Spanish, the States-General established the Dutch East India Company and granted it a monopoly of Far Eastern trade. A smaller Dutch West India Company was formed to trade in the Caribbean. These trading companies, together with the massive Dutch fishing fleet, constituted the backbone of Dutch world power. In 1610 the Dutch merchant fleet totaled almost one million tons. This figure is equivalent to almost one-quarter of the tonnage of the present-day Dutch merchant fleet and exceeds the size of the contemporary

12. Immanuel Wallerstein includes the Netherlands in his category of hegemonic powers. He defines hegemony as "momentary summit" based on financial, agricultural, and commercial superiority; see Wallerstein, *The Modern World System,* Vol. 2 (New York: Academic Press, 1980), chapter 2. George Modelski, in contrast to Wallerstein, includes Portugal as a hegemonic leader; this reflects his emphasis on seapower ("Long Cycles of Global Politics and the Nation-State," *Comparative Studies in Society and History* 20 [April 1978]). Nicole Bousquet defines hegemony somewhat more narrowly, in terms of production supremacy. Using this criterion, the Netherlands may be defined as a hegemonic power. See Bousquet, "From Hegemony to Competition: Cycles of the Core?" in Terence K. Hopkins and Immanuel Wallerstein, eds., *Processes of the World System,* Vol. 3: *Political Economy of the World System Annuals* (Beverly Hills: Sage, 1980). The Netherlands was, as Eric J. Hobsbawm notes, a "feudal business economy," geared to a role as commercial and financial intermediary, which meant that its rulers were "sacrificing Dutch manufactures to the huge vested interests of trading and finance . . . [and] encouraging manufactures in feudal and semi-colonial areas where they were not strong enough to break out of the older social framework" ("The Crisis of the Seventeenth Century," in Trevor Astin, ed., *Crisis in Europe, 1560–1660* [Garden City: Anchor, 1967], p. 45). Compared to the Netherlands, England's was a modern political economy, geared to dynamic capitalist expansion.

merchant fleets of all but a handful of LDCs.[13] The Dutch fleet dominated world seaborne trade. Heavily engaged in cross-trading, it threatened to monopolize international freight markets.

The idea of freedom of the seas expressed the interests of the Dutch trading companies and large fishing fleets. Against the fragmentation of markets and exclusive colonial spheres of influence that pertained during the heyday of Spanish and Portuguese power, the trading companies sought to create a unified world market characterized by free access to ships and cargoes. The propagandist of the new regime was Hugo Grotius, a lawyer for the Dutch East India Company.[14]

The identity between interest and ideology in Grotius's scholarship is transparent, and the evolution of his thought closely corresponded to the changing fortunes and requirements of his corporate client. The young Grotius wrote ardent nationalistic tracts celebrating military encounters with Spain and Portugal. His later, more temperate work reflects the achievement of Dutch commercial hegemony. In *De Jure Praedae Commentaris,* Grotius sought to justify the forcible seizure of Portuguese merchant vessels.[15] This work contains lengthy sections concerning the right, under natural law, to wage war at sea. It also includes a commentary on the Spanish conquest of the Netherlands, the conditions of Spanish rule and the Dutch rebellion, and the oppression of Dutch sailors by Spain and Portugal.

Despite its nationalistic fervor, *De Jure Praedae Commentaris,* written in 1606 but not published in full until 1871, does contain a chapter that foreshadows the liberal Grotius as defender of freedom of the seas. In this chapter, entitled "Mare Liberum," Grotius propounds the principle of nonaggression and develops his classic doctrine of freedom of the seas. He attacks the exclusionary practices of all states and, by focusing on Portugal's alleged occupation of the waters of the East Indies, ridicules the notion that the high seas can be territorially divided. Grotius contends that because the seas, unlike land, cannot be occupied, access to them should be open to all.[16]

---

13. Gold, *Maritime Transport,* p. 42. This figure includes the Dutch fishing fleet. By contrast, the English merchant fleet was probably less than 100,000 tons in 1610, and it did not exceed one million tons until 1788; see Davis, *Rise of the English Shipping Industry,* p. 27.

14. Gold, *Maritime Transport,* pp. 44–45; Pittman Potter, *The Freedom of the Seas in History, Law, and Politics* (New York: Longman, Green, 1924), pp. 57, 61; Edward Dumbauld, *The Life and Legal Writings of Hugo Grotius* (Norman: University of Oklahoma Press, 1969).

15. Gold, *Maritime Transport,* p. 45.

16. Ibid., pp. 45–46.

Dutch expansion constituted an immediate threat to English fishing interests. Even more ominously, it threatened the long-range development of English capitalism, which depended heavily on foreign trade and colonial windfalls.[17] Further expansion of Dutch shipping would endanger England's position in the Americas. In Europe, Dutch banking was supreme, and every increase in Dutch shipping and trade, using Amsterdam as an entrepôt, strengthened banking and commercial interests. English ships were being pushed out of the Baltic. In the Indian Ocean, Dutch warships were harassing English traders; in 1623 the inhabitants of an English settlement were massacred by Dutch raiders. Dutch shipping was gradually increasing its share of trade with the American colonies. Meanwhile, the Dutch fishing fleet was depleting the Scottish and English coastal regions. All these activities were supported by the superior Dutch navy. At the same time, Dutch shipbuilding was technologically dominant, threatening the further development of the English shipbuilding industry. The freedom-of-the-seas regime thus posed a direct threat to England's national security and to the continued momentum of two centuries of gradual economic development.[18]

Navigation Acts

Elizabeth I did not challenge the concept of freedom of the seas. However, under James I, England began to chip away at the legal foundations of Dutch maritime power. In 1609 James I declared that fishing in English waters would be reserved for English vessels. The resultant negotiations between the Netherlands and England were inconclusive, leading to a barrage of propaganda from both sides. The Englishman John Selden's *Mare Clausum* was the most consistent and scholarly defense of mercantilism and rebuttal to Dutch claims. Selden, like the Portuguese lawyers, defended the territorial enclosure of the high seas, contending that navigation was a privilege and not a natural right.[19]

Under James I, England gradually introduced new protectionist laws or began to enforce existing ones. This trend culminated in the Navigation Act of 1651, England's forceful and dramatic response to its shipping cri-

17. See esp. Hobsbawm, "The Crisis of the Seventeenth Century," pp. 53–56.
18. See Jones, *Britain and Europe in the Seventeenth Century,* p. 47.
19. Gold, *Maritime Transport,* p. 48.

sis. This act was the most extensive of a long series of measures designed to defend the merchant fleet, and it complemented other legislative measures, including subsidies to shipbuilding and the granting of exclusive right of carriage to the Crown.[20] However, given England's greatly expanded role in world trade and the considerable interdependence of the Netherlands and England, the Navigation Act of 1651, in conjunction with related acts, constituted a grave provocation to the Dutch. It indicated that England was determined to eliminate the Netherlands as an economic and military rival, although not as a trading partner.[21] The act stipulated that all imports must be carried on English ships or in the ships of trading partners. This was a clear expression of bilateralism; it eliminated the Dutch role as cross-trader in English and colonial routes and weakened the position of Dutch ports as entrepôts. The act further stipulated that only English ships had the right to trade with English colonies. Finally, it decreed that all colonial exports must be shipped to England either as the final destination or as a point of transshipment.

One year later the first Anglo-Dutch war broke out. The war was fought entirely on the seas, ending in victory for England. The Treaty of Westminster (1654) forced the Netherlands to pay a large indemnity to England. Two further wars (1665–67 and 1672–74) hastened the decline of Dutch power. In each the English naval blockade was sufficiently powerful to interfere with Dutch commerce. During the third war the Netherlands repelled a combined Anglo-French invasion only by opening the dikes. Dutch merchant shipping suffered greatly, the Dutch navy was defeated, and the Netherlands' holdings in the Americas were expropriated. A victorious England then further tightened the restrictions on open seas.[22]

As a result of these wars, England was able to create a new, mercantilistic regime suited to the requirements of English trade and shipping. Between 1660 and 1689 the size of the English fleet increased by a factor of three. As it would do often in the course of its history, England re-

20. On the Navigation Acts, see Lawrence A. Harper, *The English Navigation Laws: A Seventeenth Century Study in Social Engineering* (New York: Columbia University Press, 1939); Davis, *Rise of the English Shipping Industry*, pp. 304–7; and Davis, *English Merchant Shipping and Anglo-Dutch Rivalry*, pp. 28–36.

21. Davis, *Rise of the English Shipping Industry*, p. 307. "We can speak not merely of Anglo-Dutch rivalry, but also of Anglo-Dutch symbiosis" (Hobsbawm, "The Crisis of the Seventeenth Century," p. 45).

22. Gold, *Maritime Transport*, p. 50; Stevens and Westcott, *History of Seapower*, pp. 148–49; Jones, *Britain and Europe in the Seventeenth Century*, p. 47.

plenished its fleet with captured enemy prizes; as a result England was able
to copy Dutch shipbuilding technology, and thus another pillar of Dutch
power crumbled.[23] Victory in war and the successes engineered by the
Navigation Acts facilitated a wholesale restructuring of the international
political economy in which merchant shipping was the strategic core. This
restructuring produced tangible gains for England, paving the way for
rapid national economic development and foreign trade that could not
have taken place under the old regime. English gains included:

1. The domination of transatlantic shipping, which provided a crucial
basis for maritime progress and commercial expansion, as well as the
means of consolidating American holdings.

2. A secure basis of shipbuilding expansion and technological progress
based on a guaranteed market for the products of English shipyards.

3. Access to Baltic trade and ports.

4. Safety for British shipping.

5. The humbling of Britain's premier commercial rival.

These gains ultimately provided England with the global power to defend
most of its holdings against the challenges from France and other powers,
and so cleared the decks for the expansion of British imperialism. As Ralph
Davis has written, "The Navigation Acts gave powerful protection to English shipping through a period in which the English trading situation was
favorable to its expansion, but in which continued free competition would
have allowed the Dutch to exploit some large part of this potentiality."[24]
The return to free competition would have to await the final defeat of

23. Davis, *Rise of the English Shipping Industry,* pp. 50–52; Davis, *English Merchant Shipping and Anglo-Dutch Rivalry,* p. 32. Davis estimates that at least two thousand Dutch vessels
were captured as prizes by England during the three Anglo-Dutch wars.

24. Davis, *English Merchant Shipping and Anglo-Dutch Rivalry,* p. 32. The establishment
of an international shipping regime based on the Navigation Acts was central to the rise of
English, and global, capitalism. This chapter stresses the role played by shipping in England's
successful response to a developmental crisis. Other factors, of course, are necessary for a
comprehensive analysis of this response. It is, however, ironic that England used essentially
"atavistic" (in the Schumpeterian sense) and restrictive methods to overthrow the global
domination of "feudal business" imperialism. Hobsbawm ("The Crisis of the Seventeenth
Century," pp. 45–46) questions whether the world market was sufficiently developed to permit the simultaneous industrialization of two countries on a large scale: "British industrialization coincided with the British capture of virtually all the world's markets for certain
manufactured goods, and the control of most of the world's colonial areas. Dutch concentration thus proved extremely important, but it should not therefore tempt us to exaggerate the
'modernity' of the Dutch. If the only 'capitalist' economies available in the seventeenth cen-

France, the establishment of British commercial hegemony, and the achievement of shipping and shipbuilding superiority.

Toward Freedom of the Seas

The Navigation Acts served to define an international shipping regime because the explicit and implicit rules and procedures they mandated were followed and endorsed by most states. Mercantilist doctrine was defended not only by the Englishman Selden but also by legal scholars from France, Spain, and Portugal.[25] More broadly, because shipping was the strategic sector of the international political economy, the Navigation Acts formed the legal core of the mercantilist system. The longevity of the regime can be explained with reference to the general requirements of the mercantilist system and the particular needs of British imperialism. The more or less permanent, albeit limited, global warfare between France and England that followed the Anglo-Dutch wars focused on control of shipping and colonies. However, in contrast to the previous period, conflict now did not center on the nature of the regime (mercantilist or free) but, rather, on expansion within the given regime. Mercantilism permitted both France and England to consolidate colonial holdings and thus to expand trade using the home country as an entrepôt. Under Colbert, the French merchant fleet expanded and the French navy surpassed England's in size.[26] Although its preoccupation with Continental objectives interfered with France's attempts to consolidate a sizable global trading network, French support was, nevertheless, crucial to American independence. Through the Navigation Acts, British imperialists had sought to retard the development of American capitalism. They frustrated American merchants, who wished to widen export markets, and plantation owners, who were compelled to absorb the higher costs of transshipment of goods through Liverpool and Glasgow. The first act passed by the United States Congress, itself studded with shipowners, provided for a discount of 10 percent on tariffs for commodities imported on American vessels.[27]

Throughout the mercantilist period, England was the strongest mer-

---

tury had been like the Dutch, we may doubt whether the subsequent development of industrial capitalism would have been as great or as rapid."

25. Gold, *Maritime Transport,* p. 49.

26. Ibid., p. 52.

27. Erich W. Zimmerman, *Ocean Shipping* (New York: Prentice-Hall, 1923), p. 559.

chant shipping and naval power. However, as the American Revolution made clear, England's power was by no means unlimited. The political preconditions for shipping liberalism were the destruction of French seapower and the elimination of France as a serious imperial rival. Although French ambitions were primarily Continental, the Napoleonic wars contained an important maritime dimension. Napoleon tried to damage British commerce by attacking British merchant shipping, closing European ports to British vessels, and establishing control of trade routes to Asia.[28] After Trafalgar, however, the British navy ruled the waves and would continue to do so until the Washington Naval Agreements of 1922 and the transition to American hegemony. As Edgar Gold has noted:

> At the end of 160 years of conflict, which had begun with the first Anglo-Dutch War, and the promulgation of the Navigation Acts, Great Britain was in a position of absolute supremacy in terms of shipping, colonies, and commerce—a supremacy such as the world would not witness for at least another century.[29]

The defeat of Napoleonic France established the international political framework for free trade. The transition from mercantilism to freedom required a new hegemonic distribution of power and was facilitated by economic conditions whereby all states had incentives to relax restrictive shipping practices. During the 1830s and 1840s, the advent of the steamship sparked a tremendous expansion of world trade. Moreover, Britain's massive coal reserves and industrial and technological superiority ensured that British shipping would be the prime beneficiary of the transition from sails and wood to steam and steel.[30] These factors, in conjunction with the industrial revolution, precipitated the demand from the dominant section of the English bourgeoisie to repeal the Navigation Acts. As British capitalism developed and international trade flourished, the maze of restrictions was no longer perceived as a necessary aid but, rather, as a serious impediment to further national and international economic development.

In particular, the privileges granted to English shipping were increasingly eliciting countermeasures by foreign countries, especially the newly independent countries of South and Central America.[31] The protectionist regime limited British access to foreign ports and trade; it proscribed cross-trading, which British shipowners were now poised to dominate.

28. Gold, *Maritime Transport*, p. 77.
29. Ibid., p. 81.   30. Ibid., p. 88.   31. Ibid.

More generally, as the strategic element in mercantilism, the old regime was not compatible with the general movement toward free trade. As a British parliamentary report on shipping noted,

> In view of its great size, the British merchant marine stood to gain more from free access to foreign countries than foreign flags stood to gain from free access to British ports; and conversely a policy of mutual restriction would for the same reason have caused more harm to British than to foreign shipping.[32]

Technological developments in shipping also contributed to the free trade movement by helping to consolidate British maritime power during the 1830s and 1840s. The clipper ship, the most advanced sailing vessel, was essentially an American invention. The abundance of timber in the Americas at a time when England was being deforested provided the technical basis for a potent American challenge. However, the application of Britain's industrial prowess to shipping meant that the British steamship could relegate the United States to the status of a minor maritime nation. Britain possessed a tremendous comparative advantage in steel production and steam engines. The coal trades were the single most important basis of British maritime expansion during the nineteenth century, providing ready cargoes and cheap propulsion for British shipowners.[33]

Free trade thus reflected a return to the Grotian ideal of freedom of the seas. It implied a formally competitive regime, including

1. Abolition of preferential treatment for national flag shipping, and institution of a policy guaranteeing shipowners equal access to cargoes, and shippers equal access to vessels of all flags.
2. Freedom of passage outside a three-mile limit.
3. Equality of treatment of vessels in port.
4. Equal taxation and port charges for vessels of all flags.

32. Booth Committee Report, p. 106.
33. The Booth Committee observed that British shipping was dependent on three factors: industrial strength and free trade; the Empire with its strategically placed coal stations; and the large coal-export trade (United Kingdom, Departmental Committee on Shipping and Shipbuilding, *First Report* [Booth Committee Report], Cmnd. 9092 [London: HMSO, 1918], p. 71). Erich Zimmerman notes that "before [World War I] Germany, realizing the enormous value of coal export from a shipping standpoint, had entered mainly through the Rheinisch-Westfälische Kohlen-Syndikat, upon a systematic campaign to force England to yield, foot by foot, the markets which she had once considered her exclusive domains" (*Ocean Shipping*, pp. 231–32).

By 1830, many of these rules were being applied on a de facto basis. The tremendous expansion of world trade had, in any case, begun to limit the practical scope of the Navigation Acts.[34] Against the opposition of a protectionist faction of British shipowners who remained wedded to the security of mercantilism, the great body of laws was repealed by Parliament in 1847.[35] In 1849 English ports were formally opened to all on a reciprocal basis and, in 1853, restraints on cabotage (trading between home ports) were lifted.

International acceptance of the new regime did not depend primarily on intergovernmental diplomacy, at least among the great powers. Nor did it require state action per se, as the relevance of the Navigation Acts and the willingness and ability of governments to enforce them had gradually diminished following the defeat of Napoleon. Outside Europe, of course, free trade was often enforced by gunboat diplomacy. But the great disparities in economic development between England and other great powers tended to render free trade mutually beneficial. England possessed a decisive comparative advantage in shipping and shipbuilding, and, for England, freedom of the seas was the obvious basis of maritime expansion. For the Continental European powers and the United States, the lowered costs of transportation and the expanding market for agricultural exports, above all corn, provided strong incentives to uphold the principle of freedom. These powers were neither strong enough nor sufficiently developed economically to join in a wholesale scramble for colonies or to be unduly alarmed by the strength of British merchant shipping.

If the use of state power was not directly responsible for the international acceptance of the new regime, it was nevertheless essential to the defeat of recalcitrant sections of the English bourgeoisie. On the one hand, some British shipowners were ardent protectionists. On the other hand, British capital as a whole was reluctant to invest in new shipbuilding technology, and this gave further impetus to the forces of the old order arrayed behind the Navigation Acts. The obsolescence of the sailing ship was one condition of British support for freedom of the seas. The British govern-

34. Fayle, *A Short History,* pp. 232–33.
35. Otterson, *Foreign Trade,* p. 19. Edgar Gold emphasizes the lack of government intervention in the expansion of British steamshipping. Although this is true of the period following 1860, it is important to note that the state was actively involved in the transition from sail to steam. Otterson, writing on behalf of American shipowners in 1945, presents evidence of British government involvement in order to plead for American government aid following World War II. See Gold, *Maritime Transport,* esp. pp. 92–93.

Table 2. Development of Steam Shipping, 1850 – 80 (thousands of tons net)

	1850	1860	1870	1880
British Empire				
United Kingdom	168.5	454.3	1,112.9	2,723.5
Dominions, colonies	19.1	45.8	89.2	225.8
France	13.9	68.0	154.4	277.8
Germany	—	—	82.0	215.8
Spain	—	—	—	146.1
United States	28.1	60.8	120.3	91.6
Russia	—	—	—	89.0
Sweden	—	—	—	81.0
Italy	—	—	32.1	77.0
Netherlands	—	—	50.0	64.4
Austria-Hungary	—	—	—	64.0
Other	—	—	29.6	110.1
Total, British Empire	187.6	500.1	1,202.1	2,949.3
Total, All others	42.0	128.8	468.4	1,216.8

SOURCE. United Kingdom, Departmental Committee on Shipping and Shipbuilding, *First Report* (Booth Committee Report), Cmnd. 9092 (London: HMSO, 1918), p. 138.

ment, however, strongly supported the steamship—primarily by granting mail subsidies to steamship owners, a common pre–World War I form of subsidy. According to one observer, the British Admiralty was the "premier founder of the steamship lines. . . . By 1838 the [British] government was able to hand some of the work over to private firms, and the first regular transatlantic line, the result of a British mail contract, was really a subsidized line."[36]

The abolition of the Navigation Acts reinforced the position of London as the premier financial, commercial, and insurance center, and "the monopoly of British carriers more and more nearly approached being one of the carrying trade of the world."[37] Shipping strengthened banking by establishing London as the major entrepôt, conferring many attendant sources of profit on the City of London. The abandonment of the Navigation Acts made it possible for the British government to retreat from the affairs of the steamship lines. Table 2 shows the extent of British domina-

36. Quoted in Otterson, *Foreign Trade*, pp. 19–20.
37. Ibid., p. 49.

tion of steam transportation after 1850. By 1880 its steam tonnage was nearly three times that of the rest of the world.

Shipping in the Age of Imperialism

The steamship was the technological and geopolitical embodiment of hegemonic British capitalism. It fostered a dramatic expansion of world trade and opened opportunities to trade in a range of new agricultural commodities that required speed and regularity of transport, as well as refrigeration. As Charles Kindleberger has observed, "What the railroad was to do for increased specialization and the development of national markets in France, or for transcontinental trade in North America, the development of cheap ocean shipping has done for world trade."[38] However, political and economic forces that were called into play by the very success of the liberal regime developed in the last two decades of the nineteenth century. These forces destroyed the laissez-faire regime and inaugurated a new phase of international political economy. This new phase may be described in terms of related political and economic trends: first, the intensification of international rivalry, marked by expansionist colonial policies and the struggle to end British dominance; second, the increasing concentration and centralization of capital, both nationally and transnationally, in conjunction with a greatly enlarged role of the state in economic affairs.

These two trends were immediately reflected in changes in the organization of international shipping. Between 1880 and 1900 the liberal regime was transformed into one dominated by cartels and guided, directly or indirectly, by state intervention. Moreover, because these long-range trends were irreversible, they marked the permanent demise of shipping liberalism. Although the post–World War II regime would contain some elements of liberalism, the degree of free trade in the regime was limited; it depended on the power of cartels and was never completely free of state intervention.

The trends toward concentration of ownership and toward international rivalry were mutually reinforcing and had immediate ramifications for shipping. Politically, Anglo-German maritime rivalry led to attempts to establish economies of scale in shipping, especially in Germany, and the de-

38. Charles P. Kindleberger, *Foreign Trade and the National Economy* (New Haven: Yale University Press, 1962), p. 24.

velopment of closer relations between export firms and shipowners. The German government encouraged both these trends; it facilitated mergers to strengthen national shipping and directly or indirectly implemented cargo-reservation schemes, including the reservation of human cargo.

The prime expression of the new economic and political trends was the international shipping conference or cartel. The conference represents, in part, an idiosyncratic institution specific to international shipping. However, the development of conferences was dependent on political as well as economic forces. Conferences made it possible to rationalize freight markets and provided the means by which the leading shipowners, still predominantly the British, could protect their markets from the predations of new competitors.

A conference can be defined as "any type of formal or informal agreement between shipowners that restricts competition."[39] The origins of the shipping conference are a matter of historical debate, but these institutions became widespread and significant during the 1880s.[40] Until the development of the steamship, regular services were generally impossible, due to the vagaries of wind propulsion, although packet line services from New York to Liverpool did begin in the sailing-ship era. However, the introduction of the steamship meant that regular services could be provided. The liner sector involves services by carriers offering fixed-time schedules on specified routes (like buses or airplanes). The sector carries a low percentage of world trade by volume (approximately 20 percent), but a high percentage by value (80 percent), including virtually all manufactured commodities and some others, such as fruits, that require scheduled services.

---

39. United Kingdom, Committee of Inquiry into Shipping, *Report* (Rochdale Report), Cmnd. 4337 (London: HMSO, 1970), p. 116.

40. For general works on the conference system, see Daniel Marx, *International Shipping Cartels—A Study of Industrial Self-Regulation by Shipping Conferences* (Princeton, N.J.: Princeton University Press, 1953); B. M. Deakin, *Shipping Conferences: A Study of Their Origin, Development, and Economic Practices* (Cambridge: Cambridge University Press, 1973). The case against conferences is made in U.S. Congress, House, Committee on the Judiciary (Celler Committee), Report of the Anti-Trust Committee, *The Ocean Freight Industry*, 87th Cong., 1962; and U.S. Department of Justice, Anti-Trust Division, *The Regulated Ocean Shipping Industry* (Washington, D.C.: G.P.O., 1977). For a rebuttal to the Department of Justice study, see University of Wales, Department of Maritime Studies, *Liner Shipping in the U.S. Trades: A UWIST Study for CENSA* (London: University of Wales, Department of Maritime Studies, 1978). On the origins of conferences, see K. A. Moore, *The Early History of Freight Conferences: Background and Main Developments Until Around 1900* (London: Yale Press Ltd., 1981).

Once the steamship provided the technical means to provide regular services, liner firms sought to protect their market shares from the incursions of outsiders who might destabilize freight markets by "creaming off" lucrative cargoes without providing regularly scheduled services. In 1875 a Calcutta Conference was formed. Other conferences soon followed: China (1879); Australia (1884); South Africa (1886); West Africa (1895); northern Brazil (1895); Plate River and southern Brazil (1896); and the whole west coast of South America (1904).[41] By the turn of the century most of the world's trading routes were organized by shipping conferences, with English shipowners assuming organizational leadership. Conferences became the primary unit of power in liner shipping. They vividly exemplify the tendency toward concentration of capital which occurred during this period, and their significance was recognized by Lenin and Hobson. For Hobson, "the power of a conference is exercised by means of a 'rebate' system, which operates primarily as a bribe, partly as a menace, inducing shippers to do business exclusively with members of the conference."[42]

Although liner shipping has undergone many changes during the twentieth century, the basic purposes and functions of the conference system have not changed. Moreover, the controversy over conferences continues to focus on the same fundamental issues. The significance of conference practices is interpreted variously by governments, industry analysts, and shipping economists. States and groups have traditionally responded according to particular interests: status quo shipping powers tend to defend conferences; have-not power often seek to reform or destroy them.

As international or transnational cartels, conferences express the common interests of leading firms. The high degree of collusion displayed within conferences is, as in any cartel, conditioned by the competitive strategy of the leading firms. Thus cartelization is a "higher" form of competition. This was recognized with great clarity by the authors of the U.S. Shipping Act of 1916:

> The entire history of Steamship Agreements shows that in ocean commerce there is no happy medium between war and peace when several lines engage in the same trades. Most of the numerous agreements and conference arrange-

41. Moore, *Early History of Freight Conferences*, p. 67.
42. John A. Hobson, *The Evolution of Modern Capitalism* (New York: Scribners, 1916), pp. 175–76. See also V. I. Lenin, *Imperialism—The Highest Stage of Capitalism: A Popular Outline* (New York: International Publishers, 1939), p. 73.

ments discussed in the foregoing report were the outcome of rate wars and represent a truce between contending lines.[43]

At a minimum, conferences fix freight rates on particular trade routes. A conference is thus a cartel that eliminates price competition among its members. Most conferences engage in one or more of the following practices in order to maintain or increase the cartel's market share:

1. *Rebates to shippers.* Shippers who agree to use the conference exclusively may be offered a lower freight rate (dual rate system) than the conference tariff, or a refund (deferred rebate system), provided the shipper continues to use the conference exclusively on routes where the conference offers services. The deferred rebate is a much more effective tying device and has been outlawed by some countries, notably the United States.

2. *Restrictions on admission.* Most conferences limit membership and collaborate to reduce competition from outsiders through the use of "fighting ships" that use the superior financial resources of the conference to undercut outsiders' rates until the competition is destroyed.

3. *Rationalization.* Conferences seek to sail ships at full capacity by limiting sailings and routes.

4. *Pooling and joint services.* Highly centralized conferences may allocate cargoes and pool revenues and resources.

Even in highly centralized conferences, however, the degree of control the conference can exert over shippers is limited. Shippers (exporters or importers) can choose a shipowner, provided there is no government intervention. Not only must conference members compete among themselves on the basis of non-price factors such as service and speed, but they also must keep rates down in order to compete favorably with outsiders or independents. When freight rates rise, outsiders may choose to enter the trade route. The conference can tolerate competition, engage in protracted rate wars with outsiders, or invite competitors to join the conference.

The rapid development of the conference system in the last two decades of the nineteenth century inspired two especially prominent governmental studies, the British Royal Commission on Shipping Rings Report (1909), and the American Alexander Report (1914). Although the conference system has changed, each study remains pertinent and continues to influence

43. House Committee on the Judiciary, *The Ocean Freight Industry,* p. 11.

policy; the varying perspectives reflect differences in commercial objectives
and in domestic political and economic alignments.

Both the Alexander Report and the Royal Commission Report endorsed the conference as the most efficient and reliable institution capable
of organizing ocean transportation. While acknowledging some injustices,
the majority report of the Royal Commission strongly supported conferences. But a minority report concluded that the countervailing forces
alleged to restrain the degree of cartelization were weak and generally
ineffective. Government power to intervene in conflicts between shipowners and shippers was, therefore, necessary. Like the minority report of
the Royal Commission, the Alexander Report proposed extensive governmental regulation of conferences. The conclusions expressed the prevailing
antitrust philosophy of the time. Based on these conclusions, the U.S.
Shipping Act of 1916 prohibited "closed conferences," the deferred rebate
system, and "fighting ships."

Proponents of conferences argue that such anticompetitive practices are
necessary because shipping is unique among businesses. Once a liner is
ready to sail, taking on extra cargo is profitable at any freight rate greater
than the cost of handling plus the cost of loading and discharging ballast
(20–30 percent of average rate). Rather than sail with empty space, the
shipowner will accept freight at any rate above cost. In a freely competitive
system, rates will be forced downward because of the "dumping" of cargo
space whenever a surplus of shipping appears. Such practices result in unstable freight rates damaging to shipowners, shippers, and consumers. Instability accelerates the monopolistic tendencies inherent in liner shipping,
as only the strongest, most highly capitalized shipping firms survive.[44]

There is little practical evidence to support the contention that the absence of conferences makes for excessively chaotic conditions. Available
evidence suggests that on routes in which conferences are weak or nonexis-
tent, freight rates are lower and somewhat less stable; to the extent that
shippers favor regular sailings throughout seasonal and business fluctuations over lower rates, shipper and shipowner interests in conferences are
identical.[45] However, it is plausible to claim that the greater rationalization

44. See esp. Marx, *International Shipping Cartels,* p. 21.
45. R. O. Goss, ed., *Advances in Maritime Economics* (London: Cambridge University
Press, 1968), pp. 13–24.

achieved through closing conferences and limiting outside competition would not necessarily lower freight rates. Shipowners charge what the market will bear; rationalization of services on this basis may increase profits for the most strongly entrenched shipowners while reducing shipper options.

Opponents of conferences cite the lack of evidence that open conferences lead to a deterioration of services, or, in the long run, a lack of stability. They also argue that, in the absence of significant competition, freight rates will be set at the level of the least efficient operator, who then has little incentive to modernize.[46] In contrast, the existence of competition in non-price factors may cause the shipper to pay higher rates for services of higher quality than is required. There is no necessary connection between shipowner profit and costs; if profits are high, this does not guarantee that costs have been minimized.[47]

The New Protectionism

Shipping conferences were the most obvious form of restraint on competition. Their monopolistic and anticompetitive nature was masked not only by the lack of overt state involvement in the affairs of conferences, but also because cartels could be presented, with some plausibility, as necessary to the functioning of a stable and at least partially free freight market. But many other anticompetitive practices also appeared during the late nineteenth century. These included shipper-shipowner collusion, flag discrimination as government policy, and various forms of subsidies and promotional measures designed to assist national flag shipping. Of course these practices were not, strictly speaking, new; they originated during the mercantilist era. But they became general during the late nineteenth century and, in conjunction with the conference system, marked a decisive turning point in international shipping.

A country wishing to increase the size of its merchant fleet will endeavor to buy foreign goods on a free-on-board (f.o.b.) basis, where the

46. U.S. Department of Justice, *The Regulated Ocean Shipping Industry*, pp. 224–25.

47. Ibid., pp. 225–27. Conference operators are encouraged to invest in "service extras" such as speed, which may cause resentment among shippers who prefer to minimize costs. See UNCTAD, *Level and Structure of Freight Rates, Conference Practices and Adequacy of Shipping Services*, TD/B/C.4/38/Rev. 1 (Geneva: United Nations, 1969).

price of the commodity includes the cost of loading but excludes transportation charges. This system enables the importer to choose the shipowner. Exporters, however, might seek to sell goods on a cost-insurance-freight (c.i.f.) basis, thus allowing the exporter to select the vessel. The possibility of carrying out these operations will, in practice, depend on the supply and demand for particular commodities. In its iron ore trade with Peru, for example, Japan has traditionally purchased on an f.o.b. basis. One-half of Peru's iron ore is exported to Japan, whereas only 3 percent of Japan's iron-ore imports originate from Peru. Thus the Japanese importers—the big steel producers—have the leverage to ensure their choice of carrier; not surprisingly, it is Japanese lines that transport the bulk of Peruvian ore exports to Japan.[48] If shippers purchase f.o.b. and sell c.i.f. to favor less competitive domestic shipowners, then some form of state intervention will be required in the long run to subsidize either shippers or shipowners. The expansion of the British fleet in the eighteenth and nineteenth centuries and the current increase in Soviet shipping can, in part, be attributed to the collusion of shippers and shipowners and the practice of selling c.i.f. and buying f.o.b.

Cooperation between shipowners and shippers also increased dramatically in the bulk sector. Whereas conferences "enforced" such cooperation through rebating, cooperation in tramp shipping occurred primarily through direct business relationships, including joint ownership of ships and raw materials. The oil trades provide the clearest example of this type of linkage, which was often overseen and encouraged by governments. The integration of shipping into overall trading activities thus marked a return to the practices of trading companies under the mercantilist system.

The ability of a firm or group of firms to control shipping depends, in part, on the supply and demand for particular commodities and, more generally, on the degree of market power a firm possesses. The British coal trades were a crucial means of expanding the British merchant fleet, and contracts usually provided for coal to be exported c.i.f. In oil and cotton, Britain's market power enabled it to demand that cargo be imported f.o.b., thus strengthening British control over the shipment. Britain's use of conferences and collusion was an important component of its commercial supremacy, and the practice elicited intense hostility from competitors. The

48. UNCTAD, *Iron Ore Trade from Latin America to Japan: A Study by the UNCTAD Secretariat,* TD/B/C.4/AC.2/2 (1981), p. 5.

effect of these measures was ably described by W. Averill Harriman, president of American Shipping and Commerce Corporation, in 1920:

> We are operating a service from New York to Alexandria and the Levant. . . . One of the important commodities which is imported from Alexandria is Egyptian cotton. This country [the United States] consumes about one-third of the Egyptian crop. All the Egyptian cotton brought to this country is today carried in foreign bottoms and is shipped to us through European ports. Although we have been operating the service for eighteen months, it has been impossible for us to obtain a single pound of Egyptian cotton for our bottoms. The shipment of the entire crop is controlled by a British Conference in which a number of British shipowners participate. The British Conference makes a contract once a year with the Alexandria cotton merchants by which they agree to sell cotton only c.i.f., and to route all their shipments over the Conference lines and the rate is fixed for the season. . . . Our consumer is not allowed to go into Alexandria and buy his cotton f.o.b. and ship at the lowest rate he can obtain. Our efforts to obtain a share of this business by working both in London and in Alexandria has [sic] so far been unsuccessful. The only result of our efforts last spring was that the contract for this year's crop was made five months earlier than it had been made the year before.[49]

After World War II, the role of European and especially British shipping in raw-materials trades, buttressed by the collusive practices Harriman had condemned, was to represent a serious challenge to the architects of the Pax Americana.

A variety of practices, known collectively as *flag discrimination*, reserve cargoes for vessels under the national flag. One form of flag discrimination is achieved by enacting laws mandating that a certain proportion of export and import cargo in various trades be carried by the national flag vessels. Other forms include the reservation of government-financed exports, military-related cargoes, or foreign aid shipments to ships of the national flag. Cabotage, the reservation of coastal shipping for the national flag, is so widespread that it has become a noncontroversial norm. In practice, of course, all forms of flag discrimination presuppose a national flag fleet large enough to transport a significant portion of exports and imports.

A second way to restrain international competition is through subsidies,

---

49. Zimmerman, *Ocean Shipping*, pp. 16–17. For a comprehensive survey and analysis of protectionist methods see Ademuni Odeke, *Protectionism and the Future of International Shipping: The Nature, Development and Role of Flag Discriminations and Preferences, Cargo Reservation and Cabotage Restrictions, State Intervention and Maritime Subsidies* (Dordrecht: Martinus Nijhoff, 1984), esp. parts 1–3.

which indirectly discriminate against foreign shipping. Subsidies may be granted directly and generally to national shipowners, or they may be applied selectively to specific shipowners or in individual trades. Mail contracts were the classic expression of this policy. State aid to shipbuilding is another effective method of protection, especially if it is combined with restrictions on foreign access to ships built in domestic yards.

A third basic form of protection is achieved by adjustments in government fiscal policy. When taxation is reduced below the world average, then national shipowners are favored; even flags of convenience, despite their transnational character, have been said to be discriminatory because of the tax advantages their owners receive. A liberal depreciation allowance is a popular form of support because it encourages new investment in shipping. Outright investment grants represent a more traditional form of government support. Indirect forms of government aid include exchange controls, labor legislation, and government loan guarantees. This list is not exhaustive; it includes only the basic forms of state intervention, the ones that are apt to foster disagreements among states.

Anglo-German Rivalry

After 1880, international shipping rivalry intensified. The barrage of anti-competitive practices and the growth of government intervention were both cause and effect of this rivalry. Threatened by growing competition, British shipowners and the state sought to insulate traditional markets from competitors; challengers, in contrast, used the advantages of backwardness to perfect new forms of state intervention and financial organization of national flag shipping. Britain faced challenges from many powers, including the United States, France, Italy, and Japan, but the key antagonist was Germany. Table 3 compares the expansion of British and German shipping between 1850 and the outbreak of World War I. As the table shows, Britain retained a sizable lead over Germany even in 1914. At that time, the tonnage of the combined British and colonial fleet equaled that of the rest of the world, and three-quarters of world tonnage was built in British yards.[50] However, the table also indicates the rapid expansion of German shipping. Between 1900 and 1914, the steamship fleet more than doubled in size, paralleling the growth of the German navy. These simple tonnage figures,

50. Salter, *Allied Shipping Control,* p. 361.

Table 3.   Comparative Expansion of the British and German Merchant Fleets, 1850 – 1914 (thousands of tons net)

	British Empire	Germany
1850	187.6	—
1860	500.1	—
1870	1,202.1	82.0
1880	2,949.3	215.8
1890	5,413.7	723.7
1900	7,739.8	1,347.9
1910	11,369.1	2,396.7
1914 (June)	12,439.8	3,096.0

SOURCE: United Kingdom, Departmental Committee on Shipping and Shipbuilding, *First Report* (Booth Committee Report), Cmnd. 9092 (London: HMSO, 1918), p. 138.

impressive though they are, still underestimate the seriousness of the challenge that German merchant shipping posed to Britain: the German fleet was organized by the big German banks and the state to strike at the heart of British commerce and imperialism and to complement the German drive for colonies and a greater share of world trade.

The British parliamentary report on shipping and shipbuilding (the Booth Committee Report), prepared during World War I, provides a vivid and authoritative account of the importance of shipping in world politics. The report is notable for its candor: despite its pro-British bias, it offers a penetrating review of the crisis in British and world shipping. The committee, made up of prominent businessmen and politicians, was chaired by Alfred Booth, the director of Cunard Lines. The report detailed the increasing pre–World War I use of cargo protection measures and large government subsidies. More generally, it observed the growing tendency for states to use merchant shipping as an instrument of foreign economic policy. State intervention, according to the study, was popular in Germany:

> It is important to appreciate the close connection between political and economic aims in German expansion before the war, since the German mercantile marine was an instrument well suited to the furtherance of German objects. German shipping was, in fact, the spearhead of German aggression. It was used to force a way into markets to which access would have otherwise been difficult, and so to pave the way for German penetration.[51]

51. Booth Committee Report, p. 100.

The report documented German penetration into "four principal markets": Near and Middle East, and the Persian Gulf; Equatorial Africa; South and Central America; China and the Far East.[52] Although the authors contended that "in this respect the position of British shipping was different," they acknowledged the universality of the trend toward government subsidies to shipowners; the establishment of promotional shipping services; freight rate competition as a method of destroying rival lines; and the use of freight rates as indirect tariffs.[53]

The German government was crucial to the expansion of German merchant shipping. It promoted the interests of shipping firms not only by providing subsidies and coordinating the affairs of shipowners and exporters but also by seizing control of much of the transatlantic emigrant traffic. Through the establishment of Control Stations, ostensibly designed to prevent the spread of infectious diseases, not only Germany but also Austria-Hungary channeled emigrants destined for North and South America into German vessels. This form of protectionism enabled German shipping to enter what had previously been largely a British commercial sphere.

The Booth Committee emphasized the overwhelming contribution that merchant shipping could make to Allied victory. The possession of maritime supremacy was especially significant given American weakness in this area. It also allowed Britain to entice neutrals to become allies: "The British mercantile marine has been the pivot of Allied resistance throughout the war; it has enabled us not only to carry on the struggle but gradually to mobilize the world's resources against the Central Powers."[54] According to the Booth Committee, Germany had considered the sinking of the British merchant fleet to be an important war aim. By 1918 the German press was already calling for extensive postwar aid to German shipowners "in order that the German mercantile marine may be reconstituted as early as possible."[55]

Given these findings, and the basic hypothesis of the committee that Britain's maritime ascendancy must be preserved, the conclusions of the report were not surprising. As a precondition of negotiations at Versailles, Germany was to surrender its whole merchant fleet.[56] The ships were to be used to replenish the British fleet and those of its allies: "The seizing of

52. Ibid., p. 101.   53. Ibid., pp. 3–8.   54. Ibid., p. 61.
55. Ibid., p. 67.   56. Ibid., pp. 114–15.

enemy shipping is, in our view, just as vital to this country as is the recovery of Alsace-Lorraine to France."[57]

World War I did not end the intense international shipping conflict that had erupted after 1880, but it did temporarily halt German expansion and buy time for Britain. During World War I, the superior British navy defeated the German navy and sealed off the continent, frustrating Germany's plan to drive eastward through the Mediterranean and control shipping lanes to the Middle East. The British blockade severed Germany from its overseas trading partners, forcing it to rely on Continental resources. But World War I also accelerated the long-range decline of British seapower. In the Far East, the Japanese navy quickly rose to prominence, and Japanese merchant shipping and shipbuilding began to penetrate traditional British markets. The United States rapidly expanded shipbuilding capacity and created a huge and menacing merchant marine and navy.

World War I failed to bring about a sharp break with the principles and practices of the British imperialist regime because it did not resolve the basic issues that had led to war. The range of conflictual practices actually increased during the interwar period, as most governments were drawn more closely into the affairs of national maritime industries. In the United States, shipping was established under the direct supervision of the government and Congress seriously considered nationalizing it during the 1930s. The Axis powers sought to organize shipping as a central element of a national military and economic policy. Even in the traditionally liberal shipping nations, the degree of state intervention increased. In most cases, the main form of intervention was the subsidy, ostensibly granted for mail carriage. A secondary form of state intervention was subsidization of shipbuilding and assistance to national shipping firms purchasing in domestic shipyards.

Table 4 charts the expansion of the merchant fleets of the major powers from 1914 to 1937. During this time the world fleet increased by almost 20 million gross registered tons. All countries shared in this expansion with the exception of Germany—whose fleet was expropriated and distributed among the Allies under the supervision of British shipowners—and Britain, which experienced a small decline in tonnage. The United States, Japan, and Norway account for almost two-thirds of the interwar

57. Ibid., p. 60.

Table 4.   Merchant Shipping Shares of the Major Powers, 1914 and 1937

	1914		1937		% Increase or Decrease 1914 – 37
	Thou- sands grt	% of World Fleet	Thou- sands grt	% of World Fleet	
British Empire	20,524	47.6	20,398	32.5	−0.6
Germany	5,135	11.9	3,928	6.2	−23.5
United States	2,027	4.7	9,347	14.9	+361.1
Norway	1,957	4.5	4,347	6.9	+122.1
France	1,922	4.4	2,844	4.5	+48.0
Japan	1,708	4.0	4,475	7.1	+162.0
Italy	1,430	3.3	3,174	5.0	+121.9
Russia/U.S.S.R.	852	2.0	1,254	2.0	+47.2
Total, Major powers	33,598	77.9	45,420	72.2	
Total, All countries	43,118	100.0	62,763	100.0	

SOURCE: C.B.A. Behrens, *Merchant Shipping and the Demands of War* (London: Longman, Green, 1959), Appendix I.

increase. Much of the Norwegian expansion, however, can be presumed to have been financed by Britain and integrated into Britain's global raw-materials trades.

World War I had a major impact on the Japanese maritime industries. The Japanese merchant fleet avoided serious losses during the war and was poised not only to play the leading role in postwar Japanese trade but also to expand into areas that had been controlled by Germany and Britain before the war. Such expansion was encouraged by Japanese government policy; it was aided by the rapid increase of Japanese trade and the occupation of parts of China. The advantages of backwardness also came into play: the Japanese fleet developed during the era of steam and steel. By the late 1930s, Japan was building fast steamships frankly designed to support military conquest.[58]

58. Stanley G. Sturmey, *British Shipping and World Competition* (London: Athlone, 1962), chapter 2. For a general survey of shipping during the interwar period see also Gold, *Maritime Transport,* pp. 188–202; and Jesse Saugstad, "Ocean Shipping in World Economics: That Burning Matter of Shipping and Shipbuilding Subsidies," in *Marine News: America's Postwar Merchant Marine Forecast* (New York: Marine News Company, 1944).

The other Axis powers also integrated their maritime industries into military plans under state supervision. After World War I the German government immediately sought to reestablish its merchant fleet by making substantial direct grants to shipping and shipbuilding and also by creating a large loan fund. By 1934 the fleet had surpassed its pre–World War I level. Under the Nazis a complex system of subsidies was established. Although shipping firms were granted a degree of commercial autonomy, they were linked to central planning bodies through the system of subsidies, aid to shipbuilding, and currency operations.[59]

Most other maritime powers experienced increases in government intervention, primarily through subsidies. French shipping in particular was highly subsidized, although the French merchant fleet decreased relative to most of its rivals. One exception to the rule was Norway, whose government did not intervene in the affairs of shipowners. However, Norwegian shipowners received substantial indirect benefits from the worldwide increase in subsidies to shipbuilding. Such programs increased as the Depression wore on and world trade sharply declined. Although Britain vigorously opposed the use of government aid, correctly attributing the decline in freight rates and surplus capacity to such measures, the British government was indirectly aiding its own fleet through granting mail contracts and substantial aid to shipyards.[60] Moreover, Britain's imperial connections and market power in the cotton and oil trades allowed it to fend off competition through monopolistic practices which themselves inspired government intervention from rival maritime nations.

The United States practices represent a special case of government intervention during the interwar period. America's geopolitical position, its relatively late entry into international trade on a grand scale, and its lack of colonies make it a separate bloc in international shipping. The historical origins of United States shipping policy will be discussed at greater length in Chapter 8; however, a brief summary of developments is necessary in any account of international shipping during the interwar period. During the 1920s and 1930s, the United States emerged as a major actor in world shipping, and Anglo-American shipping rivalry was a key focus of international shipping conflict between the world wars.

59. Osborne Mance and J. E. Wheeler, *International Sea Transport* (London: Oxford University Press, 1945), pp. 72–73.
60. Ibid., pp. 120–21. See also Otterson, *Foreign Trade*, pp. 29–33.

Lack of merchant shipping was one factor that limited America's international ambitions largely to its own hemisphere until World War I. In 1900 the United States merchant fleet was approximately the size it was in 1807.[61] Most United States trade was carried by foreign, especially British, vessels. During the Spanish-American War, large numbers of ships had to be chartered from Britain to supply U.S. forces in Cuba and the Philippines.[62] Nascent antagonisms in the Far East between the United States and Britain in the aftermath of World War I were muted by the lack of an effective U.S. merchant marine. American politicians and military planners noted the problem of lengthy supply lines stretching from California to the Philippines. The problem was especially acute because of the potential for naval collaboration between Japan and Britain.

World War I had a dramatic impact on the United States maritime sector. Shipping and shipbuilding were expanded in hothouse fashion with the aid of massive subsidies. At the same time, a legislative phase was inaugurated that had major international repercussions. Under the pressure of freight rate increases due to the war, the U.S. Shipping Act of 1916 was passed. This act and subsequent legislation enacted during the 1920s and 1930s were the basis for an elaborate system of subsidies to shipping and shipbuilding. Moreover, as was noted above, the 1916 Act outlawed the use of the deferred rebate in United States trades, blunting the power of liner conferences and antagonizing European shipping firms.[63]

The tremendous expansion of United States shipping during and immediately after World War I was a grave threat to Britain and was perceived as such on both sides of the Atlantic. It made wartime collaboration difficult and contributed to Anglo-American tensions during the 1920s. In the month of October 1918, 158 American shipyards launched 391,000 tons of merchant shipping. During the course of the war, the United States government contracted for 17 million tons of shipping. As Jeffrey Safford

61. H. David Bess and Martin T. Farris, *U.S. Maritime Policy: History and Prospects* (New York: Praeger, 1981), p. 7.

62. Samuel A. Lawrence, *U.S. Merchant Shipping Policies and Politics* (Washington, D.C.: Brookings Institution, 1966), pp. 34–35. High freight rates resulting from the diversion of British shipping to the Boer War effort meant that, in the words of a congressional committee, American exporters "paid for the Boer War" (ibid., p. 34).

63. U.S. Shipping Act, 1916 (39 Stat. 728, chapter 451, approved 7 September 1916). The text of this act, as amended, is reprinted in U.S. Department of Justice, *The Regulated Ocean Shipping Industry,* Appendix A.

observed, "The world watched in amazement one of the greatest production feats in industrial annals."[64]

This tonnage represented more than simply a contribution to the Allied war effort. During the period of American neutrality, shipping was a means by which the United States attempted to penetrate foreign markets vacated by the combatants. At the same time, the Shipping Act of 1916 was a defensive reaction to British and Allied agreements "to subject the neutrals, most clearly the United States, to post-war trade discrimination" and "to recapture their former trade privileges and holdings."[65] The question of how this tonnage would be employed after the war preoccupied shipowners and government officials of all the major powers. Edward Hurley, chairman of the United States Shipping Board, voiced a typical American attitude: "My whole thought is to get a fleet of large-sized ships . . . so that we may be able to compete with Germany and England after the war. . . . Instead of being associated with England in the fight against Germany [the United States should] watch England to prevent her from gaining commercial advantage at the present time, and particularly after the war."[66] Hurley's successors, John Barton Payne and Admiral Benson, were even more rabidly nationalistic and Anglophobic. In 1919 they were described as being "bent upon eliminating [Britain] from competition by driving it into bankruptcy."[67] Benson, according to the secretary of war, dreamed of a "fierce and final competition" between British and American merchant shipping.[68]

The dramatic expansion of American shipping led to an increase in the amount of U.S. cargoes carried in U.S. vessels, from 10 percent in 1913 to 35 percent in 1935.[69] This development fundamentally shifted the balance of international maritime power and constituted an important element in the overall United States bid for world power. At the same time, however, the hothouse nature of the wartime and postwar efforts led to such serious domestic problems as systematic corruption and massive inefficiency. After the war, tonnage was sold to private firms. However, without subsidies, such tonnage could not be employed profitably. Government aid resulted in a vicious cycle of subsidy–inefficiency–further subsidy, and this cycle

64. Jeffrey J. Safford, "Anglo-American Maritime Relations During the Two World Wars: A Comparative Analysis," *American Neptune* 41 (October 1981), p. 264.
65. Ibid., p. 265.   66. Ibid., p. 267.   67. Ibid., p. 268.   68. Ibid.
69. Saugstad, "Ocean Shipping in World Economics," p. 206.

became a permanent feature of United States shipping and shipbuilding. It had a progressively greater impact on the international regime as American power and America's role in world trade expanded.

Thus during the interwar period America found itself in the paradoxical position of premier maritime nation bedeviled by a grossly inefficient and parasitic maritime sector. During World War II an even greater expansion of the maritime industries was to occur, which would have an even more far-reaching impact on the structure of the international regime. In 1945 the recognition of the responsibilities and opportunities of American hegemony would inspire American policymakers, in conjunction with their allies, to design a new regime for shipping and, at least temporarily, to resolve traditional U.S.-European conflicts.

During the interwar period, the tendencies in shipping that had their origin in the final two decades of the nineteenth century—intensified competition, government intervention, protectionist policies, and monopolistic agreements—were accentuated by the general crisis of world politics. Surplus capacity was large, although not nearly as large in either absolute or relative terms as that following the 1973–74 oil crisis. After 1934, policies were implemented by most governments to cut back this capacity. With the exception of the United States, which was a prisoner of its massive government shipping programs, most shipping nations did manage to reduce capacity.

Conclusion

This chapter has examined the succession of shipping regimes in the modern history of international relations. International shipping has been extremely important from both economic and political standpoints. Although shipping no longer serves as the strategic organizing principle of the international political economy, as it did before repeal of the Navigation Acts, it remains a crucial factor in international trade and in many national economies. On the basis of this historical sketch, three conclusions can be drawn concerning shipping's general role. First, there is an obvious correlation between free trade or the Grotian principle of freedom of the seas and the presence of a hegemonic power. Second, fundamental change in shipping is a function not only of basic transformations in the international distribution of power but also of basic changes in international capitalism. Third, shipping regimes contain the seeds of their own destruction: the success of various regimes in promoting interdependence and economic growth has undermined stability, by accentuating the tendency toward uneven development of national economies and by creating power shifts. Challenges to regimes have emanated from lesser or have-not powers. But hegemonic powers have also flouted the rules, prolonging their power but contributing to the demise of the regime and intensifying international conflicts.

The concept of freedom of the seas reflected the interests of Dutch commerce. The Netherlands enjoyed a brief period of military and economic ascendency. Its navy ruled the waves, its shipping was commercially and technologically superior to that of all other states, and the Dutch fleet was depleting European and British coastal fishing. Given the small size of the Dutch economy, the trading companies had an overwhelming interest in freedom to cross-trade. By 1650, freedom of the seas came into conflict with the requirements of England's economic and political development. Had it depended on Dutch hegemony, the expansion of the world capitalist system would have been problematic. England relied on colonial markets and participation in the Baltic trades. But a free-seas regime was subject to Dutch monopoly and threatened to stunt the growth of British shipping and, indirectly, the development of the British economy. Moreover, the expansionist impulse the maritime industries were providing to English capitalism would have been dissipated. Politically, bereft of a strong merchant fleet or navy, England would have been unable to secure its colonies from the encroachments not only of the Netherlands but also of France. Of course, once it was capable of controlling the seas, Britain was able to establish the political conditions for a new era of free trade under British hegemony.

The correlation between free trade and hegemony breaks down after 1880. At that time, changes in modern capitalism, including the greatly expanded role of the state and the concentration of ownership, precluded free trade in the strict sense, as markets were managed by states and groups of firms. The have-not powers, especially Germany, began before World War I to challenge British shipping. Britain also undermined the regime by engaging in collusive practices designed to defend its share of markets. Following 1945, the United States as hegemonic leader established a more open and cooperative system; this is the subject of Part II, which follows.

Such a system was desirable for America's leaders because a continuation of the intense shipping nationalism characteristic of the interwar years would have limited the expansion of international trade and damaged the American economy. However, the task of the new hegemonic leader was not simply to establish a freedom-of-the-seas regime. Rather, victorious America was charged with establishing a political and economic framework conducive to generalized growth and national development of a coalition of states. The United States faced the challenge of creating a relatively open system of shipping that was compatible not only with its own aims and traditions but also with those of its trading partners.

PART TWO

The Atlantic Order

3

The Creation of an
Atlantic Regime

The post–World War II international economic order was born out of conflict between two competing principles of organization: liberal internationalism and national capitalism.[1] This conflict, which raged within and among most advanced industrial nations, had specific implications for the shape of the international shipping regime. After World War II most European governments initially pressed for a national capitalist solution to the problem of reconstruction. They feared the raw power of the American economy and the strength of the left; they wished to retain empires. In the United States, nationalist forces, although important in the New Deal coalition, were thrown into disarray by the death of Franklin Roosevelt. When the coalition broke apart, they lost any hope of participating in the strategic formulation of foreign economic policy. Nevertheless, through Congress and public opinion they continued to ex-

1. The distinction between "liberal internationalism" and "national capitalism" is made by Fred L. Block, *Origins of International Economic Disorder: A Study of U.S. International Monetary Policy from World War II to the Present* (Berkeley and Los Angeles: University of California Press, 1977), esp. pp. 32–42.

Table 5.   Wartime Shares of Merchant Ship Construction (as percentage of
               Allied and neutral grt)

	1940	1941	1942	1943	1944	1945
United States	30	36	71	83	86	86
British Common- wealth	52	52	26	15	12	9
Other Allied and neutral	18	12	3	2	2	5

SOURCE: Report of the U.S. War Shipping Administration to the President, *The U.S. Merchant Marine at War* (Washington, D.C.: G.P.O., 1946).

ercise considerable leverage. In both the international and the national arenas, the victory of the liberal internationalists was incomplete and costly. Concessions to nationalism were necessary to promote stability and retain popular approval, yet these concessions set in motion forces that tended to undermine the international economic order.

America's general commitment to liberalism stemmed partly from the convictions of most statesmen and intellectuals that the autarchic drift of the 1930s was responsible for the depth of the Great Depression and the drive to war.[2] The postwar blueprint called for an open world market, which would obviate the need for rival powers to create exclusive commercial spheres. Imperial blocs would be broken up and the formal sovereignty of nations would be buttressed by international organizations capable of policing and legitimizing the new order. Free trade would also maximize benefits for the United States, which was situated to reap the rewards of a system based on equal opportunity for all nations.

The wartime mobilization of America's maritime industries meant that the United States had the power to dictate the rules of the postwar shipping regime. The tremendous strength of American industry was exemplified in shipbuilding, as Table 5 indicates. Had the United States chosen to exercise all of its power, and had the shipowners been permitted to preserve their influence over maritime policy, the ensuing regime would undoubtedly have been cast in a highly protectionist or national capitalist mold, representing

2. See esp. Herbert Feis, *The Sinews of Peace* (New York: Harper and Row, 1944). For a critique of this perspective, see the essays in Benjamin Rowland, ed., *Balance of Power or Hegemony: The Interwar Monetary System* (New York: New York University Press, 1976).

an accentuation of the international trends of the interwar period. As was indicated in Chapter 2, the American shipping industry developed under the wing of the government in a climate of Anglo-American hostility. American shipowners, unlike their banker and manufacturer compatriots, had not had their protectionist sentiments softened by the successful but limited pre–World War I expansion into world trade. On the contrary, the drive for foreign markets had confirmed and enhanced their nationalist instincts as inefficient shipowners entered an environment monopolized by the stronger Europeans. In shipping, the most ardent nationalists were American, whereas the free traders or oligopolists were European.

This historical legacy was a serious obstacle for the architects of the Pax Americana in the area of shipping policy. The importance of shipping to the European allies meant that general protection would conflict with the needs of European reconstruction. Moreover, a nationalistic regime was inconsistent with a generally liberal trading order, not only because it would raise the costs of international transportation by promoting inefficiency, but also because it would conflict with the principle of free trade, which the United States was seeking to apply wherever feasible. Internationally, American planners needed to reconcile the interests of two antagonistic shipping blocs. Domestically, they had to contend with the nationalism of shipowners and maritime unions. These groups, moreover, had gained enormous prestige in the course of the war and had powerful backers in Congress. Finally, American planners had to balance the interests of Europe with the U.S. strategic requirement of maintaining a substantial merchant marine. In contrast to all former hegemonic powers, despite its impressive wartime build-up, the United States was traditionally a very weak shipping power.

Considering these obstacles, the establishment of a relatively stable postwar shipping regime was a major accomplishment. It demonstrated the impressive political and diplomatic skills of American policymakers as well as the considerable resources available to them. In shipping, as in most other areas, American hegemony entailed a unification of the world freight market. It did not, however, result in free trade in the classical sense. Rather, the regime fulfilled the two partially contradictory objectives of openness and equilibrium, while maximizing long-range American interest.

The establishment of a privatized international shipping regime reflected both conscious design on the part of American officials and an unwillingness to oppose the reassertion of the traditional order in shipping. Moreover, such a regime was by no means inimical to the desires of American shipowners once a full-blown protectionist regime—their preference—was ruled out. In the liner sector, conferences were allowed to operate largely outside the sway of governments, including the U.S. government with its considerable body of regulatory legislation. Conferences were thus ceded key decision-making functions, including the determination of freight rates and the distribution of shipping shares. The system was oligopolistic but not formally closed. It certainly did exploit the comparative advantage of Western and Northern European nations in shipping, and so facilitated the expansion of world trade. But it also acted as a barrier to Third World fleet expansion and hastened the decline of U.S. liner shipping. In so doing it established strong incentives for the U.S. government to grant ever-increasing subsidies to U.S. liner operators and to expand the scope of protective legislation. In bulk shipping, of course, the principle of privatization served both immediate and long-range U.S. interests, for flags of convenience provided the means for the dramatic expansion of beneficially owned U.S. bulk shipping.

World War II

Command of the sea was crucial to Allied victory over the Axis powers, and America's new role was evident in the nature of Allied wartime shipping collaboration. One of Germany's weaknesses was the inability to control sea lanes. This forced Germany to adopt a strategy of rapid territorial conquest, whereas Britain and the United States could afford to pursue a strategy of attrition. Japan sought to protect access to its overseas conquests through a single, decisive blow against U.S. naval forces. Allied maritime cooperation was not immune to the frictions and rivalries that characterized relations during World War I. However, the nature of this collaboration demonstrated not only the greater magnitude of American seapower during World War II but also the ability and the willingness to use that power to maximize long-range or hegemonic interests.

The ability of the Allies to conduct anti-submarine warfare, an increasingly effective naval blockade, and the breakdown of the blitzkrieg in Russia deprived Germany of the war materiel necessary for protracted warfare. At the same time, maritime supremacy permitted the United States to deliver vast quantities of war materiel to Britain and the Soviet Union.[3] The unprecedented deployment of manpower and industrial resources on a global scale primarily through merchant shipping made possible the defeat of Japan and Germany.

Despite its overall maritime superiority, Britain's temporary inability to defend its shipping against the U-boats during the first part of World War II would have isolated it from the Empire if the U.S. maritime industries had not interceded. Britain's dependence on U.S. shipping during these years was an important factor in American diplomacy and was used as a spear to penetrate the British Empire. In September 1939, Britain and the Commonwealth possessed 17.8 million gross registered tons (grt) of merchant shipping; three months later 2.9 million grt had been sunk by German submarines. Between 1 January 1940 and 1 April 1941, 6.3 million grt of dry cargo tonnage was lost, an average of 420,000 tons per month. In the second quarter of 1941 an additional 2.4 million tons went down. In eighteen months, U-boats had sunk over 20 percent of the world merchant shipping tonnage.[4]

British shipyards were not able to replace the lost ships. In 1941 Churchill and Roosevelt agreed to trade British military bases in the Western hemisphere for 50 United States destroyers. In October 1940, Britain negotiated the purchase of 60 dry cargo vessels. In early 1941, Roosevelt decided to build 200 dry cargo vessels for American use. The standard adopted was the Liberty ship of 10,800 deadweight tons (dwt). (A few of these ships still remain in operation.) In April 1941, the United States Maritime Commission was authorized to build an additional 306 vessels, including 111 Liberty ships and 72 standard T-2 tankers. Many ships of both types were immediately transferred either to the British or the Panamanian flag, to circumvent American neutrality laws.[5]

3. Report of the War Shipping Administration to the President, *The United States Merchant Marine at War* (Washington, D.C.: G.P.O., 15 January 1946). For wartime histories of merchant shipping war, see Felix Rosenberg, Jr., *Sea War: The Story of the U.S. Merchant Marine in World War II* (New York: Rinehart, 1956); and C. B. A. Behrens, *Merchant Shipping and the Demands of War* (London: Longman, Green, 1959).

4. United States Office of Naval Operations, *Aircraft and Merchant Shipping in World War II, with Indicated Trends* (Washington, D.C.: G.P.O., October 1949).

5. Daniel Levine and Sara Ann Platt, "The Contribution of United States Shipbuilding and the Merchant Marine to the Second World War," in Robert A. Kilmarx, ed., *America's Maritime Legacy: A History of the U.S. Merchant Marine and Shipbuilding Industry Since Colonial Times* (Boulder: Westview, 1979), p. 179.

   Allied shipping collaboration created the need for international organizations. Roosevelt and Churchill agreed to pool all shipping resources, and
the Allies established the Combined Shipping Adjustment Board in early
1942. The United States accepted responsibility for shipping requirements
in the Western hemisphere, while Great Britain organized transportation
throughout the rest of the world. During World War II, the United States
merchant marine carried 268 million long tons and ferried 7 million
troops.[6] U.S. shipping also carried a steady stream of raw materials crucial
to the war economy, including bauxite from Latin America, rubber, copper,
tin, scrap iron, and crude oil. American shipping was critical to Britain's
defense of the Middle East, the Indian Ocean, and the Persian Gulf. From
May to December 1941, American ships transported 49,000 vehicles,
302,000 tons of dry goods, and 814 airplanes to these regions.[7]

   Although the Washington Naval Treaty of 1922 and the wartime expansion of American merchant shipping signified the end of British maritime
supremacy, it was the tremendous expansion of shipping and shipbuilding
capacity during World War II that finally established the United States
as the premier world maritime power. Britain would, however, remain a
strong shipping power even during its long postwar economic decline.

   Despite Anglo-American wartime collaboration, shipowners on both
sides of the Atlantic remained well aware of their economic rivalry and the
implications of wartime developments for postwar commercial plans. The
frictions of World War I and the interwar years were not forgotten. In
1943 Lord Rotherwick, chairman of Clan Line, expressed the opinion of
the majority of British shipowners in urging that after the war the British
merchant marine should rapidly be expanded to prewar tonnage levels
through the transfer of enemy shipping and the construction in enemy
shipyards of vessels for British owners. In addition to this, Rotherwick in-
sisted that the American government "hand over such vessels built, under
construction, or arranged for, under their flag, to their allies as necessary
to bring up the proportion of shipping owned by them at the outbreak of
hostilities."[8]

   American shipowners countered by reiterating their historical grievances against European owners, specifically referring to the Axis powers.

   6. Ibid., p. 204.
   7. Behrens, *Merchant Shipping,* pp. 301–7.
   8. Quoted in J. Hans Adler, "British and American Shipping Policies: A Problem and a
Proposal," *Political Science Quarterly* 59 (June 1944), pp. 201–2.

In a statement issued by the American Merchant Marine Institute, U.S. shipping firms contended that "the enemy nations have for two generations used their merchant fleets as spearheads of world penetration" and urged that "these nations should not be permitted to resume such a position."[9] In January 1944, the National Federation of Shipping Companies, the new shipowners' organization, launched an educational campaign to instruct the public on the need for a "strong postwar merchant marine capable of transporting 70 percent of America's foreign trade."[10]

World War II thus interrupted but did not completely eradicate Anglo-American shipping rivalry, which was rooted in more general commercial antagonisms and the historical position of the United States as primarily a consumer of shipping services, as opposed to Britain's role as both consumer and supplier. However, the comparison of Allied shipping collaboration during the two world wars provides a striking illustration of the transformation of America from opportunistic, upstart power to world leader. Jeffrey Safford's comparison of these collaborative efforts reveals that

> in the great conflict of 1914–18, and directly beyond, Anglo-American maritime relations were fraught with extraordinary rivalries, suspicions, and enmity. While corresponding patterns seemed possible for the Second World War, a similar tack was spurned successfully on the part of a small number of high-minded men determined to mend the ways of the past.[11]

Transatlantic hostility between shipowners remained but, in contrast to World War I, it did not now resonate in government or leading corporate circles. "High-mindedness" aptly describes the conviction of a domestic power bloc—given political and ideological leadership by Cordell Hull, William Clayton, and Averill Harriman—that America's postwar potential was best served through internationalism and leadership. The influence of these "business internationalists" derived from their political ascendancy over protectionist forces who either lacked a sophisticated understanding of hegemonic duties and possibilities or represented particular interests that were destined to lose out under the new order.

The victory of this new bloc was immediately reflected in United States

9. *New York Times*, 31 August 1943, p. 19.

10. *New York Times*, 30 January 1944, p. 37. J. E. Otterson (*Foreign Trade and Shipping* [New York: McGraw-Hill, 1945]) discusses the survival of Anglo-American antagonisms in shipping; see esp. chapters 2, 7, and 14.

11. Jeffrey J. Safford, "Anglo-American Maritime Relations During the Two World Wars: A Comparative Analysis," *American Neptune* 41 (October 1981), p. 262.

shipping strategy. In contrast to their World War I predecessors, the leading War Shipping administrators were committed to "shipping liberalism," which meant, in practical terms, a pro-English stance. Lewis Douglas, chairman of the War Shipping Administration and protégé of Cordell Hull, headed "the most potent pro-British team in the United States War Administration."[12] The sale of Liberty ships to Britain exemplifies the new attitude of the United States, and many other decisions reflect the hegemonic vision. For example, in contrast to the narrow nationalism displayed during World War I, the United States agreed to provide ships for British owners to maintain their services in cross-trading markets in the South Pacific on a "caretaker" basis.[13]

The issue of coal provides another illustration. During and immediately after World War I, Britain was unable to deliver coal to Italy, a traditional market for British exports, because of industrial militancy; despite British protest, the United States eagerly stepped into the breach, and Colonel House observed that the United States was "hitting at two of [England's] most lucrative industries."[14] During World War II, a similar situation arose because of coal shortages in Britain. This time, however, Lewis Douglas steadfastly refused to exploit the situation by exporting American coal or even by committing American vessels to carry British coal to Italy.

Of course, the new Anglo-American relationship was also made possible because of Britain's recognition of the new balance of power, in which Britain was compelled to play a subordinate role. As Arthur Salter, director of the British Merchant Shipping Ministry, noted in 1942,

> in the last war . . . there was one centre, London. Now there are two. Of these Washington has already an equal authority and its authority must increase. The great bulk of the new ships will be American. . . . To proceed as if [maritime policy] can be made in London and "put over" in Washington; or as if British policy can in the main develop independently and be only "incorporated" with American;—is merely to kick against the bricks.[15]

Designing a Postwar Regime

The nature of Allied collaboration during World War II foreshadowed the shape of the postwar regime, just as it had during World War I. American internationalism was reflected in attitudes toward shipping. Despite the

12. Ibid., p. 269.   13. Ibid., p. 275.   14. Ibid.   15. Ibid., p. 273.

best intentions, however, shipping policy was fraught with problems and contradictions. On the one hand, the tremendous wartime expansion of the United States maritime industries meant that America's general intentions and specific situation in shipping could determine the main contours of the postwar regime. As a report to the Royal Institute of International Relations observed in 1946, "the world shipping position is dominated by the enormous American fleet . . . and the future of world shipping must depend on the use the Americans make of that fleet." [16]

Yet America was relatively backward in shipping, and the effects of this backwardness—state intervention and a mercantilist tradition—made their mark on the organization of postwar shipping. As a result, certain contradictions were present in the regime from the beginning, although they did not create major disturbances until the 1960s.

Despite its mercantilist tradition and the still-virulent protectionist outlook of American shipowners, the official United States attitude toward postwar shipping was liberal and thus consistent with general commercial philosophy. Policymakers sought to organize a regime based on free trade. An open world shipping market would further the expansion of world trade by establishing a rational division of labor. The law of comparative advantage would enable the most efficient shipowners to expand their operations, causing a decline in ocean freight rates as a result of the optimal employment of all factors of production. Specialization of countries and regions with a comparative advantage, notably Britain, Scandinavia, and Greece, would be an integrative force discouraging the use of subsidies, which had promoted conflict during the interwar years. William Clayton, undersecretary of state for economic affairs, explained United States attitudes in a speech to the United Maritime Council in 1947:

> Our proposals are designed to bring about a great expansion in world economy—increased production and consumption, and a great increase in the exchange of goods between nations. . . . We confidently expect that the shipping interests of the world, for the most part, will actively support our proposals to expand free trade.[17]

16. John S. Maclay, "The General Shipping Situation," *International Affairs* 22 (October, 1946), p. 487.

17. U.S. Department of State *Bulletin* 25, no. 383 (Washington, D.C.: Department of State, 3 November 1946), pp. 817, 822. See also Eula McDonald, "Toward a World Maritime Organization—Half a Century of Development in Ocean Shipping," and John M. Cates, Jr., "United Nations Maritime Conference, Geneva, 1948," Department of State Publication

This approach, which reflected the perceived need to accommodate Western European shipping interests, represented a significant shift in traditional U.S. maritime philosophy. It was made possible by the new power of the American economy, the recognition of America's hegemonic role in the Atlantic community, and the quieting of isolationist and protectionist voices in the United States.

After World War II, the victorious internationalist coalition worked to promote an international shipping policy to restore the European shipping powers to their traditional positions. Clayton, Edward Stettinius (later a prominent shipowner), and Lewis Douglas, who realized that for Western and Northern Europe shipping was "the nerve center of their national life,"[18] took the lead in suppressing the domestic forces of maritime nationalism. This meant curbing the power of shipowners as an interest group and circumscribing the role of the Federal Maritime Board, the shipowners' main base of support within the government. The most tangible expression of the internationalists' victory was the rapid disposition of American shipping. Against the wishes of shipowners, the Merchant Ship Sales Act of 1946 was passed, authorizing the sale of American vessels to allies.[19]

The governments and shipowners of most traditional maritime powers readily supported Clayton's vision as it applied to shipping. This vision corresponded to the views and objectives of most European shipowners. Although service industries were not covered under the General Agreement on Tariffs and Trade (GATT), most Western governments sought, through their activities in the OEEC (later OECD), to apply the principles of nondiscrimination, reduction of tariff barriers, and multilateral coordination of policies to shipping.[20] The Maritime Transport Committee became an important working body within the OEEC, and the OEEC

3196, International Organization and Conference Series IV (Washington, D.C.: G.P.O., 1948).

18. Safford, "Anglo-American Maritime Relations," p. 276.

19. The Merchant Ship Sales Act of 1946 provided for sales abroad of U.S. vessels and the establishment of a United States Reserve Fleet. Between 1 July 1945 and 30 June 1953, eleven million tons of U.S. shipping were sold abroad, primarily to Greek, Norwegian, British, and French interests. See Stanley G. Sturmey, *British Shipping and World Competition* (London: Athlone, 1962), pp. 155–56.

20. For a review of the GATT, see Gerald Curzon, *Multi-Lateral Commercial Diplomacy: The General Agreement on Tariffs and Trade and Its Impact on National Commercial Policies and Technique* (London: Michael Joseph, 1965).

Code of Liberalization of Current Invisible Operations called for the progressive removal of restrictions in shipping.[21] The universality of the public commitment to shipping liberalism is indicated by the rhetorical expression of support for free trade as late as the first UNCTAD conference in 1964. In most areas of the world economy, the dismantling of restrictions did not occur until the late 1950s, when European economies were capable of competing in trade on an equal basis and convertibility was possible. Shipping was no exception to the general rule that barriers to trade should be removed. It was unusual, however, in that the typical postwar inclinations of Europe and America were reversed: Europe favored a privately organized regime, without government intervention; America was the country with a strong protectionist lobby.

As was shown in Chapter 2, before World War II international coordination of shipping was minimal and tended to be limited to the consideration of technical matters deemed important to shipping firms. International conventions were established on a range of issues affecting commercial relations; a few diplomatic conferences were also held on an ad hoc basis to consider legal problems. The main impetus to international organization, however, came from war. During World War I the allied organization of shipping was piecemeal and incomplete, especially prior to the United States entry. The World War II Allied body, the Combined Shipping Adjustment Board, was not much more effective than its World War I prototype, the Allied Maritime Transport Council. However, a remarkable degree of Anglo-American wartime collaboration was achieved despite the limitations of formal international organizations.[22]

International organizations were at the core of American plans for the postwar order. Although shipowners from the United States and some other countries, notably Norway and Sweden, opposed the establishment of an international shipping organization, the U.S. State Department advocated such a body and was supported by France and Britain. The United States sought, among other objectives, "to supply continuity of effort necessary for effective international cooperation in shipping in place of the present practice of sporadic diplomatic conferences" and "to contribute to world peace by the establishment of a forum where differences of opinion

21. Henry C. Aubrey, *Atlantic Economic Cooperation: The Case of the OECD* (New York: Council on Foreign Relations, 1967), pp. 63–64.
22. Behrens, *Merchant Shipping*, pp. 448–49.

on shipping questions could be discussed and resolved by persons familiar with the problems."[23]

The origins of the Intergovernmental Maritime Consultative Organization (IMCO) lay in the United Maritime Authority (UMA), which succeeded the Combined Shipping Adjustment Board and was charged with extending coordination of Allied shipping in the final months of the war. At the recommendation of the United States, the United Maritime Consultative Council (UMCC) convened to plan the establishment of IMCO as a United Nations specialized agency. In 1948 the United Nations Maritime Conference met in Geneva. Following negotiations, IMCO was formally established, although its ratification would take another decade.

Despite a climate conducive to multilateral agreements, the original hopes for IMCO, now succeeded by IMO, proved to be too ambitious. The convention required the agreement of twenty-one states, of which seven should possess one million tons of merchant shipping, for ratification; ratification was delayed until 1959, when Japan finally acceded. Opposition to IMCO hinged on the original mandate to investigate charges of discrimination and unfair practices, a condition that the conferences and traditional maritime nations, committed to the principle of privatization, could scarcely have been expected to accept with equanimity. As a result, IMCO remained in limbo for a decade, with the bloc of Western and Northern European states refusing to ratify it.[24]

With a budget of approximately one million dollars, IMO has functioned largely as a weak regulatory body, the poorest specialized agency within the United Nations. It is dependent on scientific personnel who are limited to a range of questions that are more technical than political. As a consequence, despite its limited successes in the fields of safety and pollution, it operates on the margins of international shipping politics. Even its highly technical conventions have not fared well in national policy; its ratification record is low, and compliance has been lower still.[25] IMO has been the province of administrators, not foreign office officials. External

23. Cates, "United Nations Maritime Conference," p. 18.
24. On IMCO, see esp. Harvey Silverstein, *Superships and Nation States—The Transnational Policies of IMCO* (Boulder: Westview, 1978); and R. Michael M'Gonigle and Mark W. Zacher, *Pollution, Politics, and International Law: Tankers at Sea* (Berkeley and Los Angeles: University of California Press, 1979).
25. See esp. M'Gonigle and Zacher, *Pollution, Politics, and International Law,* pp. 336–38.

political issues seldom penetrate IMO proceedings. This does not mean that shipping affairs have been depoliticized; national governments simply do not permit IMO to make political decisions.

The fate of IMO vividly exemplifies the essentially private character of the postwar regime: the emasculation of international organizations meant that the principal political economic issues of world shipping would be decided through the workings of the marketplace, with its oligopolistic structure, and by maritime diplomacy among the major powers. Thus the analysis of IMCO and IMO decision-making reveals only a part of the political economy of international shipping because so much of the action lay elsewhere. The establishment of such an organization with a clear mandate to address the principal issues of the regime would have to wait for UNCTAD's Committee on Shipping, in 1964. The committee very quickly rejected the principle that the state should be excluded from international shipping.

Thus, during the postwar regime no advanced industrial power challenged the principle of privatization. The natural protectionist, the United States, defended privatization as a component of general commercial policy, despite a legislative history of shipping nationalism and protectionist sentiments within the shipping industry as well as in Congress. In Western and Northern Europe, shipping industries were insulated from national capitalist approaches to reconstruction that created friction between the United States and Europe in important areas such as trade and finance. With the exception of the Japanese, shipping industries outside the Western hemisphere were relatively insignificant before the mid-1960s.

Contradictions of the Regime

Agreement on the principle of privatization established a basis for stability. But it by no means eliminated the conflicts of interest that surfaced as various states interpreted privatization according to particular interests and sought to define rights and obligations. Special characteristics of the shipping industry made it possible for states to deprive the word *marketplace* of much of its meaning even as they celebrated its alleged virtues. In the name of free competition, shipping conferences were both attacked and defended, while government regulation of obvious anticompetitive practices was criticized as a device for subverting market forces.

Despite agreement in principle on the desirability of the free market in shipping, Europe diverged from the United States on a host of practical issues. Although Japan did not play an important role in shipping diplomacy, its interests, as it rebuilt its fleet, usually coincided with those of the Europeans. Western European and Scandinavian countries, with the exception of France, favored an interpretation of the marketplace that sanctioned shipping cartels. The United States, in contrast, increasingly sought to justify government involvement while carefully upholding the principle of market discipline. Areas of disagreement increased over time and became institutionalized as American vessels were transferred abroad, Europe's shipping industries recovered, and the underlying weaknesses of U.S. shipping, despite the immense wartime build-up, became more acute.

In the aftermath of World War II, the demand for world shipping exceeded supply in many trades. Available tonnage limited the expansion of world trade, and United States and European ships competed for cargoes on an equal basis in a seller's market. By 1948, however, competition between European and American shipping was again beginning. As the traditional maritime powers increased their tonnage, the chronic weaknesses of the U.S. maritime industry—largely a result of relatively high labor costs—began to reappear. This made it difficult for the United States to resist implementing at least some protectionist measures.

Citing national security objectives, the United States government began to interpret shipping principles so as to incorporate an array of regulatory and promotional policies aimed at maintaining a substantial U.S. flag merchant fleet. Thus, for example, at the IMCO convention in 1948, the United States successfully included the following qualifications to the antidiscriminatory clauses: "Assistance and encouragement given by a Government for the development of its national shipping does not in itself constitute discrimination, provided that such assistance and encouragement is not based on measures designed to restrict the freedom of shipping of all flags to take part in international trade."[26] A proposal to clarify this rather ambiguous interpretation of discrimination was defeated. While the legitimacy of flag discrimination was in doubt throughout the postwar period, the practice and justification persisted. A United Nations study undertaken

26. Convention of the Intergovernmental Maritime Consultative Organization, Article 16, United Nations Document, E/cont. 4/61 of 6 March 1948 (Geneva: United Nations, 1948).

in 1967, for example, concluded that "there is no definite negative judg-
ment on flag discrimination."[27] Subsidies were accepted, reluctantly, by all
countries, in accordance with the guidelines of the GATT, which noted,
however, that subsidies constituted a lesser evil than protectionism in the
form of tariff barriers or quotas. In contrast to America's nationalistic proclivities, the commitment of European governments to free trade was expressed in the OEEC Code of Liberalization. The code, which mandated
the establishment of liberalization in shipping markets, was redrafted in
1961 under OECD auspices, with United States, Canadian, and Japanese
membership. Only the United States entered significant reservations regarding shipping.

Conclusion

The reconstruction of a cooperative international shipping regime, largely
purged of the nationalism of the 1930s, represented a major accomplishment for American policymakers. Shipping had historically been dominated by the traditional maritime powers of Western Europe. American
shipping, in contrast, was backward, and American shipowners were
fervently nationalistic. America's hegemonic ascendancy was expressed
not through supplanting the European powers and filling the oceans
with American flag vessels but, rather, through constructing a system in
which the European merchant fleets could flourish but in which core
American interests were safeguarded. The contrast between Allied cooperation in World War I and World War II is instructive. During and immediately after World War I, the United States confronted the Europeans—
especially the British—in maritime policy. Three decades later, however,
hegemonic America largely abandoned nationalism in favor of a more
internationalist approach. Domestically, the forces of nationalism were
bought off and not allowed to chart the strategic course of national maritime policy.

In the negotiations over the postwar regime, both Western Europe and
the United States expressed a strong commitment to competition in shipping. Broadly, the postwar regime certainly did reflect this objective: the
maze of government promotional devices that characterized the interwar

27. Economist Intelligence Unit, *Ocean Shipping and Freight Rates and Developing Countries* (Geneva: United Nations, 1964), p. 88.

period was lifted; shipowners formally had free access to cargoes; and cross-trading, the opposite of mercantilism in shipping, flourished. International organizations were not allowed to interfere with the activities of shipping firms or to address political or redistributive questions.

I have adopted the term *privatization,* rather than *liberalism,* as the most accurate description of the constitutive principle of the postwar regime. *Privatization* indicates the key role played by shipping firms in decisions concerning freight rates and shipping shares, as well as a minimum of state intervention and America's renunciation of its traditional antitrust philosophy. Although private companies were the key actors in the regime, the marketplace they dominated was not free in the classical sense but, rather, oligopolistic. Moreover, government intervention was greatly reduced but not eliminated. In the liner trades, Europe favored privatization because it allowed "conference power" in keeping with its traditions and interests. The United States, however, never completely abandoned the regulatory philosophy expressed in the Alexander Report and the U.S. Shipping Act of 1916. Nevertheless, it was content to accept privatization during the 1950s and 1960s.

In the bulk trades, as Chapter 4 will show, the situation was reversed. Here, the Europeans would have preferred national regulation as an alleged defense of the marketplace as well as a means of preserving a strong European presence in bulk shipping. But the United States celebrated the unregulated flags of convenience as embodying the highest virtues of the marketplace. On both sides of the Atlantic, interests determined ideology.

4

The Bulk/Raw Materials Sector: The Flag of Convenience Issue

In the twentieth century, the locus of power in the shipment of bulk materials, including oil, has gradually shifted from independent shipowners to transnational firms and, indirectly, to large financial institutions in the United States and to a lesser extent in Britain and Japan. This shift has been a natural outgrowth of the strategy of multinational corporations for controlling not only the extraction or harvesting of raw materials, but also transportation, refining, and marketing. Vertical integration facilitated the establishment of economies of scale in the transportation of oil and other bulk materials. It also ensured that shipping tonnage was sufficient to accommodate the greatly expanding trade in bulk commodities, especially oil. The degree of integration is not absolute and varies for different commodities. These changes have certainly not caused the death of independent bulk shipping, but they have led to the progressive incorporation of the activities of independent shipowners into the strategies of the multinationals.

The promotional and regulatory measures designed to assist the United States merchant fleet were traditionally aimed at the liner sector. Until the

amendment of the Merchant Marine Act in 1970, U.S. legislation provided no direct subsidies to bulk vessel owners. Such limited government
support as has been available has been targeted narrowly at the *national*
trade in bulk materials. Until World War II, the *global* trade in raw materials was relatively unimportant for the United States, which was a net exporter of bulk cargoes and not heavily involved in the international oil
industry.[1] Bulk exports such as grain were shipped in a relatively open market, and American exporters were not unduly troubled by European leadership. Indeed, it was European and especially British innovations (in
steam and refrigeration) that enabled American farmers to enter the world
market so successfully. Similarly, cargo-sharing arrangements in this sector
were not favored by the United States government; until recently, it has
not been practical, given the general tendency for bulk shipments to travel
from periphery (or colony) to center (or colonial power).

However, as American multinationals spread across the globe in the
wake of World War II, raw materials became increasingly important.
United States policy gradually shifted from a relatively narrow concern for
national trade to the more ambitious objective of dominating the general
regime for the transportation of bulk commodities. But the high wages
and operating costs for U.S. shipping and the relative backwardness of the
industry created a fundamental dilemma for American policymakers: because of cross-trading, either Western Europe would control the bulk sector or massive subsidies would have to be granted to equalize United States
and Western European costs.

Flags of convenience represented an alternative means of guaranteeing
economical, U.S.-controlled bulk shipping. They became the key manifestation of American maritime policy and the determining feature of the
bulk sector of the postwar regime. The establishment and defense of flags
of convenience constituted a competitive U.S. policy, aimed primarily at
Western Europe and defended with reference to the principle of privatization. In a largely unregulated environment in which labor markets were
subject to market forces and taxation was minimal, flags of convenience
would allow American extractive and agribusiness industries to integrate
transportation as a part of their operations. Western Europe and global labor, in contrast, favored the regulation of bulk shipping, which required a

---

1. See, for example, the President's Materials Policy Commission (Paley Commission),
Resources for Freedom (Washington, D.C.: G.P.O., June 1952).

substantial link between ownership and flag. As American multinational corporations (MNCs) moved to a position of dominance in world extractive industries, they helped shift the center of power in shipping from Western Europe to the United States.

In formal terms, flags of convenience are the result of foreign direct investments by multinational corporations or independent bulk carrier operators such as Aristotle Onassis or Daniel K. Ludwig. The term *flag of convenience* refers to the registration of ships on the "open" registries of countries

> whose laws allow—and indeed make it easy for—ships owned by foreign nationals or companies to fly these flags. This is in contrast to the practice in the maritime countries (and in many others) where the right to fly the national flag is subject to stringent conditions and involves far-reaching obligations.[2]

Such flags have been attacked as "free flags," "runaway flags," "bogus flags," "private flags"; they have been defended as "flags of attraction" or "flags of necessity."[3] The role of the host state is, by definition, minimal; actions deemed "inconvenient" by shipowners would defeat the purpose of the institution. Therefore, it is possible to conceive of the open registry as a disguised form of mercantilism, an element of a competitive national shipping policy of a great power (or powers) willing and able to resort to such flags. This view is, in fact, implicitly adopted by international legal scholars. According to John Colombos, "Another form of competition is the growth of the system of flags of convenience whereby some countries . . . allow the use of their flags by a simple administrative formula."[4]

The use of flags of convenience arose out of post–World War I economic and political conditions in shipping but did not become widespread until after World War II. In 1924, fifteen ships, including several owned by oil companies and passenger ships owned by Averill Harriman, were transferred to Panamanian registry to take advantage of foreign crews. In 1935, Esso Petroleum registered twenty-five tankers under the flag of the Free City of Danzig, crewed by German sailors. Anticipating war, Esso re-

---

2. OEEC, Maritime Transport Committee, *Study on the Expansion of the Flag of Convenience Fleets and on Various Aspects Thereof* (Paris: OEEC, 1958), p. 2.

3. See Boleslaw Adam Boczek, *Flags of Convenience: An International Legal Study* (Cambridge, Mass.: Harvard University Press, 1962).

4. C. John Colombos, *The International Law of the Sea*, 6th ed. (New York: David McKay, 1967), p. 387.

moved the German crews, transferred the ships to Panamanian registry, and hired American crews. Following the passage of the Neutrality Act, Esso employed British crews, thus permitting them to continue to trade with Britain. Between 1939 and 1941 Roosevelt urged American ship-owners to circumvent neutrality by adopting the Panamanian flag, en-abling them to trade with future allies.[5]

Since World War II the main open registries have been Panama and Liberia, but Honduras and Costa Rica were at one time important flags of convenience; hence the term PanLibHonCo. More recently, Cyprus, Singapore, the Bahamas, and even the Isle of Man have opened their regis-tries, in large part to Greek and West German interests. Flag-of-convenience countries charge shipowners a nominal registration fee and an annual tax on tonnage. Typically, all phases of registration of a ship can be conducted in New York City or some other major commercial center within a forty-eight-hour period. In 1949 Liberia charged a registration fee of $1.20 per net registered ton and an annual tax of $0.10 per ton. In 1981 the tax was raised to $0.30 per ton, and in 1985 to $0.40 per ton. In 1978, Liberia's revenues from flags of convenience were $11 million.[6]

Open registries confer four major types of benefits on shipowners. In descending order of importance, they are: (1) lower labor costs; (2) tax reduction; (3) ability to evade safety and environmental regulations; and (4) freedom from government intervention for political, economic, and military purposes. At any given time, of course, any one of these benefits may be the predominating motive of a shipowner seeking open registry.[7] It

5. For reviews of the period see Boczek, *Flags of Convenience,* pp. 9–24; Stanley G. Sturmey, *British Shipping and World Competition* (London: Athlone, 1962), pp. 210–33.

6. UNCTAD, *Action on the Question of Open Registries,* TD/B/C.4/220 (Geneva: United Nations, 1981), p. 21; Robert Kappel, "Liberia's International Shipping Strategy—The Role of Flags of Convenience and the Repercussions for National Development" (Bremen: Insti-tute of Shipping Economics and Logistics, 1985) (mimeographed).

7. To register a vessel under a flag of convenience, "the entrepreneur (whether one or more persons) creates a Panamanian Company usually for each one of his vessels. The Pana-manian Company is legally represented in Panama at a certain fee per annum. The Panama-nian Company applies to the Panamanian, Costa Rican, Liberian, or Honduran Government (whichever is the case) for the registration of the vessel in question under its national flag. . . . All these formalities can be and are completed by correspondence from London, New York, Piraeus, or Athens. The fiscal obligations of the firm towards the country of registration of the ship (i.e., registration fees, tonnage taxes, cost of other formalities) are relatively small. Once a vessel is purchased it can be operated by one or two or more shipbroking offices that act as

is also important to point out that the traditional maritime powers also differ significantly in national shipping policies. Britain, for example, has been identified as a "quasi–flag of convenience" due to a benign fiscal climate and relatively low labor costs.[8] The presence of open registries has undoubtedly had a significant—albeit difficult to assess with precision—impact on national legislation throughout the world. If there were no open registries, national and international shipping regulations would likely be far less favorable to shipowners and more favorable to sailors. Thus flags of convenience are a result not only of international rivalry but also of conflict between shipping capital and labor.

U.S. Policy

Despite innovations leading to spectacular increases in economies of scale, the cost of bulk shipping continues to be greatly affected by the level of wages for seamen. This characteristic, coupled with the lack of government restraints and low taxes, makes wages an important determinant of costs and, therefore, competitiveness. According to the Exxon Corporation, "For most categories of a tanker's operating costs, the nation of registry has little influence. The principal category for which it matters is manning."[9] Even following dramatic increases in the cost of fuel, the cost of labor still represented over one-fifth of operating costs for the average tanker. Labor costs were significantly lowered by the development of supertankers in the 1960s, "very large crude carriers," followed by "ultra-large crude carriers."

In 1953, monthly crew costs on a vessel in OEEC countries ranged from $5,541 (Britain) to $10,274 (Scandinavia). The monthly cost for an American crew was $29,426.[10] In 1954, a report prepared by the Department of Transportation and the Maritime Administration found that one reason for these differentials was the freedom of many traditional ship-

---

agencies of the owners and are located in the above-mentioned cities or in the south of France, East Coast, United States, and so on" (Basil N. Metaxas, *Economics of Tramp Shipping* [London: Athlone, 1971], p. 157).

8. *Economist,* 19 March 1966, p. 65.

9. Exxon Public Affairs Department, *Tankers and the Flags They Fly* (New York: Exxon, 1979), p. 13.

10. Wytze Gorter, *United States Shipping Policy* (New York: Harper and Row, 1955), p. 100.

Table 6.   Comparison of Wage Costs Aboard United States and Foreign Flag
            Vessels, 1953

	Number of Crew	Total Monthly Wages (U.S. $)
United Kingdom, mixed crew	80	5,541
United Kingdom, white crew	54	6,444
Japan	56	6,273
Norway	43	7,145
Netherlands	55	7,567
Italy	41	7,713
Denmark	43	7,990
France	47	10,274
United States	48	29,426

SOURCE: U.S. Department of Commerce, Maritime Administration, Office of Government Aid, *Study of the Operations of the Maritime Administration and the Federal Maritime Board* (Washington, D.C.: G.P.O., 1953), p. 281.

owners, notably the British, to employ non-nationals.[11] According to U.S. law, 75 percent of the crew on American registered ships must be American citizens. Flags of convenience thus permitted American owners to employ seamen from other countries. Most seamen on ships flying flags of convenience were in fact Europeans, and many European shipowners deeply resented these raids on their traditional labor pool. The figures in Table 6 suggest that although open registries permitted U.S. shipowners to be competitive in terms of wages, differences in taxation would be a crucial factor in determining overall competitiveness, as wages in Europe and Japan were relatively low.

By 1945 Panama had emerged as the leading flag of convenience; in 1949 it became, technically, the fourth largest shipping nation, following the United States, Britain, and Norway. Of 462 ships of Panamanian registry, 306 were U.S.-owned and 90 were British-owned.[12] In 1947, United

11. U.S. Department of Commerce, Maritime Administration and Under-Secretary of State for Commerce and Transportation, *Maritime Subsidy Policy* (Washington, D.C.: G.P.O., 1954), p. 54.
12. Boczek, *Flags of Convenience*, p. 12.

States shipowners and corporations, led by Edward Stettinius, who had served as Roosevelt's secretary of state during World War II, decided to create an open registry in Liberia. As Boleslaw Boczek observed in his seminal study:

> The introduction of Liberia to the shipping world seems to have been due to the Stettinius Associates of New York who, having secured a flexible concession for the development of the Liberian economy, arranged the formalities for granting Liberian registration terms still more liberal than those of Panama.[13]

And the Liberian fleet grew even more rapidly than that of Panama. By 1959 it had surpassed Panama's fleet, increasing to almost 12 million grt. American shipowners were particularly fond of the Liberian flag. As Vander Clute, managing director of Gulf Oil, told a Senate subcommittee in 1957, "Liberia we regard as the godson of the United States."[14]

The establishment of flags of convenience on a large scale made a sharp break in U.S. shipping policy. The traditional linkage of shipping to shipbuilding through "buy American" legislation, and relatively high labor costs, had imposed serious constraints on American policymakers. The resolution of the problem by a reorganization of international shipping demonstrated the strength of extractive multinationals in national and international affairs. Edward Stettinius played a key role in the development of the Liberian registry precisely because he was the ideal liaison between government and New York financial and corporate interests.[15]

The wartime experience with Panama served as a precedent for the creation of the Liberian flag. Liberia would be even more accommodating to the big corporations. Seeking to develop rubber and ore, Stettinius recognized the possibilities in a Liberian flag and enlisted the support of large independent shipowners—Esso, Standard Oil of New Jersey—and the Chase Manhattan Bank. In 1948, these interests collaborated in drawing up a Liberian code of laws.[16] They established the International Trust Company in New York to handle flag registration.

13. Ibid., p. 13.

14. U.S. Congress, Senate, Committee on Interstate and Foreign Commerce, *Ship Transfers to Foreign Flags: Hearings Before the Merchant Marine and Fisheries Subcommittee of the Committee on Interstate and Foreign Commerce*, 85th Cong., 1957, p. 115.

15. See Rodney P. Carlisle, "The American Century Implemented: Stettinius and the Liberian Flag of Convenience," *Business History Review* 54 (Summer 1980).

16. Rodney P. Carlisle, *Sovereignty for Sale: The Origins and Evolution of the Panamanian and Liberian Flags of Convenience* (Annapolis: Naval Institute Press, 1981), pp. 119–33.

The initial State Department reaction to flags of convenience was negative, reflecting the residual influence of pure multilateralists such as Cordell Hull and Adolph Berle, who viewed open registries as a subterfuge. However, the State Department review of the Maritime Code in 1949 implicitly sanctioned flags of convenience. Stettinius's meticulous preparations and extensive government contacts ensured that officials from the army, navy, State Department, and CIA had participated in the planning.[17] Dean Acheson and Allen Dulles gave further support to the concept. In 1950, the Department of Defense endorsed flags of convenience; the United States Maritime Commission coined the phrase "effective United States control" (EUSC), referring to clauses in the Liberian Maritime Code (and in treaties with Panama) that placed U.S.-owned ships under the control of the State Department. In 1952, the Maritime Administration, now based in the Department of Commerce, established official guidelines and regulations governing EUSC ships. Thus open registries were explicitly endorsed at government level.

Using the Liberian and Panamanian flags enabled American shipowners to utilize relatively cheap foreign labor. At the same time, more productive foreign shipyards were used; eventually United States shipping legislation was amended to permit the "trading out" of U.S.-built tonnage to foreign (mainly Liberian and Panamanian) flags. The creation of an international labor market enabled owners to subvert the national gains won by militant seamen's unions internationally and, especially, in the United States.

Flags of convenience thus placed America's maritime unions on the defensive. Moreover, they further eroded maritime labor's political clout, which had been declining since the mid-1930s. A Committee for Flags of Necessity was established by the leading multinational corporations in 1958 to defend flags of convenience against domestic opponents and to parry the legal maneuvers sponsored by European shipowners.[18] As it did internationally, the United States government remained neutral in the domestic struggle over flags of convenience, except when the system faced serious threats. A succession of congressional investigations was begun in

17. Ibid., p. 133.
18. At the organizational meeting the following companies were represented: Alcoa Steamship, American Oil, Atlantic Refining, Standard Oil, Bethlehem Steel, Cities Service, Gulf, Richfield Oil, Sinclair Oil, Mobil Oil, Standard Oil of New Jersey, Texaco, Tidewater Oil, United Fruit (Erling D. Naess, *The Great PanLibHon Controversy: The Fight over Flags of Convenience* [London: Exeter Press, 1972], p. 50).

1949. Flags of convenience were condemned, but Congress took no legal action. Rodney Carlisle's recent study concludes that "congressional inaction reflected political and ideological deadlock over maritime issues, a deadlock that reflected a widespread impasse over maritime issues in American society."[19] Congressional inactivity nevertheless implicitly endorsed the system, as did the Law of the Sea Convention in 1958. Neither Congress nor the Supreme Court challenged the route taken by the big oil companies and the executive branch of government. And flags of convenience continue to be supported by the same coalition in the United States: extractive multinationals, large independent shipowners, and the executive branch.

Europe's Legal Challenge

Throughout the 1950s, the war against flags of convenience was waged on a global scale by shipowners, governments, and seamen organized in national unions and the International Transport Workers Federation. The primary sponsors of legal and, to a limited extent, trade union challenges were Western and Northern European shipowners and governments, who sought to establish the principle of regulation by requiring a "genuine link" between the vessel and the flag of registry. Battles raged in the United Nations, IMCO, the International Court of Justice, and on the waterfront. Opposition to flags of convenience culminated in an unprecedented international strike in 1958.[20]

Defenders of flags of convenience have portrayed postwar opposition to the legality of such flags as an "attack on the traditional principle," namely, that the concept of freedom of the seas establishes the right of sovereign states unilaterally to determine conditions of registry.[21] In fact, the principle has been vague enough that individual states have developed their own interpretation of the meaning of "freedom of the seas." As Sir Hersh Lauterpacht observed: "The purely legal aspect of the problem revealed

19. Carlisle, *Sovereignty for Sale*, p. 141.
20. See Naess, *The Great PanLibHon Controversy*, for one prominent shipowner's account. For a recent account of the International Transport Workers Federation, see Herbert Northrup and Richard L. Rowan, *The International Transport Workers Federation and Flags of Convenience* (Philadelphia: Wharton School, University of Pennsylvania, 1983).
21. For the legal defense of open registries, see Boczek, *Flags of Convenience*, esp. chapter 10.

once again that although in any field of international law there is, as a rule, a consensus of opinion on broad principles . . . there is no semblance of agreement in relation to specific rules or problems."[22]

In 1896 the Institute of International Law, reflecting Western European attitudes, ruled that conditions of registry "should not depart too much from the principles which have been adopted by the great number of states and which may, therefore, be considered to constitute the basis of international law in this respect."[23] In 1947, the General Assembly of the United Nations established the International Law Commission (ILC) in order to "initiate studies and make recommendations for the purpose of . . . encouraging the progressive development of international law and its codification."[24] The ILC was assigned the task of preparing the agenda for the Geneva Convention on the Law of the Sea. At this time flags of convenience were becoming controversial and emerged as one of fifteen issues considered formally by the ILC in 1949. Debate centered on the meaning of the phrase "freedom of the seas," and legal views reflected national interests. Panamanian delegates argued the states' rights position: "Every sovereign state shall be entitled to decide to whom it will give the right to fly its flag and to establish the regulations governing the granting of that right."[25] European representatives repeated the position of the Institute of International Law: because in the overwhelming majority of states registration required national ownership and national crew, at least one of these two conditions should be met. The ILC thus recommended that for registration to comply with international law "there must be a minimum national element, since control and jurisdiction by a state over shipping flying its flag can only be effectively exercised where there is in fact a relationship between the state and the ship other than is based on mere registration."[26] The ILC's conclusion expressed the intention of the majority of its members to curtail the use of flags of convenience. In 1955 the ILC submitted proposals to governments limiting states' rights by criteria of ownership. But the timidity of the ILC was revealed in the gaping

22. Sir Hersh Lauterpacht, "Codification and Development of International Law," *American Journal of International Law* 49 (January 1955), p. 51.
23. Quoted in Boczek, *Flags of Convenience,* p. 210.
24. Ibid., p. 216.
25. International Law Commission, *Yearbook, 1950,* Vol. 1, p. 188.
26. International Law Commission, *Yearbook, 1955,* Vol. 2, pp. 22–23.

loopholes in clauses defining ownership; as a result, even the Panamanian delegate was able to vote for the articles.[27]

In 1956 the ILC, under mounting pressure from trade unions and European governments, again confronted the problem. This time it attempted to establish general principles rather than detailed definitions of ownership. The final article, a synthesis of British and Dutch drafts, expressed the notion of a "genuine link." The clause containing this notion is worth quoting, because it has provided the basis of all opposition to flags of convenience, including the recent activities of the UNCTAD secretariat, yet it does not define "genuine link."

> Each state shall fix the conditions for the grant of its nationality to ships, for the registration of ships in its territory, and for the right to fly its flag. Ships have the nationality of the State whose flag they are entitled to fly. Nevertheless, for purposes of recognition of the national character of the ships by other states, there must exist a genuine link between the State and the ship.[28]

The first two sentences were passed unanimously; the third passed by a vote of 9 to 3, with Syria, Mexico, and Bolivia opposing.

In 1958, the Law of the Sea Conference convened in Geneva. Literature on the law of the sea has emphasized the disputes arising over territorial limits and, more recently, the exploitation of the seabed; however, the issue of flags of convenience is an important component of the law of the sea. At the Geneva Conference the resolution of this issue revealed important economic and political divisions in international politics. The issue of flags of convenience involved organization and control over transportation of raw materials, including oil, on a global scale. At Geneva, all states agreed that the phrase "genuine link" was imprecise. Government interpretations of the phrase reflected the interests of national shipowners. As in the ILC, Netherlands led the anti–flag-of-convenience group, with strong assistance from Britain and Norway. U.S. shipowners and the U.S. government were the sole genuine forces in their defense, although delegates from Panama and Liberia were, not surprisingly, the most fervent backers. Both sides sought to cloak their interests in the rhetoric of freedom of the seas, thus anticipating the present conflict over flags of convenience between South

27. Boczek, *Flags of Convenience*, pp. 225–26.
28. International Law Commission, *Yearbook, 1956*, Vol. 2, p. 15.

Library
Lakeland College

and North, in which both sides also claim to uphold free trade principles. Liberia's representative exhorted delegates to "accept freedom as the guiding principle of its deliberations—the freedom of the high seas," [29] whereas the OEEC retorted that flags of convenience were a threat to freedom because they "contained nuclei of disorder and anarchy" and needed to be regulated.[30] The irony of this debate is that over questions of liner shipping Europe and America adopted the reverse position: the United States argued that regulation of conferences enhanced free trade, whereas the Europeans claimed that regulation was destroying it.

Ultimately, the "genuine link" provision enunciated by the ILC was endorsed unanimously at Geneva. The clauses were not considered to be legally binding, however, because the proposals permitting nonrecognition of flags of convenience and a formal identification of ownership and "genuine link" were rejected. The rejection of the nonrecognition clause was due to extensive lobbying by the United States. In the absence of effective sanctions, the vague notion of "genuine link," although it represented the force of world opinion, was unenforceable, as shipowners recognized. In any case, despite widespread opposition to flags of convenience, in 1960 the International Court of Justice, in a dispute over the inclusion of Liberia in the Maritime Safety Committee of IMCO, ruled that registry was the sole test of nationality of merchant vessels.[31] By 1960, therefore, flags of convenience had weathered all legal attacks; legal sanction and the failure of the International Transport Workers Federation strike left no force strong enough to engage in more than minor skirmishes with shipowners. The OECD continued to condemn flags of convenience, although it shied away from concrete action. The United States, Liberia, and Panama conceded only the obligation to increase surveillance of health and safety standards, but even this was outside the purview of national and international law.

The Transformation of the Regime

The ambiguity contained in the "genuine link" resolution at Geneva in 1958 strengthened the position of flags of convenience, despite the exigen-

29. Quoted in Boczek, *Flags of Convenience,* p. 258.
30. OEEC, Maritime Transport Committee, *Study on the Expansion of the Flag of Convenience Fleets,* p. 3.
31. Advising Opinion of the International Court of Justice, 8 June 1960.

Table 7.   Flag of Registration of Tankers, 1939 – 85 (million dwt)

	1939	1956	1962	1966	1968	1979	1985
Liberia	—	5.7	10.9	20.6	25.6	114.3	66.8
Norway	3.2	6.9	10.2	14.6	16.0	30.1	14.2
United Kingdom	4.5	7.8	11.1	11.9	13.7	33.1	12.3
Japan	0.6	1.3	3.5	8.7	11.8	35.0	25.9
United States	4.3	5.9	6.9	6.8	7.0	14.3	15.9
Panama	0.7	3.3	3.4	4.1	5.0	11.7	18.8
France	0.3	2.0	3.9	3.9	4.5	15.8	8.3
U.S.S.R.	0.3	0.6	1.4	3.8	4.3	7.2	7.9
Greece	0.0	0.3	2.6	3.1	3.5	21.4	15.9
Others	3.1	9.4	15.0	19.4	23.9	70.1	71.0
Total	17.0	43.2	68.9	96.9	115.3	353.0	257.0

SOURCES: United Kingdom, Committee of Inquiry into Shipping, *Report* (Rochdale Report), Cmnd. 4337 (London: HMSO, 1970); Exxon Public Affairs Department, *Tankers and the Flags They Fly* (New York: Exxon, 1979); Institute of Shipping Economics and Logistics, *Shipping Statistics* 29, no. 12 (Bremen: Institute of Shipping Economics and Logistics, December 1985).

cies of public opinion. The practical immunity from sanctions achieved at Geneva was reinforced by the 1960 ruling of the International Court of Justice. And United States law contained none of the ambiguity of the Geneva Convention. In 1953, Supreme Court Justice Robert H. Jackson argued for the majority: "Each state under international law may determine for itself the conditions on which it will grant its nationality to a merchant ship, thereby accepting responsibility for it and acquiring authority over it."[32] A decade later the United States Supreme Court ruled that it was illegal for unions to picket in an attempt to organize and represent crews on foreign flag shipping.[33] Thus, the practical effect of the international law of the "genuine link" was negligible, as was evident in the proliferation of flags of convenience, and U.S. law unambiguously defended their practice.

Table 7 presents data on the expansion of tanker shipping between 1939 and 1985 by flag of registration. The figures underscore the tremendous increase in world trade in petroleum after World War II and the sharp decline in tanker tonnage resulting from the oil crisis of 1978–79 and the

32. Lauritzen vs. Larsen, 25 May 1953.
33. Incres vs. NCRA, 18 February 1963.

world recession of the early 1980s, and they give some indication of the expanding American role in oil transport in conjunction with Liberia and Panama. Tonnage figures indicate that even if all Liberian and Panamanian shipping could be assumed to be U.S.-owned, the United States share increased only from one-quarter of the world total before World War II to one-third in 1968. By the late 1960s, approximately one-third of flag-of-convenience shipping was owned by Greek, Japanese, and British–Hong Kong interests.[34] In 1968, 36 percent of the world tanker fleet was owned by oil companies, 62 percent by independents, and the remaining 2 percent by governments.[35]

Tonnage figures do not, however, tell the full story of United States control of bulk shipping. A qualitative analysis reveals two related processes: first, a shift of ownership and control from Europe to the United States; second, an increasing tendency for effective control of shipping to pass from independent shipowners to large multinational corporations or banks. The shift from Western Europe to the United States and, eventually, Japan was inevitable, given the weight of American and Japanese business abroad. It is revealed less in tonnage statistics than in the determination of effective financial control and market power; control of shipping corresponds generally to control of cargoes. After World War II, most of the tonnage registered under the Norwegian and Greek flags was financed by United States and British banks.[36] Exchange controls prevented Norwegian independent owners from ordering ships overseas; American and British banks provided loans, while Norwegian owners chartered ships back to the multinationals or carried U.S. cargoes. Between 1948 and 1959 the Norwegian fleet expanded by 250 percent. Virtually all Greek tanker construction was financed with American capital. A typical arrangement provided for the securing of a time charter from an oil company as collateral, issuance of a 95 percent mortgage from U.S. financiers, and then the construction of the tanker in either Western Europe or Japan. Norwegian owners were legally prohibited from registering their ships under flags of convenience,

34. United Kingdom, Committee of Inquiry into Shipping, *Report* (Rochdale Report), Cmnd. 4337 (London: HMSO, 1970), p. 52.

35. Ibid., p. 157.

36. Sturmey, *British Shipping and World Competition,* p. 223. Virtually all Greek shipping was U.S.-financed; much Norwegian shipping was financed by British banks. On this, see Chapter 9, below.

but U.S. banks and corporations encouraged Greek owners to do so, because of political instability in Greece, especially during the 1950s.[37]

In addition to American financing of the Norwegian and Greek bulk fleets, substantial portions of the British, French, and West German bulk fleets were owned by subsidiaries of U.S. multinationals. This reflected the fact that much American direct investment in Western Europe was in marketing, refining, and transportation of oil. Before World War II, 90 percent of Europe's energy was derived from coal, and 8 percent was petroleum-based. By 1973, however, oil accounted for 60 percent of Europe's energy use.[38] The shift from coal to oil reinforced American power and was a source of Atlantic tensions. By 1950, 11 percent of shipments to Europe under the Economic Cooperation Act (Marshall Plan) consisted of oil. According to Walter Levy, these shipments helped to "maintain for American oil . . . a competitive position in world markets."[39]

Beyond financial control or ownership, the sheer weight of market power ensured that American multinationals would dominate international bulk shipping. The international oil cartel, dominated by a few large American (and British) firms, controlled tankers and oil. In 1949 the "Seven Sisters" (Exxon, Gulf, Texaco, Socal, Mobil, British Petroleum, and Shell) owned 92 percent of reserves outside North America and the Soviet Union. These firms and the larger independents followed a strategy aimed at maximizing market power and stability without tying up excess amounts of capital in shipping. Oil companies directly owned enough open registry tonnage to carry between one-third and one-half of their shipments; additional tonnage was supplied through long-term charters or the spot market.

The tonnage owned and controlled by the Seven Sisters declined somewhat during the 1960s and 1970s. Recent UNCTAD studies show that in 1977 the Seven Sisters owned approximately 22 percent of the world

37. This process may be reversing. Greek shipowners appear to be returning to the Greek flag as they seek a more independent or Eurocentric role in the international economy. See M. Serafetinidis et al., "The Development of Greek Shipping Capital and Its Implications for the Political Economy of Greece," *Cambridge Journal of Economics* 5 (September 1981).

38. N. J. D. Lucas, *Energy and the European Communities* (London: Europa, 1977), p. 1; D. Schmidt, "Alternatives to Oil Imported from OPEC Countries: Coal as a Substitute?" in F. A. M. Alting von Geusau, ed., *Energy in the European Communities* (Leiden: A. W. Sijthoff, 1979), p. 92.

39. Quoted in Joe Stork, *Middle East Oil and the Energy Crisis* (New York: Monthly Review Press, 1975), p. 62.

tanker tonnage; international oil companies collectively owned 40 percent; independent shipowners owned 60 percent.[40] A strategy of limited ownership is rational from the point of view of oil firms. Charter rates fluctuate widely in response to supply and demand. During recessionary periods large amounts of tonnage are laid up as rates fall below the break-even point. Excessive investment in tanker tonnage caused the collapse of Burmah Oil, a sizable British independent, in 1974. During expansionary phases, in contrast, rates soar. The large oil firms have been willing to concede not only the risks but also the potential windfall profits to independent tanker owners.

The case of Erling Naess, one of the largest bulk carrier owners, reveals the close ties between independent shipowners and large oil companies. Despite the size of his Norness Shipping, Naess "regarded it as vital to establish a close relationship with a major bank and not to trade each individual ship purchase around the money market."[41] He worked closely with Morgan Guaranty and also concluded agreements with Equitable Life Insurance of New York, Northwestern Mutual, and Prudential in London. These institutions would provide the mortgage of 60 to 80 percent of a ship's price. The remainder of the purchase price was put up by other financial backers. In Naess's company, for example, there were partners from Kidder Peabody, and from Loeb, Rhoades and Company. In 1962, Naess Shipping became a public company through its merger with Anglo-American. In the new firm, Anglo-Norness, Naess owned the largest number of shares but did not control it. In 1968, Naess was bought out by the international oil firm Zapata. Ultimately, even the largest of the independent owners fell under the sway of MNCs and banks.

Control over transportation was a necessary component of U.S. foreign policy on all raw materials. Just as Rockefeller's Standard Oil achieved preeminence in the United States through controlling railways, so U.S. transnational oil firms, in conjunction with Shell and British Petroleum, used control of shipping to consolidate their holdings against outside competi-

40. UNCTAD, *The Maritime Transport of Hydrocarbons*, TD/222/Supp. 3 (Manila: 1979), p. 20. In 1949 the Seven Sisters controlled two-thirds of the world tanker fleet. M. A. Adelman gives a low estimate of approximately 25 percent (including beneficial ownership) for 1972 (*The World Petroleum Market* [Baltimore: Johns Hopkins University Press, 1972] pp. 104–6).

41. Erling D. Naess, *My Life: Autobiography of a Shipping Man* (Colchester: Seatrade, 1977), p. 215.

tion and Middle Eastern nationalism. In 1952, for example, Mossadegh's attempt to nationalize British Petroleum's holdings in Iran failed, to a large extent because Iran's lack of a national flag fleet enabled the oil companies to impose a boycott on Iranian oil and to induce independent tanker owners to enforce the boycott. According to Louis Turner, the Iranian experience demonstrated that "the problem had never been one of producing or refining the oil. [That would have been within Mossadegh's capabilities.] The question was to find tankers and markets."[42]

The joint Saudi Arabian–Onassis attempt to penetrate the Arabian American Oil Company (ARAMCO) cartel even more dramatically exemplified the power of the multinationals and showed that the free market in bulk shipping operated within the confines of an Anglo-American cartel. Eager to exercise greater control over oil and aware of Iranian mistakes, Aristotle Onassis and certain members of the Saudi monarchy agreed to establish a Saudi Arabian Maritime Company, registered under the Saudi flag. Onassis was to provide a 500,000 dwt tanker fleet. In return he was guaranteed access to 10 percent of Saudi oil output, to be carried at a freight rate exceeding the market level. Onassis would, furthermore, be permitted to carry a progressively greater proportion of Saudi oil exports, enabling both Onassis and the monarchy to increase the size of the national flag tanker fleet. If carried out, the project would have helped the Saudis achieve a greater measure of independence from the ARAMCO cartel.

ARAMCO responded to the challenge through high-level diplomacy. In representations to the National Security Council, Onassis's project was characterized as "a wedge that could be driven between the United States government and the Saudis, thus leading to a serious erosion of American influence in the Middle East."[43]

America's diplomatic efforts to persuade the Saudis to pull out of the deal were reinforced by the power of oil companies to boycott Saudi oil shipments. According to Secretary of State Dulles's cable of 16 July 1954:

> Present position is that parent companies will refuse cargo . . . although realize shut down and eventual nationalization could result. . . . From practical busi-

42. Louis Turner, *Oil Companies in the International System* (London: Allen and Unwin, 1979), p. 93.

43. Nicholas Fraser, Phillip Jacobson, Mark Ottaway, and Lewis Chester, *Aristotle Onassis* (New York: J. B. Lippincott, 1977), p. 138.

ness viewpoint United States believes Saudi Government would run grave danger substantial loss by implementation. Financial benefits to Saudi Government bound to be infinitesimal compared potential loss oil revenues. Loss of markets for only one million barrels of oil would roughly cancel contemplated annual financial benefits.[44]

Dulles's arguments did seduce the monarchy away from Onassis, once a face-saving means of cancellation was found: in arbitration, the International Court of Justice ruled that the proposed deal violated ARAMCO contracts and, hence, international law.[45]

Stabilization of the Regime

The foregoing discussion indicates that U.S. multinationals, tacitly supported by their government, sponsored and successfully defended a regime based on the principle of privatization. The lack of a genuine link between ship and flag, the mobility of capital, and the physical mobility of ships allowed owners of flag-of-convenience fleets to take advantage of a global supply of cheap labor. At the same time, efforts to unionize open registry crews were inhibited by national law, as in the United States, and by nationalism among crews. For American shipowners, open registries were necessary because they equalized wage costs with those of their principal competitors. There is no evidence that wages aboard open registry vessels have been significantly different from the European average. Indeed, many officers and crews were Western European, especially Italian and British, lured by marginally higher wages than were available under their national flags. Moreover, periods of labor shortage ensured that the large transnational corporations would be willing to pay wages approximately equal to the world average aboard their open registry ships.

Wages on flag-of-convenience ships were, however, significantly below the levels achieved by American seamen as a result of years of labor mili-

44. Ibid., p. 144.
45. See Robert Engler, *The Politics of Oil: A Study of Private Power and Democratic Decision* (New York: Macmillan, 1961), p. 180; OEEC, Maritime Transport Committee, *Maritime Transport, 1954* (Paris: OEEC, 1955), p. 54. Despite its victory, ARAMCO evidently sought to punish Onassis by imposing an international boycott on new charters for his fleet. The closing of the Suez Canal and the ensuing leap in demand for oil tankers saved him. Joachim Joesten contends, without supplying documentation, that Onassis (who built the ships in Hamburg) had close ties to West German industrialists, who sought access to Middle Eastern oil supplies (*Onassis: A Biography* [New York: Abelard-Schuman, 1963]).

tancy and the disincentives to counter that militancy given to shipowners in the form of operating-differential subsidies and other government assistance. The International Transport Workers Federation, dominated by the United States, sought to establish wages on the basis of nationality of owner, reflecting the fact that most open registry vessels were owned by U.S. interests. Shipowners, however, naturally favored wage scales based on crew nationality, thereby benefiting from Italian, British, and Greek wage scales. The importance of relatively lower wages as a motive for the proliferation of flags of convenience was emphasized by leading U.S. oil companies during Senate hearings in 1957. Vander Clute, managing director of Gulf Oil, expressed the prevailing industry attitude:

> The fundamental reason for Gulf's operation of foreign-flag tankers is competition. . . . We cannot remain competitive with [European companies] by operating our tankers exclusively under the American flag, because our costs of operation under the United States flag would exceed their costs by some 70 percent. In any business which is as highly competitive as the international oil industry it is impossible to absorb such increased costs if one is to stay in business.[46]

Flags of convenience not only enabled American shipowners to compete with European shipowners by lowering labor costs, but they also affected wages throughout the world. Indeed, it is plausible to assume that, following Europe's recovery from the effects of World War II, European wages would have gradually increased to approximate U.S. levels, as they did in other industries, in the absence of flags of convenience. Open registries thus may have helped to suppress wages throughout world shipping, including the liner trades, as the historical militancy of American unions was largely neutralized.

The positive influence of flags of convenience on world labor markets was not lost on the Europeans, for whom the issue of taxation was the immediate concern.[47] Flags of convenience benefited the United States

46. Senate Committee on Interstate and Foreign Commerce, *Ship Transfers to Foreign Flags*, p. 104.

47. For example, the International Shipping Federation opposed the 1958 boycott on the grounds that the "advantage of flags of convenience lies essentially in lower taxation, not bad employment conditions" (*Financial Times*, 5 November 1958, quoted in Sturmey, *British Shipping and World Competition*, p. 220). Open registries ultimately influenced the regime in ways favorable to shipowners; classification societies, for example, relaxed safety and manning rules. See R. S. Doganis and B. N. Metaxas, *The Impact of Flags of Convenience* (London: Polytechnic of Central London Transport Studies, 1976), pp. 105–14. See also Chapter 9, below.

relative to Europe, but also conferred absolute gains on shipping capital as a whole. From the European perspective, the fact that the United States government did eventually tax profits repatriated from open registry countries was irrelevant. Title 35 of the Liberian Code of Laws states that the income of a Liberian corporation owning a vessel registered under the Liberian flag is exempt from Liberian income tax.[48] The freedom from taxation by the host government thus enabled American bulk shipowners to use a greater proportion of their profits for reinvestment and expansion than could European shipowners, who were subject to traditional corporation taxes.[49] This cumulative advantage was especially significant in an industry that was becoming increasingly capital-intensive as the size and sophistication of ships increased. Flag-of-convenience operators found greater access to credit; once begun on the "virtuous cycle" of accumulation, independent shipowners could expand by obtaining time charters from the major oil and mining companies and using them as collateral. This pattern contributed to the creation of the bulk shipping empires of some of the world's wealthiest men: Daniel K. Ludwig, Y. K. Pao, C. Y. Tung, Aristotle Onassis.

Just as open registries defined the upper limits of labor costs, so the hidden subsidies available to their owners gradually altered the role of government in the bulk trades. Government either permitted shipowners to utilize open registries or else established a fiscal climate where national flag shipping could survive. Thus, by 1967, governments had established a range of policies indirectly compensating shipowners. Britain led the way and others, notably the Scandinavian countries and Japan, emulated British policy. By 1961 Erling Naess, a leading independent, open registry owner, could cite the liberal fiscal climate in Western Europe as a reason to maintain tax deferment for United States owners. Speaking to the House Ways and Means Committee, and perhaps unaware of the irony of arguing that the United States should grant fiscal support comparable to that supplied by traditional European powers, Naess stated:

> Taking into account the capital gains taxes and gift taxes which either do not exist or are levied to a lesser extent, in the principal European countries, than is the case in the United States, I do not believe that this tax deferment has, in

48. Carlisle, *Sovereignty for Sale,* p. 129.
49. OEEC, Maritime Transport Committee, *Study on the Expansion of the Flag of Convenience Fleets,* p. 4.

Table 8. Structure and Host Countries of Some Greek and Greek-American Shipping Families, 1970

	No. of Companies	No. of Ships	Registry		
			Panamanian	Liberian	Greek
Onassis	65	65	45	5	—
Niarchos	53	53	1	50	—
Livanos	49	52	4	46	—
Chandris	43	50	37	4	—
Coloctronis	27	29	—	—	29
Karageorgis	27	27	—	—	27
Latsis	10	15	6	—	9

SOURCE: *Shipping and Shipbuilding Record* (London, 1972).

the long run, been materially greater than it is in the country of our chief competitors.[50]

Flags of convenience have also defined the limits of national and international rules governing pollution and the safety of life at sea. These two issues are closely related: unsafe working conditions and insufficient training lead to accidents that pollute the environment. The unwillingness or inability of open registry countries to regulate shipping permits shipowners to ignore established standards.

Table 8 indicates the extent to which flags of convenience permitted ownership to be hidden in a maze of separate corporations. This practice is enormously beneficial to shipowners. Although all ships can be used as collateral for loans, setting up separate companies ensures that the empire as a whole cannot be threatened by lawsuit. In 1970, for example, the 11,000-ton Onassis-owned *Arrow*, registered in Liberia, sank off the coast of Nova Scotia, spilling 11,000 gallons of crude oil. The Canadian government inquiry blamed the captain for "improper navigation . . . while proceeding at virtually full speed through waters unfamiliar to him."[51] The *Arrow*, however, was technically owned by Sunstone Marine of Panama, operated by Olympic Maritime of Monte Carlo, chartered by Standard

50. Naess, *The Great PanLibHon Controversy*, p. 148. See also UNCTAD, *Action on the Question of Open Registries*, pp. 8, 9, 28.
51. Fraser et al., *Aristotle Onassis*, p. 285.

Table 9.   Loss Ratios of Merchant Ships, 1964 – 73 (world as a whole = 1.00)

	Liberia	Panama	Lebanon	All FOC	OECD	East Europe	Rest of World
1964	2.57	5.52	4.76	3.57	0.67	0.23	1.73
1966	2.22	5.00	6.94	3.53	0.73	0.15	1.16
1968	1.92	4.05	6.84	2.57	0.80	0.25	1.43
1970	1.43	4.74	2.92	2.76	0.75	0.07	1.54
1972	1.78	4.13	2.86	2.67	0.60	0.16	1.98
1973	1.32	3.83	4.35	2.53	0.63	0.23	1.62
1964–73	1.95	4.20	6.04	2.83	0.69	0.19	1.62

SOURCE: OECD, Maritime Transport Committee, *Maritime Transport, 1974* (Paris: OECD, 1975).

Tankers of the Bahamas, and in turn subchartered to Imperial Oil of Canada. Sunstone's shares were held anonymously; no proof of ownership could be established. Even if proof could have been found, the company's sole assets had sunk to the bottom of the sea. Onassis thus avoided liability.

The overall safety record of open registries has been relatively poor, especially in the 1950s and 1960s, as Table 9 shows. Flag-of-convenience ships have traditionally been older than the world average, with lower standards of maintenance, crew training, and social conditions aboard ship, and a higher intensity of work. It should be noted, however, that aggregate statistics are not sensitive to the wide discrepancy between the generally old Greek and independently owned tonnage, and the modern tonnage owned and chartered by the large international oil and mining firms.

U.S. Power and Flags of Convenience

The establishment of flags of convenience and the ability of the United States to defend their use transformed the structure of power in bulk shipping. The principle of privatization, embodied above all in flags of convenience, underwrote American power in the regime; it forced the Europeans to adapt to their use by adjusting maritime strategies and policies. As noted above, open registries were valuable to the United States not simply because of relatively lower wages but also because of tax policy; it was here, predictably, that Europe attacked open registries. In 1958, an OEEC study warned that "owners of these ships are able to devote to development and expansion of their fleet that proportion of their profits which their competitors in other countries have to set aside for tax payments."[52] Freedom from taxation created a cumulative advantage for flag-of-convenience owners: larger fleets earned higher profits; the more rapid pace of capital accumulation facilitated fleet expansion. Owners of flag-of-convenience fleets had privileged access to the United States capital market, especially the New York banks.[53] They enjoyed the patronage of international oil companies, provided they cooperated with their clients' political and commercial strategies.

Thus, the postwar growth of open registry fleets outstripped the growth of European fleets. This process was accelerated by buoyant demand created by the expansion of trade in raw materials. American financial institutions favored flags of convenience. Yet recessions offered no respite from the squeezing process to the Europeans, who were less able to balance losses in bad years with profits in boom years. The process created, from the OEEC point of view, "a diminishing degree of influence in world shipping on the part of the maritime countries with their generally accepted standards of effective maritime jurisdiction and authority."[54]

The OEEC critique, reflecting the Western European position, foreshadowed current UNCTAD views. Proponents of flags of convenience argued that greater efficiency and lower costs resulted in lower freight rates, and lower rates in turn catalyzed the expansion of world trade. But the traditional maritime powers argued that freight rates did not vary according to the flag distribution of tonnage and owner costs but, rather, according to the law of supply and demand; in other words, there was no reason why flag-of-convenience owners should pass their savings on to their clients. The European argument in essence claimed that flags of convenience had no overall effect on world freight rates or expansion of trade: tonnage and profits were simply being redistributed from the Western Europeans to

52. OEEC, Maritime Transport Committee, *Study on the Expansion of the Flag of Convenience Fleets*, p. 8.
53. Naess, *The Great PanLibHon Controversy*, p. 43.
54. OEEC, Maritime Transport Committee, *Study on the Expansion of the Flag of Convenience Fleets*, p. 8. Or, as Vander Clute of Gulf Oil argued, "Our foreign competitors, knowing that the high-cost United States–flag ships cannot compete with them, broadcast their propaganda for the sole purpose of eliminating the competition so they can have the field to themselves" (Speech to the American Legion, 10 April 1958, quoted in Naess, *The Great PanLibHon Controversy*, p. 25).

open registry operations and the United States sphere. "Indeed it can be assumed that their orders have merely replaced orders which otherwise would have been placed by owners in the maritime [i.e., European] countries."[55] The traditional maritime powers also criticized open registries for setting lower standards of safety and environmental protection, although there is little evidence that this was a matter of deep concern. Evidence presented in Chapter 9 suggests the ways that open registries affected not only wages but also general social and environmental policies throughout the world, including Europe.

Flags of convenience thus helped the United States establish merchant shipping primacy through substantial control over raw materials, best illustrated in the statistics on oil. Although less dramatic, statistics on American ownership and control over other significant raw materials suggest a similar pattern. These realities contributed to the unwillingness of the Western Europeans to develop a serious strategy for opposing open registries, and so fatally weakened the "unholy alliance" of shipowners and unions. After Algeria won independence, no Western European country was able significantly to penetrate or circumvent the Anglo-American oil monopoly. Before the oil crisis, the Seven Sisters controlled 71 percent of world oil; with the aid of open registries, they secured a virtual monopoly. This monopoly over transportation weakened European overtures to Middle Eastern rulers. American oil interests perceived flags of convenience in exactly this context. As the American Merchant Marine Institute warned in 1958:

> Their [Western European] propaganda and conspiracies against United States–controlled ships under Panamanian and Liberian flags are unfriendly acts against the United States, and it should be made clear to them that they are so regarded by the United States Government, business community, and public. A country like Norway is too dependent on the good will of the United States to afford to persist in unfriendly agitation and one-sided propaganda against important United States interests. The reservoir of good will enjoyed by Norway is great, but not inexhaustible.[56]

Thus, Western European shipowners, including the British, were compelled to adapt their business strategies and shipping laws to the dictates of

55. OEEC, Maritime Transport Committee, *Study on the Expansion of the Flag of Convenience Fleets,* p. 8.

56. Statement of the American Merchant Marine Institute, 17 March 1958, quoted in Engler, *The Politics of Oil,* p. 180. See also "A Serious Warning by the Oslo Shipowners Association," *Norwegian Shipping News* 14 (10 February 1958), pp. 137–40.

the U.S.-dominated regime.[57] In 1958, Viscount Runciman summed up
the new attitude of British owners:

> If it can be shown that taxes on shipping are still so heavy as to make her com-
> petitive position difficult . . . surely it is a matter for the British owners to take
> up with their government. I'm sure that efforts in this direction would be more
> productive and beneficial than maligning the competition.[58]

In Europe, as in Britain, fiscal policy, already favorable to shipping, was
made even more attractive. In the late 1960s and the 1970s, Hong Kong
shipping, financially linked to United States and United Kingdom banks
and oil companies, began to seek open registry and experienced tremendous growth.

Conclusion

The establishment and preservation of flags of convenience reflected American hegemony and the position of U.S. multinational corporations in raw-
materials industries, especially oil. The corporations were unwilling to
cede control of their transport functions to non-U.S. shipping. The utiliza-
tion of Liberian and Panamanian registries buttressed a competitive shipping policy directed at the traditional maritime states. Through ownership,
financing, or long-term charters, American banks and multinational corporations gradually took control of world bulk shipping. Control of transportation was an important element in the overall strategy of the multinationals, and it had the effect of reinforcing Europe's dependence on the
United States.

Nevertheless, from the point of view of the expansion of the international system, flags of convenience were preferable to various alternative
policies. Given the inherent competitive weakness of American-flag shipping, either widespread cargo reservation or massive subsidies, alternative
means of establishing a strong American presence, would have proved ex-

57. The tables of contents in the OEEC-OECD Maritime Transport Committee's annual, *Maritime Transport,* are revealing in this respect. Between 1954 and 1960 flags of conve
nience were discussed under the heading "Basic *Problems* Confronting Shipping" (italics
mine). After 1960, reflecting American entry, the heading was changed to the more diplomatic "International Shipping *Developments.*" By 1975, the OECD called only for "common
action against the *negative effects* of flag of convenience fleets" (italics mine). See OECD,
Maritime Transport Committee, *Maritime Transport, 1974* (Paris: OECD, 1975), p. 19.

58. Quoted in Naess, *The Great PanLibHon Controversy,* p. 32.

tremely costly. Flags of convenience allowed the organization of bulk shipping to conform to the requirements of an expanding world economy. Efficient, economical transportation contributed to the progressive decline in
the real cost of raw materials, including oil.

The organization of bulk shipping after World War II corresponded
to the principle of privatization. The scope of national or international
regulation was sharply limited because of the widespread use of flags of
convenience. International organizations proved unable or unwilling to
challenge the leadership of large multinationals and shipowners. Flags of
convenience made it extremely difficult for national governments to monitor safety standards, environmental protection, or the conditions of labor.
Ironically, the United States, historically an advocate of regulation in shipping, was the most ardent defender of privatization in the bulk trades.

The major actors in the bulk trades were the large multinationals, to
which even the large independent shipowners owed their fortunes, and the
key practices of the regime corresponded to the interests of these actors.
Freight rates were formally determined by the workings of the marketplace, although this marketplace was oligopolistic in structure and strongly
influenced by the multinationals. Similarly, the allocation of shares to various shipping firms and national flag fleets was formally conducted through
the marketplace. However, as Western European governments (and later
the UNCTAD secretariat) noted, the characteristics of this marketplace ensured that beneficially owned American shipping, closely connected to
multinationals, would flourish. Finally, flags of convenience represented a
special form of promotion, but one that could be reconciled with the principle of privatization. Firms able to take advantage of Liberian or Panamanian registry received substantial indirect, promotional benefits, including tax breaks and avoidance of costs associated with government
regulation.

5

The Liner Sector

As Chapter 2 showed, the liner sector of shipping has been dominated by conferences or cartels since the latter part of the nineteenth century. The cartelization of liner shipping was made possible by technical and organizational changes, and it reflected the specific alignment of international forces. As a result of division into tightly knit cartels, the liner sector has displayed a politics quite different from that of the bulk sector. In liner shipping, America's strong regulatory tradition, manifest in the U.S. Shipping Act of 1916 and the dense thicket of protectionist laws and subsidy provisions, attests to the wide separation between Europe and America before World War II. These politico-economic differences, anchored in fundamentally opposed attitudes to shipping cartels, reflected the position of Western Europe and the United States in international freight markets and the delayed entry of the United States as a major trading power. Despite this unpropitious legacy, America's general strategy in this sector in the postwar years was hegemonic, that is, the United States made important concessions to Europe in the interests of systemic cohesion.

The problem of global influence faced United States policymakers in liner as well as bulk shipping. After World War II, the system of liner conferences was reconsolidated on the basis of principles and practices reflecting the desires of Western and Northern European shipowners and governments. As in the bulk sector, the regime may be characterized as privatized; America's statist traditions were not allowed to intrude into the regime in any fundamental way, and Third World shipping was quantitatively unimportant, although significant from the point of view of individual countries and firms. Liner shipping was dominated by cartels and relatively immune from government attempts either to regulate it or foster it.

In principle, the obstacles imposed by higher wages and operating costs might have been overcome through pursuit of a flag-of-convenience strategy in the liner sector. However, in liner shipping, cargoes were already parceled out among lines and states; Western European firms were heavily entrenched in cartels and would have resisted U.S. efforts with the considerably greater resources at their disposal. Most important, U.S. firms did not exert the same type or degree of control over liner cargo as over bulk. American corporations dominated the raw-materials trades, from extraction to market, on a global scale: the United States was clearly the dominant power in those trades. This was not the case for liner cargoes. Trading partners could easily block attempts to cross-trade with the aid of integrated operations, as the United States was in effect doing in bulk trades.

Consequently, America's decision to establish a modus vivendi with Europe that was slanted to the needs of European shipping was not based on altruism. Rather, it reflected a recognition of the costs of alternative policies to the integrity of the system. The United States government recognized the importance of shipping for European reconstruction, including the balance of payments. As Lewis Douglas noted, shipping was the "nerve center" of European political economy.[1] The alternative, a generalized system of protection, was favored by many shipowners in the United States. However, such a protectionist regime would have been costly and thus deleterious to the expansion of world trade; it was also antithetical to the prevailing liberal trade doctrine. At the same time, European-style conferences were by no means unappealing to American shipowners, many of whom welcomed the shelter of monopoly. The United States government

1. Jeffrey J. Safford, "Anglo-American Maritime Relations During the Two World Wars: A Comparative Analysis," *American Neptune* 41 (October 1981), p. 276.

was willing to establish a relatively modest system of subsidies, limited cargo-protection, and related programs that appeased American shipowners, who otherwise would have demanded a full-blown protectionist regime. These violations of the liberal norm were resented by Europe; they introduced a subversive undercurrent of protectionism in the regime. Yet they were in effect side payments to U.S. shipping firms. They facilitated international integration because they guaranteed the compromise equilibrium that characterizes hegemonic power.

The history of liner shipping since the mid-1960s is the chronicle of the gradual demise of a Eurocentric system that was artificially prolonged under the wing of American hegemony and the tremendous postwar expansion of international trade. The decline of this system now portends sweeping changes in the domestic maritime structures of both Europe and the United States. The postwar regime temporarily alleviated certain disintegrative tendencies in world shipping; Atlantic rivalry was dampened, although not eliminated. Three such tendencies were particularly evident in the regime:

1. The tendency of the United States, as Europe extended control and expanded its presence in liner shipping, to increase subsidies, to create promotional programs, and to make bilateral or protectionist shipping deals.

2. Challenges from independent shipowners to conference monopolies, and the related challenge from the have-not states of the Third World.

3. Growing conflicts in the United States (and, to a lesser extent, in Europe) between shippers and shipowners in response to conference practices and perceived rate discrimination against have-not shipping countries, including LDCs and the United States.

The Reestablishment of Strong Liner Conferences

Liner shipping regimes can be described and evaluated in terms of the nature and degree of government regulation and promotion. *Regulation* refers to state control over the activities of conferences; *promotion* refers to government support of national flag shipping through subsidies and related fiscal measures. In practice, regulatory and promotional measures are closely related. Through various regulatory activities, states can directly or indirectly promote national fleets. Conversely, promotional measures can serve as substitutes for regulation. Through granting side payments to par-

Table 10.   Volume of U.S. Seaborne Foreign Liner Trade, 1956 – 72
                 (millions of long tons)

	All Carriers		Liners	
	Total	U.S. Flag	Total	U.S. Flag
1956	260.1	53.9	46.4	18.0
1958	253.3	30.9	43.4	14.0
1960	277.9	31.0	50.7	14.5
1962	296.8	29.6	48.3	12.7
1964	332.8	30.5	50.3	14.2
1966	392.3	26.2	49.9	11.4
1968	418.6	25.0	46.1	11.1
1970	473.2	25.2	50.4	11.8
1972	513.6	23.8	44.6	9.9

SOURCES: U.S. Department of Commerce, Maritime Administration, *Annual Report of the Maritime Administration for Fiscal Year 1971* (Washington, D.C.: G.P.O., 1972); U.S. Department of Commerce, Maritime Administration, *Annual Report of the Maritime Administration for Fiscal Year 1981* (Washington, D.C.: G.P.O., 1982).

ticular shipping firms or the national flag fleet as a whole, promotional policies can compensate for elements in the regime that are unfavorable to national shipping. The postwar regime in the liner sector was built on a foundation of side payments: U.S. promotional activities were a supplement to the benign neglect shown by the U.S. government to the practices of liner firms. This promotional activity simultaneously propped up the regime and subverted it.

Table 10 indicates American liner trade by volume from 1956 to 1972, and the relative decline in the size of the U.S. liner fleet during this period. The precipitous decline during the 1950s was in part a natural result of postwar reconstruction of Europe and Japan. However, it also demonstrated the determination of Europe and Japan to return to positions of prominence in this area, and the inability of the United States flag fleet to compete successfully in international shipping markets, despite its substantial initial postwar advantages. The increasing disparity between the value of U.S. trade relative to the rest of the world and the proportion of exports and imports carried on American flag vessels was a perennial source of protectionist demands by shipowners and unions, representing a continuation of prewar attitudes. This disparity also demonstrated America's vast underlying power and its potential to modify the regime to suit the needs of both U.S. industry and shipping. However, such power was not fully exploited during the postwar period. Its use would have proved highly problematic; in particular, changing the regime in accordance with narrowly defined American interests would prove difficult, because the interests of shippers and shipowners are by no means identical.

Shipping conferences promote the common interests of the most powerful, but not necessarily the most dynamic, shipping firms. In the postwar period, the conference system was dominated by the Europeans and Japanese. By the late 1960s European and Japanese firms had returned to the forefront of global liner shipping, both quantitatively, in tonnage, and also qualitatively, in their ability to shape the rules of the regime according to their particular interests. These firms played the leading role in the conferences, and thus in the organization of the worldwide transportation of manufactured goods.

Despite subsidies, the competitiveness of United States flag shipping declined sharply during the postwar years. In 1956, United States flag liners carried 8.5 million tons of commercial cargo; by 1962 the figure was 3.8 million tons. In both years approximately 32 million tons were shipped from U.S. ports. In 1956, American vessels carried 13.7 million tons, of which 38 percent was government-sponsored. By 1962 they were carrying only 11.2 million tons, two-thirds of which was government-sponsored.[2]

The declining performance of U.S. shipping in relation to Western European and Japanese rivals was reflected in the weak position of American lines within the conferences. Table 11 documents this weakness. In the most important superconferences, the United States was outnumbered 190 to 36. As one congressional witness testified in 1960, "In some 93 of today's 113 [United States—related] shipping conferences Americans are outnumbered by foreign shipowners."[3]

The numerical predominance of the lines of traditional maritime powers was reinforced by the organizational structure of conferences and the tendency for administrative functions to overlap. In 1962 investigations undertaken by the House Anti-Trust Subcommittee found considerable

2. Samuel A. Lawrence, *U.S. Merchant Shipping Policies and Politics* (Washington, D.C.: Brookings Institution, 1966), p. 179.
3. U.S. Congress, House, Committee on Merchant Marine and Fisheries (Bonner Committee), *Steamship Conference Study*, 86th Cong., 1959, p. 166.

Table 11.   American and Foreign Members of Superconferences in the Foreign
             Commerce of the United States

Superconference	Number of Foreign Lines	Number of American Lines
Great Lakes Overseas Freight Conferences	12	0
Latin American Freight Conferences	28	3
Associated Latin American Freight Conferences	18	7
East Coast of South America Conferences	15	2
Pacific Coast Committee of Inward Trans-Pacific Steamship Lines	18	5
New York Committee of Inward Far East Lines	25	6
Gulf Associated Freight Conferences	26	5
Trans-Atlantic Associated Freight Conferences	48	8
Total	190	36

SOURCE: U.S. Congress, House, Committee on the Judiciary (Celler Committee), Report of the Anti-Trust Committee, *The Ocean Freight Industry*, 87th Cong., 1962, p. 53.

evidence of bloc voting by national shipowners within various conferences. The effect of bloc votes was increased by indirect linkages between conferences. According to the investigators, "The large number of ostensibly independent conferences in the United States foreign trade actually is belied by the solidarity and unity that is effectuated among many of the most important conferences."[4] These linkages naturally resulted from the market strength of a few large shipowners and their ability to elect the same chairman to many conferences in order "to coordinate harmoniously the general affairs of the respective conferences associated under his aegis."[5]

The "high degree of power within the conference system" led by 1961 to a few "highly centralized groups of superconferences" dominating the U.S.-European trades and able "to determine policies with respect to almost the entire foreign commerce of the United States with European nations."[6] Three such superconferences were identified in 1961: Pacific Coast European, Gulf Associated Freight, and Trans-Atlantic Associated Freight.

4. U.S. Congress, House, Committee on the Judiciary (Celler Committee), Report of the Anti-Trust Committee, *The Ocean Freight Industry*, 87th Cong., 1962, p. 57.
5. Ibid.
6. Ibid., p. 81.

All were dominated by European and Japanese lines. The Pacific Coast European Conference coordinated all trade between the Pacific coast ports of the United States and all European ports; of twenty-four lines, only two were American.[7]

A similar lack of American representation can be found in other super-conferences. Even in the Latin American trades, European lines predominated. In 1961, eleven of twelve conferences serving the Pacific Coast and South America, Central America, and the Caribbean were informally affiliated in the Latin American Freight Conferences, headed by R. F. Burley, who was also chairman of each individual conference. In all, only three of thirty-one carriers were American.[8]

American opposition to conference practices originated from independent liner operators and shippers. The difficulty of reconciling the interests of U.S. shippers, conference operators, and other operators is a continuing theme in U.S. maritime politics. The Shipping Act of 1916, the foundation of American policy, was developed in the context of a weak U.S. merchant marine and conflict between U.S. exporters and European shipowners. Restraints on conferences, especially the necessity of openness, were mandated to help U.S. firms compete favorably in world markets. American businessmen generally believed that European owners discriminated against American shippers through freight rate differentials. In this they anticipated more recent claims of less developed countries.

Despite this regulatory tradition, the two decades following World War II were the heyday of unrestrained conference control over ocean liner transportation. Conferences extended control over services and rates and, outside U.S. trades, acted independently of government intervention. Even in U.S. trades the rebating system flourished, despite its illegality. Through this system conferences were able to extend their control over American commerce. Writing in 1962, the House Anti-Trust Committee noted that "the prohibition of the Shipping Act of 1916 against 'deferred rebates' has been violated in one way or another almost continuously since the law was passed."[9] These systematic violations were permitted despite the fact that the Federal Maritime Board (FMB), charged with regulation, possessed "a veritable arsenal of weapons which could have been brought to bear" against the conferences.[10]

7. Ibid. 8. Ibid., p. 61. 9. Ibid., p. 396. 10. Ibid., p. 330.

Table 12.   Comparison of Conference Ocean Freight Rates Effective May 1963 on Iron and Steel Products for U.S. – Foreign Trade Routes ($ per ton)

	U.S. North Atlantic Ports and West Germany		U.S. Gulf Ports and North Atlantic French Ports		U.S. Pacific Ports and Japan	
	Rate on U.S. Exports	Rate on U.S. Imports	Rate on U.S. Exports	Rate on U.S. Imports	Rate on U.S. Exports	Rate on U.S. Imports
Angles, beams, girders	31.25	17.75	33.50	13.50	31.10	15.50
Bolts	31.25	16.25	33.50	17.00	33.35	25.25
Castings and forgings	44.75	26.25	47.35	34.00	58.50	n.a.
Billets and blooms	13.25	17.25	15.55	13.50	33.35	15.50
Rails	37.00	17.75	39.40	13.50	39.35	15.50
Rods, wire, plain	25.50	16.50	31.45	13.50	33.35	15.50
Screws	45.75	21.50	49.10	17.00	33.35	23.75
Pipes, iron and steel, 6" diameter	56.75	18.75	60.25	14.50	33.35	18.00

SOURCE: U.S. Congress, Joint Economic Committee, *Discriminatory Ocean Freight Rates and the Balance of Payments*, 88th Cong., 1965, p. 10.

Thus, given the weight of American commerce in world trade, the free rein of the conferences had its necessary counterpart in United States shipping policy. The FMB supported the interests of subsidized shipowners who sought shelter from more competitive foreign lines in conferences to which access was guaranteed and from domestic independent lines, who had fought unsuccessfully since the early 1950s against the rebate system. Conference membership enabled United States subsidized lines to stay afloat but, paradoxically, reinforced their weakness and so increased the level of subsidy. Hence the confusion of regulation and promotion by the FMB, a charge heard frequently from U.S. shippers and European lines. The latter's complaints were muted, however, by the recognition that the gentle remonstrances of the FMB were preferable to the intervention of the Department of Justice and stricter enforcement of U.S. shipping law.

Thus the challenge to conference autonomy and power in the United States was rooted in the historical evolution of U.S. maritime policy and preceded UNCTAD efforts in this direction. In the United States the immediate cause of challenges to conferences in the 1960s was opposition to rebating by independent lines, which culminated in the Isbrandtsen case, heard before the Supreme Court in 1958.[11] Underlying this legal battle and congressional efforts to increase regulatory activity was the recognition of growing problems in the U.S. balance of payments. American exporters resurrected traditional charges that European-dominated conferences were discriminating against American exports due to "the discrepancy between rates from United States ports to foreign destinations and from foreign ports to these same foreign destinations for the same commodity."[12] For example, European automobiles imported to the United States were granted rates less than half of those of U.S. auto exports, all other factors being roughly equal.[13] As Table 12 shows, a similar situation was found to exist across a significant number of commodities. The U.S. shippers' case for enforcing prohibition of dual rebates and thus blunting

11. Federal Maritime Commission vs. Isbrandtsen, 1958.
12. House Committee on the Judiciary, *The Ocean Freight Industry*, p. 124.
13. For impressive documentation, see U.S. Congress, Joint Economic Committee, *Discriminatory Ocean Freight Rates and the Balance of Payments*, 88th Cong., 1965, esp. pp. 238–41, 333–39. CENSA responded to evidence of rate discrepancy for exports and imports by noting the greater demand for shipping on the outbound leg, leading to higher rates. Even if true, such differentials as are documented in Table 12 were damaging the competitiveness of American exporters.

the power of conferences was enhanced by the lessening of cold war tensions, which weakened the case for making concessions to European allies, and the recognition of a serious balance-of-payments problem. As a result of this pressure, in 1961 the Federal Maritime Board was reorganized into the Federal Maritime Commission (FMC), and regulation gradually began to reflect U.S. shipping law, the basis of European-American tensions.

Third World Shipping and Liner Conferences

Conferences were established to maintain stability in shipping. Like any cartel, the conference was intended to discourage or destroy competition arising from outside forces. Moreover, the entrenchment of national shipping lines indirectly furthered the competitiveness of the national economies of the traditional maritime powers. Therefore, it was quite natural for the conference system to be attacked by all countries outside the Western European bloc that gave birth to the system. A simple model of conflict in liner shipping resembles a life cycle: from outright opposition, to reformist goals, to vigorous defense of the system by those states whose national lines have become entrenched and have thus acquired a vested interest in monopoly profits.[14]

Less developed countries have traditionally perceived the conference system to be an institution that sanctions and complements an unequal international division of labor. Whereas American attitudes during the postwar period were ambivalent, the Third World, along with the Soviet bloc, opposed conferences. The following description of Polish foreign trade by the Polish economist Ignacy Chrzanowski indicates that opposition was not based on abstract ideological goals:

> In view of the fact that the small [pre-war] Polish fleet could not cope with the growing needs of the national trade and that it was necessary to attract to Gdynia and Gdansk several well-established shipping companies who were most likely conference members, the relationship with the conference was described as that between a weaker and a stronger partner. . . . The main criticism of the conferences from the Polish point of view was the concentration of services

14. It is possible to devise a crude life-cycle model of a state's attitude to flag discrimination simply on the basis of fleet size relative to trade. States with very small fleets and large, cross-trading states oppose discrimination. States that fall between these poles favor it, all other things being equal. On this, see esp. Olav Knudsen, *The Politics of International Shipping* (Lexington, Mass.: D. C. Heath, 1973), p. 79.

in the ports of Western Europe and the avoidance of more distant ports which had to bear a "range addition" to the conference rate applicable to the basic ports . . . which affected the competitiveness of Polish goods abroad. . . . During the early years after the Second World War the attitude of the Conference to Polish shipping and ports was distrustful and discriminating, for example, in the application of zonal surcharges to the tariffs fixed for the base conference ports. The small Polish fleet was not seen as a suitable conference partner. . . . In order to secure for conference members a suitable margin of profit through a reduction of costs achieved by a smaller number of calls and the concentration of cargoes, minimum cargo tonnages had to be guaranteed by Polish shippers to secure the calls by conference ships. The tariff surcharge affected the competitiveness of Polish goods on foreign markets. The necessity for the accumulation of cargoes in ports also increased the warehousing and other loading costs.[15]

The Polish experience exemplifies the effect of shipping cartels on less developed countries. A full list of grievances would include:

1. Discriminatory freight rates.
2. Lack of access to shipping.
3. Perpetuation of routes linking center and periphery.
4. Lack of consultation on a range of technical matters.
5. Excessive costs due to unnecessary technological advances.
6. Arbitrary withdrawal of services (e.g., during political crises and war).
7. Rejection of membership of national shipping lines.

Moreover, the champions of Third World fleet expansion have argued that, regardless of putative claims concerning the comparative advantage of European lines, the insufficiency of Third World shipping, which is indirectly a partial result of conferences, is itself detrimental to less developed countries simply because of the drain on the balance of payments caused by imports of shipping services. From this point of view, even inefficient national shipping would be preferable to foreign shipping, regardless of appeals to the functioning of the international division of labor as a whole. An early Economic Commission for Latin America study, for example, revealed a balance-of-payments deficit for transport of $527 million for Latin America in 1963.[16]

15. Ignacy Chrzanowski, Maciej Krzyanowski, and Krzystof Luks, *Shipping Economics and Policy—A Socialist View* (London: Fairplay, 1979), pp. 157–59.
16. Between 1961 and 1963, "invisible services"—shipping, insurance, debt service, repatriation of profits, etc.—transferred 61 percent of Latin America's foreign exchange earnings out of the region. See André Gunder Frank, "Services Rendered," *Monthly Review* 13 (June 1965).

Shipping spokesmen from the traditional maritime countries dispute most critiques of the conference system. They argue that despite the net outflow of foreign currency that results from shipping expenditure, investment in shipping by most LDCs tends to contravene the principle of comparative advantage and so constitutes an inefficient allocation of resources. Rate discrimination violates the principles of profit maximization; furthermore, from the point of view of any single country, conferences are foreign-dominated; no country has the capability to determine conference practices unilaterally.[17]

These arguments will be addressed at greater length in Chapter 6, which deals specifically with the Code of Conduct for Liner Conferences. Clearly, however, the LDCs play a subordinate role in shipping, and the structure of conferences has, at least until recently, helped to maintain this situation. The keenest defenders of conferences, such as Karl Fasbender and Wolfgang Wagner, have acknowledged that LDCs' "power to influence decisions is . . . rather limited."[18] And the authors of the Rochdale Report themselves felt compelled to recommend significant reforms.[19] As Alexander Yeats has argued, even if conferences themselves could be considered neutral on trade and development issues, the structural context in which they function guarantees that their effects constrain Third World development:

> The demand schedules facing a given developed country are likely to be very elastic unless the country is an important source of supply and the commodity has no close substitutes. This, coupled with inelastic supply, means that developing countries' expenditures normally bear the major burden of freight costs, and any increase in freights may be expected to produce equivalent decline in net export receipts.[20]

Tables 13 and 14 show, respectively, the percentage of goods loaded by region and the percentage of world shipping shares by region, between 1957 and 1984. It is clear that during the postwar period Third World countries have been underrepresented in liner shipping. Between 1960

17. Karl Fasbender and Wolfgang Wagner, *Shipping Conferences, Rate Policy, and Developing Countries: The Argument of Rate Discrimination* (Hamburg: Weltarchiv GMBH, 1973), p. 53.
18. Ibid., p. 50.
19. United Kingdom, Committee of Inquiry into Shipping, *Report* (Rochdale Report), Cmnd. 4337 (London: HMSO, 1970), p. 136.
20. Alexander J. Yeats, *Trade Barriers Facing Developing Countries* (New York: St. Martin's Press, 1979), p. 182.

Table 13.   Goods Loaded in Seaborne Trade, by Region, 1957 – 84
            (percentage of world trade)

	1957	1962	1965	1970	1982	1984
Developed market economy	46.8	33.7	31.3	31.1	41.3	44.1
Eastern Europe	3.9	6.7	6.9	5.6	6.1	6.1
Developing	49.3	59.6	61.8	62.8	51.3	48.5

SOURCES: United Nations, *Statistical Yearbooks* (New York: United Nations, annual); UNCTAD, *Review of Maritime Transport* (Geneva: United Nations, 1979, 1983, 1985).

Table 14.   Shipping Shares, by Region, 1957 – 84 (percentage of world grt)

	1957	1962	1965	1970	1980	1984
Developed market economy	68.8	63.2	69.6	65.1	49.7	45.4
Eastern Europe	2.8	4.2	7.0	8.9	7.8	8.1
Developing	6.4	5.3	7.4	6.7	14.3	16.5
Open registry	11.5[a]	13.1	15.1	18.8	25.4	26.6

SOURCES: United Nations, *Statistical Yearbooks* (New York: United Nations, annual); UNCTAD, *Review of Maritime Transport* (Geneva: United Nations, 1979, 1983, 1985).

[a] 1956.

and 1971, the growth rate of Third World shipping amounted to 172 percent, compared to an average rate for world merchant shipping of 90 percent. However, LDCs had not, at that time, engaged in container shipping; tonnage figures do not take technological change into account. In 1970 developing countries still possessed only 6.7 percent of the world fleet by tonnage, roughly half of which was registered in seven newly industrializing countries.

Throughout the 1950s and 1960s cargo reservation laws passed by prominent shipping nations of the Third World such as Argentina and Brazil were largely ineffective, because these countries possessed insufficient tonnage to avoid relying on conference services. Their ability to influence conference decision-making was severely constrained by lack of the tonnage that would have given them a voice in conferences or given credibility to laws mandating flag discrimination. In 1971, liners from LDCs had a share in 198 of a total of 368 conferences in world trade. But in only 24 cases were half or more members from LDCs, whereas in most conferences rates and other decisions are made formally by majority decision and, less formally, by the strongest members.[21] Less developed countries claimed conferences refused admission to their national lines; this was especially true in the Indian and Nigerian trades. According to Stanley Sturmey, "Many subsequent troubles would have been avoided if the traditional maritime countries would have bowed to the inevitable; instead, when the new and expanded fleets became significant, attempts were often made to stifle their further growth by refusing to admit the fleets to the relevant conferences."[22]

In the years immediately after World War II, LDCs were able to show modest gains in shipping. This reflected the development of nationalism and self-reliance, in part imposed by the wartime removal of ships and perhaps also by the slowness of the United States and other advanced industrial countries in reconsolidating economic ties with the Third World, especially Latin America. In Argentina, for example, a period of state-induced shipping expansion occurred under Perón but lost steam in the mid-1950s. Throughout the 1950s and 1960s, however, the fleets of LDCs failed to keep pace with the expansion of world shipping. This both relative and absolute decline of Third World shipping was to elevate shipping questions to high priority in UNCTAD and in the foreign trade ministries of many Third World governments.

Flag Discrimination

During the interwar years, subsidies were the principal means of government intervention in shipping (see Chapter 2). In the postwar period, however, cargo preference, known as flag discrimination, became widespread. During periods of overcapacity such as the 1930s and 1970s, freight rates decline, thus encouraging subsidies; during periods of expansion, when freight rates are relatively high, cargo protection may be necessary to protect national flag fleets from stronger competitors. In the immediate aftermath of World War II, protection was unnecessary because the growth of world trade quickly reached the limit of shipping capacity.

During the postwar period, among advanced industrial states only the United States formally protected its shipowners. Western European gov-

21. Fasbender and Wagner, *Shipping Conferences,* p. 50.
22. Stanley G. Sturmey, *British Shipping and World Competition* (London: Athlone, 1962), p. 195.

ernments were bound by the OEEC Code of Liberalization of Current Invisible Operations, which covered maritime transport. The code mandated
free trade in shipping and charged the Maritime Transport Committee
with the task of policing the system. Cargo protection was not permitted
and overt forms of flag discrimination have not been available to the Europeans since World War II.

In attempting to generalize shipping liberalism, the OEEC countries
encountered opposition from less developed countries and, even more
forcefully, from the United States. During the war, shipping nationalism
had developed in the Latin American countries, primarily as a response to
the dislocation of trade caused by the withdrawal of shipping tonnage by
the United States and Europe. Less developed countries thus sought to
establish their own fleets, to avoid the threat of future disruptions. This
desire was enhanced by the fact that American aid could be used to purchase U.S.-built ships.[23] It resulted in attempts by LDCs to protect infant
shipping industries.

Protectionist measures emanating from Third World countries, although extensive from their own point of view, had only a limited influence on the postwar regime as a whole. In general, the quantitative significance of participation in trade by LDCs was not great. The practical effect
of protectionist laws was even less because of the relatively small size of
most Third World fleets, and the barriers to their expansion: Western-
dominated conferences, lack of access to shipping capital, and competing
claims on available capital. The significance of Third World cargo reservation lay in its relation to U.S. shipping policy rather than its immediate
impact on the regime. In theory, for example, the mandate that the U.S.-
sponsored Latin American Free Trade Area (LAFTA) had to reserve cargo
was, in the view of the Rochdale Report, a "dangerous precedent."[24] This

23. Ibid., p. 193. For surveys of the historical role of shipping in LDCs, see Michael
Morris, "Brazilian Ocean Policy in Historical Perspective," *Journal of Maritime Law and Commerce* 3 (April 1979); Dag Tresselt, "Shipping and Shipping Policy in Latin America," *Nor-
wegian Shipping News* 23 (25 November 1967); and L. M. S. Rajwar et al., *Shipping and Devel-
oping Countries* (New York: Carnegie Endowment for International Peace, 1971).
    24. Rochdale Report, p. 46. For studies of LAFTA and shipping, see Sidney Dell, *A
Latin American Common Market?* (Oxford: Oxford University Press, 1966), chapter 6; Enrique
Angelo, "Transportation and Intra-Latin American Trade," in Miguel Wioncek, ed., *Latin
American Economic Integration: Experiences and Prospects* (New York: Praeger, 1966); R. T.
Brown, *Transport and the Economic Integration of South America* (Washington, D.C.: Brook-
ings Institution, 1966).

tendency was all the more threatening, from the European point of view, because of the connection between overt protection from less developed countries—primarily in Latin America—and U.S. shipping law.

After the brief period when demand for ships outpaced supply, the statist tradition in American maritime policy gradually began to reappear. The U.S. Shipping Act of 1916 provided a broad base for shipping nationalism: "It is hereby declared the policy of the United States to do whatever may be necessary to develop and encourage the maintenance of . . . a merchant marine . . . sufficient to carry the greater portion of its commerce." [25] The 1936 act gave an even more explicit mandate to initiate protectionist measures. Throughout the 1950s and 1960s a progressively greater proportion of U.S.-generated cargo was being reserved for American flag shipping. Technically, these cargoes were government-related, enabling the United States to deny charges of protectionism. In 1948, Marshall Plan shipments to Europe were scheduled to be transported on United States flag shipping "at reasonable rates." [26] After the shipping boom induced by the Korean War, further provisions of this type were implemented. In 1954, cargo preference law was expanded to include food shipments under Public Law 480 (Food for Peace), AID shipments, and cargoes financed by the Export-Import Bank. [27]

United States flag discrimination in the liner trades was viewed with alarm by Western European shipowners not only because of the size of the U.S. trade and the importance of its market, but also because of the example the United States set for the less developed countries. The U.S. government responded to European complaints by arguing that cargo preference was justified by the need to preserve the national flag fleet and that it did not violate the principles of the regime as interpreted by the United States. The United States did, in fact, comply with the IMCO Charter, which mandated only that states should avoid intervention "designed in a manner which restrains the freedom of all flags to take part in world trade." [28] U.S. diplomats and policymakers could cite the government's re-

---

25. U.S. Shipping Act of 1916, 41 Stat. 988.

26. Lawrence, *U.S. Merchant Shipping,* p. 168.

27. Hadley Arkes, *Bureaucracy, the Marshall Plan, and the National Interest* (Princeton, N.J.: Princeton University Press, 1972), pp. 166–70; Lawrence, *U.S. Merchant Shipping,* pp. 168–72.

28. IMCO, *United Nations Maritime Conference, Geneva, 1948—Documents,* E/Conf. 4/1–63 (London: United Nations, 1948), Article 1(b).

fusal to apply any form of discrimination to purely commercial cargoes, which constituted the bulk of American exports and imports. The U.S. position was clarified by acting secretary of state C. Douglas Dillon during meetings with high-level Western European shipping officials in Washington in 1959:

> Cargo preference as we define it, therefore, differs widely from flag discrimination in the accepted sense of the term, which we believe properly refers to government measures to control the routing of normal commercial cargoes in which that government has no proprietary interest. Our cargo preference statutes, then, apply to a very limited and clearly defined class of cargoes which would, in fact, be non-existent if they had not been generated by our government under specific programs authorized by statute.[29]

The transition from OEEC to OECD highlighted shipping problems among advanced industrial countries. The new organization decided to renew the Code of Liberalization of Current Invisible Operations. The code provided for complete freedom of maritime commerce:

> As the shipping policy of the Governments of the Members is based on the principle of free circulation of shipping in international trade in free and fair competition, it follows that the freedom of transactions and transfers in connection with maritime transport should not be hampered by measures in the field of exchange control, by legislative provisions in favour of the national flag, by arrangements made by governmental or semi-governmental organizations giving preferential treatment to national flag ships, by preferential shipping clauses in trade agreements, by the operation of import and export licensing systems so as to influence the flag of the carrying ship, or by discriminatory port regulations or taxation measures—the aim always being that liberal and competitive commercial and shipping practices and procedures should be followed in international trade and normal commercial considerations should alone determine the method and flag of shipment.[30]

The United States accepted the code as a whole, but had reservations regarding application of the shipping clauses. The council of the OECD, in an annex to the code, accepted that the code would not apply to commercial practices under the jurisdiction of the U.S. government.[31]

29. U.S. Department of State *Bulletin*, Vol. 41 (Washington, D.C.: Department of State, 6 July 1959), p. 13.

30. OECD, *Code of Liberalization of Current Invisible Operations* (Paris: OECD, 1961), Annex A, note 1.

31. Ibid., Annex C. See also OECD, Maritime Transport Committee, *Maritime Transport, 1960* (Paris: OECD, 1961), pp. 7–9.

Table 15.   World Trade Subject to Flag Discrimination, 1957 (million metric tons)

	Exports		Imports	
United States	155	(16.5%)	168	(18.0%)
Nondiscriminators[a]	452	(48.0%)	618	(66.0%)
Known discriminators[b]	98	(10.5%)	95	(10.0%)
Possible discriminators[c]	55	(6.0%)	43	(4.5%)
Unaccounted	170	(19.0%)	6	(1.5%)
Total trade	930	(100.0%)	930	(100.0%)

SOURCE: Stanley G. Sturmey, *British Shipping and World Competition* (London: Athlone, 1962), p. 205.

[a] OEEC countries, except for Portugal, Spain, and Turkey; British Commonwealth, except for South Africa, India, and Pakistan; oil exporters in respect of all shipments.

[b] Most South American countries, French and Portuguese possessions, the Soviet bloc.

[c] Countries for which no definite information is available for 1957; India, Pakistan, and South Africa, where discrimination is frequently alleged.

The influence on the postwar regime of flag discrimination in less developed countries and the United States should not be overestimated. Despite discriminatory practices and tendencies, shipping markets were, in fact, largely open—as they remained in 1986, albeit less so and with increasingly important qualifications. The rules mandating openness were enshrined in the OEEC and OECD codes, in the spirit of the IMCO Convention, in the GATT Convention clauses applying to shipping, and in the limitations of U.S. protection to government-related cargo. Furthermore, existing flag discrimination applied almost solely to the liner trades. The combined interests of the Atlantic Alliance nations and the inability of the less developed countries to develop significant bulk fleets created a largely open market in this sector.

It is impossible to measure precisely the amount of cargo removed from the open market by flag discrimination. Table 15, originally compiled by Stanley Sturmey, groups countries according to attitudes toward discrimination, treating the United States separately. Sturmey calculated that less than 5 percent of world trade in 1957 was "captive" because of official policies.[32] The Rochdale Report estimated that no more than 3 percent of cargo was government-controlled in 1966, although it conceded that perhaps 8 percent of trade by weight on liner shipping was affected.[33] These

32. Sturmey, *British Shipping and World Competition*, p. 206.
33. Rochdale Report, pp. 42–46.

figures do not include cargo reserved by tacit agreement, or Soviet bloc shipping. Nor, because of their aggregate form, do they convey the impact on carriers in particular trades. For example, according to Rochdale, "Before World War II U.K. liners carried four-fifths of the liner traffic on the Calcutta to United States North Atlantic ports route; ten years ago the last two U.K. operators withdrew their services."[34] Nevertheless, despite significant influence in particular trades, especially those linking less developed countries and the United States, the overall impact of flag discrimination was not heavy during the 1950s and 1960s.

Subsidies and Fiscal Aids

Direct or indirect subsidies have traditionally been a preferred form of government intervention in shipping markets. Like any other fiscal measure, subsidies indirectly influence trade flows. Just as deflationary fiscal policy can be a form of indirect protectionism because it increases the ratio of exports to imports, so aid to shipping in excess of the world average protects national shipowners at the expense of foreign competitors.

Subsidies tend to increase during recessions as freight rates plunge below the break-even point. This trend has been especially clear since World War II, when multilateral agreements have prohibited direct protectionist measures. Subsidies have been considered "lesser evil" forms of intervention; they do not directly impose trade barriers, their effects are most easily gauged, and they discriminate equally against all foreign shipowners. Whether direct or indirect in form, subsidy levels constitute an easily quantifiable form of government intervention in shipping.

In general the level of subsidy was low in the postwar period and tended to decrease, except in the special case of the United States. Even the authors of the Rochdale Report, ever jealous of encroachments upon the cross-trading so necessary to British liner shipping, concluded as late as 1970 that they did "not consider that operating subsidies in total are significantly affecting the profitability of world shipping."[35] Although in the United States subsidies have been extremely high throughout the postwar period, they have not engendered the level of conflict and international opposition that regulatory policy and flag discrimination have. However, if

34. Ibid., p. 45.
35. Ibid., p. 50.

the tax advantage to flag-of-convenience owners is considered to be an indirect subsidy, then this has represented a serious conflict, a point that will be addressed below.

The most significant government aid in the postwar period was granted by the United States and by Britain. In the United States, subsidies have traditionally been the essential component of state intervention in shipping. The 1936 act provides for operating-differential subsidies to be paid to owners of United States flag vessels. The difference between the average cost in foreign countries and U.S. cost is made up by the government in the form of subsidies to liner trades. In return, subsidized shipowners are bound to provide services on Essential Trade Routes. The number of Essential Trade Routes was extended considerably in the postwar period, and U.S.-subsidized liners were able to fill the vacuum in the Pacific trades caused by the ejection of Japanese lines during and immediately after World War II.

The cost to the United States Treasury of operating-differential subsidies has been enormous. Between 1936 and 1973 it exceeded $3.6 billion. Between 1948 and 1958, U.S. shipowners received $788 million. During the 1950s, the annual operating-differential subsidies to U.S. shipowners averaged over $100 million. The figure rose to 200 million during the 1960s, increased to $396 million in 1976, and has not been below $300 million since that time.[36]

Provisions of the 1936 act guaranteed a close relationship between American shipbuilding and the subsidized shipowners. This relationship reflected the relatively higher U.S. costs throughout the maritime industries. American liner owners who wish to receive subsidies must, in addition to providing scheduled services on Essential Trade Routes, purchase ships built in American yards. The construction-differential subsidy equates the costs of foreign and domestic shipbuilding; the difference is paid directly to shipbuilding companies. Between 1948 and 1958 over $100 million was paid in construction-differential subsidy; between 1936 and 1973 the total payments exceeded $1.8 billion.[37]

British shipowners have not generally received direct subsidies. How-

36. U.S. Department of Commerce, Maritime Administration, *Annual Report, 1979* (Washington, D.C.: G.P.O., July 1980).
37. Ibid.

ever, in 1954 the government granted an investment allowance to ship-owners, permitting accelerated depreciation that resulted in a 20 percent reduction in the cost of new ships. This aid was granted without regard to British shipbuilding and, combined with special privileges for British shipowners, it represented the most explicit response by the traditional maritime powers to the challenge from flags of convenience. Indeed, by 1970 it was "the view of the industry that a U.K. public company would probably prefer, in present circumstances, the combined worth of free depreciation and investment grants to the possibility of operating under a flag of convenience."[38]

Of maritime subsidies, only British and American government aid was important in quantitative terms through the late 1960s; in general, a buoyant freight market made it possible to operate without subsidy. In both Japan and West Germany expansion was occurring in accordance with market principles, although for Japan, close links between shippers and shipowners were important in reestablishing its power in the Pacific conferences. In the case of France, subsidies were paid to shipowners and shipbuilders, demonstrating the government's intention of developing a coherent maritime strategy. However, during the postwar period as a whole "the total amount currently paid in aid to French shipping appears to be less than the tax relief from the investment allowances of British shipowners."[39] In the cross-trades, France has traditionally conceded supremacy to British and Scandinavian lines. French maritime power was, to a great extent, built on links to colonies; the loss of Vietnam and Algeria thus had a significant impact on French liner shipping.

The generally low level of subsidies in the postwar period conforms to the expectation of a privatized regime. Although most governments extended some form of assistance such as low-interest loans or credit to shipbuilders, the total was not large. In some countries, notably Britain, the presence of open registries indirectly benefited shipowners by compelling governments to create a more favorable fiscal policy. Moreover, it is probable that in the absence of open registries the system of government regu-

38. Rochdale Report, p. 54. Britain's traditional commitment to shipping liberalism must be reappraised in this context.

39. Sturmey, *British Shipping and World Competition*, p. 189. For information on subsidies and other government aid, see U.S. Department of Commerce, Maritime Administration, Office of International Activities, *Maritime Subsidies* (Washington, D.C.: G.P.O.) (biannual).

lation would have been more extensive in such areas as labor protection and environmental policy.

Conclusion

After World War II, a new system of liner shipping was established. The United States did not dominate this system in shipping tonnage, but its presence was felt indirectly in all aspects of liner shipping. The system can be described as privatized because shipping firms, organized in cartels, were the key powers in the regime. To be sure, the principal institution of the regime, the shipping conference, restrained competition and, at the very least, distorted the functioning of the law of comparative advantage. Moreover, most states intervened directly or indirectly on behalf of national shipping. Nevertheless, the scope of intervention was limited even in the United States, where it was most extensive.

The system reflected America's hegemonic response to domestic and international realities. The full-blown mercantilism of the interwar years was successfully overcome. Within the context of the oligopolistic structure of shipping conferences, the marketplace for cargo was open. Domestically, the United States government suppressed or bought off protectionist forces with "side payments" that did not affect the regime in fundamental ways. The system provided an efficient means for the transportation of world trade, and it facilitated the reconstruction of Western Europe and Japan, whose national fleets flourished and provided a crucial means of earning foreign exchange. National shipbuilding was also a key factor in postwar Japanese and European industrial development.

The great freedom that was allowed to liner conferences reinforced the principle of privatization. Decisions concerning freight rates were made by the conferences themselves, most of which were dominated by Western European firms. The availability of strong loyalty devices, either endorsed or tolerated by governments, greatly limited the role of outsiders or independents, leaving shippers little choice but to accept conference decisions concerning freight rates and routes. In most cases, the level of government interest was low; the conferences themselves, not surprisingly, advocated self-regulation. Few governments pursued grand interventionist schemes in order to promote the development of national flag shipping and redistribute shipping shares. In general, flag discrimination was not practiced, and the level of subsidies was modest. Of course, the liner sector was never as free of state intervention as the bulk sector. Some governments, such as that of the United States, did pursue limited strategies of protectionism. Moreover, the fact of a "genuine link" between flag and vessel in liner shipping made it possible for governments to exercise a greater degree of surveillance of safety and labor standards than in bulk shipping; oversight was aided by the concentration of most liner tonnage under a relatively small number of flags. Nevertheless, the fact that decisions were made by conferences eventually elicited hostility from some governments, shippers, and shipowners, not only in the Third World but also in the United States.

As Chapters 6–8 show, the contradictions inherent in the regime were to grow increasingly serious and, eventually, begin to undermine the regime. First, the expansion of European and Japanese shipping elicited progressively higher levels of support for U.S. shipping. As subsidies gradually increased, protectionist solutions to the problems of U.S. shipping gained credence, especially as subsidies failed to create a more competitive U.S. merchant marine. United States shipowners began to favor bilateral arrangements; Third World countries, especially in Latin America, were willing partners.

A second set of contradictions concerned changes in conference practices. As European shipping expanded, the European model of conferences was becoming more firmly implanted; cartels were becoming tighter, more closed to outside competition; most U.S. shipowners colluded in such practices. However, a strong reaction against monopoly was developing in the Third World, where the end of colonialism had removed the paternalistic shelter of colonial shipping services and exposed LDCs frontally to market forces. Some American shipowners who wished to expand as outsiders also began to attack conference practices. More generally, although the postwar regime was conducive to Atlantic harmony, it stacked the cards against the development of a competitive U.S. flag liner fleet. Finally, both Third World and U.S. shippers began to respond to increasingly restrictive monopoly practices. They sought to document rate discrepancies and other forms of discrimination against national trade, and they demanded basic reforms in the structure of conference activities.

The subversive potential of each of these contradictions for U.S.-European maritime relations was magnified during the mid-1960s by the waning of the cold war and by the increasingly serious U.S. balance-of-payments problem. As the perception of Soviet threat diminished, the hegemonic compromise no longer seemed necessary. Western Europe began to be perceived as an economic competitor, not just an ally requiring economic support. As the balance-of-payments situation deteriorated, concern for the dollar led to a greater appreciation of the role of shipping in the national economy, both as a provider of foreign exchange and, equally important, as an instrument of industrial strategy and international competitiveness.

Change has been greater in the liner sector than in the bulk sector. As Part III will show, whereas in liner shipping regulation was minimized during the postwar regime, the principles of the new regime favored national and international regulation. States have joined conferences as the fundamental units of power in the regime. Yet at least some of this new regulatory activity may be said to enhance, rather than restrict, market forces: states can blunt the power of quasi-monopolistic actors, thereby creating basic change in the balance of power among shipowners, shippers, and governments. This change is closely related to the altered objectives and position of the United States in the international political economy.

PART THREE

The Challenge to the Old Regime

6

The UNCTAD Code
of Conduct
for Liner Conferences

The postwar international shipping regime reflected the intellectual commitment to free markets, refracted through the reality of cartels. As was shown in Chapters 4 and 5, the operation of international shipping markets during the postwar period may be said to have been characterized by the principle of privatization and to have conformed to the generally liberal, although by no means strictly laissez-faire, system of international economic relations. An Atlantic shipping order, sponsored by the United States, was an essential component of the constellation of economic regimes that formed the Bretton Woods system. The analysis of shipping highlights underlying conflicts during this period and demonstrates how these conflicts were resolved or intensified as America's role in the world political economy changed.

One version of the theory of hegemonic stability predicts that as United States hegemony erodes, a straightforward tendency toward protectionism or bloc politics will reappear, as it did during the 1930s after the collapse of the British regime.[1] However, as noted in Chapter 1, current devel-

1. See esp. Robert Gilpin, *U.S. Power and the Multinational Corporation* (New York: Basic Books, 1975), p. 72.

opments in shipping cannot be described by a simple openness-closure scheme. Indeed, it is difficult to identify a definite tendency toward either openness or closure. Some changes point to a strengthening of the market; others reveal a strong movement toward protectionism. Moreover, no definition of *free trade* in shipping commands general support in an era of cartels and state intervention. Finally, as shown in Chapter 2, wars have swept aside specific ideas and interests associated with maritime regimes. War has been a necessary but not sufficient condition of regime change. Historically, new regimes were distinguished from the old with some degree of clarity; they reflected the new configuration of power. Moreover, war settlements established the ascendant classes and interest groups of victorious powers, allowing them to reshape the domestic structures of the defeated states according to the requirements of the new regime.

At the present time, the ambiguities of the new order are pronounced. In the absence of a sharp break with the past, the distinguishing features of the new regime do not reveal themselves with great clarity, and it incorporates many elements of the previous regime. The new regime might more properly be called an incipient regime. The impact of change in some areas of the system has not yet spread throughout the system as a whole. Ideologically, liberalism and nationalism compete. Yet the discrepancy between stated principles and actual practices reveals an even greater tension than existed during the postwar regime. Put another way, a greater degree of anarchy exists. As one Western European shipping official remarked, "We'll interpret the Code of Conduct to mean what we think it should mean."[2]

This chapter describes the assault on the postwar shipping order that began during the 1960s and continues today. Although change has its origins in many factors, technological and commercial as well as political, it can be summarized as an attack on the concept of privatization, or the progressive replacement of self-regulation with state regulation. Such a change can be identified in new attitudes toward the role of liner conferences and in the proliferation of protectionist laws and subsidies. Although the change has been heralded by the UNCTAD Code of Conduct for Liner Conferences, the code only partially expresses the nature of the revolution in liner shipping. The challenge from the United States will ultimately prove more revolutionary and have a much greater impact on the regime.

2. Author's interview, London, 1980.

The Emerging Challenge to the Old Order

The New International Economic Order (NIEO) attempts to relate the shipping policies of LDCs to general development strategy. Third World attitudes toward the market in shipping reflect the general design for a NIEO: shipping policies are evaluated in a wider framework of goals stressing equity and development. In practice, therefore, market principles, but not capitalism, are viewed with suspicion except where their absence is seen as a form of discrimination violating the "natural" trend toward comparative advantage of LDCs in shipping.[3]

At the first UNCTAD, in 1964, the Common Measure of Understanding provided that all states should follow "sound economic criteria" in implementing policies of maritime expansion. Western shipowners concluded, with some relief, that their success in including this clause would ensure that shipping was viewed as an industry relatively insulated from concerns about development. By 1971, however, the Third World had made its own interpretation. According to a Brazilian spokesman:

> Obviously there was no doubt that economic considerations should be taken into account by any country planning the establishment or expansion of its merchant marine—no rational planner could consciously base decisions on unsound criteria. . . . Interpreted in this restricted sense, it would encompass the establishment of a merchant marine in a developing country only as an industry among others, losing sight of the all important implications of shipping for national security and the development of the economy as a whole.[4]

Shipping nationalism in Latin America stemmed logically from the reformist critique of international capitalism popularized by Raul Prebisch and the Economic Commission for Latin America (ECLA). Prebisch asserted that the exploitative terms of trade arising from the secular decline of prices of raw materials relative to manufactured goods would lock Third World states in a structure of dependency. Neoclassical economists claimed to refute this thesis, partly on the grounds that the secular decline in ocean

3. A summary of the objectives of the New International Economic Order can be found in Edwin P. Reuben, ed., *The Challenge of the New International Economic Order* (Boulder: Westview, 1981).

4. M. G. Valente, "The Participation of Developing Countries in Shipping," in L. M. S. Rajwar et al., *Shipping and Developing Countries* (New York: Carnegie Endowment for International Peace, 1971), p. 38. See also UNCTAD, *Establishment or Expansion of Merchant Marines in Developing Countries*, TD/26/Supp. 1 (Geneva: United Nations, 1967).

freight rates would tend to equalize terms of trade in the primary goods and manufacturing sectors. Prebisch's critique assumed that the cartelization of liner shipping precluded this possibility.[5]

In subsequent theoretical and empirical writing, the structure of liner shipping was identified as a key mechanism promoting dependency relations between North and South. Liner conferences were attacked for imposing excessively high freight rates, for denying Third World lines admission to conferences, and for excluding them from consultation on decisions that affect basic trading strategies and policies. Liner services were also indicted for reinforcing neocolonial ties. They have traditionally established routes linking center and periphery; these patterns have discouraged the efforts of many LDCs to develop lines of communication and trade among themselves. Finally, the lack of national shipping necessitated expenditure of scarce foreign exchange for shipping services, exacerbating balance-of-payments problems.[6]

Shipping was thus to serve as both a defensive and an offensive weapon in the development policies of LDCs that stressed national rather than market criteria. On the one hand, a presence in shipping markets would give less developed states the muscle to negotiate with conferences. As the president of the Brazilian Commission of the Merchant Marine declared in 1969, "The decision of a foreign government is not open to discussions by private organizations."[7] On the other hand, shipping would also activate the development process, through both its potential for opening up new markets and its spillover into the economy as a whole. Of course, Western

5. Dag Tresselt, *The Controversy over the Division of Labor in International Seaborne Transport* (Bergen: Institute for Shipping Research, 1970). See also *Statement made by Dr. Raul Prebisch, Secretary General of UNCTAD, at the 14th Plenary Session of the Committee on Shipping*, TD/B/C.4/14 (Geneva: United Nations, 1966). Olav Knudsen makes the point that the relatively high cost of transportation during the nineteenth century served as a protective barrier, indirectly promoting the infant industries of the day (*The Politics of International Shipping* [Lexington, Mass.: D. C. Heath, 1973], p. 34).

6. See especially André Gunder Frank, "Services Rendered," *Monthly Review* 13 (June 1965); and many of the articles in Rajwar et al., *Shipping and Developing Countries*.

7. Macedo Soares Guimaraes, "Obsolete Regulations in Maritime Transport," *Intereconomics* 4 (March–April 1969), p. 39. For surveys of Latin American shipping, see Michael Morris, "Brazilian Ocean Policy in Historical Perspective," *Journal of Maritime Law and Commerce* 3 (April 1979); and Michael Morris, "The Domestic Context of Brazilian Maritime Policy," *Ocean Development and International Law: The Journal of Maritime Affairs* 2, no. 4 (April 1977).

spokesmen and academicians have challenged the utility of shipping as an infant industry.[8]

From the LDC perspective, the new order thus generally expresses neo-mercantilist intentions. At its root, shipping is viewed not as a separate, profit-making industry but, rather, as a guarantor of national autonomy. The implications of this approach presage an assault on the open freight market in the form of cargo reservation, subsidies, the elimination or restriction of cross-trading, and the strengthening of conferences under state regulation. As shipping becomes more closely integrated with general economic planning, the ability to export replaces "efficiency" as the guide to possession of tonnage. Cargo generation thus becomes the principal criterion for the allocation of national shipping shares.

These general principles are by no means limited to the Third World; they are also espoused by Soviet bloc states. The growing importance of the Soviet Union in economic affairs contributes to the advance of shipping nationalism. Soviet endorsement of the UNCTAD Liner Code, which preserves a limited role for cross-traders, in theory challenged traditional Soviet doctrine by constraining the movement toward pure bilateralism. In practice, however, the Soviet Union's own cross-trading interest and presence in some conferences limit its willingness to champion Third World causes.[9]

8. See Hans Böhme, *Restraints on Competition in World Shipping*, Thames Essay No. 15 (London: Trade Policy Research Centre, 1978), pp. 33–54, for an excellent account of ideological currents in shipping, and pp. 83–85, for a defense of the status quo. On traditional approaches, see (in addition to Böhme) especially Brian Griffiths, *Invisible Barriers to Invisible Trade* (London: Macmillan, 1975), pp. 83–112; and Karl Fasbender and Wolfgang Wagner, *Shipping Conferences, Rate Policy, and Developing Countries: The Argument of Rate Discrimination* (Hamburg: Weltarchiv GMBH, 1973). See also L. G. Hudson, "Prospects for the Liner Industry," in M. P. B. Ranken, ed., *World Shipping in the 1990s, Greenwich Forum VI: Records of a Conference at the Royal Naval College* (Guildhall, Surrey: Westbury House, 1981), pp. 19–34.

9. For statements of Soviet views, see Böhme, *Restraints on Competition*, pp. 48–52; Böhme, "Eastern Bloc Competition and Freedom of the Seas," *Fairplay International Shipping Weekly* 258 (9 September 1976), pp. 7–8; and Ignacy Chrzanowski, Maciej Krzyanowski, and Krzystof Luks, *Shipping Economics and Policy—A Socialist View* (London: Fairplay, 1979), pp. 200–205. The proliferation of Soviet transnational corporations, led by shipping, is reflected in recent Soviet literature on the international economy that stresses the positive role of multinationals and the principle of mutual advantage. See Elizabeth K. Valkenier, "Development Issues in Recent Soviet Scholarship," *World Politics* 32 (July 1980); and Elizabeth K. Valkenier, *The Soviet Union and the Third World: An Economic Bind* (Boulder: Westview, 1983).

The economic nationalism emanating from the Third World and the Soviet bloc elicits echoes from the advanced industrial countries. This is true not only of states with strong protectionist lobbies, such as the United States and, to a lesser degree, France, but also of West Germany and even Britain. The shipping nationalism of the West thus competes with the defense of the liberal status quo, reflecting the theoretical and policy confusion that exists among and within OECD states. This is most evident in American attitudes toward UNCTAD's Liner Code. In 1982 the secretary of state for transportation, Drew Lewis, characterizing the views of the Reagan administration, stated:

> The Administration believes that—to the greatest extent possible—the members of the ocean lines industry should be free to conduct their business as they see fit, free of government intervention in the form of unnecessary regulations, vague standards and threatened penalties under changing interpretation of antitrust law.[10]

At the same time the Federal Maritime Commission has openly called for protectionism: "As the United States confronts maritime nationalism and solidarity of purpose in every foreign market, bilateral agreements negotiated between the United States and foreign governments . . . become an increasingly attractive option."[11] Even in the bulk trades protectionist sentiment has increased, although it is rejected by major corporations and the executive branch. American attitudes reflect divisions within the government, between the liner industry and export interests, and even among subdivisions of the liner sector.

In both Japan and Western Europe the loss of tonnage has alerted governments to the economic and political value of shipping; the increasing interest in maritime policy is reflected in private and public responses to UNCTAD pressures. According to Shizho Kondoh, president of Mitsui OSK Lines, "The means of transportation constitute the artery of the Japanese economy. In that sense, it can be said that the shipping industry is one

10. *Fairplay International Shipping Weekly* 282 (4 March 1982), p. 8.
11. U.S. Congress, House, Committee on Merchant Marine and Fisheries, *Omnibus Maritime Bill: Hearings Before the Subcommittee of the House Committee on Merchant Marine and Fisheries*, 96th Cong., 1980, pt. 1, p. 79. Ronald Reagan has said that "maritime policy should be an integral part of foreign policy. If it is not, our national interests cannot be served and protected" (*Container News* [December 1980], p. 8).

of the basic industries."[12] The French government has recently sponsored measures directed at increasing "Franco-French solidarity," open cooperation between shippers and shipowners to "ship French," and wholesale bilateral agreements with Third World countries within the provisions of the UNCTAD Liner Code.[13]

A trend toward neo-mercantilism in shipping can be identified even in Britain and Scandinavia, bastions of shipping liberalism. This trend is expressed in speeches by government officials, academicians, and leading shipowners.[14] Attempts to defend the principles of the old order and salvage a sphere where cross-trading interests can survive coexist uneasily with government intervention in the form of increasing subsidies and other aid. State intervention involves the traditional shipowners in a contradiction: their increasingly close relationship with governments is noted by proponents of Third World nationalism. Tradition is still defended. Increasingly, however, state activity at national and international levels limits the operation of market forces and undermines the liberal order it once helped to create.

Western Europe and the Defense of the Old Regime

The neo-mercantilist trend reflects both the worldwide tendency toward centralization of ownership and control, and government attempts to shield the maritime industries from severe recession. It has been encouraged by three additional factors. First, states traditionally hostile to liberal principles by virtue of economic backwardness or ideology have gained economic and political power and are playing a more active role in international shipping politics. Second, the OECD bloc has broken ranks.

12. *Business Japan* (July 1981).

13. Vanya Walker-Leigh, "Will French Shipping's Brave New World Ever Be Built?" *Sea trade* (February 1982), p. 19.

14. See especially Ademuni-Odeke, *Protectionism and the Future of International Shipping: The Nature, Development and Role of Flag Discriminations and Preferences, Cargo Reservation and Cabotage Restrictions, State Intervention and Maritime Subsidies* (Dordrecht: Martinus Nijhoff, 1984); and Böhme, *Restraints on Competition*. The president of the General Council of British Shipping, Lord Inchcape of P & O, asserted, "If cargo generation is to be the governing factor, as it has been before in our affairs up to the repeal of the Navigation Acts, might we not lean upon our membership of what is the largest and most powerful trading group in the world, the EEC?" (quoted in *Times* [London], 30 June 1976, p. 19).

Third, an energetic UNCTAD secretariat and Committee on Shipping have mobilized a vocal constituency against the status quo. The enemies of the status quo have introduced institutional and legal innovations: in liner shipping, the Code of Conduct, itself a "visionary code" from which specific rules must be derived; in bulk shipping, the renewed attempts to abolish flags of convenience through a comparable code supplemented by cargo-sharing in this sector. Positions have crystallized and are articulated publicly through the UNCTAD bloc system: Group B (OECD), Group D (Soviet bloc), and the Group of 77. However, the OECD is divided on many shipping issues.

Efforts to establish international regulation of conferences coincided with national policies directed toward this end and preceded by a decade the drafting of the UNCTAD Code of Conduct in 1972. Extensive negotiations and modifications of the code were necessary to win the requisite number of votes for ratification in October 1983. The formal ratification brings debate over the code into a new phase, as states claim to discover their own practices embodied in its ambiguous language.

The *Common Measure of Understanding on Shipping Questions,* adopted at the first UNCTAD, in 1964, not only embraced the "sound economic criteria" doctrine, which upheld the principle of privatization, but also praised conferences as "necessary in order to secure stable freight rates and regular services." However, it also called for close cooperation between shippers and conferences and recommended that appropriate consultation machinery should be established. Consultation between shippers and shipowners would provide an effective counterweight to conferences and would "improve and promote exports of developing countries and . . . intraregional trade."[15] The early work of the Committee on Shipping thus focused on the regulation of conferences without challenging the integrity of established institutions and practices.

The debate between North and South in shipping has been ideologically charged and acrimonious. Shipping elites in the traditional maritime nations have enjoyed great prestige, stemming from their pivotal role in imperialist expansion and from the importance of shipping to national economies. Writing in 1965, Sidney Dell observed that "ideas regarding

15. UNCTAD, *Common Measure of Understanding on Shipping Questions* (Geneva: United Nations, 1964), Articles 1 and 1(f).

the economic development of underdeveloped countries that have by now come to be accepted quite widely in governmental and business circles of the industrialized countries have still scarcely penetrated the anachronistic outlook of shipping circles."[16]

Throughout the 1960s and early 1970s, Western European shipowners sought to outflank UNCTAD's Committee on Shipping and generally to appease the Third World while retaining the principle of privatization. They sponsored the establishment of a voluntary code of conduct that was the first of many efforts to anticipate the conclusions of the Committee on Shipping and to disarm the opposition by proposing minimal, voluntary reforms that would leave the essentially private structure of liner shipping intact. In 1963, Western European foreign ministers, meeting in London, recognized increasing opposition to conference power. They realized that defense of the status quo would be more difficult in the absence of formal machinery designed to respond to shipper grievances. Three main threats to the conference system were identified:

1. Threats from shippers and governments.
2. Flag discrimination.
3. Government interference in "day to day operation of the conference system."[17]

European shipowners declared that the principal threat was flag discrimination. But they viewed the activities of the U.S. Federal Maritime Commission as especially ominous: "In the view of the European Conference Lines, unless there is a radical change in the present position, the time is rapidly approaching when the maintenance of the conference system in the United States trades will become impracticable."[18] Western European shipowners responded to these perceived threats by establishing a European Shippers Council (ESC), comprising individual national shippers' councils, and by forming the Council of European and Japanese National

16. Sidney Dell, *A Latin American Common Market?* (Oxford: Oxford University Press, 1966), p. 105.
17. "Western European Ministers Resolution of 15 March 1963, Memorandum from Western European Shipowners," reproduced in Chamber of Shipping of the United Kingdom, *Annual Report 1963–64* (London: Chamber of Shipping of the United Kingdom, 1964), pp. 225–26.
18. Ibid., p. 226.

Shipowners Associations (CENSA).[19] The centralized consultation procedure would not supersede negotiations between conference and individual firms, nor would the shippers' councils usurp the role of trade associations in various industrial sectors in negotiating with conferences. They would, however, provide a permanent forum for the dissemination of information and a negotiating structure facilitating "collective consultation" between conferences and shippers.

Sensitive to growing criticism, CENSA stated that it regarded shippers' councils not "as condemnation of past shortcomings, but rather as an awareness of the need to keep abreast of the complexities of international trade in the twentieth century."[20] European shippers' councils, for their part, largely accepted CENSA's approach; the negotiations or "consultations" were to be concerned primarily with technical matters. For example, notification of freight rate increases and cargo handling procedures were within the scope of consultation; freight rate increases as such were not. Given the historical identity of interest between European shippers and the shipping industry, it was not surprising that the shippers' councils would not fundamentally affect the traditional behavior of conferences. Nevertheless, both the councils and CENSA saw their consultation machinery as a model for the rest of the world. The British Shippers' Council put the matter bluntly in its *Annual Report* of 1965. Referring to the impending work of UNCTAD's Committee on Shipping, it warned: "It is expected that the real work of this Committee will begin in the Autumn of 1966, and that a broad choice will confront it between world-wide governmental regulation on the American pattern, or a world-wide establishment of shippers councils on a European pattern."[21]

A predictable lack of enthusiasm was shown for this model outside Europe. It conflicted with both American and Third World aspirations to regulate conferences. Less developed countries such as Australia, India,

19. UNCTAD, *Consultation in Shipping: Report by the Secretary General,* TD/B/C.4/20 Rev. 1 (Geneva: United Nations, 1967), pp. 29–50. The consultation machinery was institutionalized in the *Note of Understanding Reached between European Conference Lines and the European Shippers following the Adoption of the Resolution of 15 March 1963 by the Western European Ministers,* reproduced in Chamber of Shipping of the United Kingdom, *Annual Report 1963–64,* pp. 230ff. See also CENSA, "Sailing in Harmony: Self-Regulation in Shipping Works—and Works Well" (London: CENSA, 1968).

20. CENSA, "Memorandum on Shipowner-Shipper Consultation in Response to UNCTAD Letter of 16 July 1965," reproduced in UNCTAD, *Consultation in Shipping.*

21. British Shippers Council, *Annual Report 1965.*

and South Africa, with the most (and worst) experience with conferences, had already begun to develop shippers' councils armed with governmental powers. They perceived their councils as truly adversarial bodies, backed by law, not consultative, and having a mandate to negotiate on questions of freight rates as well as quality of services.

In the United States, the Federal Maritime Commission, prodded by the Department of Justice and exporting interests, was adopting an increasingly interventionist policy toward conferences. Throughout 1963 and 1964, it sought to collect information on rates and rebates from European lines. The British government responded by passing legislation forbidding shipowners to comply with Department of Justice requests. In 1965 a truce was arranged by OECD officials.[22] But these conflicts fractured all hope of a common front between Europe and America over liner shipping negotiations within UNCTAD. The shippers' council model was not suitable from the American point of view. The collusion implicit in consultation procedures violated antitrust law. More important, shippers' councils as conceived by the Europeans represented a step backward in regulatory policy because they lacked legal sanction. In any case, America's export interests are highly concentrated: 85 percent of United States trade is controlled by one hundred shippers.[23] So it was not clear that the lack of a centralized shippers' council was responsible for the allegedly inferior bargaining position of shippers.

Table 16 summarizes three positions on the conference system. Throughout the 1960s the U.S. government grew increasingly hostile toward traditional conference practices. Here the United States and the Third World find common ground. American attitudes, however, are deeply rooted in antitrust philosophy. Because of its socialist history, the Soviet bloc makes no distinction between shipping and industry, at least in theory, and its trading takes place on a bilateral basis. In the 1960s it did not engage significantly in cross-trading and its views did not diverge substantially from those of the UNCTAD secretariat.

In general, Third World countries did not consider shippers' councils

22. OECD, Maritime Transport Committee, *Maritime Transport, 1965* (Paris: OECD, 1966), p. 10.

23. Reported by Richard J. Daschbach (chairman of the FMC), in U.S. Congress, House, Committee on Merchant Marine and Fisheries, *Closed Conferences and Shippers' Councils in U.S. Liner Trades: Hearings Before a Subcommittee of the House Committee on Merchant Marine and Fisheries,* 95th Cong., 1978, p. 7.

Table 16.   The Role of Liner Conferences

	Restraints on Conferences	Type of Conference Desired	Role of Government	Policy Statement
Third World	Shippers' council; government	Closed	Participant	UNCTAD Code of Conduct
Western Europe	Shippers' council; market	Closed	Minimal	CENSA Code
United States	Government; prohibition of deferred rebate	Open	Regulatory	Shipping Act of 1916 and subsequent antitrust laws

without governmental powers to be a sufficient counterweight to conferences.[24] They lacked the commercial muscle to break the quasi-monopoly of conferences. And even relatively highly concentrated commercial power was not enough, as the American experience seemed to demonstrate. Throughout the 1960s the Committee on Shipping relied heavily on U.S. experience and documentation of conference practices. It appropriated theoretical justifications from the United States for regulation of conferences.[25] The establishment of indigenous merchant fleets would improve the Third World's position in bargaining with Western shipowners and would also serve as an engine of general economic development. In Latin America, shipping became an important component of LAFTA and the Alliance for Progress. The establishment of shipping would require regional cooperation and, at least in the initial stages, flag discrimination.

The establishment of Third World merchant fleets thus posed a further threat to Western European shipowners; any modus vivendi with the Third World would now have to encompass not only consultation procedures but also the role that flag discrimination would play in liner trades and the admission of new lines to conferences. In the long run, any agreement would

24. UNCTAD, *The Effectiveness of Shippers' Organizations: A Report by the UNCTAD Secretariat,* TD/B/C.4/154 (Geneva: United Nations, 1976). This report argues that, in the absence of government intervention, shippers' councils are ineffectual.

25. See, for example, UNCTAD, *The Liner Conference System,* TD/B/C.4/62/Rev. 1 (New York: United Nations, 1970).

have to be acceptable to the United States as well as to the Third World. Thus it would have to accommodate divergent legal and philosophical approaches to regulatory activity. By 1970, moreover, even the governments of some other developed countries, especially France, were no longer willing to unequivocally endorse the conference system.[26]

Further defense of the past was organized under British leadership. The Rochdale Report, completed in 1970, went beyond all CENSA statements in conceding "certain defects" in conference organization. It acknowledged that "conferences need to be both respectable and respected" and that "the public interest is wider than the interests of shippers and shipowners."[27] While asserting the partial success of the existing consultation machinery, the report surpassed the Note of Understanding between CENSA and ESC in calling for a formal international code of conduct. At the initiative of the British government, CENSA convened in Tokyo in February 1971. It sought to preempt the anticipated UNCTAD code of conduct through its own code of practices, the CENSA Code. This document incorporated some of the suggestions of the Rochdale Report. It urged, for example, that conferences "keep in step with the efforts of the governments of developing countries to ensure the establishment of shipper representation."[28] In general, however, it did not depart substantively from the perspective of the Note of Understanding. The "sound economic criteria" phrase was retained as the basis for the fleet expansion. Conferences, not national governments, were to control conference membership. Disputes between shippers and shipowners were to be referred to voluntary conciliation at a "commercial level." Thus, the CENSA Code actually retreated from the modest reforms suggested in the Rochdale Report.

The UNCTAD Code of Conduct for Liner Conferences

Less developed countries asserted that a code prepared by Western Europe "without direct involvement of the developing countries will not fully

---

26. UNCTAD, *Report of the Committee on Shipping in Its Fourth Session, 20 April–4 May 1970*, TD/B/C.4/73 (Geneva: United Nations, 1970), pp. 9–10.

27. United Kingdom, Committee of Inquiry into Shipping, *Report* (Rochdale Report), Cmnd. 4337 (London: HMSO, 1970), p. 133.

28. CENSA and European Shippers Councils, *Code of Practice for Conferences* (London: CENSA, 1971), p. 5.

meet their needs and interests."[29] In April 1971, UNCTAD's Committee on Shipping, following the recommendation of its Working Group on International Shipping Legislation, decided to include the issue of a code of conduct in the agenda for the third session of UNCTAD in Santiago, Chile. Groups A (Asian and African) and C (Latin American) submitted preliminary drafts to the Working Group. Afro-Asian states envisaged an internationally binding code. The Latin Americans presented a detailed code that would be subject to national law. The two versions were unified and considered in January and June 1973. During late 1973 and early 1974, a Conference of Plenipotentiaries adopted a final Code of Conduct, passed by a vote of 72 to 7. The code was opposed by Denmark, Finland, Norway, Sweden, Switzerland, Britain, and the United States. Five states abstained: Canada, Greece, Italy, the Netherlands, and New Zealand.

The final text of the code resulted from intensive public and private negotiation. With minor exceptions, it reflected the perspective of the Group of 77, the bloc of less developed countries in UNCTAD. The code mandates a sharp break with traditional conference practices, reflecting the shift from privatization to regulation in three major areas:

1. *Consultation.* The code surpasses the weak reforms proposed by CENSA. It is designed "to ensure a balance of interests between suppliers and users of shipping services." Freight rates are to be fixed at "as low a level as is feasible from the commercial point of view."[30] Conferences are to give shippers 150 days notice of rate increases. A system of consultation on matters such as freight rates, loyalty agreements, quality of shipping services, information, and promotional freight rates is instituted. Government participation is mandated. The code upholds the deferred rebate, a point of considerable importance. Although the code curbs conference autonomy, it sanctions a higher level of monopolistic organization. Disputes between shippers and conferences are to be resolved through "international mandatory conciliation," a highly ambiguous procedure, especially in light of the provision that decisions concerning trade between two states cannot be made without the approval of national shipping lines of both states.

29. UNCTAD, *United Nations Conference of Plenipotentiaries on a Code of Conduct for Liner Conferences: Reports and Other Documents,* TD/Code/13 (Geneva: United Nations, 1974), p. 2.
30. Ibid., pp. 4, 9.

2. *Conference membership*. National shipping lines have automatic right of entry into conferences serving national trades. In theory, conferences are no longer automatically open to the lines of third countries. All conference members have the right of admission to shipping pools or other trade-sharing agreements. National lines may be established through joint ventures or through charters, thus enabling less developed countries to acquire sufficient tonnage to take advantage of the code's provisions. This also creates a loophole that could enable Western liner owners to establish subsidiaries in Third World countries that charter ships from the parent firm, thereby indirectly preserving trade shares.

3. *Flag discrimination*. The cargo-sharing provisions of the code generated the most controversy. Article 2(a) mandates that "the group of national shipping lines of each of two countries the foreign trade between which is carried by the conference shall have equal rights to participate in the freight and volume of the traffic generated by their national foreign trade and carried by the conference." Article 2(b) divides the trade: "Third country shipping lines, if any, shall have the right to acquire a significant part, such as 20 percent, in the freight and volume of traffic generated by the trade."

These clauses give rise to the "40–40–20" formula; 80 percent of the trade is distributed on a bilateral basis between importing and exporting states. This measure shifts the balance of power in favor of those states generating large trade volumes and represents a direct assault on cross-traders.

The Code of Conduct has been attacked not only politically and economically but also on legal grounds. It is unclear on many points, and important issues await resolution in practice. Some of the more important problems are arbitration procedures; rules concerning joint ventures and rights of cross-traders in decisions concerning particular trades; and, as conferences weaken, the role of non-conference lines.[31]

The completion of an UNCTAD draft code caused the various blocs in international shipping to enter protracted negotiations, during which

31. For legal commentary, see M. J. Shah, "The Implementation of the United Nations Convention for Liner Conferences 1974," *Journal of Maritime Law and Commerce* 4 (October 1977); Hudson, "Prospects for the Liner Industry"; Stanley G. Sturmey, *The Code—The Next Five Years* (Bremen: Institute of Shipping Economics and Logistics, 1980); and Stanley G. Sturmey, "The UNCTAD Code of Conduct for Liner Conferences: A 1985 View," *Journal of Maritime Policy and Management* 13 (October–December 1985).

states tended to adopt positions in accordance with interest and tradition. The code has thus served as a catalyst for regional and international attempts to respond to changes in shipping and, more generally, in the international division of labor. It has forced the European Community (EC) to design a shipping policy and has stimulated attempts by Washington to develop a more coherent approach to international liner shipping issues. It has also contributed to parallel efforts to eliminate flags of convenience and establish cargo preference in the bulk sector.

The formal negotiations at the Conference of Plenipotentiaries give some indication of the nature and extent of bloc conflict in world shipping. In general, the Soviet Union and its bloc supported the Group of 77. Soviet concepts of bilateralism have harmonized with the views of Latin America. As noted above, the code represents a modest retreat from the traditional Soviet position because it retains a domain of third-country access that did not exist under pure bilateralism. Soviet bloc delegates both encouraged and gave technical assistance to the UNCTAD secretariat and Third World delegates. Their contradictory roles as ideological advocate of bilateralism and as cross-trader contributed to their willingness to compromise on issues between the Group of 77 and Group B (the OECD in UNCTAD). This was true in both public and private negotiations.

OECD unity collapsed in 1973. Although formally a member of Group B, the United States in practice remained aloof. In the early phases of UNCTAD activity the United States had sympathized with the Group of 77.[32] As U.S. and Third World goals converged, U.S. experience in regulation and information-gathering came to be of considerable importance. However, as the drafting reached more advanced states, United States philosophical and legal opposition to the code became more pronounced. As one U.S. delegate reported: "The FMC seemed to be preoccupied with ensuring that the Code would in no way detract from the pre-eminence of the Commission as the world's leading shipping regulator, and the State Department seemed to be locked in a philosophical straitjacket because of its commitment to free trade."[33] Opposition focused on the imprimatur the code granted to closed conferences through the deferred rebate and the cargo-sharing clauses. The first contravened U.S. shipping legislation and

32. See, for example, the testimony of Richard Sharood, in House Committee on Merchant Marine and Fisheries, *Closed Conferences*, pp. 129–39.
33. Sharood's testimony in ibid., p. 321. See also the memorandum from Sharood to the House Committee on Merchant Marine and Fisheries, reproduced in ibid., p. 321.

tradition; the second obviously related not to U.S. practice, but to more general foreign economic policy concerns. As the leader of the American delegation declared, expressing State Department views: "An international cargo-sharing scheme . . . constitutes a form of bilateralism which also runs directly counter to the above-described mainstream of multi-lateralism. It could also serve as a precedent for bilateralist tendencies in other economic fields." [34]

These more general concerns, and not simply resistance to bilateralism in shipping, led the State Department to oppose the code. However, not all U.S. delegates shared the State Department's philosophy. As will be shown in Chapter 8, bilateralism is retained as one means of resolving U.S. shipping problems if an accommodation with the European Community cannot be reached. In European shipping circles, it was felt that practical American opposition to the code stemmed not from opposition to bilat-eralism but, rather, from the fact that the UNCTAD Code of Conduct would interfere with U.S. attempts to regulate shipping unilaterally. Never-theless, opposition on ideological grounds prevented the United States from participating in the private negotiations over changes in the final text of the code.

The CENSA countries, led by Britain, made a last-ditch attempt to integrate CENSA/ESC procedures into the framework of Third World proposals. The attempt centered on a Swedish proposal to create a Free Maritime Trade Area among the CENSA countries in 1973. The failure of this proposal marked the decline of CENSA as the power center in global liner shipping. At the same time, French and West German acquiescence to bilateral demands from individual Third World countries corroded residual Western unity. These countries had less to lose and could even secure long-term gains from cargo-sharing agreements. Thus France failed even to attend the Free Maritime Trade Area discussions. As the West German spokesman acknowledged: "The hope of establishing two different re-gimes, one for trade among developed countries and one for trade with developing countries, did not materialize." [35]

At Geneva, Group B tended to divide over questions of cargo-sharing and conference decision-making. One group, led by France and sometimes

34. Ron Webb, U.S. State Department Shipping Coordinating Committee, "Some Gen-eral Foreign Economic Policy Considerations Relating to Cargo Sharing," in ibid., p. 320.

35. Christoph Hinz, "Protectionism in Shipping—Some Current and Future Trends," *Marius* (Oslo) 42 (May 1979), p. 3.

including Japan, Italy, Spain, and Belgium, tended to vote with Group D (the Eastern bloc) and the Group of 77. With the exception of Italy, all these states ultimately voted in favor of the code. A second group, composed of the traditional liberal states, Britain, Sweden, Norway, Denmark, and Switzerland, generally refused to compromise. As a result, their influence on the final document was minimal, despite the fact that most of these countries have tended to champion Third World causes in other areas of world trade.[36] West Germany was positioned between these two groups. It eventually voted in favor of the code and became one of its most ardent defenders. Unlike France, however, West Germany consistently maintained that its support for the code was conditioned by fear of even greater protectionism and instability if a compromise with Third World views was not reached.[37]

The Development of Protectionism

Protectionism in shipping can be measured by the amount of world seaborne trade subject to various forms of flag discrimination. As noted above, indirect forms of protectionism include government subsidies and related forms of state sponsorship of shipping enterprise. In general, the maritime industries are becoming increasingly integrated into national economic planning; this is especially true of shipbuilding, where nationalization is occurring in Western Europe as well as in the Third World. Another indicator of the neo-mercantilist trend is the increasingly close relationship between shipping and shipbuilding. As shipping policy begins to blend with national industrial policy, the relationship between shippers and shipowners also becomes closer, and the balance of power shifts in favor of the former.

Protectionism in its various guises influences the distribution of power throughout the various shipping blocs. From the point of view of OECD countries, the threats from the Soviet bloc and the Third World demand a united front. Instead, however, the division between the United States and Western Europe weakens the OECD, creating opportunities for Soviet

36. See UNCTAD, *United Nations Conference of Plenipotentiaries,* esp. pp. 42–44 for voting patterns.

37. See, for example, Lienhard Schmidt, "The International Shipping Policy Issues at UNCTAD V, Manila, May 1979" (Hamburg: Hapag-Lloyd, 1979) (mimeographed), esp. pp. 7–9.

shipping and Third World flag discrimination. Atlantic disunity has also inspired the EC's efforts to establish a stable regime. However, EC success has been limited both by America's opposition to its policies and by intra-European conflicts. Thus, the United States remains the dominant force in world shipping, and the main obstacle to stability.

Chapter 3 outlined the main types of flag discrimination in the postwar regime. The most important forms included United States reservation of government-sponsored cargoes to national flag vessels, a practice which the Latin Americans increasingly followed. In the heyday of the postwar regime, however, flag discrimination was not practiced extensively. Plausible estimates, cited in Chapter 3, indicate that less than 5 percent of cargo in 1960 was formally subject to discrimination.

The UNCTAD Code of Conduct reserves up to 80 percent of liner cargoes to exporting and importing nations; in practice, the degree of effective cargo reservation will depend on the size of the merchant fleets in protectionist states. In many Third World countries, shipbuilding is expanding rapidly; at the same time the code, by mandating captive cargoes, favors merchant fleet expansion. In theory, this type of protection-based expansion is excluded from the EC and OECD blocs. However, as will be shown in Chapter 8, the ambiguities of EC shipping policy suggest that some form of cargo reservation may eventually appear in EC trades.

The extent to which the code simply reflected—and even restrained—the legal and economic trend toward nationalism can be gauged from the many national cargo reservation laws and bilateral treaties that began to appear during the late 1960s and early 1970s, before the drafting of the UNCTAD Code of Conduct. Table 17 lists these cargo reservation laws. Table 18 documents the development of bilateral shipping agreements concluded since 1969. In 1969, Argentina and Brazil pioneered the development of strict cargo reservation. Before this, formal bilateralism had been limited mainly to trade involving the United States and the Soviet bloc states. In the United States, Public Law 664, the Cargo Preference Act of 1954, had formed the basis of nine subsequent congressional acts expanding preference and widening the interpretation of government involvement in seaborne trade. Preference was extended to 50 percent of food shipments under Public Law 480, military cargoes, and cargoes sponsored by the government. These laws were interpreted broadly to pertain to cargo indirectly related to the government, such as shipments covered under government loan guarantees.

Latin American governments modeled cargo protection laws on United States experience. As the data in Tables 17 and 18 indicate, flag discrimination is most advanced in this region. Initially, Latin American governments seeking to expand their fleets relied on fiscal inducements and the reservation of relatively small portions of government-related cargoes to the national flag. These laws applied primarily to the liner sector. In the 1970s, however, outright bilateralism was sought, in conjunction with unilateral

Table 17.   Significant Cargo Preferences Under National Law, 1984

Algeria	50% carriage of oil and LNG exports
Argentina	50% carriage of all government-financed, -owned, or -concessionary cargoes; 50% carriage of goods under any international trade agreement
Australia–New Zealand	Trade reserved to national flag vessels
Brazil	100% carriage of government-related goods
Chile	50% carriage of exports
Colombia	50% carriage of imports and exports
Dominican Republic	40% of general imports and exports
Ecuador	30–50% of imports and exports
Egypt	30% of imports and exports
Indonesia	45% of European imports and exports
Iran	All government imports
Mexico	Preference to Latin-flag lines and government-impelled cargoes
Morocco	40% of imports; 30% of exports
People's Republic of China	50% carriage of exports
Peru	30% of imports and exports
Philippines	Monopoly of government-sponsored or -financed cargoes
South Korea	Mandatory Korean-flag preference
Turkey	All public sector cargo
United States	All military cargoes, 50% of Ex-Im Bank and government-financed cargoes; 50% PL 480 exports
Uruguay	50% of export cargo
U.S.S.R.	Sell c.i.f., buy f.o.b.
Venezuela	50% of imports and exports

SOURCES: U.S. Federal Maritime Commission, *Annual Report* (various) (Washington, D.C.: G.P.O.); trade literature (various); OECD, Maritime Transport Committee, *Maritime Transport* (various) (Paris: OECD).

Table 18.   Development of Intergovernmental Bilateral Agreements, 1969 – 84
             (50 – 50 or 40 – 40 – 20)

Algeria	U.S.S.R., G.D.R., Guinea, P.R.C., Brazil, France
Argentina	Uruguay, Peru, Brazil, Chile, Colombia, U.S.S.R., Cuba
Brazil	Argentina, Chile, Peru, Uruguay, Nigeria, Mexico, Panama
Chile	Argentina, Brazil
Colombia	Argentina, Uruguay
Egypt	U.S.S.R.
France	Ivory Coast, Tunisia, Algeria
Greece	U.S.S.R.
India	U.S.S.R., Egypt
Indonesia	U.S.S.R.
Ivory Coast	France, West Germany
Japan	P.R.C., Taiwan, South Korea
Mexico	Brazil
Pakistan	Poland
People's Republic of China	U.S. (33 – 33 – 33)
Peru	Argentina, India, Brazil
Philippines	U.S.
Portugal	U.S.S.R., Mozambique
South Korea	U.S., Japan, West Germany
United States	P.R.C. (33 – 33 – 33), Philippines, South Korea
Uruguay	Argentina, Brazil, Colombia
West Germany	South Korea, Ivory Coast

SOURCES: U.S. Federal Maritime Commission, *Annual Report* (various) (Washington, D.C.: G.P.O.); trade literature (various); OECD, Maritime Transport Committee, *Maritime Transport* (various) (Paris: OECD).

reservation of up to 50 percent of government-related cargoes if the offer of bilateral pacts was rejected by the trading partner. Most states in the region maintain a high degree of involvement in exports and imports. Between 1970 and 1983 government ownership of Latin American shipping increased from 56 to 64 percent.[38]

All Latin American governments have instituted cargo reservation. Although the laws vary, shipping policies share three major characteristics:

38. Seatrade, *Latin American Shipping 1981—A Seatrade Guide* (Colchester: Seatrade, 1981), p. 35; and Seatrade, *Latin American Shipping 1983—A Seatrade Guide* (Colchester: Seatrade, 1983), p. 30.

1. A certain proportion of government-sponsored imports and exports are reserved for the national flag. The emphasis on imports reflects the greater leverage in liner shipping enjoyed by the importer who can specify f.o.b. purchase.

2. Non-government cargoes have a target of 50 percent for imports and exports.

3. State-owned fleets are granted special privileges such as internal cargo preference.[39]

The success of protectionist policies can be measured by the development of national flag fleets and the increasing percentage of cargo they have carried during a decade when exports and imports expanded rapidly. In 1982 Latin American fleets carried from 30 to 50 percent of imports and 20 percent of exports.[40] In liner shipping, many Latin American countries transport more than 50 percent of imports and exports,[41] and Latin American shipping has increased from 6.4 million grt in 1970 to 14.3 million grt in 1983.[42] Success has been greatest in the liner trades; in bulk shipping the barrier to entry caused by the greater degree of external control of cargoes is higher. The Latin American experience serves as a model for other newly developing countries such as South Korea, Singapore, and Taiwan, where maritime expansion has played an important role in national economic development.

In principle the United States opposes bilateralism, and opposition from the State Department has been a major obstacle to U.S. endorsement of the UNCTAD Code of Conduct. In practice, however, the American response to bilateralism has been permissive. Under Section 15 of the Shipping Act of 1916, the FMC is authorized to approve practices that would otherwise be prohibited by antitrust statutes. Section 15 reflects the conclusion of the Alexander Report that the anticompetitive activities of conferences, including bilateral agreements, require government regulation. All anticompetitive agreements must be filed and receive FMC approval before their implementation.

During the late 1960s, Latin American lines sought to capture a greater

39. Michael Morris, *International Politics and the Sea: The Case of Brazil* (Boulder: Westview, 1979), pp. 267–82.

40. Seatrade, *Latin American Shipping 1983,* p. 30.

41. Seatrade, *Latin American Shipping 1981,* p. 43.

42. UNCTAD, *Review of Maritime Transport, 1984* (Geneva: United Nations, 1985).

share of inter-American trade. Once the resistance of American lines was broken through unilateral action on the part of Latin American governments, Latin American and United States lines reached a series of pooling and equal access agreements in conference trades. These agreements essentially divided cargoes on a 50–50 basis. Initially the FMC refused to approve these agreements because of their anticompetitive nature. However, in August 1970, Brazilian and U.S. lines brought two such agreements before the FMC and, despite European opposition, they received prompt approval.[43] Pooling or equal access agreements typically encompass all liner conference traffic from Latin ports to separate U.S. coasts (Atlantic, Gulf, Pacific). Trade is divided among lines of the trading partners, excluding third flags. The FMC has taken the position that approval of bilateralism is preferable to legal action against Latin American countries:

> Experience has shown that pooling or equal access agreements are acceptable alternatives to retaliatory steps which could be taken in opposing this type of discrimination. The objective is to forestall any governmental action which might adversely affect the operations of United States shipping lines in these regions.[44]

Pooling and equal access agreements have been bitterly opposed by Western European lines because they limit cross-trading in Latin American trades.[45] American lines have secured a leading position in many trades, often at the expense of Western European lines. Thus, for example, by 1979 the FMC had approved nineteen equal access and pooling agreements between the United States and Argentina, Brazil, Chile, Colombia, and Peru, including agreements between Empresa Lineas Maritimas Argentinas (ELMA) and Moore-McCormack Lines about cargoes between Argentina and the U.S. East Coast and Great Lakes ports, and between ELMA and Delta Steamship Lines about cargoes between Argentine ports and U.S. Gulf ports.[46]

United States participation in bilateral cargo-sharing has not been limited to Latin American trades. The FMC has approved pacts with South

43. FMC, *Annual Report, 1971* (Washington, D.C.: G.P.O., 1972); Carlos Oswaldo Saraiwa, "Brazilian International Shipping Policy," *Lawyer for the Americas* 4 (February 1972), pp. 37–40.

44. FMC, *Annual Report, 1970* (Washington, D.C.: G.P.O., 1971), p. 28.

45. Seatrade, *Latin American Shipping 1981*, p. 49.

46. FMC, *Annual Reports* (various).

Korea, the Philippines, and some ports of India and Bangladesh. Inter-governmental bilateral agreements have been concluded with the Soviet Union (1972) and People's Republic of China (1980).[47] Substantial bene-fits to American liner shipping did not occur in U.S.-Soviet trades, because of the low level of liner trade. In China, the bilateral agreement was sought in order to promote long-term expansion of liner trades between the two countries. American delegates used UNCTAD committee meetings to plan bilateral deals with foreign shipowners even as they made speeches against bilateralism.[48] The FMC has become an increasingly strong ad-vocate of bilateral policy. As a former chairman, Richard Daschbach, testified:

> My personal opinion is we should start from a 50–50 point of view. In keeping with our notion that cross-trading is a privilege, not a right, it seems that if you start negotiating or bargaining from a 40–40–20 point of view, you have con-ceded the point of privilege vs. the right.[49]

Significantly, however, with the exception of Soviet and Chinese bulk trades, the United States has not initiated cargo protection or bilateralism in bulk shipping beyond the extremely limited scope of PL 480 cargo. Bi-lateralism has applied primarily to the liner trades; although Third World states formally extend protection to non-liner cargoes, the practical effect of this policy is limited by their lack of ships and power over cargoes.

The UNCTAD Code of Conduct restricts the extent of protectionism in some cases, because it formally preserves the right to cross-trade. Conse-quently some states, notably West Germany, favored the code as a moderat-ing influence.[50] This demonstrates the extent to which national economic policies and interests have anticipated international legal developments.

47. Ibid.; OECD, Maritime Transport Committee, *Maritime Transport* (various); Peter Goldman, "National Policies Recognized as United States and China Enter Sea Trade Pact," *Seatrade* (October 1980), p. 89.

48. Author's interview with a U.S. shipping official, London, 1980. Howard Saxner cites the opinion of a lawyer that the U.S. shipping lines he represented, and not the Brazilian lines, had conceived the 1970 bilateral agreements ("On Troubled Waters: Subsidies, Cartels, and the Maritime Commission," in Mark J. Green, ed., *The Monopoly Makers* [New York: Grossman, 1973], p. 129); U.S. lines and officials dispute this claim. The FMC has been one of the strongest government advocates of bilateral policy.

49. U.S. Congress, Senate, Committee on Commerce, Science, and Transportation, *Ocean Shipping Act of 1979*, 96th Cong., 1979, p. 67.

50. See, for example, Schmidt, "International Shipping Policy Issues," pp. 27–29.

Table 19.   World Trade Subject to Flag Discrimination, 1978 (million metric tons)

	Exports		Imports	
United States	296	(8.3%)	618	(17.5%)
Nondiscriminators[a]	1,902	(54.0%)	1,954	(55.4%)
Known discriminators[b]	1,007	(28.0%)	603	(17.1%)
Possible discriminators[c]	229	(6.5%)	180	(5.1%)
Unaccounted[d]	116	(3.2%)	170	(4.8%)
Total trade	3,550	(100.0%)	3,525	(100.0%)

SOURCES: United Nations, *Monthly Bulletin of Statistics* (New York: United Nations); UNCTAD, *Review of Maritime Transport, 1980* (Geneva: United Nations, 1981).

[a]OECD countries, except for the United States, Portugal, Spain, Turkey; Yugoslavia; OPEC countries; Bahrain, Cyprus, Democratic Yemen, Iran, Iraq, Jordan, Kuwait, Lebanon, Qatar, Saudi Arabia, Syria, United Arab Emirates.
[b]COMECON bloc, People's Republic of China, South American countries, South Korea, Philippines, North African countries, West African countries.
[c]India, Pakistan, South Africa, Portugal, Spain, Turkey, Indonesia, Caribbean, Central American countries.
[d]Some countries of Southern and Eastern Asia, Oceania.

Many countries, especially in Latin America and the Eastern bloc, expressed reservations on this point about the code; Soviet bloc states declared that the provisions of the code "do not apply to joint shipping lines established on the basis of intergovernmental agreements to serve bilateral trade between the countries concerned."[51]

In Chapter 4, two estimates of the quantitative impact of discrimination were cited. The authors of the Rochdale Report concluded that as late as 1967, less than 5 percent of world trade by weight was subject to cargo protection laws. Stanley Sturmey divided states into various categories ranging from "non-discriminator" to "known discriminator." Based on world trade data from 1957, he concluded that less than 15 percent of trade flowed to or from discriminating countries and that no more than 5 percent of this fraction was actually subject to discrimination, because most countries with protectionist laws lacked the ships to enforce them (see Table 15).

Table 19 presents an estimate of the extent of flag discrimination in 1978 based on Sturmey's procedures. It serves an an index of the increase in protectionism since the middle 1950s. The table indicates the decrease

51. UNCTAD, *Status of the Convention on a Code of Conduct for Liner Conferences—Note by the UNCTAD Secretariat,* TD/B/C.4/206 (Geneva: United Nations, 1980), p. 5.

in American trade as a percentage of world trade and reveals significant increases, both absolute and relative, in the trade of "known discriminators." It also shows a decline in the percentage of trade imported by "free" countries. "Free" country exports increased primarily because most OPEC states are included in this category.

A rough calculation of the quantity of trade subject to protection has been made by adding 50 percent of the imports of "known discriminators," 25 percent of the imports of "partial discriminators," and 10 percent of American exports. This essentially repeats Sturmey's procedure, with some modifications. It yields an estimate of 12 percent of world trade by weight flowing to or from discriminatory countries. In this case, however, the figure can be maintained on the assumption that, contrary to the situation in the 1950s, "discriminators" now possess sufficient tonnage to put their laws into practice.

Table 19 is useful as a crude indicator of the increase in discrimination. But any conclusions to be drawn from it must be qualified. First, the categories reflect subjective impressions concerning the real impact of cargo reservation on trade in many countries. Second, and equally important, the aggregate trade data do not discriminate between bulk and liner shipping. Because more than half of world trade by weight consists of liquid and dry bulk cargo, most of which is technically "free," the 12 percent figure could perhaps be doubled if value rather than tonnage were used. Unfortunately, data for seaborne trade by value are not available. Finally, the table includes only cargo officially subject to flag discrimination. Collusion between shippers and shipowners, government pressure on shippers, and other discriminatory practices are gaining momentum worldwide.

As Sturmey has noted: "The question of the effects of discrimination cannot be observed only in static terms, as it is always possible for a single country, the shipping of which is being barred by discrimination, to lessen that harm by adopting discrimination itself."[52] Cargo reservation has a crucial effect on all aspects of the regime. It influences government fiscal and subsidy policies, and intervention "downstream" into shipbuilding and "upstream" into insurance. The consequences of beggar-my-neighbor policies are felt throughout the maritime industries and are reinforced by the

52. Stanley G. Sturmey, *British Shipping and World Competition* (London: Athlone, 1962), p. 207.

high cost of ships and the increasing bargaining power of importers during the global recession.

Thus, a substantial trend toward flag discrimination can be identified; indeed, for some countries the process appears to have just begun. The UNCTAD Code will encourage protectionism. This is demonstrated in the growing shipbuilding capacity in those countries, such as the Soviet bloc, South Korea, Brazil, Argentina, and India, that have embraced shipping nationalism. As ships are forced to abandon traditional trade routes, they gravitate to the free market, notably in the U.S. Atlantic and Pacific trades, where the conferences remain open. Thus, Third World protection, though not quantitatively large, has indirectly provoked internal competition in the traditional maritime bloc and sharpened the conflicts between Western Europe and America. Most advanced industrial states have resisted flag discrimination in favor of its functional equivalents, informal collusion between shippers and shipowners or massive aid to shipping and shipbuilding.

The Limits of the Soviet Challenge in Liner Shipping

Soviet foreign economic expansion in the post–World War II era established the conditions for the parallel development of a global transportation network. According to Admiral Sergei Gorshkov, commander of Soviet naval forces, "The Soviet merchant marine, like that of any country, is a component of the sea power of the Soviet Union, and the continuous expansion of its foreign trade links has resulted in a rapid development of the maritime shipping ability of the Soviet Union."[53] Much of the Soviet transportation system is land-based, and the largely continental transport of oil and gas requires pipelines rather than ships. In shipping, Soviet expansion has been limited mainly to the liner sector, one part of which is the integrated land/sea bridge made possible by the construction of the Trans-Siberian Container Link (TSCL). Despite the collapse of U.S.-Soviet détente, Soviet shipping continues to compete favorably in many Western

53. Quoted in Atlantic Council of the United States, *The Soviet Merchant Marine: Economic and Strategic Challenge to the West* (Washington, D.C.: Atlantic Council, 1978), p. 8. For Soviet views, see esp. S. G. Gorshkov (Admiral of the Fleet of the U.S.S.R. and Commander-in-Chief of the Soviet Navy), *The Sea Power of the State* (Annapolis: Naval Institute Press, 1979), pp. 29–46.

Table 20.   Participation of Soviet Merchant Fleet in International Carriage of
                 Goods by Sea, 1970 – 84 (millions of tons)

	1970	1976	1978	1980	1984
Cargo carried worldwide	2,605.0	3,355.0	3,468.0	3,778.0	3,320.0
World fleet (dwt)	326.1	601.2	662.8	682.8	674.5
Soviet fleet (dwt)	12.0	16.0	18.4	19.0	27.9
Soviet fleet as percentage of world fleet	3.7	2.7	2.8	2.8	4.1

SOURCES: "East Bloc Survey," *Norwegian Shipping News* 38 (2 April 1982); Institute of Shipping Economics
and Logistics, *Shipping Statistics* 29, no. 12 (Bremen: Institute of Shipping Economics and Logistics, December
1985); UNCTAD, *Review of Maritime Transport, 1984* (Geneva: United Nations, 1985).

markets. The lack of a common response to Soviet incursions in liner shipping highlights the fragmentation of the OECD and the North Atlantic
Treaty Organization (NATO). According to Karl-Heinz Sager, chairman
of Hapag-Lloyd, Soviet shipping has "involuntary aides" in the U.S.
government.[54]

The growth of the Soviet fleet and its ability to penetrate world markets
have undoubtedly been exaggerated by Western academicians and shipowners. Nevertheless, its growth has been impressive, especially in certain
specific sectors of shipping. Table 20 depicts the modest overall expansion
of the Soviet merchant fleet. Although the size of the fleet more than
doubled between 1970 and 1984, it only kept pace with the development
of the world fleet. Predictably, Soviet growth has been concentrated in the
liner sector, where the entry barriers are lower and foreign exchange can
readily be earned. In 1984, the Soviet fleet included 7.9 grt of general
cargo vessels, making it the world's second largest fleet (below only Panama) in this category. A limited expansion of bulk shipping is anticipated
during the late 1980s, and the Soviet Union's container capacity has expanded steadily.

Like the United States, the Soviet Union follows an opportunistic and
somewhat inconsistent strategy. In its national trades, the Soviet Union is

54. Karl-Heinz Sager, *A West European Shipowner's Reply to Mr. Averin and to His Involuntary Aides in the United States* (London: Hapag-Lloyd, 1979). For a Soviet statement, see
Timofei Guzhenko, "Soviet Merchant Marine and World Shipping," *Marine Policy* 1 (April
1977).

highly protectionist. However, because of its involvement in cross-trading, it supports the principle of free access to cargoes. As was noted in Chapter 4, Soviet shipping firms rely more heavily on cross-trading than do their American counterparts. The nationalistic tradition combined with extensive participation in Western markets and cross-trades explains Soviet ambivalence toward the UNCTAD Code.

Soviet nationalism is expressed in bilateral agreements with trading partners where these are appropriate and, where possible, buying cargoes f.o.b. and selling c.i.f. Except for grain, most Soviet imports are of liner cargoes. Because Soviet shipping costs are well below those of Western competitors and there is no competition among Soviet importers, it is virtually impossible for Western shipowners to challenge the policy of purchasing f.o.b. (and thereby directing cargo to Soviet ships). In 1978, 95 percent of EC seaborne trade with the U.S.S.R. was carried by Soviet vessels. In 1978, the Soviet merchant marine transported 84 percent of Soviet-British trade, 75 percent of Soviet–West German trade, and 97 percent of Soviet-Japanese trade.[55] In 1976, Soviet vessels carried 2.9 percent of the total U.S. liner trade by weight, a not insubstantial portion of world trade; U.S. foreign commerce accounts for 14 percent of world seaborne trade by weight, but 66 percent by value.[56]

The main Soviet commercial threat to Western European shipping stems from cross-trading and the Siberian land bridge. Soviet participation in some important cross-trades has become significant. By the late 1970s, the Soviet Union had acquired 13 percent of the carryings between the United States and Northern Europe, including 25 percent of U.S.–West German trade. The Far Eastern Shipping Company of Vladivostok carried 23 percent of cargoes in the trans-Pacific trade route, more than any other line. In addition, Soviet shipping carried 35 percent of Northern Europe–Mediterranean cargoes, 25 percent of Northeastern Europe–African West Coast trade, and 20 percent of the traffic between the Gulf of Mexico ports and the Mediterranean.[57]

55. *Economist*, 18 June 1977, p. 85; Herbert E. Meyer, "The Communist Internationale Has a Capitalist Accent," *Fortune* 45 (February 1977), pp. 141–42.

56. U.S. Department of Commerce, Maritime Administration, *Expansion of the Soviet Merchant Marine into U.S. Maritime Trades* (Washington, D.C.: G.P.O., 1977), p. 4.

57. *Economist*, 18 June 1977, p. 85. For Western European views, see GCBS, *Red Ensign vs. the Red Flag* (London: GCBS, 1975).

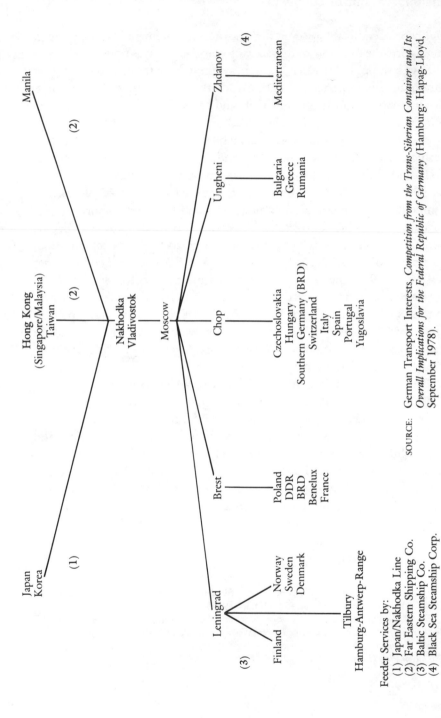

Figure 1 The Soviet Container Transport System

Japan
Korea

(1)

Hong Kong
(Singapore/Malaysia)
Taiwan

(2)

Manila

(2)

Nakhodka
Vladivostok

Moscow

Brest

Chop

Ungheni

Zhdanov

(4)

Poland
DDR
BRD
Benelux
France

Czechoslovakia
Hungary
Southern Germany (BRD)
Switzerland
Italy
Spain
Portugal
Yugoslavia

Bulgaria
Greece
Rumania

Mediterranean

Leningrad

(3)

Finland

Norway
Sweden
Denmark

Tilbury
Hamburg-Antwerp-Range

Feeder Services by:
(1) Japan/Nakhodka Line
(2) Far Eastern Shipping Co.
(3) Baltic Steamship Co.
(4) Black Sea Steamship Corp.

SOURCE: German Transport Interests, *Competition from the Trans-Siberian Container and Its Overall Implications for the Federal Republic of Germany* (Hamburg: Hapag-Lloyd, September 1978).

Soviet shipping achieved these shares through an aggressive marketing strategy aimed at shippers and freight-forwarding agents. Acting mainly as non-conference outsiders, Soviet firms charge freight rates from 10 to 40 percent lower than do conferences. Soviet lines focus on the highly valued cargoes and are helped by their flexible rate structure. Gradually, modern tonnage in the form of container and ro-ro ("roll-on-roll-off" car carriers) vessels is replacing conventional cargo ships.[58] Soviet (and Polish) firms are also aided by their large size. The largest firms (Baltic, Black Sea, Far East, POL, PSC) are comparable in size to the largest Western firms. Their competitive strength is enhanced because they do not have to compete among themselves for cargo.

A parallel threat to Western European shipowners is the TSCL. This is a combined rail/sea link offering containerized services between Western Europe and Asia. Figure 1 depicts its massive scope. The TSCL competes directly with the Far Eastern Freight Conference, which is made up of the major Western European and Japanese consortia. In 1977, the TSCL carried 10 percent of Western European/Far East liner traffic, and the Soviet Odessa Line handled an additional 5 percent. Soviet freight agents concentrate on the major exporting countries, West Germany and Japan.[59] In 1982, TSCL transported 12 percent of Western European/Far Eastern liner trade. According to the *Norwegian Shipping News,* Soviet firms hope eventually to capture 50 percent of the traffic.[60]

The growth of Soviet shipping has accentuated the effects of the recession on Western shipowners. Since 1975, British and West German owners have taken the lead in urging a common Western response. They have identified the problem as "noncommercial" competition; unconcerned with Western profit-loss calculations, Soviet firms can undercut the Western lines to fulfill their objectives of increasing foreign exchange and political influence.[61]

58. "Russians Steady on New Five-Year Course," *Norwegian Shipping News* 38 (2 April 1982), p. 16.

59. German Transport Interests, *Competition from the TSCL—and Its Overall Implications for the Federal Republic of Germany* (Hamburg: Hapag-Lloyd, 1978).

60. "Russians Steady," p. 16; and Richard Bell, "European Shipowners Demand Action Against Trans-Siberian Box Line," *Container News* 11 (April 1981), p. 12.

61. Atlantic Council, *The Soviet Merchant Marine,* p. 28; Bell, "European Shipowners," p. 12. However, a recent report by the European Commission ("Aspects of the Competition between EC Maritime Shipping and the TSR on Europe–Far East Routes") concludes that charges of price-cutting are not justified.

Despite the strenuous efforts of British and West German shipowners, little action has been taken against Soviet shipping. Competition is more serious for some fleets (United Kingdom, West Germany, and France, where despite a bilateral treaty 90 percent of cargo carried between the U.S.S.R. and France is transported in Soviet vessels) than for others. Moreover, low freight rates are beneficial to shippers in both Western Europe and Japan, who have provided much TSCL investment capital.[62] U.S. regulatory policies designed to assist U.S. shippers, including the government as a shipper, also favor Soviet shipping in its efforts to displace Western competitors. Prohibition of the deferred rebate disarms the conferences in their battles with Soviet shipping firms. In 1978, the United States purchased five hundred buses from West Germany with Urban Mass Transit Administration funds and shipped them on Soviet vessels at $3,000 per bus less than the lowest American bid.[63] In 1977, the North Atlantic Freight Conference invited the Soviet Balt-American Line to join the conference. The Department of Justice, however, refused, on antitrust grounds, to approve the agreement.[64]

After intensive lobbying, the Controlled Carrier Bill passed as part of the Ocean Shipping Act of 1978. Aimed at the Soviet fleet, it outlawed freight rates below a level determined to be "just and reasonable." Although the language is ambiguous, the bill authorizes the FMC to restrict access of state-owned fleets to U.S. ports. In any case, after the Soviet invasion of Afghanistan, most Soviet tonnage was forced out of the United States trades by longshore and shipper boycotts.[65] This tonnage emigrated primarily to Western European routes, where the shipowners were vulnerable to an aggressive competitor.

Like the less developed countries, the U.S.S.R. opposes conferences only to the extent that they injure the competitive position of Soviet lines. The Soviet firms join conferences when compelled to do so or when they have secured a favorable percentage of trade, the basis for a satisfactory car-

62. "Soviets a Focal Point of Georgia Conference," *Container News* 7 (June 1977), pp. 40–44.

63. Colin Morrison, "FMC Rings a Bell on Soviet Bus Shipment," *Seatrade* (May 1978), p. 21.

64. Atlantic Council, *The Soviet Merchant Marine*, p. 31.

65. See U.S. Congress, Senate, Committee on Commerce, Science, and Transportation, *Ocean Shipping Act of 1978: Hearings Before the Senate Subcommittee on Merchant Marine and Tourism of the Senate Committee on Commerce, Science, and Transportation*, 95th Cong., 1978.

tel division. Thus, the Soviet Union, acting within the framework of the regime, poses a significant challenge to the status quo. The regime thus becomes less acceptable to Western European shipowners. The highly unpredictable conditions created by both superpowers have led the EC to favor the UNCTAD Code as a means of preserving trade shares and strengthening the position of conferences.

Conclusion

This chapter has reviewed the challenge to the principle of privatization in liner shipping, which was dominant from the end of World War II to the mid-1960s. In liner shipping, the principle of regulation was articulated by all have-not shipping blocs, although regulation has meant different things to different blocs. The efforts of both the Third World and the U.S.S.R. reflect not only general developmental objectives, expressed in the New International Economic Order, but also the typical views of have-not states in shipping. Each bloc has favored national and international regulation as a means of establishing greater control over their activities. Yet each bloc is also essentially opportunistic, seeking to gain entry to conferences and re-shape them in accordance with national objectives.

In general, the U.S.S.R. has not been a major force in international shipping politics. Despite their formal adherence to bilateralism, Soviet firms have tried to exploit conferences, not to bury them. Morflot is a highly efficient, profit-seeking multinational corporation. Although the development of Soviet shipping undoubtedly serves military objectives, its primary purpose is to earn foreign exchange. Soviet liner shipping is heavily engaged in cross-trading. It is not linked to a strategy of penetrating foreign markets, although it could be deployed in this fashion. This conclusion seems equally valid for the relatively small Soviet bulk fleet. Of course, Soviet-bloc expansion in the liner trades does represent a commercial threat to some Western European shipping firms. For the structure of global transportation, the TSCL may have long-range implications which require further analysis.

The UNCTAD Code of Conduct for Liner Conferences represents a rare legal and diplomatic achievement for the Third World. The principle of regulation or authoritative allocation is both a means of establishing greater control over national trade and also an instrument for reshaping conference practices in order to redistribute income from North to South. The code is essentially nationalist and regulatory; it restricts the freedom of conferences and allows states to influence freight rates and allocate shipping shares in accordance with national objectives. Hence, it represents a frontal challenge to the principles and practices of the postwar regime. The Third World, in contrast to the United States, does not seek to regulate conferences in order to increase competition. Indeed, the monopolistic practices of conferences may be considered attractive, provided Third World lines have representation within them. Therefore, like Western Europe, the Third World generally does not oppose closed conferences.

Ultimately, the code gives international legal expression to the maritime strategies of a small number of newly industrializing countries that have the resources to sponsor national merchant fleets and, in many cases, national shipbuilding industries. However, the extent to which the development of shipping and shipbuilding has reduced global dependency must not be overestimated. Shipping is a highly capital-intensive service industry, and scarce resources that are being devoted to shipping might be better utilized elsewhere. Moreover, in establishing liner fleets, Third World countries are reinforcing many elements of the current international division of labor. The UNCTAD Code of Conduct strengthens the role of conferences, although LDCs are guaranteed access. It seems doubtful that new trading routes will be established through the use of shipping. In many cases, Third World maritime fleets are financed and owned by multinationals and linked to Northern industrial strategies.[66] Finally, the capital-intensive nature of shipping acts against the urgent need of less developed

---

66. LDC shipbuilding is closely linked to Japan and, to a lesser extent, the Netherlands. Japanese shipbuilding has extensive links to Brazil through the Japanese-financed Ishibras, the second largest Brazilian shipbuilder (Verolme, Dutch-owned, is the largest). Cheap labor (in 1980 South Korean shipbuilding workers received $55 per week) is one reason for Japanese participation. In addition, only a fairly small portion of marine equipment is produced in LDCs; thus shipbuilders are often closely integrated into Japanese marine industries. See Andrew J. Cornford and Raymond B. Glasgow, "The Process of Structural Change in the World Economy: Some Aspects of the Rise of Shipbuilding Industry in Developing Countries," *Trade and Development* 1 (Winter 1981), esp. pp. 106, 112–15. In 1975 South Korean shipbuilding workers worked a nine-hour day with every third Sunday off. See "Hyundai Shipbuilding: Large Hypermodern Shipyard with Great Flexibility," *Norwegian Shipping News* 31 (25 April 1975), p. 6. In 1983, hourly wage costs in South Korean shipbuilding were 16 percent of West German costs and approximately 25 percent of British and Japanese costs (Commission of the European Communities, answer given by Mr. Davignon on behalf of the commission to written question no. 1491/83 by Miss Quin).

countries to develop technology that is appropriate to conditions of massive unemployment.

The significance of the Third World challenge in liner shipping must be viewed in the context of growing maritime conflict between Europe and America, the subject of Chapters 7–9. In quantitative terms, if the scope of the Code of Conduct is limited to North-South trades, which appears probable, it will govern only a fraction of world trade: estimates range from 10 to 25 percent. Moreover, a large and growing proportion of LDC trade in manufactured goods is with the United States.[67] Since these trades are a traditional province of European cross-traders, this trend indicates the centrality of U.S.-European relations and the pivotal role of the United States in the political economy of liner shipping.

67. A detailed analysis of the potential impact of the Code of Conduct on U.S. trades is presented in Lawrence Juda, *The UNCTAD Liner Code: U.S. Maritime Policy at the Crossroads* (Boulder: Westview, 1984), esp. chapter five. For the high estimate of world trade actually affected by the Code (25 percent), see ibid., p. 148. For the low estimate (10 percent), see *FACS Forum* (June 1983), p. 4.

7

United States Shipping Policy: State Power and Cartels

The United States plays a key role in the structural changes occurring in international liner shipping. With declining industrial competitiveness and resulting balance-of-payments problems, and decreasing concern for the special role of Western and Northern European shipping in the world economy, revisionist attitudes toward the conference system gained adherents in the United States. In this context, the United States was unwilling to make concessions to its rivals. The regulatory strategy that the United States began to pursue during the late 1960s was viewed as a means of increasing export competitiveness and thereby arresting the adverse trend in the balance of payments. It also facilitated the introduction of new technologies that were beneficial to the U.S. merchant marine as well as to U.S. trading interests. The increasing significance of America's domestic structure for regime development is consistent with the expectations of the theory of hegemonic stability. As the United States became less concerned with the effects of its policies on other countries, it was natural that the regulatory traditions and statutes of U.S. maritime policy, embodied in the U.S. Shipping Act of 1916, the Alexander Report, and much subsequent legislation would make their mark on the international regime.

Development of U.S. Maritime Policy

National shipping policy may be defined as

> the totality of economic, legal and administrative measures by means of which the state influences the position of its national fleet, that is, its place and role in the national economy and in international freight markets. The attitude of the state to its own merchant fleet as a rule reflects indirectly its attitude to the fleets of other countries.[1]

Geography and national security are constants that play an important role in national shipping policy. Island trading nations tend to be prominent in shipping. Military interests dictate a merchant fleet with overseas supply capabilities; periods of imperialist expansion coincide with merchant fleet development. Beyond this, there are wide variations in national shipping attitudes and policies, which can be explained in terms of the politics of the maritime sector and its responses to constraints and opportunities presented by the international regime. The most dramatic example is the serious internal debate within Norway during the 1950s, when shipping capital was pitted against industrial capital. The debate focused on the allocation of resources to shipping and affected Norway's internal development and interrelation to the international economy, especially to the United States and Britain. The victory of the shipowners resulted in an economy geared to shipping and foreign capital.[2]

The international regime shaped Norwegian policy. There is a considerable amount of evidence, however, that U.S. policy shapes the interna-

---

1. Ignacy Chrzanowski, Maciej Krzyanowski, and Krzystof Luks, *Shipping Economics and Policy—A Socialist View* (London: Fairplay, 1979), p. 246. Stanley Sturmey gives the following definition: "A nation may be said to have a shipping policy when it encourages, permits, or formulates measures to interfere with or control the free play of market forces in regard to the employment of shipping" ("A Consideration of the Ends and Means of Shipping Policy," in Sturmey, *Shipping Economics: Collected Papers* [London: Macmillan, 1975], p. 178). Yet it is difficult to define "market forces" in shipping, an observation that informs much of Sturmey's own work. "Free market" national shipping, however defined, is itself a "policy."

2. Dag Tresselt, *The Controversy over the Division of Labor in International Seaborne Transport* (Bergen: Institute for Shipping Research, 1970); and V. D. Norman, *Norwegian Shipping in the National Economy* (Bergen: Institute for Shipping Research, 1971).

tional regime. The historical development of U.S. maritime policy reflects conflicts of interest between shipping firms and shippers, yet the ability of the state to influence international freight markets in the interests of shippers requires a strong United States flag merchant fleet. The shipper-shipowner dichotomy has been compounded by institutional weaknesses. The shipping sector has, until recently, suffered from retarded development, nurtured by a state too weak to help it overcome its backwardness.

In the first half of the nineteenth century, shipping was in the forefront of U.S. economic development. Stimulated by the availability of timber and shipbuilding expertise, U.S. shipping achieved sufficient strength to challenge Britain for maritime supremacy. Then, as noted in Chapter 2, in the 1840s the development of the steamship gave Britain, with its abundant coal reserves and advanced steel industry, a strong advantage. The discovery of gold and the preoccupation with internal development transferred resources away from the U.S. shipping sector; even the clipper ship eventually succumbed to steel and steam.[3] The United States was unable to meet these new technological challenges, and its shipbuilding and steel industries remained backward, protected by steep tariffs. During the nineteenth century relatively high freight rates also served as a protective tariff for infant industry, an advantage no longer available to less developed countries.

The advent of the steamship established the conditions of British merchant seapower. As shown in Chapter 2, it allowed the repeal of the Navigation Acts. British shipping no longer needed protection. During the American Civil War, Confederate raiders, supported by Britain, further damaged U.S. shipping. They sank 110,000 tons and, more significantly, forced many American shipowners to transfer vessels to foreign flags, including that of Britain.[4] From a peak of 2.4 million tons in 1865, the fleet

3. For reviews of American shipping policy, see H. David Bess and Martin T. Farris, *U.S. Maritime Policy: History and Prospects* (New York: Praeger, 1981); Samuel A. Lawrence, *U.S. Merchant Shipping Policies and Politics* (Washington, D.C.: Brookings Institution, 1966); Paul M. Zeis, *American Shipping Policy* (Princeton, N.J.: Princeton University Press, 1938); Ernest Frankel, *Regulation and Policies of American Shipping* (Boston: Auburn House, 1982); Robert A. Ellsworth, "Liner Conferences: Evolution of United States Policy," *Marine Policy 7* (October 1983); and Clifton H. Whitehurst, Jr., *The U.S. Merchant Marine: In Search of an Enduring Maritime Policy* (Annapolis: Naval Institute Press, 1983).

4. In 1868 the U.S. government received a settlement of $15 million from Britain for shipping losses suffered during the Civil War.

declined to 817,000 tons in 1900, the same size as the merchant fleet in 1807.

United States interventionism highlighted its shipping weakness and stimulated government activity. In 1900, American flag ships carried only 9.3 percent of the U.S. seaborne trade. During the Boer War, Britain withdrew tonnage from the U.S. trades. The resulting high freight rates meant, according to a congressional commission, that American exporters "paid for the Boer War."[5] In 1908, President Roosevelt sent the navy to the Far East in an effort to intimidate Japan. Because of a lack of merchant shipping, "this grand demonstration of American power was attended by a motley array of colliers, tankers, and tenders bearing the flags of the world."[6]

America's movement away from isolationism coincided with the worldwide consolidation of conferences. The development of shipping conferences stemmed from the general tendency to form trusts and cartels, part cause and part effect of increasing economic rivalry at the international level. The reaction of U.S. shippers to conferences and the ensuing Senate investigation that ended in the Alexander Report reflected the intention of American industry to resist European-dominated cartels. United States regulatory actions exempted conferences from the Sherman Act but made the deferred rebate illegal. This decision elicited intense hostility from American shipowners, delaying the passage of the Shipping Act of 1916 for three years.

The Shipping Act, along with the Alexander Report, remains topical because it serves as the doctrinal and legal basis of U.S. shipping policy. Moreover, the cleavages that marked its debate and passage are still important elements of American shipping policy. The Shipping Act established the United States Shipping Board, an independent agency with a mandate both to promote shipping and to regulate conference practices. The combination of regulation and promotion, reflecting and accentuating the shipowner/shipper dichotomy, as will be explained, has been the main source of inconsistency in American policy. The work of the Shipping Board was interrupted by World War I and the ensuing rapid expansion of U.S. shipping. The Shipping Board promoted and, to a great extent, spon-

5. Lawrence, *U.S. Merchant Shipping*, p. 34.
6. Ibid., p. 35.

sored this expansion. In 1922, it owned or controlled 13 million tons, over five times as much as prewar American tonnage, an expansion that created the need for further elaboration of policy. The Merchant Marine Act of 1920 sought to increase the role of U.S. shipping in world trade and to develop, with government aid, a viable private shipping sector capable of operating without subsidies. But attempts to create a rationalized merchant marine foundered when the postwar shipping boom ended. At the same time, foreign shipowners sought to win back their prewar share of U.S. trade. American shipping firms were poorly capitalized; they lacked the experience and stature within conferences to respond to intense international competition without government support.

The result was increasing subsidization during the 1920s and 1930s, carried out by the institution responsible for regulating the industry. The Shipping Board became increasingly intertwined with private industry, prompting congressional surveillance during the early years of the Roosevelt administration. The results of Senate investigations revealed, according to Senator Hugo Black, that

> private ownership of merchant and aerial transportation with governmental subsidy has resulted in a saturnalia of waste, inefficiency, unearned and exorbitant salaries, and bonuses and other so-called "cooperation," corrupting expense accounts, exploitation of the public by sale and manipulation of statutes . . . and a general transfer of energy and labor from operating the business to "operating on" the taxpayer.[7]

The performance of the Shipping Board in part reflected the backwardness of American shipping. Lacking capital and experience, shipowners were compelled to rely on government support. At the same time the dual regulatory/promotional task of the board was unwieldy because it invited the agency to work at cross-purposes with itself. As long as American shippers could compete favorably in international markets, the colonization of the Shipping Board and its successors by the shipping industry could be tolerated. The situation of shipping reflected the paradox of "external strength and internal weakness."[8] The weakness of state institutions

7. Ibid., p. 37.
8. Stephen Krasner, "United States Commercial and Monetary Policy: Unravelling the Paradox of External Strength and Internal Weakness," in Peter J. Katzenstein, ed., *Between Power and Plenty: Foreign Economic Policies of Advanced Industrial States* (Madison: University of Wisconsin Press, 1978).

was not detrimental to the domestic economy and was of little note in world economic affairs.

In 1935, Senator Black and other congressional Democrats recommended nationalizing the shipping industry, on the grounds that government-business connections were already close. The government was heavily subsidizing losses, according to Black, but it was not participating in profits. Plans for nationalization were eventually abandoned, but a new Federal Shipping Commission, initially chaired by Joseph Kennedy and subsequently by Admiral Emory S. Land, was established as part of the 1936 Merchant Marine Act. This act institutionalized and regulated the ad hoc pattern of subsidies that had developed since World War I. It accepted realistically that the maritime sector was backward, inefficient, and in need of permanent assistance. It provided for both operating-differential subsidies and construction-differential subsidies. Thus the fortunes of shipping were linked to shipbuilding by guaranteeing that any subsidized United States flag ship must have been purchased from a domestic yard. This highly protectionist legislation further bound shipowners to the government; the subsidy provisions discouraged innovation and encouraged management to make concessions to labor, to be paid for by the government. At the same time, the Federal Shipping Commission was increasingly drawn into the day-to-day operation of shipping lines because of its promotional mandate. This "New Deal settlement" partially insulated U.S. shipping from world competition. Although it was highly protectionist, it minimized the possibility of conflict.

The mobilization of the maritime industries on a massive scale during World War II did not fundamentally alter the structure of domestic shipping politics. But postwar planning led to a major shift in U.S. international shipping policy as administrators adopted an internationalist or hegemonic perspective. As was discussed in Chapter 3, the architects of the Pax Americana pleaded for moderation in shipping and acceptance of an international division of labor based on comparative advantage. Nationalist and protectionist forces, reflecting the views and interests of shipowners, pressed for bilateralism. Shipowners responded by calling for a large governmental role on the grounds that "foreign trade follows the flag."[9] The

9. Albert V. Moore, "Tomorrow's Shipping and Trade Channels: Foreign Trade Follows the Flag," in Marine News, *America's Postwar Merchant Marine Forecast* (New York: Marine News, 1944).

American Merchant Marine Institute, the shipowner lobby, favored a policy reserving 50 percent of trade to U.S. shipping, the takeover of traditional Axis shipping markets, and the minimization of vessel sales to allies. These policies were supported by the United States Maritime Commission, which acted essentially as the bureaucratic instrument of the shipowners.[10] The Merchant Marine Act of 1936 stipulated that the U.S. merchant marine should be sufficient to carry "a substantial portion" of U.S. cargoes. Maritime Commissioners interpreted this to mean 50 percent.[11]

However, internationalism ultimately prevailed over the parochialism of the shipping community. Leo Crowley of the Foreign Economic Administration summarized the hegemonic strategy:

> We hope to see a postwar trade with other nations that will exceed that of any prewar year, but the ability of other nations to pay for the goods we produce is one of the most important factors in the development of a greater export and import trade. And the dependence of some nations on the sale of services is as great as our own dependence upon the sale of manufactured goods where foreign trade is concerned. If no artificial restrictions are placed on shipping, it would be natural to find essentially maritime nations, such as Norway, furnishing shipping services to the world. There is every reason why this should be so. Norway's economy is virtually entirely dependent upon shipping.[12]

No means were found, however, to help American liner shipping become more competitive internationally. Subsidies and limited cargo reservation artificially maintained the size of the fleet, but these side payments discouraged innovation and efficiency, portending future instability.

The underlying weakness of the liner sector, heavily dependent on subsidies, discouraged the United States from attempts to curtail the power of conferences; cartels, after all, could shelter American as well as European shipping. At the same time, subsidies did not provide incentives for either the shipping or the shipbuilding industry to modernize. America's inability to institute technological innovations in shipping in the 1950s, as it did in other industries, may account for the chronic backwardness of U.S.

10. New York Trust Company, "A Bank Views Our Merchant Marine," in Marine News, *America's Postwar Merchant Marine Forecast*, p. 175.

11. Ibid.

12. "International Trade and Post-War Shipping," in Marine News, *America's Postwar Merchant Marine Forecast*, pp. 43–44.

shipping compared to that of countries possessing cheaper labor. Yet it could be argued that the structure of the American maritime sector itself discouraged technological innovation and meant that new technologies would have to develop largely outside the subsidized sector. Shipping firms remained highly dependent on government subsidies, including the indirect subsidy of freight revenues from heavy shipments of U.S. military cargoes. The Federal Maritime Board (FMB), like the United States Shipping Board of prewar days, to a large extent eschewed its regulatory tasks in favor of promotion of shipping. A community of interest developed between the Confederation of American Shipping Lines (CASL), representing the subsidized firms, and the FMB.

Throughout the 1950s the competitiveness of American industry relative to its trading partners muted historical international tensions over maritime policies. As long as export markets remained strong, the closed conferences (described in Chapter 4) were not viewed as a serious problem for shippers. The government recognized the contribution of shipping to European economies. As a result shippers tolerated the cozy relationship between the FMB and shipping firms; indeed, the strong conferences that were developing were viewed as a potential means for reducing the subsidy requirements of American shipping.

In the late 1950s and early 1960s, three separate but related developments profoundly changed the balance of forces in American shipping. As the United States began to acquire balance-of-payments deficits, American policymakers sought ways to stem the dollar outflow. Shipping services were identified as an important method of improving the payments position. Sensing the possibility of higher subsidies, CASL commissioned a study to support its requests. However, the problem was increasingly recognized as primarily involving trade competitiveness, a view that would ultimately reduce, not enhance, CASL's influence. This led the government and Congress to focus on rate disparities and the role of conferences in United States and world trades. As the competitive lead of American industry diminished, the balance of power began to shift from shipowners to shippers.

The increasing scrutiny of conference practices also resulted from attacks by independent liner owners on the system of deferred rebates. In 1958 the Supreme Court ruled that the dual rebates system was discriminatory. This ruling stimulated extensive investigations by Congress and the Department of Justice.[13] Subsequent Supreme Court rulings further weakened conference powers. Challenges from independent owners (especially Isbrandtsen) and the balance-of-payments problem eventually led to a full-blown investigation of the Federal Maritime Board that precipitated sweeping institutional changes.

The conclusions of Congress regarding the role of conferences were summarized in Chapter 4. Recognizing that the FMB had been "captured" by the subsidized shipping firms and that its regulatory and promotional tasks were contradictory, the Federal Maritime Commission (FMC) was established as a purely regulatory agency. The Maritime Administration (MARAD) inherited promotional responsibilities. The destruction of the FMB stripped the subsidized shipowners of their base within the government. The FMC, like the United States Shipping Board and the FMB, has tended to act as the voice of subsidized shipping firms, albeit with much less consequence, again demonstrating the continuity of the political network.[14]

Containers: Technology and Power

The advent of container shipping in the early 1960s constituted a destabilizing force in United States and, eventually, international liner shipping, and its effects continue to be felt as the revolutionary technology spreads to all world trades. The container originated in the U.S. trucking industry during the 1950s. It was then gradually and sporadically adopted by some U.S. liner firms and imposed on Europe and Japan. It continues to spread today in the Third World. The technology of container shipping is an element in America's competitive maritime strategy, although it has never been specifically articulated as such.

13. These investigations were discussed in Chapter 5. They include U.S. Congress, House, Committee on Merchant Marine and Fisheries, *Steamship Conference Study*, 86th Cong., 1959; U.S. Congress, House, Committee on the Judiciary (Celler Committee), Report of the Anti-Trust Committee, *The Ocean Freight Industry*, 87th Cong., 1962; and U.S. Congress, Joint Economic Committee, *Discriminatory Ocean Freight Rates and the Balance of Payments*, 88th Cong., 1965.

14. Congressional committees dealing with the U.S. merchant marine have traditionally acted as the voice of the shipowners, but their power has diminished in recent years as shippers have played a more important role in maritime politics. In 1977 Congressman Paul

As noted above, the relatively high cost of labor is the principal barrier to U.S. maritime strategy. With respect to labor costs, the development of container systems was a functional equivalent to flags of convenience in the liner sector. The concept of the container, although it has profoundly influenced world trade, is a simple one. General cargo ships carry breakbulk goods, loaded in crates or comparatively small packages, whereas container shipping employs large steel boxes of uniform size (20 or 40 feet long). This greatly simplifies loading and unloading and permits multimodal transportation, or using the same container on ships, trains, and trucks, thus breaking down the barrier between land and sea. Container shipping is highly capital-intensive and displaces both shipboard and dockside labor. This increased capital requirement for large economies of scale stimulated the formation of international consortia or ultra-cartels.[15]

During the 1950s, shipowners introduced the container sporadically on individual trade routes, where its potential for altering economic and political relationships gradually became evident. In 1959 a U.S. government study of the effects of containers assumed "an eight fold increase in tons handled per ship-hour working cargo . . . using only one third the number of longshoremen per ship."[16] The American firm Sea-Land pioneered the systematic introduction of containers in the intercoastal trades and then on the North Atlantic. The concept spread rapidly, and today a number of less developed countries are building facilities to accommodate second- and third-generation container vessels.

Industry analysts saw containers as a means of reversing the decline in the United States flag fleet. In 1970 authors of one study noted:

McCloskey of the House Merchant Marine Subcommittee acknowledged, "There is no secret that the industry has control over this committee" (*Container News* 7 [September 1977]).

15. Ignacy Chrzanowski, *Concentration and Centralization of Capital in Shipping* (Westmead: Saxon House, 1975), esp. pp. 105–10. See also Figure 2, below.

16. National Academy of Sciences, National Council, *Maritime Transportation of Unitized Cargo—A Comparative Analysis of Breakbulk and Unitized Services* (Washington: National Academy of Sciences, 1959), p. 66. In comparison, in conventional or breakbulk U.S. liner trades, direct labor costs (including crew and dock labor) rose by 8 percent compound throughout the postwar era, with no increase in productivity. A similar situation pertained in the United Kingdom, where during the 1960s labor costs (dock and shipboard) tripled. See Bernard Gardner, "The Container Revolution and Its Effects on the Structure of Traditional U.K. Liner Shipping Companies," *Journal of Maritime Policy and Management* 12 (July–September 1985).

Table 21. Development of the World Container Fleet, 1970 – 84 (millions grt)

	1970	1971	1972	1973	1974	1975	1976	1977	1978	1979	1982	1984[a]
World	1.9	2.8	4.3	5.9	6.3	6.2	6.7	7.5	8.7	10.0	12.9	16.9
United Kingdom	0.4	0.6	1.1	1.3	1.4	1.3	1.3	1.5	1.8	1.8	1.5	1.5
West Germany	0.2	0.3	0.5	0.6	0.6	0.6	0.6	0.7	0.9	1.0	1.1	1.7
France	n.a.	n.a.	0.1	0.1	0.1	0.1	0.2	0.3	0.3	0.4	0.5	0.6
European Community	0.6	1.1	1.9	2.5	2.6	2.6	2.9	3.3	3.9	4.3	5.1	5.9
Japan	0.2	0.4	0.7	1.0	1.0	1.1	1.1	1.3	1.3	1.4	1.7	1.8
United States	0.9	1.1	1.1	1.7	1.9	1.8	1.8	1.7	1.7	1.8	2.5[b]	3.4

SOURCES: United Kingdom, Department of Industry and Trade, *General Trends in Shipping: A Report on the U.K. Merchant Fleet, World Shipping, And Seaborne Trade*, Series 2, No. 6 (London: Department of Industry and Trade, November 1979); UNCTAD, *Review of Maritime Transport, 1982* (Geneva: United Nations, 1983); UNCTAD, *Review of Maritime Transport, 1984* (Geneva: United Nations, 1985); Seatrade, *United States Yearbook 1983* (5th ed.) (Colchester: Seatrade, 1983).

[a]Includes ships on order, June 1985.

[b]1983.

[Container ships] can generate far greater annual revenues at about the same wage costs as a comparable fleet of breakbulk vessels. This in return reduces the significance of wage costs to a relatively small proportion of total expense which will also allow the United States–flag fleet to compete vigorously with foreign flag vessels and carry a greater share of United States foreign trade.[17]

Between 1966 and 1969 the number of seafaring shipboard jobs decreased from 52,000 to 27,000, with a comparable reduction in longshore labor. At the same time the total tonnage carried by United States flag lines increased from 11.4 to 15.6 million. Dramatic increases in the wage differentials between 1965 and 1970 favored U.S. production workers over seamen as the use of containers eroded the bargaining position of maritime labor.[18]

Other characteristics of container systems contributed to the rapid growth of their popularity in the United States. Multimodalism has helped establish conditions favorable to U.S. shipping: the container is shipped door-to-door, eliminating the need for intermediate handling of cargo in transit. In addition to cost savings, multimodalism tends to reduce competition from smaller, independent lines and enhances the position of liner operators with superior organizational capabilities.[19] Container shipping shifts the financial burden from labor to capital, driving out smaller operators. Moreover, the cost advantage of multimodalism is greater for countries with large land masses, where the distance between port and ultimate destination is great. In small European countries the cost advantage of multimodalism may be outweighed by the scale of capital investment involved. In less developed countries especially, where labor is abundant and relatively cheap, containers and other advanced technologies are not cost-effective. The United States and the Soviet Union are the prime beneficiaries of container shipping.

By 1970 the United States owned approximately one-half of world container tonnage; it sustained its lead throughout the 1970s and was caught only temporarily by Britain in 1978 (see Table 21). The container revolu-

17. James C. Barker and Robert Brandwein, *The U.S. Merchant Marine in National Perspective* (Lexington, Mass.: D. C. Heath, 1970), p. xv.
18. Data on employment and cargoes are derived from U.S. Department of Commerce, Maritime Administration, *Annual Report* (Washington, D.C.: G.P.O.) (various years); on wage differentials, see John Kilgour, *The U.S. Merchant Marine: National Maritime Policy and Industrial Relations* (New York: Praeger, 1975), p. 40.
19. UNCTAD, *Unitization of Cargo*, TD/B/C.4/75 (Geneva: United Nations, 1970), pp. 37–38.

tion accelerated the tendency toward concentration, driving many U.S. and European firms into bankruptcy or takeovers. By 1980 five American firms—Sea-Land, Farrell, Lykes, United States Lines, and American President Lines—owned two-thirds of all United States flag liner tonnage. Sea-Land alone owned more than one-fifth of U.S. tonnage and is now the world's largest container operator in maritime trades.[20] The shakedown in liner shipping will continue. It is probable that by the end of the 1980s the United States liner sector will consist of no more than three or four large firms, or perhaps consortia, heavily engaged in cross-trading and "around the world" services.[21]

The introduction of container technology, like flags of convenience, was a commercial threat to Western European shipowners. Writing in 1970, the authors of the British Rochdale Report concluded that "the technological changes now so evident in the world shipping industry are probably no less significant than the replacement in the nineteenth century of the wooden ship with that of iron, and of sail by steam."[22] The introduction of containers rendered existing tonnage obsolete, thus imposing massive new capital requirements on shipowners (see Figure 2). This capital intensity partially explains the proliferation of subsidies in Western Europe and Japan in the late 1960s and early 1970s. Even with these aids, however, the new capital requirements exceeded the resources of the largest firms. Western European shipowners responded by establishing international liner consortia, new and higher forms of cartelization or ultra-cartels.

The capital requirements of containers and other new maritime transport technology (for example, roll-on-roll-off, and complex barge systems) strained the resources not only of European owners but also of American subsidized lines. By 1970 a two-tier structure was developing in United

20. On Sea-Land's performance, see the testimony of Sea-Land officials in U.S. Congress, House, Committee on Merchant Marine and Fisheries, *Omnibus Maritime Bill: Hearings Before the Subcommittee of the House Committee on Merchant Marine and Fisheries*, 96th Cong., 1980, pt. 1, p. 490. United States Lines' recent acquisitions include twelve large container vessels, built in South Korea and scheduled to be placed in "around the world" trades.

21. See U.S. Government Accounting Office, *Changes in Federal Maritime Regulations Can Increase Efficiency and Reduce Costs in the Ocean Liner Shipping Industry* (Washington, D.C.: G.P.O., 1982), esp. pp. 14–16.

22. United Kingdom, Committee of Inquiry into Shipping, *Report* (Rochdale Report), Cmnd. 4337 (London: HMSO, 1970), p. 409. Of course, containers also presented an opportunity for British shipowners who, like their American counterparts, faced militancy from dockworkers.

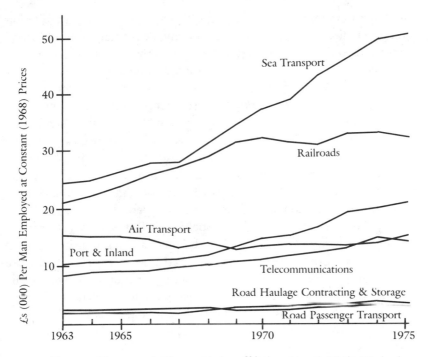

SOURCE: Thorsten Rinman and Rigmer Linden, *Shipping: How It Works* (Gothenburg, Sweden: Rinman and Linden, 1979).

Figure 2. Trends in Capital Intensity, 1963–75

States shipping: Sea-Land, which was developing outside the umbrella of government subsidies (but enjoying U.S.-directed cargo), was now capable of competing favorably with Western European and Japanese lines. U.S. regulation of conferences thus provided the ideal competitive conditions for the growth of Sea-Land and, eventually, a few other large containerized firms: United States Lines, American President Lines, and Lykes Steamship Lines. Regulation kept the conferences open to big American independents. The smaller lines, in contrast, saw their interests coinciding with those of Western Europe and Japan. They still favor closed conferences, and their optimal regime is one of generalized protectionism or bilateralism.

America's regulatory policies have helped to shift the balance of power from shipowners to shippers. However, despite serious overtonnaging and instability, the consequences of regulation have been less severe for the large American shipowners than for their foreign counterparts. Regulation has served indirectly to promote U.S. shipping by frustrating the efforts of competitors to develop a concerted response to the container challenge.

Western European, Japanese, and subsidized American lines have sought to cope with the capital burdens of container technologies by rationalizing services. Above all, this requires the deferred rebate, thus encouraging even higher levels of cartelization, including division of market shares and pooling of cargoes, capital, and, in some cases, profits. Captive cargo makes possible high levels of investment. This is particularly true for West German lines that based their capital-investment programs of the 1970s on the possibility of rationalizing the North Atlantic trades. In 1965, for example, the Atlantic Container Line was established. By 1967 it included Svenska Amerika Linien AB, Rederiaktiebolaget Transatlantic (Denmark), Wallenius-Redierna (Sweden), Holland Amerika Lign, Cunard (United Kingdom), and Compagnie Générale Transatlantique (France). By the late 1960s, consortia were operating on all major liner routes.[23] However, the application of U.S. antitrust laws to the activities of conferences has effectively limited the extent of rationalization; shipping firms have been subjected to felony proceedings and large fines for systematic, illegal rebating to shippers.

Increasing capital intensity drastically raised the stakes of competition. It made losses of market share much more costly to shipping firms. By decreasing the importance of labor costs in overall operations, it made laying a ship up more expensive. The higher level of collusion desired, combined with greater risk and capital involvement, gave impetus to further demands for rationalization, the stricter closing of conferences to outsiders. In this context American regulation became increasingly significant. It represented the main obstacle keeping traditional operators from establishing the strong conferences that could minimize the threat from outside competition and thereby tie shippers to the conference. At the same time, the United States is attempting to impose its regulatory policy on non-American trades, a development of great importance to those American firms that are beginning to engage in a substantial amount of cross-trading.

The situation in U.S. trades thus differs from that in virtually all other world trades. Western European (and Japanese) shipowners have formed

23. Chrzanowski, *Concentration and Centralization,* pp. 105–10.

"cooperatively organized and appropriately rationalized" (closed) conferences in non-American trades. These conferences have permitted an orderly reduction of cargo space to allow optimal use of ships. Studies show they permit greater efficiency than the open conferences, mandated by U.S. shipping law in American trades. For example, in the closed conference serving Australia and the United Kingdom/Continent, the average load factor increased from 90 percent in 1958 to 95 percent in 1968.[24] Despite recent attempts to amend the 1916 Shipping Act, including the reformist U.S. Shipping Act of 1984 (to be discussed in detail in Chapter 10), the FMC and the Department of Justice have continued to apply antitrust statutes to shipping. In practice this has prevented the use of the deferred rebate and has significantly weakened the power of conferences, contributing to "rate wars" and intense competition from outsiders. In 1977, the Department of Justice began successfully to prosecute seven major U.S. and foreign lines for illegal, secret rebating. European governments reacted strongly to these steps. Their legislation to block national shipowners from cooperating with U.S. courts repeats the legal and diplomatic maneuvers of the 1960s.[25]

Shipowners, both United States and European, have responded by seeking repeal of antitrust laws as applied to shipping. This would pave the way for multimodalism, closed conferences, and shippers' councils that would in effect replace the FMC. Such legislation would bring United States policy in line with that of its major trading partners, and it would facilitate ratification of the UNCTAD Code of Conduct.[26]

Pointing to low profitability and excess capacity on U.S. trade routes, shipowners convincingly demonstrate that their cost structures would be considerably lower if rationalization were allowed. According to Hapag-Lloyd, for example, in 1975 seven major conference lines were operating thirty-six ships in the North Atlantic–European trades. Because of their inability to rationalize, an average of only 68 percent of capacity was

24. University of Wales, Department of Maritime Studies, *Liner Shipping in the U.S. Trades: A UWIST Study for CENSA* (London: University of Wales, Department of Maritime Studies, 1978), p. 48.

25. For a summary of individual governmental responses, see ibid., pp. 71–114.

26. Karl-Heinz Sager, *Shipping Conferences: A Form of Maritime Cooperation to Which There Is No Alternative* (Hamburg: Hapag-Lloyd, 1979); and Hans Dieter Drugg, *Why We Consider Consultation the Superior System to Regulation in United States Liner Shipping* (Hamburg: Hapag-Lloyd, November 1978).

reached in seventy-six weekly calls. A simulation of the consequences of rationalization showed that closed conferences would require only sixteen vessels making thirty-three weekly calls and operating at 85 percent capacity. In theory, this would allow freight rates to be reduced by 29 percent.[27]

Demands for reforming U.S. regulatory policy, which would curb the power of the Department of Justice, have been rejected until recently by successive administrations, despite intensive lobbying by subsidized shipowners and widespread congressional support for reform. Serious overtonnaging has not been a concern for American shippers. Perhaps equally important, some dynamic American liner firms are thriving in a climate of uncertainty and the virtual collapse of conferences in some trades. The Department of Justice, with support from the executive branch, has persistently rejected the claim that efficiency and cost reduction translate into lower freight rates. Only where supply of shipping services is not artificially restricted can efficiency lead to a lowering of rates: "A price-discriminating cartel will set rates according to the elasticity of demand for its services."[28] Freight rates are seen ultimately to be determined by what the market will bear.[29]

The Evolution of Policy: Toward Maritime Reindustrialization

The reform of U.S. shipping policy and promotional measures have not by themselves been sufficient to stem the decline of the United States flag liner fleet. Promotional policies have mostly been in the form of increasing sub-

27. Hapag-Lloyd, *The Organization of Liner Shipping in the Container Age Illustrated by the North Atlantic Trade* (Hamburg: Hapag-Lloyd, 1975).

28. U.S. Department of Justice, Anti-Trust Division, "Analysis of the Booz, Allen, and Hamilton Study of Ocean Freight Rate Discrimination for the House Committee on Merchant Marine and Fisheries," in House Committee on Merchant Marine and Fisheries, *Omnibus Maritime Bill*, p. 202.

29. On the efficiency potential of closed conferences, see University of Wales, Department of Maritime Studies, *Liner Shipping*, p. 48; Hapag-Lloyd, *The Organization of Liner Shipping;* and Manalytics, Inc. (for the Maritime Administration), *The Impact of Bilateral Shipping Agreements in the United States Liner Trades* (Washington, D.C.: G.P.O., 1979). See also Department of Justice, Anti-Trust Division, *The Regulated Ocean Shipping Industry* (Washington, D.C.: G.P.O., 1977), esp. pp. 209–15 and 240–56. For the views of shippers, see "Written Testimony of the Chemical Manufacturers Association Submitted to the Subcommittee on Monopolies and Commercial Law, United States House of Representatives," for the 18 May 1983 Hearing Record on H.R. 1878, Shipping Act of 1983 (mimeographed).

sidies or extending the scope of cargo reservation, and the result has not been especially conducive to the expansion of the United States flag fleet. However, those policies that have encouraged the emergence of a non-subsidized American sector have contributed to the resurgence of United States flag liner shipping. The changing emphasis in policy is evident in the comparison of two major legislative reforms, the U.S. Merchant Marine Act of 1970 and the U.S. Shipping Act of 1984. The former, largely promotional in emphasis, had little impact on national or international trends; the latter, directed to international change, promises to have a major effect on international regime developments and to contribute to the resurgence of the U.S. liner sector.

The Merchant Marine Act of 1970 was designed to streamline and reform U.S. policy within the framework of existing traditions and practices. It greatly enlarged the capital construction fund for American ship operators and extended favorable tax treatment to nonsubsidized as well as subsidized operators. Recognizing the need to promote U.S. shipbuilding, it increased the construction- and operating-differential subsidies, extending them to dry and liquid bulk carriers for the purpose of increasing the United States flag bulk fleet.

The 1970 act also provided ship operators with incentives to minimize labor costs. Previously, the operating-differential subsidy had equalized U.S. and foreign wages at no cost to the operator; the 1970 act indexed wages and established limits for subsidy payments, thereby compelling operators to absorb at least some of the cost of wage increases. In addition, limits were established for crew size. The authors of the 1970 act predicted that these reforms would promote the building of three hundred ships during the 1970s. These projections proved highly optimistic, however; the cost of subsidies incurred by the Treasury continued to increase, while the United States continued to decline as a producer of merchant ships. In fact, fewer than seventy new vessels were completed. The resurgence of U.S. liner shipping has come about largely outside the framework of incentives and promotional measures created by the 1970 act and previous legislation. Moreover, it has not resulted in a comparable resurrection of U.S. shipbuilding. Indeed, recent legislation has, in keeping with the deregulatory emphasis of the Reagan administration, tended to sever the link between shipping and shipbuilding as America's international liner operators, in reaction to the abolition in 1981 of the construction-differential subsidy, are building ships abroad.

In 1984 a reform bill, the U.S. Shipping Act of 1984, was finally enacted after seven years of intensive lobbying. This bill received support from all U.S. shipping operators and most shippers. It marks a departure from previous policy initiatives, for it reduces the role of the Department of Justice and, to a lesser degree, the powers of the Federal Maritime Commission, and it relaxes antitrust standards. These aspects of the bill do reflect the aspirations of European and some American shipping firms. But despite the hopes of would-be reformers, U.S. shipping policy continues to prohibit closed conferences. Although the act will give American steamship lines greater latitude in commercial strategies and may facilitate the rationalization of U.S. trades, it will not close the very wide gap between European and American shipping.

The vigorous application of antitrust law in conjunction with container shipping has continued America's revisionist assault on the postwar regime. Interpretations of statistics about the performance of the United States liner sector are subject to great controversy. Many studies, relying on aggregate data, paint a dark picture based on the loss of tonnage, lack of profitability, and increasing average age of the fleet.[30] But aggregate data do not reveal the significant gains that the American liner sector has made in recent years. In terms of its share of U.S. liner cargo carried, by value and tonnage, the U.S. liner sector declined during the postwar period. Since the early 1970s, as Table 22 indicates, the development of container shipping and increased regulatory activity has coincided with a modest reversal of this trend. Put into context, however, the statistical picture shows more progress. First, the amount of cargo carried increased despite the significant penetration of new merchant fleets (LDC and Soviet) into U.S. and world trades. It follows that the national flag share of most traditional maritime countries has declined relative to that of the United States.[31] Sec-

30. Often these are public relations exercises, sponsored indirectly or directly by shipping firms in search of government support. For an alternative argument to mine, see Lawrence Juda, *The UNCTAD Liner Code: United States Maritime Policy at the Crossroads* (Boulder: Westview, 1984), esp. chapter 2.

31. Japan's share increased to over 50 percent, if chartered tonnage is included; U.K. imports declined from 31 to 29 percent and exports from 47 to 37 percent between 1970 and 1978. West Germany experienced a sharp decline, from 26 to 18 percent of imports and 39 to 27 percent of exports between 1969 and 1975; France declined from 48 percent of total trade by weight to 31 percent between 1966 and 1978. These figures are taken from the U.S. Department of Commerce, Maritime Administration, Office of Policy and Planning, *The Maritime Aids of the Six Major Maritime Nations* (Washington, D.C.: G.P.O., 1977), pp. 1–15;

Table 22.   U.S. Oceanborne Foreign Liner Trade, 1972 – 83 (millions of dwt tons)

	Total	United States Flag	United States Flag as % of Total
1972	44.6	9.8	22.0
1974	51.4	15.3	29.8
1976	49.8	15.4	30.9
1978	56.5	16.0	28.3
1980	59.3	16.2	27.3
1982	54.5	14.3	26.2
1983	56.8	14.0	24.6

SOURCES: U.S. Department of Commerce, Maritime Administration, *Annual Report, 1981* (Washington, D.C.: G.P.O., 1982); U.S. Department of Commerce, Maritime Administration, *Annual Report, 1984* (Washington, D.C.: G.P.O., 1985).

ond, the end of the Vietnam War, with its large cargo requirements, has meant a significant decline in cargo reserved by law for U.S. ships; more cargo carried by the American fleet is commercial, and U.S. firms are competing successfully without subsidies or protection, even in third-country markets. Third, the modest relative increase in U.S. shipping shares must be seen in the context of an enlarged absolute pool of imports and exports and a dramatic increase in the significance of foreign trade for the American economy.[32] Finally, the United States flag liner sector is now significantly engaged in cross-trades. Able to purchase ships from abroad and, in some cases, to continue to receive subsidies, the large U.S. firms continue to expand relative to their foreign rivals.

These successes represent a dramatic gain if viewed in the historical context of the backwardness of the U.S. maritime sector, although of course the tenacity of competitors and their determination not to be driven out of U.S. trades are also evident. The United States is fostering a leaner, more competitive liner fleet. The wave of bankruptcies and mergers is a sign not

Lloyds List, 18 January 1980; U.S. Department of Commerce, Maritime Administration, Office of International Activities, *Maritime Subsidies* (Washington, D.C.: G.P.O.) (various years); and United Kingdom, Department of Trade and Industry, *Trade and Industry* (London: HMSO, 6 July 1979).

32. Between 1978 and 1983, the volume of inbound and outbound containerized cargo in U.S. trade increased by more than 25 percent (Institute of Shipping Economics and Logistics, *Shipping Statistics* 29, no. 12 [Bremen: Institute of Shipping Economics and Logistics, December 1985], p. 33).

of weakness but of dynamism. Since 1970 the number of basic firms in the United States flag liner fleet has shrunk from nineteen to seven. Sea-Land, now one of the world's largest liner fleets, derives one-fifth of its revenue from cross-trading.[33] Sea-Land has so far been the main beneficiary of American regulation; its ability to compete with whole conferences and consortia has allowed it to expand either as an outsider or, using its threat to withdraw from the conferences as leverage, to increase its market share from within. As observers have noted, "Open conferences with limited power of rationalization are virtually powerless against determined and financially strong outsiders."[34]

The conflict in the United States between large and small shipping firms has undermined legislative attempts to achieve regulatory reforms. The smaller U.S. lines and their European counterparts favor closed conferences. However, small American lines, unlike the Europeans, favor bilateralism, since they are engaged primarily in U.S.-LDC trades, which are increasingly being carved up on a bilateral basis. These lines receive subsidies and vigorous congressional support. Because of their political influence, they receive a sympathetic hearing from the FMC and the administration. The FMC, although charged with regulation, is sympathetic to advocacy of closed conferences. Support in the United States for the UNCTAD Code of Conduct emanates from these quarters.[35] Yet these lines are highly vulnerable to the competition from the stronger American lines—Sea-Land, United States Lines, American President Lines, and Lykes—and also to administration attempts to cut subsidies as part of general budgetary policy.

The United States and the Container Era

Conference discrimination led to increasing regulation of conferences and, hence, to a return to the principles underlying the U.S. Shipping Act of

33. House Committee on Merchant Marine and Fisheries, *Omnibus Maritime Bill*, pt. 1.

34. Nick Seaward et al., "The Eternal Debate: Independents Gain Ground," *Seatrade* (October 1980), p. 109. See also R. F. Gibney, "Outsiders Fuel Market Crisis," *Seatrade* (April 1983), pp. 97–103.

35. At the same time the Department of Justice and shippers have renewed their opposition to closed conferences. See, for example, Ralph King, "Paul O'Leary Opens an Old Wound," *American Shipper* 25 (July 1983), pp. 40–41.

1916. Containers, however, made an anti-cartel strategy workable by creating a competitive sector in American shipping. In the absence of this sector, the competition with European lines would probably have further eroded the United States presence in liner shipping. Containers thus complement the more vigorous assertion of U.S. shipping interests. According to Edgar Vierengel, director of international logistics for Ingersoll Rand,

> In the postwar era, Western Europe and Japan underwent a new industrial revolution which, during the past 15 years, has put them in a position to compete effectively for industrial product markets, not only in the United States, but also against United States producers in developing Third World markets. . . . Our past concerns in regulating international shipping focused on Americans competing against other Americans for foreign markets, on an equal footing. Today, our concern must focus on assuring that American industry as a whole is competitive with European and Japanese industry with respect to transportation.[36]

By the mid-1960s it was possible to curb the power of conferences without damaging United States shipping. Containers proved to harmonize the interests of shippers and some sections of shipping. U.S. shipping policy is rooted in antitrust philosophy. This alone divides American from European shipping. Yet, in addition to this, the structure of the industry in the United States is different from that of its trading partners. Sea-Land, American President Lines, and United States Lines are powerful enough to compete with conferences or consortia, so they oppose closed conferences. Yet smaller American lines have orchestrated bilateral treaties with South America against opposition from shippers.

But if the United States has blunted monopolistic tendencies in liner shipping, it has also played a central role in protectionist developments, in deed if not in word. Policies developed in an ad hoc fashion have nourished the systematic growth of protectionism on an international scale. The essentially opportunistic nature of U.S. policy is evident in its strict application of antitrust principles to Atlantic and Pacific trades and loose application to Latin and other Third World trades. The acquiescence of the FMC and the Maritime Administration has been defensive but at the same time permissive. With the exception of agreements with the Soviet Union and China, the United States has not actively sponsored bilateralism. Neverthe-

---

36. House Committee on Merchant Marine and Fisheries, *Omnibus Maritime Bill,* p. 495.

less, U.S. lines have benefited from it and have sought agreements with their foreign counterparts. As the vice chairman of the International Traffic Committee of the U.S. Chamber of Commerce observed,

> The United States has power [in] that it has ways to avoid being dragged into bilateral agreements if it does not wish to get involved in bilateral agreements. . . . We had those opportunities in the Brazilian case. I think there were feelings in the country, and in part of the industry involved in international trade that it might not be a bad idea to have a bilateral agreement.[37]

The history of containers vividly illustrates the extent to which technological developments depend on political factors. Within the established system of political and economic relationships, the introduction of the container was a potent source of conflict. The container system is a breakthrough in transportation—but technology did not change independently of politics. Rather, it served to restructure social and political relationships at the international and the national levels by tilting the balance of power from Europe to the United States and from labor to capital.[38] The container is just a steel box; it did not, in itself, initiate conflict. Technology led to instability *in the context* of United States regulatory policy and growing Atlantic rivalry.

Conclusion

The theory of hegemonic stability relates changes in regimes to shifts in the international distribution of power. A hegemonic system is one in which the leading state is willing and able, through a combination of inducement and coercion, to manage interdependence in such a way that the long-range viability of the system is maintained. Part II of this book showed how developments in the postwar regime, and the corresponding evolution of U.S. shipping policies, could be explained in terms of the hege-

37. Testimony of Edgar A. Vierengel in ibid.
38. On the relationship between technology and politics, see Harry Braverman, *Labor and Monopoly Capital: The Degradation of Work in the Twentieth Century* (New York: Monthly Review Press, 1975), esp. chapters 9 and 10. Another significant technological development in shipping is roll-on-roll-off carriers. I emphasize containers because of their special political importance. Containers were introduced as a response to political and economic conflicts, and those same conflicts have affected their efficiency. Other "flexible systems" might be equally or more desirable, and no less efficient. See H. W. Dick, "Containerisation and Liner Conferences: A Polemic," *Maritime Policy and Management* 10 (July–September 1983).

monic stability thesis. Privatization was a principle that applied to all aspects of shipping in the postwar period. It reflected American hegemony in diverse ways, expressing both domination, as in the bulk sector, and accommodation with trading partners, as in the liner sector. In the bulk sector, the United States organized a maritime network designed to provide maximum control over the transportation of raw materials. American policy thus diverged significantly from the narrow nationalism of the interwar period, and its new policies corresponded to the changing role and objectives of the United States in the international economy. The ensuing regime, which severed the link between ownership and flag of registry, limited the power of Western Europe in bulk shipping, illustrating that hegemony involves not only consensus and the provision of "collective goods," but also outright domination. Europe was denied a major presence in raw-materials trades. However, the cheapening of commodity prices, helped by flags of convenience, was an important determinant of the postwar economic boom of which Europe was a prime beneficiary.

In liner shipping, the United States, despite its ideological commitment to free trade, was unwilling to completely expose its shipping industry to the free market. Against European opposition, it enacted protectionist legislation in the early 1950s, and the program of subsidies that had been developed in the 1930s was not entirely dismantled. Nevertheless, throughout the 1950s and early 1960s the United States did tolerate conference practices that were detrimental to U.S. liner shipping and contravened American legal and maritime traditions. At the same time, the limited degree of protectionism the United States pursued was not a significant threat to European liner shipping. This uneasy and ultimately unstable mix of policies allowed for the provision of "collective goods." The regime was multilateral in both form and content. America possessed great underlying power, but it chose not to exercise it in ways that would undermine European reconstruction.

As hegemony declines and the former hegemonic leader is no longer able to play an effective managerial role, the concessional features of the international political economy should diminish. A comparison of the two sectors of shipping bears out this thesis. Although its raw-materials network has suffered shocks during the 1970s, most notably at the hands of OPEC, the United States remains the dominant power in this sector, especially compared to Western Europe and Japan. America's trading partners are either too weak to challenge the system or, in the cases of Britain and Japan, have bought an important, although subordinate, share in it. In the area where the United States leads the Western coalition, the Third World has been unable to effect any significant change in the system. In liner shipping, in contrast, the United States has strong incentives to seek change as it becomes less able and willing to play the role of stabilizer.

The theory of hegemonic stability anticipates that instability will increase as hegemony declines. As noted in Chapter 1, the theory also expects a greater degree of influence for domestic structures; national structures are only partially conditioned by international or system relations and under conditions of hegemonic decline these structures assert themselves with greater force. Hence, the analysis of domestic structures provides a more complete picture of regime change.

The U.S. merchant marine developed during acute international rivalry, when European powers had carved up international markets among themselves. Historically backward, U.S. shipping has required state intervention, yet the American state has been too weak and too concerned with other priorities to nurture shipping to adulthood. This historical legacy weighs heavily on the present. It appears in the current labyrinth of interest groups; the diffusion of bureaucratic responsibility and ensuing rivalry; the interpenetration of capital and state; the conflict between shippers and shipping firms; and the philosophical confusion. In recent years rapid change has exacerbated domestic conflicts. Policy has become even more incoherent, ranging, in the words of Ian Sproat, U.K. minister of trade, "from ruthless anti-trust enforcement to protectionism." [39] Most observers of shipping refer to domestic politics to explain policy incoherence; indeed, most European and American officials and shipowners reject the proposition that America has a shipping policy per se.

Certainly, the fragmentation of the state apparatus is an obstacle to consensus on the national shipping interest. Contradictions inherent in the domestic maritime sector make such a consensus highly unlikely and even politically dangerous. But in the absence of coherence, policy can be evaluated objectively, in terms of rational and predictable functions. In shipping, the leading American firms are advancing in a climate of instability. The effect of policy has been to help a process of rationalization and concentra-

39. Quoted in *Journal of Commerce* (23 March 1983), p. B1.

tion. Regulation has also been the favored policy of large exporters. The most visible interest groups, lobbies, and congressional committees are fighting a losing battle. They have been able to retard change, but not to prevent it. Thus the decline of hegemony has important consequences for domestic as well as international relations.

The analysis of domestic structure provides, in conjunction with international structure, a more comprehensive explanation for change in the regime. Construction of the postwar regime entailed suppression of the conflicts of interest inherent in the differing domestic structures of Europe and America. The growing instability in the liner sector reflects American influence and an American agenda: technological change, regulation, and ad hoc protection.

8

European Community Shipping Policy: Europe vs. America

Since World War II, the maritime powers of Western and Northern Europe have been placed on the defensive. The assault on the old regime in bulk shipping began immediately after World War II, when flags of convenience enabled the United States to achieve a dominant presence in what had hitherto been a Eurocentric sphere. Europe's primacy in liner shipping was prolonged until much later, when not only the Third World and the Soviet bloc but also the United States began to challenge the principle of privatization, proposing various alternatives, all essentially regulatory. As conflict between Western European nations and the United States has increased, the nations of the European Community have responded by developing a common maritime transport policy, part of a larger common transport policy covering rail, road, and air traffic, whose objective is to further European interests while stabilizing the situation in shipping, particularly in global liner trades.

In shipping, as in other areas, the EC is bedeviled not only by external weakness but also by differences of interest among the member nations. The maritime policies of the major European shipping powers reflect their economic policies. The French strategy is mercantilistic, characterized by

Table 23.   Share of the Shipping Industry in Gross Fixed Capital Formation, 1965 – 72

	Britain	France	West Germany
1965	1.6	n.a.	0.85
1970	3.0	0.50	1.00
1971	3.3	0.72	n.a.
1972	4.4	n.a.	n.a.

SOURCE: OECD, Maritime Transport Committee, *Maritime Transport, 1973* (Paris: OECD, 1974), pp. 94, 95.

state ownership and control; British policy is liberal, although shipowners have been heavily subsidized by the government. West Germany, although more difficult to characterize, is also a liberal maritime country; the structure of ownership and control in West Germany is highly concentrated, however. Shipping requires more capital than it contributes in proportion to other industries in the gross national product. The power of the shipping sector, and not necessarily its proportionate contribution to GNP, determines its success in competing for capital. British shipowners are the most powerful; French shipowners are the weakest.

Statistical data do not necessarily indicate the qualitative importance of shipping in the national economies of the Western European maritime powers. Investment is highly cyclical, but Table 23, which indicates the share of the shipping industry in gross fixed capital formation, is reasonably accurate in portraying the positions of "the Big Three" in terms of investment. In 1980 gross shipping revenue for West German shipping was approximately $4.4 billion; for Norway, $4.1 billion; for Denmark, $1.6 billion; for Sweden, $2.6 billion; and for Britain, $6.4 billion.[1] (Data for France are not available.) These figures do not take into account ownership of vessels under foreign registry. The merchant fleets of Norway and Greece are larger than those of the Big Three. But because these countries lack overall political and economic power, they have only limited influence over the shape of the regime. Both countries are, of necessity, primarily engaged in cross-trades and therefore are heavily dependent on the policies of other states. They are compelled to work within a regime: they cannot significantly shape its structure, nor can they flout its rules. Moreover, much of Greek and Norwegian shipping is financed abroad.

1. UNCTAD, *Review of Maritime Transport, 1982* (Geneva: United Nations, 1983), p. 40.

The City and Shipping

The success of British shipping was initially based on the shipbuilding and iron industries and on the availability of coal. Of course, British imperialism created the need for the expansion of the fleet, which in 1890 was approximately one-half the size of the world fleet. As P. T. Moon observed, "The annals of empire bristle with the names of shipowners."[2] The roles of shipping in the American and the British economies have thus diverged: in Britain shipowners are at the core of the financial and industrial elite; in the United States shipping firms are at the periphery. These differences dictate different shipping policies and a tradition of Anglo-American conflict over maritime affairs.

As the formal and informal British Empire has declined, the politico-economic power of shipowners has increased. Investigation of successful industries in Britain reveals much about the "British crisis." The pattern of relative success in shipping against the backdrop of Britain's general de-industrialization illustrates the political and economic sway over British society of externally oriented financial and service-sector capital based in "the City."[3] This bloc of capital has managed partially to disengage itself from the national economy.

Shipping is an important factor in the continuing strength of the City. According to Anthony Renouf, *Seatrade* magazine's financial observer,

> Unlike any other sphere of financial or commercial activity these days, it is in marine insurance alone that the City still exercises real power worldwide; at a conservative estimate, at least 50% of the premium income from all internationally traded hulls finds its way through London—and over 90% P & I [Protection and Indemnity] is still locked in. . . . And the fact that many U.K. shipping companies have interests in broking and underwriting concerns reaching back into history also helps to make for a good, if not downright cozy, relationship between those who operate United Kingdom–flag ships and those who pay up when they sink.[4]

Between World War II and the mid-1960s the British flag fleet underwent a steady decline in tonnage relative to the world totals and also to

2. Parker T. Moon, *Imperialism and World Politics* (New York: Macmillan, 1926), p. 61.

3. See esp. Eric J. Hobsbawm, *Industry and Empire* (London: Penguin, 1968). For a recent statement, see Frank Longstreth, "The City, Industry and the State," in Colin Crouch, ed., *State and Economy in Contemporary Capitalism* (London: St. Martin's Press, 1979).

4. Anthony Renouf, "Loss of Autonomy But Not of Ships," *Seatrade* (January 1981), p. 129.

most European countries. The decline was sharpest in tankers, but at the same time U.K. banks were active in financing the growth of the Norwegian, Hong Kong, and Greek flag tanker fleets. Then in the mid-1960s, a new cycle of investment in British shipping began: between 1968 and 1974, Britain increased its share of world shipping tonnage. The increase is especially significant if carrying capacity, rather than tonnage, is compared. Recent losses of tonnage (since the oil crisis) overstate the decline of British shipping; most losses occurred in the bulk market. During this period, too, the Hong Kong fleet, in which British interest is undoubtedly large, has increased substantially. In 1975 the *Norwegian Shipping News* summarized the results of 1974 for British shipping:

> Taken all in all, British shipping has enjoyed a successful year. Earnings have continued to rise, as well as profits, new investment has remained at substantial levels and thus new tonnage has continued to enter service to give Britain its youngest-ever fleet. Moreover, the industry has maintained its lead in a number of specialized sectors [refrigerated carriers, gas carriers, chemical carriers, containers].[5]

The dynamics of bloc politics in Britain can be illustrated by comparing government policies toward shipping and shipbuilding. A massive injection of funds to shipowners began in 1966. Notably, outright grants totaling 20 percent—later, 25 percent—of vessel cost were given to shipowners for vessel purchase. This inspired high-level protests from Scandinavian countries that Britain itself was turning into a flag-of-convenience country.[6] During the late 1960s investment flowed into shipping on a massive scale. In 1973, investment in new tonnage "amounted to 624 million pounds—the equivalent of one-quarter of the total investment of all British manufacturing industries."[7] This level of investment can be directly at-

5. *Norwegian Shipping News* 31 (31 January 1975), p. 103.

6. *Economist,* 19 March 1966, p. 65.

7. "U.K. Strong Despite Problems," *Norwegian Shipping News* 31 (3 October 1975), p. 6. The gross capital stock of the shipping industry in 1968 was approximately the same size as that of the iron and steel industry. Shipowners invested 15 percent of the gross fixed investment by British manufacturing in 1968. See United Kingdom, Committee of Inquiry into Shipping, *Report* (Rochdale Report), Cmnd. 4337 (London: HMSO, 1970), p. 39. Gross earnings of U.K. shipping totaled 2.3 billion pounds in 1978 and 2.6 billion pounds in 1977. "Their net contribution to the balance of payments in net foreign exchange earnings was 942 million pounds in 1978. In addition they accounted for gross import savings of 445 million pounds" (General Council of British Shipping, *Facts and Figures 1980* [London: GCBS, 1980]). These figures must, however, be interpreted. As Stanley Sturmey points out, "The extent to which foreign exchange can be saved by the establishment of a national shipping

tributed to government incentives. D. H. Aldcroft commented, somewhat diplomatically: "The combined effect of these terms tends to encourage a diversion of resources to shipping investment—probably to an uneconomical degree as it allows the industry to operate on lower margins than other commercial activities which are less favored."[8]

The postwar period was marked by progressive disengagement of shipping from shipbuilding. High levels of investment in shipping combined with disinvestment in shipbuilding epitomized the separation of finance and industry. Government policy under both Labour and Conservative rule encouraged this trend. In the immediate postwar period, output of British shipyards was high because of the destruction of enemy yards. By the 1960s, however, the uncompetitive nature of British shipbuilding had become evident. As early as 1958 Andrew Shonfield had presciently selected British shipbuilding as a case study of what later came to be called deindustrialization. Shonfield and official investigators recognized the problem as lack of capital investment.[9]

Government support for shipping contrasts with the "benign neglect" shown to shipbuilding. This can be demonstrated qualitatively, in government controls on shipping aid, and quantitatively, in the disproportionate amounts given to shipping. Subsidies to shipowners were granted without regard to where ships were purchased. In practice, much government aid was being channeled into Japanese yards. Shipowners and shipbuilders came into conflict over ship purchase, because the government consistently refused to link the industries. By the early 1970s, the ratio of ships exported to ships bought for U.K. registry had dropped to 1 : 3, while 80 percent of ships for British registry were purchased abroad. Shipowners point to their absorption of most British production.[10] But this only underscores

---

fleet is substantially smaller than the freight costs of imports. Using British figures, for every 100 pounds of foreign earnings of British ships, expenditure of foreign exchange is 40 pounds" (*Shipping Economics: Collected Papers* [London: Macmillan, 1975], p. 189).

8. Derek H. Aldcroft, "Reflections on the Rochdale Inquiry into Shipping: A Review Article," *Maritime History* 1 (September 1971), p. 207.

9. Andrew Shonfield, *British Economic Policy Since the War* (London: Penguin, 1958), pp. 41–43; United Kingdom, Shipbuilding Inquiry Committee 1965–66, *Report* (Geddes Report) (London: HMSO, 1966); United Kingdom, Department of Trade and Industry, *British Shipbuilding, 1972: A Report to the Department of Trade and Industry* (Booz-Allen Report) (London: HMSO, 1973).

10. See, for example, the Rochdale Report. The General Council of British Shipping adopts this position in discussions with the government and the National Union of Seamen.

the fact that British export competitiveness has been lost and the governments have not been able or willing to reverse the trend.

By the 1950s, the leading sectors of British capital had largely cast adrift the older industries such as coal and shipbuilding. In contrast to other European countries, in Britain shipowners had divested themselves of shipbuilding firms.[11] The problems of British shipbuilding stemmed from lack of capital and severe labor militancy. These trends are related. British shipbuilding workers, until recently, successfully resisted labor-displacing investment. As a former chairman of Govan Shipbuilders observed:

> It is absolutely true to say that unless money is spent the yards will never achieve the necessary competitiveness. Further, and especially in Britain, if we want to change relationships with the shop floor, which is sometimes very difficult, one of the few ways that change can be brought about is through capital investment.[12]

The sharp class conflict that lies at the root of the crisis of the British economy thus strengthened the external proclivities of British capital, enhancing the power of shipowners.

The political organization and potency of British shipowners reflect social and economic power. The General Council of British Shipping (GCBS), formerly the Chamber of Shipping, occupies what one high-level official acknowledged to be an "eccentric" position in the establishment. The GCBS is eccentric in relation to other British industrial associations, and also in comparison with its Continental counterparts. There is a continuous flow of personnel among shipping firms, the GCBS, and the Shipping Policy Division of the Department of Trade, and there is a remarkable degree of continuity between Labour and Conservative shipping policies. The GCBS did not take a formal position on the nationalization of shipbuilding. Privately, however, many from the industry expressed satisfaction.[13] Shipowners have recognized the relative weakness of the Confedera-

---

11. For a heavily documented longitudinal study of this phenomenon, see Benwell Community Project, *The Making of a Ruling Class: Two Centuries of Capitalist Development on the Tyneside*, Final Report, Series No. 6 (Newcastle-upon-Tyne: Benwell Community Project, 1978). According to the Booz-Allen Report, "It is also worth considering the benefits of forming stronger relationships between shipowners and shipbuilders in the U.K. to mutual advantage. The two shipbuilding companies who had strong formal links with shipowners in the U.K. between 1967 and 1971 are also the most successful at present" (pp. 5–6).

12. "Interview with Graham Day," *Norwegian Shipping News* 32 (25 June 1976), p. 13.

13. Author's interviews with numerous shipping observers.

tion of British Industry (CBI) vis-à-vis the City, and until recently they refused to join it. In testimony to the Commission of Inquiry into Industrial and Commercial Representation (the Devlin Committee), the Chamber of Shipping stated that "it would gain very little—and might lose its close relationship with government departments—by joining the CBI." [14] Two recent presidents of the GCBS, A. C. Swire, 1980, and E. H. Vestey, 1982, reflect both tradition and change in British maritime politics and interests. Both are members of families that have been prominent in shipping since the nineteenth century. Swire Shipping is a leading Hong Kong firm. Vestey vessels fly the Bermudan flag; the Vestey family has paid no taxes to the British government since 1920. [15]

Since 1978, the British flag merchant fleet has declined from a postwar peak of 50.4 million dwt to 20.6 million dwt. This decline reflects the general decline of Western European shipping and, as a result of relatively high labor costs, the loss of comparative advantage. However, statistics on recent losses of tonnage overstate the true decline. In liner shipping, the transition to containers and other specialized ships has inevitably led to tonnage losses as the efficiency of vessels has increased. Perhaps more important, most losses have occurred in the bulk market. At the same time, British shipowners have transferred a great deal of bulk tonnage to the Hong Kong flag. The dramatic growth of Hong Kong shipping, which is "both British and cheap," is largely a reflection of this trend. [16]

The nature of the postwar regime profoundly influenced the domestic structure of British maritime politics. Opportunities offered by a privatized regime reinforced the power of shipowners. The regime made internationalization of capital a logical plan. More than 60 percent of the earnings of British shipping are derived from cross-trading. [17] Britain has a deep commitment to the status quo. British shipping has also used its do-

14. Wyn Grant and David Marsh, *The Confederation of British Industry* (London: Hodden and Stoughton, 1977), p. 76.

15. On Vestey, see Sunday *Times* (London), 5 October 1980, p. 14. The GCBS takes note of the need to include FOC owners within its membership; see GCBS, *British Shipping Review* (1985), p. 3.

16. On Hong Kong shipping, see "Goodbye to the Red Duster, Nei Hao to the Red Flag?" *Far Eastern Economic Review,* 14 February 1985.

17. U.S. Department of Commerce, Maritime Administration, Office of Policy and Planning, *The Maritime Aids of the Six Major Maritime Nations* (Washington, D.C.: G.P.O., 1977), p. III–23.

mestic power to force upon government and society certain choices that enhance its power and profit. The extraordinary vigor and innovativeness demonstrated by the captains of an industry that displays all the trappings of tradition contradict cultural interpretations of the decline of British capitalism during the 1960s. Yet the hostility of shipowners and government to new ideas from Geneva is easily understood. After World War II, British shipping flourished, despite the decline of the British economy. As the international regime breaks down, however, British shipping must fight for survival.

France: State Capitalism and the Maritime Industries

Unlike their American counterparts, Western European shipowners are part of the financial and industrial elite. This reflects the greater centralization of Western European economies and societies. It adds to the conviction of United States and Third World shippers that conferences discriminate in favor of Western European trade. France and West Germany illustrate the centrality of shipping in the economic hierarchy, albeit in radically different ways. The interests of American and British shipping, though for quite different reasons, have appeared contradictory to the overall development of national capitalism in important respects, but in France and West Germany, shipping is subordinate to general foreign economic policy objectives. In both countries the expansion of foreign trade and shipping was centrally coordinated.

As late industrializers, neither Germany nor France could have developed a strong shipping sector without state intervention. The development of the shipping sector was heavily influenced by struggles with British imperialism. By 1890, British shipowners had completed the cartelization of international liner shipping. British shipping totaled 10 million tons, one-half of world tonnage. Germany possessed 1.5 million tons; France, 1.1 million tons.[18] Although state intervention was a primary component of French and German national maritime development, the methods by which shipping was integrated into national objectives were quite different

18. Stanley G. Sturmey, *British Shipping and World Competition* (London: Athlone, 1962), pp. 6, 14–16.

from those used in Britain. Because the shipping sector performs less independently in these countries, it is possible to deduce the broad outlines of shipping policy from a general knowledge of foreign economic policy.

French shipping developed primarily as a transportation link to the French empire, and secondarily as a passenger carrier. This reflected both the relatively low level of trade between France and other industrialized countries, and the supremacy of Britain in the conferences. The colonial trade was a protected trade. Hence French shipping never experienced a significant laissez-faire phase. After World War I the French government intervened on behalf of French shipping. By purchasing enemy tonnage and reselling it to private owners, France increased the size of its merchant fleet. This larger fleet in turn required subsidies and increasing cargo preference, and thus a nationalistic shipping policy was formed.[19] In 1924, the French government established the Compagnie Française des Pétroles. To complement the drive for energy independence it stipulated that two-thirds of French oil imports for domestic consumption be shipped in French vessels. However, the maze of restrictions, the sharp industrial conflict, and the resulting high costs of the French flag precluded expansion. By 1939 the fleet was smaller than in 1920 and incapable of meeting world competition without heavy government support.

The post–World War II objectives of French maritime policy have been remarkably consistent with prewar aims: energy independence, and consolidation of French neocolonial (francophone) ties. In the first two decades after World War II the French government placed heavy emphasis on shipbuilding, to which shipping was (in the eyes of the government) only an adjunct. French shipbuilding expanded greatly during the postwar boom and was able to hold its own against intensive Japanese competition until the early 1970s. Modernization plans were largely successful; French shipbuilding received extensive government support designed to rationalize shipyards and redirect inefficient facilities into alternative industrial activity. The emphasis on national trades and on close relations between shipping firms and shipbuilding was consistent with the French strategy of subordinating shipping to the needs of industrial modernization. Since the recession, both industries have been heavily subsidized, but shipbuilding

19. Osborne Mance and J. E. Wheeler, *International Sea Transport* (London: Oxford University Press, 1945), pp. 115–29.

has maintained a high export profile, selling two-thirds of its output abroad, much of it to former colonies.[20]

The performance of shipbuilding contrasts with the record of shipping. In tonnage, the French fleet exhibited considerable growth. However, three-quarters of the French flag fleet consists of oil tankers, some of which are British- and American-owned. The rest—except the Worms Group, which is primarily devoted to shipping—are owned by French oil firms. The increase in tanker tonnage reflects France's drive toward independence in energy, but the surplus capacity in tankers indicates the country's inability to achieve this goal despite the application of considerable public resources.[21]

In the liner sector France remains weak. This is mainly a result of its lack of presence in conferences and the high operating costs of the French flag. France was slow in developing container shipping. In 1974, the state-owned liner firm Compagnie Générale Maritime (CGM) was formed by a merger of the Compagnie Messageries Maritime and the Compagnie Générale Transatlantique. With a presence in Atlantic and Far Eastern consortia, the CGM is the "national champion" of French shipping. With its cargo base in French trade, it serves as a "vital keystone of French exporting."[22] Thus the largest firms in both the bulk and liner sectors are state-owned.

In marked contrast to Britain, the French fleet is highly national in its commercial domain. Only two firms are truly international: Louis Dreyfus, part of the international grain empire; and Gazocean, an international trader in gas. The liner sector is linked primarily to French exports because of high labor costs, which in turn can be attributed to trade union militancy and historical laws preventing the use of foreign labor. In contrast to the GCBS, the Comité Central des Armateurs de France (CCAF) is a weak trade association. In 1981 President François Mitterrand's government established a Ministry of the Sea to coordinate all relevant groups. The inexorable decline of French shipping, which decreased from 21.1 mil-

20. "Traditional Shipbuilders Fall Further Behind," *Seatrade Annual Review* (1980), p. 149.

21. For an analysis of French oil policy, see Peter J. Katzenstein, "International Relations and Domestic Structures: Foreign Economic Policies of Advanced Industrial States," *International Organization* 30 (Winter 1976), pp. 35–42.

22. Ian Middleton, ed., "Le Nouvel Age?" *Seatrade* (October 1981), p. 104.

lion dwt in 1978 to 12.5 million dwt in 1985, heightens protectionist sentiments.

West Germany: Shipping and Exports

The position the shipping sector occupies in West German society was determined historically by the rapid burst of industrialization in the last two decades of the nineteenth century and by the country's defeat in war. The formal structure of the West German maritime sector resembles that of Britain; government keeps at arm's length. In practice, however, West German shipping policies are, like France's, calculated to conform to the requirements of industry and the need to penetrate foreign markets.

French shipping was able to avoid a frontal assault on Britain's commercial supremacy. Germany, in contrast, was inevitably drawn into direct confrontation because of its complete lack of colonies and its need to enter Britain's export markets. The challenge to the liner conference system thus paralleled the Anglo-German naval rivalry. As the Booth Committee observed in 1918: "Large scale productivity not to say overproduction at home required foreign markets for the disposal of the surplus output, and the whole German system was directed to facilitate marketing abroad . . . by the action of [among other sectors] the steamship lines."[23] Shipping was to "assist the national object." As a result, shipping firms, ten of which owned 60 percent of German tonnage, were organized in cooperation with German industry and banks and with each other.[24] The two leading firms, Hamburg-Amerika and Norddeutscher Lloyd, dominated the maritime sector until they merged into the German national champion Hapag-Lloyd in 1970.

Challenging Britain in the conferences meant that, unlike France, Germany would have to acquire a sizable liner fleet, run on market principles and capable of gaining entry to conferences by penetrating trades as an outsider. As noted in Chapter 2, Germany built up its fleet by using its political and geographical position to establish "control stations" for immigrants, channeling passengers into German ships, a form of flag discrimination. For Germany, as for France, the passenger trade was an important base of

23. United Kingdom, Departmental Committee on Shipping and Shipbuilding, *First Report* (Booth Committee Report), Cmnd. 9092 (London: HMSO, 1918), p. 102.
24. Ibid., p. 96.

national shipping development during the "age of immigration." By World War I the German fleet was the main threat to British shipping. The Booth Committee claimed that the desire to limit the size of Britain's merchant fleet was a cause of Germany's entry into the war.[25]

International maritime rivalry thus accompanied the birth and early development of the German liner fleet. After each world war the fleet was dismantled, with British shipowners officiating in the process of requisition and sales. Both times, however, it gradually and tenaciously reestablished its position in the conferences. International rivalry had its greatest long-term effect on the German bulk fleet. Germany's mining concessions, especially oil, were divided among the Allies after World War I as spoils of war. Defeat in World War II precluded any serious effort to challenge the Anglo-American oil condominium. The bottling up of financial and industrial capital mandated a return to an export orientation, which has characterized German foreign economic policy since 1945.[26] This established the conditions necessary for the expansion of German liner shipping in the 1950s and 1960s. West Germany's tanker fleet, like its oil sector, remains small despite modest attempts to increase its size in the wake of the oil crisis.

In contrast to France, West German shipping firms comprise a powerful interest group within the financial/industrial elite. This is the liberal aspect of German shipping politics. However, the power of shipowners and their independence derive from, and are constrained by, the export needs of German industry. Whereas French shipping has been subordinated to the needs of shipbuilding, West German policies have achieved a balance between the two industries. This balance rests primarily on the modernization of shipbuilding and secondarily on the importance assigned to liner shipping. German shipbuilding is more competitive than that of other EC nations. Subsidies have been granted to shipowners, but the productivity of the shipbuilding industry has been instrumental in reinforcing the tacit bargain whereby German shipowners purchase from German yards. The

25. Ibid., p. 64.
26. See Frieder Schlupp, "Modell Deutschland and the International Division of Labor: The FRG in the World Political Economy," in Ekehart Krippendorf and Volker Rittberger, eds., *The Foreign Policy of West Germany: Formation and Contents* (Beverly Hills: Sage, 1980); and Willi Semmler, "Economic Aspects of Model Germany: A Comparison with the United States," in Andrei Markovitz, ed., *The Political Economy of West Germany* (New York: Praeger, 1982).

Deutsche Bank, as the "command post" of the German economy, aids this process. Hapag-Lloyd is linked to the Deutsche Bank; at least one Deutsche Bank director sits on the board of Hapag-Lloyd. The Deutsche Bank and two large insurance companies own 80 percent of DDG Hansa, West Germany's second largest liner firm, and the Deutsche Bank supervised the sale of DDG Hansa's financial assets to Hapag-Lloyd in 1979.[27]

The ambivalence of the government concerning the protectionist trend reflects the role of shipping in West Germany. Unlike the French shipowners' association, the German shipowners' association vigorously opposes shipping nationalism and the attacks on the status quo mounted by both superpowers. German liners have suffered from Third World cargo reservation; Hapag-Lloyd is heavily involved in Atlantic trades and was among the shipping firms indicted by the United States Department of Justice on felony charges for secret rebating. West German shipowners have a substantial investment, in terms of container tonnage and market share, in most important conferences and cross-trades. In contrast to the French liner sector, West German lines are heavily "internationalized" in cross-trades as well as in national trades. Although West German shipping has declined from 15.7 million dwt in 1978 to 8.4 million dwt in 1985, its liner sector has remained strong, and West German owners have led the European exodus to flags of convenience. However, the slowdown in expansion of world trade and the accompanying maritime nationalism increasingly isolate the liberal shipping sector from the rest of the economy. And even within shipping, accommodationist tendencies are surfacing. From a purely economic point of view, shipping plays a very small role in the German economy; a relatively high level of investment in shipping yields limited results on a balance sheet. This is a function of the high capital intensity of German tonnage and, more important, the productivity and profitability of German industry.

National Shipping Strategies

Changes in the postwar regime have posed a number of tangible problems for Western European shipping firms and governments:

27. Author's interviews with Hapag-Lloyd; "High Noon for Hansa," *Seatrade* (March 1980).

1. The general increase of protectionist laws and bilateral agreements.

2. Increasing competition from Third World fleets and Soviet bloc shipping.

3. America's regulatory policy.

4. The need to adapt to container technology rapidly, to maintain a competitive fleet.

These problems have resulted in a significant decline in the size of most Western European merchant fleets. Europe's response can be analyzed in terms of *national* strategies and *European* or EC policy. Of course, EC policy is an element of national strategy. However, national policy has, for the most part, stressed governmental assistance. Because individually European states are weak, national policies are not designed either to promote or to retard regime change. EC policy expresses the attempt of European states collectively to influence the nature of the regime.

West Germany

Government aid to the West German maritime industries has been substantial, although the lowest among the major maritime powers. Since 1972, aid levels have increased. In contrast to most other OECD states, in West Germany aid has been channeled to shipowners not primarily through credit assistance but, rather, through direct tax allowances and subsidies, especially subsidies for the purchase of West German–built ships. Throughout the postwar period West German shipowners and shipbuilders had a private understanding that vessels would be purchased from domestic shipyards. Governments have tended to designate shipbuilding as the major source of government assistance.[28]

Between 1965 and 1974 West German owners were eligible for a construction subsidy covering 10 percent of the cost of ships built in either West German or foreign yards. In 1975 this was increased to 12.5 percent, and in 1977 a further special subsidy was granted so that the total exceeded 17 percent. Owners using these subsidies were prohibited from adopting flags of convenience. In 1974 an additional subsidy program was

28. U.S. Department of Commerce, Maritime Administration, *Maritime Aids*, p. VI–13; U.S. Department of Commerce, Maritime Administration, Office of International Activities, *Maritime Subsidies, 1978* (Washington, D.C.: G.P.O., 1978), p. 54.

initiated to encourage West German owners to increase the size of the national tanker fleet. The government subsidized 15 percent of the cost of very large crude carriers; relatively successful, the program was terminated in 1976 after the tanker market collapsed.

Significant levels of support have also been available to West German shipowners in the form of Special Depreciation Allowances. Between 1973 and 1975 these amounted to the equivalent of 4 percent of a ship's cost. Further minor benefits included Marshall Plan loans at low interest rates and tax deferral on gains from ship sales. These aids have been supplemented by general investment grants and industrial assistance applying to the economy as a whole. Through regional state aid to shipbuilding, West Germany evades OECD and EC guidelines.[29]

Overall government assistance to West German industries has helped to maintain the competitiveness of shipping. In 1973–74, construction subsidies totaled $100 million per year, with an additional $61 million per year for the tanker program. Tax allowances for owners averaged $32 million per year between 1971 and 1975. By 1975 it was estimated that more than $200 million was spent in construction grants for West German yards. Between 1976 and 1979 $370 million was made available in construction grants under West Germany's Eighth Shipbuilding Assistance Program.[30]

West Germany's conciliatory attitude toward the Third World, reflected in its early acceptance of the principles of the UNCTAD Code of Conduct, is a function of the primacy of industry and exports in the West German political economy. West German industry as a whole does not share the shipowners' antipathy to competition from either the Eastern bloc or the Third World. Its attitude toward the NIEO is fundamentally positive, based on a desire for export markets and the fact that West Germany hopes to participate heavily in Third World economic expansion.[31] As in France, West German desire for export markets must be weighed against the needs of its shipping industry. The Ministry of Transport in Hamburg supports a narrower constituency than the Ministry of Economics in Bonn.

With one-third of EC exports, West Germany is playing an increasingly central role in the formation of EC transportation policy. Since the mid-

29. Author's interview with British Shipbuilders, 1980.

30. U.S. Department of Commerce, Maritime Administration, *Maritime Aids,* p. VI–50.

31. Ulrich Albrecht, "The Policy of the FRG Towards the 'South,'" in Krippendorf and Rittberger, eds., *Foreign Policy of West Germany.*

1970s shippers have become more reluctant to support conferences. Hence the old CENSA/ESC understandings appear to have weakened. In 1979, for example, the Bundesverband der deutschen Industrie (BDI, Association of Federal German Industry) opposed attempts by the Verband deutscher Reeder (VDR, German Shipowners Association) to limit tonnage on the Trans-Siberian Container Link, arguing that "a strangulation of TSR [Trans-Siberian Railway] traffic would have a detrimental effect on the competitiveness of German exports to the Far East."[32] Similarly, associations of West German machine and electrical industries have responded positively to attempts to develop a set of competition rules to regulate conferences.[33]

The new order in shipping does not conflict with the fundamental objectives of West German foreign economic policy. The need to maintain exports and consolidate Third World markets and Eastern bloc connections requires a policy that accommodates development in these areas. While shipowners want the government to take strong action against the Soviet Union and to make a concerted effort to reduce protectionism, shippers require low-cost shipping and international economic stability. Moreover, although a nationalist regime would require a reorganization of West German shipping, a regime that linked shipping shares to trade generation would increase the size of the liner fleet in the long run. Even in its traditional role, the threat to West German shipping comes not primarily from bilateralism, as in Britain, but, rather, from lack of stability, which prevents the consolidation of rationalized conferences carrying West German trade.

France

French aid to shipping has been explicitly linked to the objective of increasing the French flag share of national trade. This goal has become increasingly important since the mid-1960s, forming the basis of a series of Five-Year Plans for Shipping. Government aid has been comparatively heavy, reflecting the mercantilist tradition. Under the seventh plan, the Plan de Croissance, the government sought unsuccessfully to increase the

---

32. Richard Bell, "European Shipowners Demand Action Against Trans-Siberian Box Line," *Container News* 11 (April 1981), p. 17.

33. Ibid., pp. 18–19; author's interviews with shipowners and government officials in Hamburg, 1980.

size of the merchant fleet by one-third between 1974 and 1978. Recently all maritime activities have been centralized in a Ministry of the Sea, reflecting the increasingly close links between shipping and shipbuilding and the fact that in France "a realization of the international workings of the shipping market is quite a recent phenomenon."[34]

The main forms of assistance to the French fleet are interest subsidies, accelerated depreciation, construction subsidies, and equipment grants. As in West Germany, aid to shipbuilding is the focus of French maritime efforts. Although shipowners are free to utilize the world market, in practice the government enforces a policy of "buy French." For example, shipowners seeking to purchase vessels from abroad will encounter "lengthy administrative delay" of requests for import licenses. To compensate shipowners, the government increases subsidy levels.[35] In 1979, the Comité Central des Armateurs de France launched a "concours" between shipping and shipbuilding, further formalizing the cohesion of the maritime industries. Government presence is strengthened by state ownership of the Compagnie Générale Maritime, the largest shipowner.

Between 1971 and 1975 interest subsidies and accelerated depreciation provided an average of $100 million per year. Equipment grants, which constitute the main form of assistance, increased substantially. In the mid-1960s these grants provided up to 12 percent of vessel cost. Under the sixth plan (1971–75), the percentage increased to 15 percent for container ships. Between 1976 and 1980, $233 million was allocated to shipowners, and subsidies increased to 17 percent of a ship's cost. British Shipbuilders has estimated that, including all forms of aid, the French government provides up to 30 percent of a ship's cost.[36] In the 1960s, direct subsidies to shipbuilding amounted to 20 percent of construction costs per vessel.[37]

34. Paul Woodward, "French Report: International Succour," *Seatrade* (January 1985), p. 7.

35. Author's interviews with French maritime officials, 1980; author's interviews with British Shipbuilders, 1980; *Lloyds List,* 18 January 1980. In 1980 the SNCC group ordered four container ships from Japan. However, "under pressure we believe from the French shipbuilding industry, the Government adopted a dilatory approach towards granting the import licenses, signalling the intention not to do so." The order eventually went to Alsthrom-Atlantique (*Fairplay International Shipping Weekly* 278 [3 April 1980], p. 9).

36. British Shipbuilders, Corporate Planning Division, "Shipbuilding in Recession" (internal document) (1980), chapter 9.

37. U.S. Department of Commerce, Maritime Administration, *Maritime Aids,* p. VII–38.

The recent tentative steps toward liberalization in the shipping sector parallel tendencies in the French economy toward internationalization and a loosening of governmental controls.[38] In part this reflects the recognition of the limits to the state's ability to manipulate international settings to its own advantage. In both the bulk and liner sectors, France has encountered a regime that has been profoundly opposed to national objectives. Liberalization, involving the dismantling of extensive controls over wages and social policy, also reflects the desire to create a more docile labor force. Wage costs are higher than for most of France's competitors. France is unlikely to dismantle the extensive mechanisms that pervade its maritime politics and direct the majority of government funds to shipbuilding rather than shipping. In 1984 shipowners were still "frustrated that the government was directing more time and money to the crippled shipbuilders whilst shipping was being virtually ignored."[39]

French national objectives synchronize with the UNCTAD Code of Conduct. With its foreign trade as a cargo base, French liner shipping could significantly increase its share of world trade. As the minister for marine transport notes, echoing traditional French views, the "flag, i.e., our economy, does not always draw full advantage from the market share served by our enterprise."[40] The code appears actually to increase French links to former colonies. It strengthens bilateral relations and, by encouraging Third World fleet expansion, provides a market for French shipbuilding and marine equipment exports. Francophone countries of Africa (e.g., Morocco, Ivory Coast) have been in the vanguard of the New International Maritime Order and merchant fleet development. Finally, the abolition of open registries would be consistent with raw materials and energy policy, which seeks to achieve independence from U.S. multinationals.

Britain

Although the British government strenuously defends shipping liberalism, British shipowners have received much more government aid than

38. On liberalization, see John Zysman, "The French State in the International Economy," in Peter J. Katzenstein, ed., *Between Power and Plenty: Foreign Economic Policies of Advanced Industrial States* (Madison: University of Wisconsin Press, 1978).

39. Woodward, "French Report," p. 74.

40. Quoted in Hans Ludwig Beth, Arnulf Hader, and Robert Kappel, *Twenty-Five Years of World Shipping* (London: Fairplay, 1984), p. 186.

their counterparts. British shipping also enjoys a privileged position in relation to other domestic industries. As noted in Chapter 5, generous investment allowances were initiated by the government in 1954, and tax requirements for U.K. owners were "eased very considerably" at that time.[41]
In 1966, a system of direct investment grants was introduced by the Labour government. Along with low-interest loans, these grants constitute
the main form of support. Until recently the shipping and shipbuilding
industries have not been closely linked in terms of combined ownership or
control, or by comprehensive government planning. Thus aid to shipping
should not be considered a form of support for shipbuilding. The government nationalized the crumbling shipbuilding industry in 1977.

During the mid-1960s, as was noted above, the United Kingdom em-
barked on a program of massive, systematic support of shipping. The level
of aid increased dramatically throughout the late 1960s and early 1970s. In
1965, free depreciation was made available to owners. As subsidy-induced
investment soared, this depreciation became progressively more important
and encouraged the participation of major banks, which found a tax shelter
in shipping.[42] The United States Department of Commerce estimated the
benefit, based on an 8 percent interest rate, to be equivalent to 11 percent
of capital investment. The Cash Investment Grant Program, included under
the 1966 Shipbuilding Act, provided for direct payments to shipowners
of 20 to 25 percent of vessel cost between 1966 and 1971, and payments
on these grants amounted to $325 million between 1966 and 1970 and
$1.1 billion more through 1976. An additional significant support was the
Home Credit Guarantee Scheme under the Industry Act of 1972, by which
the government guaranteed loans for vessels to be added to the British flag
registry. In 1976, the British government's risk exposure on loans was $1.8
billion.[43]

Total aid to U.K. shipbuilding between 1966 and 1975 was a comparatively modest $344 million; the bulk of this sum was injected after
1970. In contrast to the West German and French policies, in Britain construction subsidies were not generally granted during the 1960s. In 1972,
a subsidy of 10 percent of ship cost was paid, but this was rescinded in
1974 in accordance with OECD guidelines. After nationalization, an inter-

41. Rochdale Report, p. 54.
42. U.S. Department of Commerce, Maritime Administration, *Maritime Aids*, p. III–13.
43. Ibid., p. III–17.

vention fund was established for British Shipbuilders to support various bids at its own discretion. In 1977, the amount was $112 million; under the Thatcher government, the level of aid has gradually been reduced.[44]

Britain's ardent defense of the status quo is based on the importance of shipping to the national economy and the role of British shipping in cross-trades. Although Britain, unlike Norway and Greece, is not wholly dependent on cross-trades, nevertheless a protectionist regime based on cargo generation would be harmful to British shipping. Hence, shipowners and the government have pressed for the maintenance of a liberal regime while rejecting the contention that high levels of governmental support contradict liberal doctrine.

During the late 1960s, the level of aid to the shipping industries of the major maritime powers began to increase dramatically, indicating the strong role of governments prior to the development of surplus capacity and the recession of the mid-1970s and suggesting that government intervention was itself a contributing factor in the subsequent expansion of excess tonnage. The amount of American aid actually exceeded the very high levels of Japanese and British support, even if the special tax exemption enjoyed by shipowners using flags of convenience (amounting to approximately $200 million per year) is not included.[45] In this context, the growing role of most European governments in national shipping affairs can be assumed to be at least partially a reaction to American policies and actions.

Europe and the Third World

The negotiations over the UNCTAD Code took place during the early 1970s and hence coincided with Britain's entry into the EC. The inclusion of this first-class maritime power, the necessity of responding to Third World and U.S. actions, and the failure of CENSA established the desir-

44. Peter Hill, "Shipbuilding Output at Lowest in Fifty Years," *Times* (London), 31 December 1980, p. 17. For a general survey of governmental intervention in shipbuilding, see Brian Hogwood, *Government and Shipbuilding: The Politics of Industrial Change* (Westmead: Saxon House, 1979).

45. UNCTAD, *Action on the Question of Open Registries,* TD/B/C.4/220 (Geneva: United Nations, May 1981), p. 11. Susan Strange cites an estimate of $50 billion in subsidies to shipbuilding since World War II ("The Management of Surplus Capacity, Or, How Does Theory Stand Up to Protectionism 1970s Style?" *International Organization* 33 [Summer, 1979], p. 325).

ability of formulating an EC shipping policy. In voting for the code in 1974, France, West Germany, and Belgium had technically violated the Treaty of Rome, which requires the adoption of a common stance on trade matters. However, through a private agreement with the European Commission, the pro-codists agreed not to proceed with ratification until the five-year ratification period elapsed or until a common position could be reached.[46]

The elaboration of EC shipping policy was itself legally questionable. On transport, Article 84, Title 4 in the Treaty of Rome stipulates: "The provisions of the Title shall apply to transport by rail, road, and inland waterway. The Council may, acting unanimously, decide whether, to what extent, and by what procedure appropriate provisions may be laid down for sea and air transport." This clause, sponsored by the Netherlands, indicates that shipping matters are not included in the terms of the treaty. However, in 1974, the commission brought a test case to the European Court of Justice, and the court ruled that the general provisions of the treaty do apply to shipping. This ruling paved the way for EC policy and the attempt to step into the political and philosophical leadership role vacated by the United States.

The formulation of EC policy created both opportunities and pitfalls for member states. It complicated the international ratification and implementation of the UNCTAD Code of Conduct. Because it sired EC competition rules and increased the potential for invoking Europe's own antitrust laws, it posed new dangers for anti-codists, who called for EC protection of free-market principles. The importance of EC shipping policy was amplified by the reluctance or inability of the United States to develop a viable multilateral response to UNCTAD, and Japan's unwillingness to offend Third World sensibilities. Ratification of the code required the accession of twenty-four states possessing 25 percent of world tonnage. European ratification would fulfill this requirement and thus compel Japan and the United States to define a long-term strategy. Clearly, the intra-European conflicts that erupted during the UNCTAD conferences at Geneva would be played out once again, with even greater urgency, in Brussels.

Within the EC, France, West Germany, and Belgium championed the

46. Anna Bredimas and John G. Tzoannis, "In Search of a Common Shipping Policy for the European Community," *Journal of Common Market Studies* 20 (December 1981), p. 100.

UNCTAD Code. Britain and Denmark opposed it; other member states were neutral. Ministers sought to reconcile the views of all member states. But the need to reach a common position against rapid external changes excluded the possibility of a stalemate. Anglo-French conflict marked the first phase of the negotiations. The debate over the broad outlines of EC policy was resolved in favor of British views. The second phase involved more practical considerations; here the protagonists were Britain and West Germany. Once again, the compromise appeared to favor Britain, at least in the short run.

The French government launched the discussion of shipping principles with a memorandum submitted to the commission in 1975. France was proposing a Grand Design for EC shipping; a "skeleton" encompassing all major aspects of shipping policy would be introduced by the European Commission and would gradually be fleshed out. The design corresponded to French interests: the Code of Conduct would be endorsed at EC level, preserving the cargo-sharing clauses. The Grand Design also called for harmonization of wages and social policies, condemnation of open registries, and stricter safety standards.[47]

The Grand Design triggered intense debate and led to the formation of a consensus on the need for an EC policy. However, the design's deductive character and broad scope were too ambitious and too obviously parochial, expressing traditional French interests and only rhetorical support for the New International Economic Order. Britain replied with what came to be known as the "mosaic approach." Like the Grand Design, this prompted extensive public debate. It argued for a gradual evolution of policy on an ad hoc basis as the need for a common position arose. Policy should only be developed by consensus; where it was unnecessary to force the pace of events in response to external pressures the commission should remain silent. This approach was favored by the anti-codists and thus endorsed by the Comité des Associations d'Armateurs des Communautés Européennes (CAACE), the European shipowners' association, and it ultimately became the basis of commission proposals.[48]

The acceptance of the mosaic approach had the practical effect of isolat-

47. See European Parliament, Ad Hoc Merchant Shipping Committee, *EEC Shipping Policy—Flags of Convenience* (Brussels: European Community, 1979).
48. Bredimas and Tzoannis, "In Search of a Common Shipping Policy," p. 113; and CAACE, *Annual Report* (1979), p. 1.

ing the question of the UNCTAD Code of Conduct from other areas of shipping such as social policy or flags of convenience. A compromise over the UNCTAD Code was considered necessary to appease the Third World and slow the pace of developments in the bulk trades. Britain's position, formulated by the GCBS, was "disapplication" of the code within the EC and among those OECD countries that could be induced to follow the community's lead. This would enable the EC to ratify the code, subject to the disapplication reservation. France and West Germany opposed what appeared to be a return to the "two regimes" position originally introduced within CENSA, on the grounds that it would alienate Third World states and thus lead to further destabilization. If Britain remained intransigent, France and West Germany threatened, they would ratify unilaterally.

By March 1978, the commission was recommending ratification on the basis of GCBS proposals. However, West Germany and France continued to balk at these modifications of the code. Moreover, U.K. officials were increasingly skeptical of the possibility of achieving a concrete agreement within the OECD. Pro-codists argued that disapplication of the code would strip the code of its meaning and practical effect. The conciliatory attitude within the EC was enhanced by serious tensions with each superpower: Soviet shipping was undercutting conference rates, and overtonnaging was becoming a serious problem in U.S. trades, where the FMC prohibited rationalization of conferences and was initiating legal action against several European (and American) shipowners for secret rebating. Meanwhile, developing countries continued to apply cargo preference laws.

Given the agreement in principle among European shipowners on the desirability of "commercial criteria," the question was how to disapply the cargo-sharing measures of the code while leaving the rest of the code intact. The British government favored a *trades* approach, which would retain commercial criteria on all intra-OECD trades. France and West Germany wanted a *lines* approach, applying only to lines engaged in OECD trades. The latter approach was compelling for two reasons. First, it preserved the spirit of the code; in theory it granted Third World cross-traders access to 20 percent of OECD trades, although the practical effect was negligible. Second, it provided the EC with a means of eliminating Soviet competition. By specifying that the lines approach applied to "national lines of developing countries," Soviet access to cross-trades would be limited.

The lines approach constituted the essence of the Schipol Memorandum, negotiated by French, West German, and British shipowners in November 1978. It represented the main body of EC shipping doctrine; French opposition to flags of convenience and the movement to curb Soviet incursions in the cross-trades had been deflected by EC agreement to monitor developments. After initially opposing the lines approach, British shipowners and the government, at the instigation of the GCBS, ultimately accepted the Schipol compromise. The lines approach thus represented an internal compromise both within the EC and between the EC and the Third World.[49]

The final agreement, known as the Brussels Package, enabled those states favoring the code to include Third World countries in their commercial sphere while, at least in principle, excluding much Soviet shipping. Anti-codists were able to carve out a large amount of trade subject to market principles. Under the terms of the EC reservation, the lines of less developed countries were to be allocated 40 percent of cargo traded with the community, while the rest was distributed according to commercial criteria. This agreement, however, was subject to several qualifications. First, the greater portion of Soviet shipping operates outside the conference structure, and it is unclear whether the provisions of the code apply to non-conference lines. Second, there is to be a redistribution of shares of trade among national lines of the EC, taking account of "the volume of cargo carried by the conference and generated by the Member States whose trade is served by it" and "the needs of the shipper whose cargoes are carried by the conference."[50] Thus even within the EC and those OECD states that can be induced to join, a degree of effective cargo reservation seems probable.

The Brussels Package, completed immediately before UNCTAD V at Manila in 1979, paved the way for the code to become part of international law. Following the formal ratification by the EC states, it entered into law in October 1983. For Europe, agreements with Japan and the United States are considered crucial. Japan has not made a decision on the

---

49. For accounts of the formation of EC shipping policy, see Sigma Services, "The U.N. Liner Code" (Farnham, Surrey: Sigma Services, 1979); Ian Middleton, "Back from the Brink," *Seatrade* (November 1978); House of Lords, Select Committee on the European Communities, *Liner Conferences*, Session 1977–78, 25th Report, R/3245/77 (London: HMSO, 1978); Paul Larsen and Valerie Vetterick, "The EC and the UNCTAD Liner Code," *Law and Policy in International Business* (March 1979); and Hans Böhme, "Current Issues and Progress in European Shipping Policy," *World Economy* 6, no. 3 (September 1983).

50. EEC Council Regulation No. 954/79 of May 1979.

code and may ratify it in its original form.[51] U.S. ratification is doubtful and official policy statements continue to reiterate opposition to protectionism in shipping. The Brussels Package has had the effect of placing conflict between Europe and America in the forefront of world shipping politics.

The United States and Europe

The Brussels Package envisions two regimes: in trade between OECD states and LDCs, 40 percent of cargo would be reserved for the LDC fleet; the rest would be open to OECD states on a commercial basis. Similarly, in intra-OECD trades, cargo would be, in principle, subject to competitive access. The Brussels Package thus seeks to satisfy LDC demands without discarding essential features of the conference system.

Europe's hope that the United States would accept the principles of the Brussels Package and ratify the UNCTAD Code of Conduct on this basis was excessively optimistic. The Brussels Package is a major challenge to the United States. Europe's acceptance, subject to its reservations, of the UNCTAD Code of Conduct means that closed conferences have been enshrined in international law. On the one hand, the EC has acceded to Third World demands for a guaranteed (40 percent) share of cargo. In return, on the other hand, the code legitimizes the deferred rebate, strengthening the monopoly powers of conferences in which European firms are entrenched.

Consequently, the United States has vigorously opposed the Brussels Package. American officials fear that U.S. lines would be denied access to EC-LDC trades and intra-EC trades by closed conferences already dominated by European shipping firms. Such a concern is one indication of the profound changes that are occurring in the U.S. shipping industry. American policy recognizes the potential for its lines to participate in "round the world" services. Moreover, the United States opposes the institutionalization of bilateralism that the UNCTAD Code sanctifies. However, it is by no means opposed to striking ad hoc bilateral agreements.[52]

51. See "Sneaking Japanese Protectionism," *Norwegian Shipping News* 36 (12 September 1980), p. 1; Japan, Ministry of Transport, *The Current Situation of Japanese Shipping, 1985* (Tokyo: Japan Maritime Development Association, 1985), pp. 32–36.

52. See Chapter 6, above. In March 1984 after two years of U.S.–EC discussions, Admiral Harold Shear, U.S. maritime administrator, proclaimed that the United States would "continue to resist cargo reservation schemes" but that such resistance "would be tempered by realism" (*Seatrade* [April 1984], p. 17).

Since 1982 negotiations have been held between the EC, led by the Consultative Shipping Group (CSG), and the United States, represented by the U.S. Maritime Administration, MARAD. The EC has pressed the United States to accept a regime similar to that envisioned by the Brussels Package, but the United States has refused to accept either the Brussels Package or the UNCTAD Code in its original form. It calls for reciprocity or equal access to all conferences, fearing a regime in which American trades are open to Europe and all other trades are, in effect, closed to American shipowners. Yet the United States refuses to accept restrictions on its right to negotiate bilateral shipping pacts with LDCs. It threatens a series of such agreements, eliminating European shipping, as the alternative to European acceptance of American policies.

America's centrality in world trade is such that a closing of trade of this magnitude would be extremely harmful to European shipping. U.S. trade constitutes about 12 percent of world trade by weight (down from 15 percent in 1950). By value, the more relevant measure for liner shipping, the figure is substantially higher, perhaps as high as 66 percent of world trade.[53] EC shipping is clearly in decline. Between 1970 and 1983 the fleet declined from 29 percent to 23 percent of the world total. These figures overstate the extent of the decline because they do not take into account the use of flags of convenience or the qualitative impact of container shipping, 39 percent of which is European. Nevertheless, despite its strong presence in world trade, European shipping is highly dependent on its position in the U.S. market. This is especially true of the liberal or quasi-liberal Western and Northern European states. America's opposition to the Brussels Package highlights the inability of Europe to make a separate peace with the Third World without American consent.

The European Community as a Global Shipping Power

The development of EC shipping policy exemplifies the reactive, defensive nature of the EC as a bloc that attempts to cope with the raw power of the American economy. All EC governments view the Common Market as a means of furthering national interests and reducing uncertainty in shipping. This is true of even the most liberal shipping countries, who previ-

53. See U.S. Department of Commerce, Maritime Administration, *Statistical Summary of Seaborne Commerce to and from the United States, 1977* (Washington, D.C.: G.P.O., 1978), p. 4.

ously resisted a common policy and who now view EC shipping policy as a tactical retreat.[54]

Evidence from shipping suggests that the concept of integration is not obsolete but, rather, very useful in understanding the growth of the EC. Integration does not run counter to national economic conflicts; rather, it expresses them against the rest of the world, between member states, and within member states. Integration and disintegration are complementary processes; the process of integration ultimately benefits the strongest states and most powerful classes and interest groups within the EC.

Attitudes of national governments toward the UNCTAD Code of Conduct were conditioned by two factors: the gains and losses that would accrue to national shipowners from cargo-sharing, and the possibility of using the weight of the EC in trade and shipping to strengthen member states in relation to the United States and the U.S.S.R. Belgium and France represented the opportunistic wing, recognizing that cargo-sharing would benefit the national fleet. Britain and Denmark reluctantly acquiesced in a common policy to further international stability. West Germany saw elements of both approaches in the common policy.

The ambiguities in the eventual directive on shipping reflected the contradictions between member states; in the short term, at least, both sides could claim victory. The opportunists invoked the clauses stipulating cargo generation as a basis for shipping shares. Belgian shipowners, for example, proclaimed, "We will interpret our share as 40 percent."[55] The big cross-traders noted with satisfaction the "disapplication" of cargo-sharing within the EC and, potentially, among OECD states. British shipowners stressed the worldwide implications of the code; yet, ironically, the British intend to use the cargo-generation criterion to exclude the Greeks from their traditional markets.[56]

The victory of the mosaic approach in the shipping debate reflected the

54. Lord Inchcape of P & O announced as early as 1976, "We are ready and willing to make practical proposals for making it [the UNCTAD Code of Conduct for Liner Conferences] a sound and effective instrument which could be the basis for a new and lasting world order in world shipping"; Michael Baily, "The Shipping Industry and the Bureaucrats of Brussels," *Times* (London), 30 June 1976, p. 19; author's interviews, London, 1980.

55. "Belgian Report," *Seatrade* (February 1981), p. 99.

56. Michael Baily, "British Shipowners Beware the Greeks," *Times* (London), 2 December 1981, p. 16. For a sharp indictment of the maritime powers of the EC by a Greek observer, see Gregory Callinoupolos, "In Search of Freedom," *Seatrade* (December 1982), p. 136.

efforts of the British government and all EC shipping firms to use the EC primarily as an externally oriented, stabilizing bloc. This has resulted in a least-common-denominator approach to EC policy even in terms of external policy. Predictably, the French effort in open registries and social policy failed, and EC efforts to counter Soviet shipping have also been frustrated by France. The main arena of EC activity has been in liner conferences, where it has been possible to gain a consensus on ratification of the code. However, policy in other areas is being made, and eventually a common transport policy, including a comprehensive approach to shipping, should evolve.

Britain's insistence on a mosaic policy also stemmed from the attempt to forestall integration, which, at the time, it believed to be a danger to the traditional system of shipping. The application of the Treaty of Rome raised the specter of application of antitrust or "competition" rules and the possibility that, even within Western Europe, the principle of privatization would be overtaken by regulation. Thus, from the standpoint of the more liberal maritime nations (the Netherlands, the United Kingdom), EC policy in shipping has promised costs as well as benefits. Preliminary commission proposals reflected Continental conceptions (paralleling the American ones) of shipper-shipowner relations. Highly regulatory in nature, these proposals called for a modified version of the FMC in the European Commission, thus superseding the CENSA/CSG consultation system even among Western European countries. Ironically, the antitrust provisions initially proposed by the commission were stiffer than those of the UNCTAD Code of Conduct. The most important regulation would have restricted loyalty agreements, making the deferred rebate optional to shippers. However, this strict interpretation of competition rules elicited intense hostility from shipowners, as well as from the British government, which feared an internal power shift from Britain to France and West Germany.

More recent proposals were more in keeping with traditional European practices, providing an automatic exemption for shipping conferences, although enabling the commission to investigate and levy fines on shipowners if it found any abuse of a dominant position.[57] A further area of

57. "Contrary to the legislation in the U.S., providing for the open conference system, the Community's proposal leaves it entirely to the conference to decide on their membership and in doing so does not deviate from the system endorsed by the [UNCTAD Liner] Code" (European Commission, *Progress Towards a Common Transport Policy: Maritime Transport* [Brussels: European Community, March 1985], p. 23).

substantive policy in which the commission has made proposals is internal liberalization or "freedom to provide services." At the present time European Community law establishes the right to free access to trade in goods but not in services such as shipping, banking, and insurance. Commission proposals to establish the right of such access in maritime transport would thus have general significance. Moreover, they would aid in the process of intra-community concentration of capital in shipping, which the commission views as essential. However, France, Italy, and Greece, while favoring measures such as the Brussels Package and action to monitor competition from the Soviet-bloc liner fleet, are less enthusiastic than Britain about the possibility of liberalization within the EC, which would render national protectionist measures, including cabotage, illegal.

Conclusion

From the perspective of Western Europe, the history of shipping since 1945 has been a series of rearguard actions in defense of the status quo. Understanding the limitations of purely national policies, the nations of Western Europe have sought as a bloc to repel commercial and political challenges from the Third World, from the Soviet bloc and, above all, from the United States. Western Europe has fought on various terrains: in the United Nations, with support from maritime unions; in the OECD against the United States; and, once again, in the United Nations against LDCs, where its support from the United States has been limited.

European countries have a set of roughly similar maritime interests and objectives; for this reason, Western Europe or the European Community can be considered a maritime "bloc." Yet there are significant differences in outlook among the nations of the EC, resulting from differences in domestic structure. This renders the formulation of EC policy problematic, because the implementation of significant policies inevitably creates winners and losers within the community. That a European shipping policy is being elaborated is evidence of the intensity of global conflict in shipping and the seriousness with which it is viewed in Western Europe.

The most visible challenge to European shipping has stemmed from LDCs. However, as Chapters 6 and 7 indicated, one reason the Third World challenge transcended the level of rhetoric was its partial convergence with American objectives. Ironically, Europe's eventual conciliatory response to the Third World has not resolved global conflict. Rather, by compelling the United States to formulate specific policies and by bringing the issue of closed versus open conferences to the forefront, it has served to deepen the division between the United States and Europe. The European Community, unlike either the Third World or the United States, would like to retain the principle of privatization. It fears that the regulation or opening of conferences will destroy the traditional ability of conferences to determine freight rates and market shares. By permitting outsiders to enter trades, regulation will pave the way for cross-trader competition in trades that European firms now dominate. Faced with this situation, Western Europe prefers the certainties of the UNCTAD Code of Conduct to the potential dangers of an open-conference regime.

The case of shipping illustrates the contradictory role played by the EC in the international political economy and the great difficulties that this body faces in the period of declining hegemony. During the hegemonic phase the EC itself represented a deliberate attempt by the United States to create an institution that could defend Western European states against the overwhelming force of the American economy. The EC is thus simultaneously a creature of American hegemony, requiring American support, and a citadel of defense against external challenges, including that of the United States. However, as American support for Western Europe's traditional principles and practices diminishes, it becomes more difficult, yet increasingly necessary, to coordinate national policies.

9

The Future of International Liner Shipping

Since the introduction of the steamship in the second half of the nineteenth century, international liner shipping has passed through a number of distinct phases. The period from 1880 to 1900 saw the rapid formation of liner conferences dominated by Western European firms and above all by the British. The interwar period was one of increasing maritime nationalism, characterized by the generalized expansion of state activity and the debut of the United States as a major shipping power. From World War II to the mid-1960s, the maritime powers of Western Europe reconsolidated their position in liner shipping under the umbrella of American power. Japanese shipping and shipbuilding also expanded rapidly during this time. Since the mid-1960s, however, international liner shipping has grown increasingly unstable under the combined impulses of containerization; the expansion of Third World and, to a lesser extent, Soviet-bloc shipping; and a new dynamism in U.S. shipping.

The preceding chapter indicated the great problems faced by the maritime powers of Western Europe both in articulating a common shipping policy and in preserving a strong European voice in world shipping affairs.

As the principle of privatization comes under attack, Western Europe is placed on the defensive. This chapter considers the role played by the new actors and challengers in international liner shipping: the Third World, Japan, and the United States. It concludes that less developed countries are very weak in this sector, despite the UNCTAD Code of Conduct for Liner Conferences. Japan, although quantitatively important, is unlikely to play a crucial political role. Rather, it is capable of adapting to the new regime just as it flourished under the old. The U.S. Shipping Act of 1984 heralds the new role and changed purpose of the United States in international liner policy. The act will have a major influence on the future of international liner shipping, perhaps even overshadowing the UNCTAD Code of Conduct.

The Limits of Third World Maritime Power

Despite the passage of the UNCTAD Code of Conduct and the elaboration of extensive cargo protection laws, less developed countries as a whole have been able to do little more than arrest the relative decline of tonnage they experienced during the 1950s and 1960s. The LDCs' maritime goal for the United Nations Second Development Decade was extremely modest: 10 percent of world tonnage. Between 1970 and 1984 the participation of LDCs in world trade remained approximately the same. By weight, exports declined from 62.8 to 48.5 percent of the world total. This decline was compensated for by an increase in imports, from 16.7 to 25.4 percent. Between 1970 and 1984 the Third World share of all shipping increased from 6.7 percent to 16.5 percent, including 14.5 percent of container tonnage.[1] Fleet expansion in some Third World states has been impressive. Twelve newly industrializing countries possess approximately 78 percent of total Third World liner tonnage. Latin Americans own 28 percent of the total. As Table 24 shows, container capacity has grown among developing countries. However, 98.3 percent of such capacity is owned by the newly industrializing countries in Asia: Hong Kong, South Korea, Singapore, Taiwan, and Indonesia. Taiwan's Evergreen Line, financed in part by Japanese interests, is becoming a major force in Pacific trades and plans to establish "round the world" services.

1. UNCTAD, *Review of Maritime Transport, 1984* (Geneva: United Nations, 1985).

Table 24.   Distribution of Capacity of Fully Cellular Container Ships, 1980 – 84
              (% share)

	Capacity		
	1980	1982	1984
Developed market	76.0%	69.0%	64.0%
Open registry	11.1%	15.8%	12.0%
Socialist countries of Eastern Europe and Asia (People's Republic of China)	3.1%	2.7%	4.0%
Less developed countries	7.6%	9.0%	14.5%
Unallocated	2.2%	3.5%	5.5%
World total	100.0%	100.0%	100.0%

SOURCES: UNCTAD, *Review of Maritime Transport, 1983* (Geneva: United Nations, 1984); UNCTAD, *Review of Maritime Transport, 1984* (Geneva: United Nations, 1985).

The maritime objectives of LDCs must be assessed in the context of overall development strategy and, in particular, of the effect of shipping policy on the balance of payments and general economic development. To comprehend the impact of shipping expansion, empirical analyses of individual countries and value judgments concerning various modes of development are required. In all countries where merchant fleets are domestically owned, payments to national shipowners represent a net decrease in outflow of foreign exchange. However, the immediate gains may be offset by the cost of buying ships and expertise from abroad, or inefficiencies (or discrimination) necessitating protectionism or subsidies. Moreover, shipping is highly capital-intensive; capital invested in shipping as an "infant industry" might be more productive—and therefore have a more positive effect on the balance of payments—if applied elsewhere. (These considerations, of course, apply equally to developed and less developed countries.)[2]

The infant-industry argument is most convincing when applied to those countries where shipping is linked to a general maritime expansion including shipbuilding and repair. Here shipping is directly related to the

2. See R. O. Goss, "Investment in Shipping and the Balance of Payments: A Case Study of Import Substitution Policy," in R. O. Goss, ed., *Studies in Maritime Economics* (London: Cambridge University Press, 1968), pp. 46–60. For a general discussion of this issue, see R. T. Brown, *Transport and the Economic Integration of Latin America* (Washington, D.C.: Brookings Institution, 1966), pp. 107–9. See also UNCTAD, *Establishment or Expansion of Merchant Marines in Developing Countries,* TD/26/Supp. 1 (Geneva: United Nations, 1967).

development of basic industries, especially steel. Given the relatively high degree of labor intensity and the availability of foreign technical aid (and capital), Third World shipbuilding industries can compete favorably on the world market. There is, in fact, a high correlation between the development of shipping and of shipbuilding in the newly industrializing countries. In theory it is possible that even in these countries investment in shipping does not represent the best use of capital. Moreover, the shipbuilding industries of some less developed countries are closely linked to developed states, notably Japan. In practice, however, the barriers to expansion in shipping are probably lower than in most other sectors of the world economy. As Adib Al-Jadir, former head of UNCTAD's Shipping Division, noted before UNCTAD V in Manila,

> several spokesmen have suggested to us that instead of expanding into shipping, developing countries should expand into some other industrial sector which is more appropriate to their abilities. In reality, though, developing countries are being prevented from expanding in practically all other industrial sectors by reason of tariff and non-tariff barriers.[3]

Strong opponents of conferences in the 1960s, many LDCs have now become their ardent defenders. The UNCTAD Code endorses the deferred rebate, the ultimate conference weapon. At the same time, development of the shipping industry as an end in itself appears to have overtaken the original objective of influencing freight rates and trading patterns. Recent data, reproduced in Table 25, seem to document the persistence of a discriminatory freight rate structure. But these data must be interpreted with some caution: discrepancies in freight rates between the Third World and advanced countries reflect, in part, the relatively cheaper transport costs of raw materials, a factor that became more noticeable as the cost of oil rose. Moreover, although it is true that the development of Third World merchant fleets may provide their governments and shippers with the power to negotiate effectively with conferences over rates and services, protectionism may also contribute to high freight rates damaging to Third World exports and consumers. Table 25 thus reflects the persistence of an inter-

3. *Seatrade* (July 1979), p. 164. "Where a country meets import quotas, tariffs, or inconvertible currencies which prevent it from adopting the most economical way of earning or saving foreign exchange, recourse to a second-best solution, the use of domestic resources uneconomically to economize on foreign exchange, becomes an attractive policy" (Stanley G. Sturmey, *Shipping Economics: Collected Papers* [London: Macmillan, 1976], p. 189.

Table 25.   Freight as a Percentage of Import Value, 1970 – 83

	1970	1977	1980	1981	1982	1983
Developed countries	7.3	5.6	5.6	5.4	5.3	5.4
Less developed countries	10.0	10.1	10.4	10.0	10.6	10.8
World total	7.7	6.6	6.6	6.6	6.6	6.6

SOURCES: UNCTAD, *Review of Maritime Transport, 1980* (Geneva: United Nations, 1981); *Review of Maritime Transport, 1984* (Geneva: United Nations, 1985).

national division of labor in which less developed countries export raw materials and import manufactured goods. Changes in shipping have in some respects reinforced this structure. Shipping was originally viewed as a major force for Latin American and Asian economic integration. In practice, however, the shipping strategies of less developed countries continue to be shaped by external forces. For example, as George Lauriat has noted regarding the Association of Southeast Asian Nations (ASEAN), "Each country has developed its own maritime policy which is frequently at cross purposes with its neighbors. . . . The number of ASEAN-owned ships will increase but the uncoordinated nature of these purchases will not effectively alter ASEAN dependence on foreign shipping."[4]

In adapting to the needs of the conference system, less developed countries are compelled to adopt highly capital-intensive container systems, entailing the use of scarce foreign currency. This involves the transformation of the infrastructure of transport through integration into a wider world network, and it necessitates costly investment in port systems in which the use of labor is decreased. There are certainly substantial benefits to be enjoyed from the conversion to container-based transport systems, for gains in productivity facilitate modernization. Nevertheless, introduction of containers and the whole package of multimodal sea/rail systems is not without costs, including the displacement of labor and the uneven development resulting from concentration of activity at a few major ports. Of course, these costs also occur in developed countries, but with less impact on the economy as a whole.[5]

4. George Lauriat, "Self-Interest Becalms ASEAN Maritime Plan," *Far Eastern Economic Review,* 15 July 1977, p. 29.

5. George Lauriat, "Containerisation Is Now Much More Effective," *Far Eastern Economic Review,* 9 February 1979, pp. 35–37. See also UNCTAD, *Multimodal Transport and*

Global Impact of the U.S. Shipping Act of 1984

The passage of the U.S. Shipping Act of 1984 was the culmination of a decade of legislative attempts to simplify American maritime law and policy and to institute reforms demanded by the advent of the container age. The act does not, contrary to the wishes of Western European shipowners, represent a fundamental departure from America's traditionally strong regulatory stance. It does, however, seem likely to reinforce the power of American exporters and large, independent liner operators at the expense of those lines whose ability to compete favorably is now reduced by their inability to establish closed conferences.

The U.S. Shipping Act of 1984 is not a "regime document" like the UNCTAD Code of Conduct; it does not consciously seek to articulate basic international principles. Nevertheless, in practice the act may prove to be much more influential than the code. In contrast to previous legislative efforts such as the U.S. Merchant Marine Act of 1970, the 1984 act is intended to be global in scope. It will not only serve to promote—or attempt to promote—the expansion of United States flag merchant shipping within the confines of a given regime, as previous legislation did, but it will also have a great influence over the shape of the new international regime. Given the weight of the United States in international commerce, it thus represents an unprecedented challenge to Western Europe and Japan.

Chapter 7 described the progressive intrusion of the Department of Justice and regulatory philosophy in liner shipping, beginning with the Isbrandtsen, Svenska, and Carnation cases and culminating in felony indictments of a number of Western European, Japanese, and American liner operators in 1978. The progressive tightening of U.S. antitrust standards facilitated change in the liner sector by encouraging major American lines to act independently of the conference system. Nevertheless, the enforcement of antitrust legislation provoked great conflict within the American

---

Containerization: Guidelines on the Introduction of Containerization and Multimodal Transport and the Modernization and Improvement of the Infrastructure of Developing Countries, TD/B/C.4/238 (Geneva: United Nations, 1982). For an optimistic survey, see Ross Robinson, "Containerization in Ports of Third World Asia: An Overview of Present Patterns and the Direction of Future Growth," *Journal of Maritime Policy and Management* 12 (October–December 1985).

maritime sector. Not only European and Japanese but also some American lines favored closed conferences and therefore desired immunity from the antitrust provisions of U.S. shipping law. The 1984 act followed several unsuccessful attempts to reform U.S. maritime law to provide safeguards for conferences and prevent the Department of Justice from directly intervening in international shipping affairs. However, although the act introduced important reforms and perhaps eliminates the tactical role of the Department of Justice, it is not a mandate for closed conferences.

The reform elements of the act are significant. It greatly eases antitrust restrictions. The notorious "public interest" requirement, which placed the burden of proof on the shipowner, has been eliminated. The new act simply "establishes a threshold for prompt approval of most generally accepted joint conduct in shipping."[6] The FMC, although still charged with regulatory duties, is no longer authorized to disapprove agreements between lines. It can either approve such agreements or else file suit, allowing federal courts to have the final say. Thus the burden of proof of compliance shifts from the ship operator to the FMC. Finally, conferences are granted the right to establish intermodal tariffs.[7]

The Shipping Act of 1984 has been welcomed by European and Japanese as well as American shipowners, primarily because it does ease antitrust standards. The bill will undoubtedly provide relief from the Department of Justice, thus permitting conferences greater latitude in their commercial activities. Nevertheless, in the long run the act is unlikely to bridge the gap between the United States and Europe over the issue of closed conferences. Indeed, it will support the competitive strategies of the largest United States flag liner firms. By protecting the commercial strategies of independent shipowners, the bill may accelerate the concentration of United States flag liner shipping. In the long run, therefore, it may pave the way for the formation of giant international shipping consortia in which American firms play a leading role.

6. U.S. Congress, House, *Shipping Act of 1984 — Conference Report 98-600,* 98th Cong., 2d sess., 23 February 1984, p. 32.

7. On the role of the FMC, see ibid., particularly Section 6. According to the *Conference Report,* Section 6(g) and (h), "The conferees agree that selective provisions limiting joint ventures or pooling agreements might discourage arrangements that often enhance the quality, frequency, or efficiency of transportation services. These agreements, just as any others, should be permitted unless the FMC demonstrates that they are likely to cause concrete competitive harm."

The 1984 act was a "shippers' bill"; that is, shippers contributed to its drafting and lobbied for its passage. Their support, absent in previous legislative efforts, explains the ultimate passage of the bill into law. The growing concern of American shippers for competitive ocean freight rates and services and their greater desire to exercise surveillance over global shipping issues are major developments of the 1980s.[8] As a result, the 1984 act, in contrast to earlier reform proposals, contains strong safeguards for shippers. First, shippers are to be permitted to sign "service contracts" with conferences. Such contracts, made possible by the easing of antitrust standards, will work to the benefit of large shippers; smaller shippers will be permitted to combine and negotiate jointly with conferences. Service contracts will thus supersede loyalty contracts, striking a balance between shippers and shipowners. For their part, conferences will be allowed to undertake "service rationalization," which may, in the long run, lead to greater competition among ports and, ultimately, to abandonment of the least competitive ports. The second major safeguard for shippers is the right of independent action for shipowners: conferences may not prevent members from engaging in independent action. The resulting competition may work to the benefit of shippers, especially those in a strong bargaining position by virtue of large volumes to be transported.[9]

The 1984 act clearly preserves the right of independent action, not only in U.S. trades but also in trades between third countries. This global orientation, reflecting the interest and ability of the large American lines to expand their share of cross-trades and initiate "round the world" services, has brought the United States into conflict with the European Community and some Third World countries. The act provides the FMC with power to take action against foreign shipowners or governments that deny U.S.

8. Peter A. Friedman and John A. Devierno, "The Shipping Act of 1984: The Shift from Government Regulation to 'Shipper's Regulation,'" *Journal of Maritime Law and Commerce* 15 (July 1984). On the specific role of shippers, see esp. Tony Beargie, "Future Role of Shippers," *American Shipper* 26 (August 1984). One indication of the growing involvement of shippers is the formation in 1984 of Shippers for Competitive Ocean Transportation (SCOT). Heavily oriented toward market principles, including the right of independent action, SCOT was formed explicitly to influence U.S. maritime policy.

9. Beargie, "Future Role of Shippers," p. 3. Conference agreements must "provide that any member of the conference may take independent action on any rate or service item required to be filed in a tariff . . . upon not more than 10 calendar days notice to the conference and that the conference will include the new rate or service item in its tariff for use by that member" (*Shipping Act of 1984*, Section 5[8]).

shipowners access to trade. It specifically gives the FMC power to impose sanctions in the event of discriminatory treatment of United States flag vessels in the form of fees, charges, requirements, or restrictions that hinder competitive access; cargo reservation that prevents "reasonable competitive access to cargoes by U.S. vessels"; and "predatory practices," including closed conferences using the deferred rebate or employing fighting ships.[10]

The granting of extraterritorial power to the FMC is clear evidence of the new intentions of the United States in international liner shipping, including the enhanced competitive abilities of American liner firms and the determination of the U.S. government to sustain a competitive environment that corresponds to the interests of these lines. The 1984 act does not seem likely to resolve basic conflict between Europe and the United States. The act will, to be sure, mollify European lines because it will restrict, although not eliminate, the role of the Department of Justice, particularly in U.S. trades. However, the act will also pave the way for further expansion of U.S. liner shipping, thereby providing a challenge to the traditional maritime nations and some protectionist Third World states.

Japan as a Maritime Power

Japan enjoys high stature in world freight markets by virtue of its prominence as both consumer and major provider of international shipping services. Nevertheless, Japan has not received a great deal of attention here, least of all in the analysis of liner shipping. This lack of attention matches Japan's low-key approach to international shipping politics. Japan is a major shipping nation, ranking first in overall tonnage among advanced industrial states, yet it has sought to minimize its political role. This policy is unlikely to change, for a number of reasons. First, after its defeat in World War II Japan was compelled to shape its maritime law and policy to accommodate the dictates of the international regime, and Japanese shipping continues to be flexible. Second, Japan is a major consumer as well as operator of shipping services, and its shipping firms are closely linked to

10. *Shipping Act of 1984*, Section 10. See also Tony Beargie, "Long Arm of the New FMC," *American Shipper* 26 (July 1984).

industrial and export interests. Consequently, Japanese lines are favored with a large cargo base to which they enjoy privileged access. Moreover, divisions between shippers and shipowners do not figure prominently (although they exist) in domestic maritime debates. Third, as a major exporter of industrial products and consumer of raw materials, Japan is careful to remain on good terms with the Third World. Like West Germany, Japan has chosen a path of conciliation concerning the UNCTAD Code of Conduct for Liner Conferences. Japan's prominence as an exporter of ships reinforces the desire for compromise: if Third World countries are to purchase ships from Japan, they must be able to operate them at a profit. Japan has been instrumental in the development of shipbuilding in South Korea and Brazil, two of the largest Third World shipping nations.

As indicated in Chapter 2, Japanese shipping grew dramatically before World War II. After the war, Japan quickly reestablished its bulk and liner fleets, with shipping closely linked to shipbuilding. It was able to utilize Hong Kong capital and the Liberian flag of convenience to create an economical and reliable system for transportation of bulk commodities and oil. In liner shipping, industrial evolution and government policy led to a concentration of ownership and increasingly close cooperation between exporters and shipping companies.

The organic relationship between state and big business in Japan was instrumental in reasserting Japanese maritime power. In 1963 the Law for Shipping Reconstruction organized ninety-five shipping firms into six giant groups totaling 10 million dwt, over 80 percent of Japanese tonnage. These measures were outlined in a White Paper issued by the Ministry of Transportation in 1964; the government described them as the "turning point in Japan's shipping history which will from then onwards regain brightness."[11] The Development Bank of Japan made the sun shine by initiating a two-tier loan policy that, by granting lower interest rates to Japanese shipowners, gave them privileged access to Japanese shipyards.[12] The concentration of Japanese shipping was assured by the stipulation that only the merged groups would have access to investment financing assistance.

11. Erling D. Naess, *Tanker Industry: Problems and Prospects* (Bergen: Institute for Shipping Research, 1965), p. 25. For a summary of Japan's postwar shipping, see H. Sasaki, *The Shipping Industry in Japan* (Geneva: I.L.O., 1972).
12. Naess, *Tanker Industry*, pp. 18–20.

This type of aid was the principal engine of fleet expansion in the 1960s and early 1970s. The Japanese government provided considerable aid in the form of interest subsidies and tax allowances. This support supplemented aid to shipbuilding through low-interest loans by the government-owned Export-Import Bank. Between 1971 and 1975 government aid to shipbuilding was approximately $200 million per year. During this period shipbuilding was one of Japan's leading export industries.[13]

Japanese shipping law has reflected American influence: first, the American occupation, with its emphasis on breaking the formal power of cartels; later, the American preoccupation with antitrust provisions pertaining to shipping conferences. However, despite both this anti-cartel legacy and some strongly worded anti-cartel legislation, Japan's maritime outlook more closely resembles that of Western Europe than that of the United States. Although the Anti-Monopoly Law appears, in principle, to prohibit combinations such as liner conferences, in practice they are sanctioned by the government. The Maritime Transport Act establishes the minister of transportation as regulator of conferences; and the Federal Trade Commission retains the right to administer regulation if there is "undue enhancement of freight rates."[14]

Despite the dense and contradictory legal maze, inspired in part by the U.S. example Japan has followed the closed conference system. To the extent that Japan has sought to defend closed conferences in the international political arena, it has done so primarily through its membership in CENSA and the CSG. However, Japan has sought to remain on good terms with Third World maritime nations. Although the Japanese government initially opposed the UNCTAD Code of Conduct for Liner Conferences, it did not play a major role in UNCTAD deliberations. Japan has delayed formal ratification, but it appears willing to accede to the code when its domestic legislation is revised. Moreover, despite its membership in CENSA and CSG, Japan is likely to eventually ratify the code without the disapplication provisions of the Brussels Package. Japan can accept the code, including its

13. U.S. Department of Commerce, Maritime Administration, Office of Policy and Planning, *The Maritime Aids of the Six Major Maritime Nations* (Washington, D.C.: G.P.O., 1977), pp. II–8, III–15, 16.

14. Ronald G. Brown and Akinori Uesugi, "Japanese Regulation of Ocean Freight Shipments," *Journal of Maritime Law and Commerce* 11, no. 3 (April 1980), p. 297.

protectionist elements, although it is reluctant to sacrifice its competitive advantages to the code's cargo-sharing provisions.[15]

The United States and Japan

Because Japanese shipping firms have favored closed conferences and self-regulation, Japan has experienced many of the same frustrations and difficulties in dealing with the United States as its Western European counterparts have. Japanese shipowners were among those indicted for illegal rebating in 1977. Correspondingly, American efforts to establish greater control over international shipping have been partly a result of friction with Japan. As a result of American pressure, the Japanese government has sought to play a greater role in the regulation of conferences, particularly over the level of freight rates. Some evidence suggests that greater regulatory activity by the Federal Trade Commission has resulted in lower freight rates.[16]

The future of Japanese shipping will depend greatly on American policies. Primarily as a result of American pressure, including the determination to maintain or enhance access to trades for independent lines, the nature of the Japanese shipping industry is changing. Since 1968 the six major Japanese lines have cooperated closely in Japanese–U.S. West Coast trades, operating a space charter agreement and pooling revenues. However, this degree of cooperation has antagonized American independents. In late 1984 the Federal Maritime Commission notified the Japanese companies that a further five-year exemption from antitrust law had been made impossible by passage of the U.S. Shipping Act of 1984. Such exemption was to be granted only if the six lines agreed to discontinue pooling revenue and to freeze the level of carrying capacity.[17]

American pressure has coincided with competitive forces within the Japanese economy and shipping industry. The Japanese Council for the Rationalization of Shipping and Shipbuilding Industries, supported by the

15. Ibid., p. 317; Japan, Ministry of Transport, *The Current Situation of Japanese Shipping, 1985* (Tokyo: Japan Maritime Development Association, 1985), pp. 32–36.
16. Brown and Uesugi, "Japanese Regulation of Ocean Freight Shipments," p. 316.
17. For surveys of Japanese shipping policy, see "Shipping 84," *Far Eastern Economic Review,* 16 February 1984; and "Shipping 85," *Far Eastern Economic Review,* 14 February 1985.

Ministry of Transportation, contends that a greater degree of competitiveness should be introduced into Japanese liner shipping. Japanese firms should operate independently and be permitted the freedom to enter into agreements with foreign lines. In the long run, therefore, it is possible that external and internal pressures will lead to the further concentration of the liner sector and to closer cooperation between Japanese and American firms.[18]

At the present time Japan does not appear likely to seek to play a more visible role in international shipping politics. Although its maritime industries flourished under the postwar regime, its large cargo base, its relative lack of presence in cross-trades, its interest in Third World shipbuilding and shipping, and its adaptability make it possible for Japan to retain its quantitative role in world shipping. Since the 1973–74 oil crisis, Japanese flag liner tonnage has carried a steadily decreasing amount of Japanese cargo. However, much of the difference has been made up by Japanese-operated flag-of-convenience and charter tonnage or Third World shipping firms in which Japanese capital maintains an interest (for example, Evergreen of Taiwan). Ultimately, U.S. shipping policy, rather than the UNCTAD Code of Conduct, will provide the greatest challenge to Japan and prove to be the catalyst for internal change and adaptation.

Conclusion

Chapters 6–9 have described the development of conflict among the major power blocs in international liner shipping since the mid-1960s. The difficult birth of the new order and the role of the United States as midwife—however reluctant and inept—confirm the central hypothesis of this book: although many factors must be included in a comprehensive analysis of what is happening in world shipping, American power and interest are central to all significant developments. Neither less developed countries nor the European Community appears capable of establishing or maintaining a regime that is acceptable to the international community and also corresponds to their basic interests. Although each bloc disagrees with American views, the emerging principles and practices governing

18. On internal and external influences on Japanese shipping, see "Japanese Lines Feel the Heat," *American Shipper* 26, no. 10 (October 1984).

liner shipping reflect American domestic structures and are consistent with America's post-hegemonic approach to foreign economic policy. Change in the liner sector contrasts with relative stability in the bulk sector, lending further support to the argument: where the United States favors stability, the challenge from less developed countries has proved to be very weak.

Under conditions of hegemonic decline, there is a closer correspondence between American domestic structures and the international regime. The U.S. Shipping Act of 1984 gives legal expression to the most important changes that have occurred in both U.S. and international shipping and signifies America's intent to establish a regime that is more consistent with American traditions and interests. The 1984 act does not simply seek to promote the U.S. merchant marine in a given international environment. In addition, the regulatory power it confers on the government enables it to restructure the environment according to the preferences of the leading shippers and liner firms: hence the extraterritorial dimension of American law and policy, which provokes such concern among trading partners. Together with the virtual abolition of subsidies to shipbuilding, the act indicates the "internationalization" of U.S. liner shipping and the corresponding penetration of the American government into conference decision-making.

By the mid-1980s the UNCTAD Code of Conduct for Liner Conferences was beginning to show its age. The document, drafted in the early 1970s, at a time when conferences were strong, did not clearly specify whether its provisions applied to non-conference lines acting as outsiders. Yet as conferences have become progressively weaker and more disorganized, the code has lost much of its relevance. According to Stanley Sturmey, one of its principal defenders, within a decade the code will no longer be meaningful because the conference system it was supposed to organize will have been transformed beyond recognition.[19]

Clearly, the heyday of closed conferences is at an end. Nevertheless, although conference power has been curbed, it would be premature to declare that it will never recover. Already new consortia are forming, even as

19. Stanley G. Sturmey, "The UNCTAD Code of Conduct for Liner Conferences: A 1985 View," *Journal of Maritime Policy and Management* 13 (October–December 1985). Sturmey believes the code still has an important role to play as a temporary set of rules and guidelines to effect a smooth transition to a code that addresses the new situation.

international liner shipping is concentrated in fewer hands. If historical experience is a guide, once a period of intense competition has occurred it is
possible that the larger survivors will eventually seek once again to close off
trades to outsiders through various de facto loyalty devices and that governments—including that of the United States—will once again acquiesce
in these practices. The major, irreversible change in liner shipping is not
the legal blunting of conferences as such but, rather, the ascendancy of the
principle of regulation, which is a natural result of the expanded role of
American shipping and the American government in the regime.

10

Flags of Convenience: The New Assault

The stability of the postwar regime in the bulk sector rested, as was argued in Chapter 4, on the capitulation of the "unholy alliance" of European shipowners and international seamen's unions to the United States government and multinational corporations on the issue of flags of convenience. Trade unions were demoralized by legal rulings in favor of open registries at The Hague and in the United States Supreme Court, and by the early 1960s union opposition to their use had become sporadic and ineffective. European shipowners and governments adapted to, and in some cases took advantage of, the opportunities created by the regime. Thus by the 1960s opposition focused on the effects of open registries rather than on their existence. Efforts were made to unionize open registry ships and to enforce stricter safety and environmental standards. In the late 1960s environmentalists, inspired by the spate of oil spills, joined the fray. Similarly, trade unions adopted a strategy of fighting local skirmishes over union certificates on individual ships rather than attempting to recreate worldwide strike opposition.

Capital inevitably flowed into Liberian and Panamanian registry shipping, and into a host of newer open registries such as Cyprus and the Bahamas. Given America's diplomatic successes, Western European and Japanese shipowners faced increasingly strong pressure to follow their American counterparts if they wished to survive in such a competitive climate. As will be shown in this chapter, Britain gained access to open registries through Hong Kong. Japan, similarly, took advantage of flags of convenience either directly, or indirectly, through links to Hong Kong. More recently, a number of Western European shipowners, led by the West Germans, have begun to transfer tonnage to open registries.

Use of flags of convenience (FOCs) exacerbated the tendency toward a cyclical economy in the shipping industry by encouraging shipowners to invest heavily in new tonnage during booms. At the same time, the availability of open registries encouraged many governments to increase subsidies and other forms of aid in order to preserve a sizable national flag fleet. This also had the effect of stimulating shipbuilding artificially, contributing to excess capacity.[1]

UNCTAD and the New Attack

Third World states are heavily dependent on raw-materials exports. With the exception of a few semi-peripheral or newly industrializing countries that have made a partial transition to industrialization, LDCs are more involved with bulk shipping than with liner trades. Even the most advanced of the newly industrializing countries, such as Brazil and India, remain heavily dependent on raw-materials exports. Consequently, the specter of flag discrimination has always been present in this sector. It has exerted a subtle influence over UNCTAD's work ever since the Committee on Shipping was set up in 1964, although the initial thrust of the committee's work was directed to liner shipping. OECD governments and shipowners were relieved when this sector was ignored at the first UNCTAD in 1964. They hoped that a favorable settlement in the liner trades would satisfy Third World aspirations, leaving the bulk owners to proceed with business as usual.[2]

1. UNCTAD, *Action on the Question of Open Registries*, TD/B/C.4/220 (Geneva: United Nations, 1981), p. 11.

2. Dag Tresselt, *The Controversy over the Division of Labor in International Seaborne Transport* (Bergen: Institute for Shipping Research, 1970), p. 14.

However, in 1974, UNCTAD's Committee on Shipping instructed the secretariat to examine "the economic consequences for international shipping of the existence or lack of a genuine link between vessel and flag of registry."[3] Following reports from the secretariat, an Ad Hoc Intergovernmental Work Group convened in 1977. In February 1978, it concluded that a "genuine link" between ship and country of registry would require economic ties such as ownership or recruitment of labor.[4] This conclusion, rejecting the accepted interpretation that had grown out of the 1958 Law of the Sea Conference, served notice of a new effort to abolish or "phase out" flags of convenience.

The Group of 77's efforts in the early stages coincided with expressions of opposition to flags of convenience as EC policy was being formulated. France, supported by Belgium and Italy, was asserting its Grand Design, which included the issue of flags of convenience. In both 1974 and 1975, the French government presented to the UNCTAD secretariat its opposition to open registries. At the same time, an OECD report on flags of convenience published data that revealed a significantly higher casualty rate for such vessels. Finally, trade unions in the EC sought to capitalize on the greater attention to open registries in the European Parliament and Economic and Social Council.[5] These efforts illustrate the residue of opposition to FOCs not just from European labor but also within governmental and business circles.

As late as 1979 the Ad Hoc Merchant Shipping Committee of the European Parliament strongly condemned flags of convenience. It reflected French attitudes and was heavily slanted to trade union views. The committee advocated ratification of the UNCTAD Code, enforcement of safety standards throughout the European Community, and shipbuilding subsidies. It protested that shipowners "treat flag of convenience crews in despotic fashion since they are deprived of all rights . . . tapping the enormous reserves of cheap labor in the Third World."[6] The committee also

3. UNCTAD Committee on Shipping, "Resolution," 9 August 1974.
4. UNCTAD Committee on Shipping, "Resolution," 10 February 1978.
5. UNCTAD Committee on Shipping, "Resolution," 9 August 1974; UNCTAD, *Report of the Committee on Shipping, Seventh Session* (Geneva: United Nations, November 1975), pp. 14–15; OECD, Maritime Transport Committee, *Maritime Transport, 1974* (Paris: OECD, 1975), pp. 88–105.
6. European Parliament, Ad Hoc Merchant Shipping Committee, *EEC Shipping Policy— Flags of Convenience* (Brussels: European Community, 1979), p. 10.

emphasized the high proportion of tanker tonnage controlled by multi-national corporations: "This, together with the fact that certain countries have insufficient national tanker capacity, means that in emergencies these member states are dependent on the multinationals for their vital energy supplies."[7] In 1979, the EC gave rhetorical support for cargo-sharing in the bulk trades in the Lomé Convention, which states that "the Community recognizes the aspirations of ACP [African, Caribbean, and Pacific] states to have a greater share in the carriage of bulk cargoes."[8]

Before UNCTAD V in Manila, in 1979, the UNCTAD secretariat took the logical step of linking the question of open registries to cargo-sharing in the bulk trades. At Arusha in February 1979, the Group of 77 asserted the principle that a country's participation in transportation should be proportionate to that country's participation in foreign trade. In a report prepared for UNCTAD V, the secretariat told delegates that

> the traditional maritime nations have conceded the right of developing countries to participate in the liner trades, which account for 20% of world cargoes, but, except in very general and indirect terms, they have not recognized the rights of developing countries to participate in world bulk trades, which account for 80% of world cargoes, and in practice many developed market economy countries (which are the major importers of bulk cargoes) appear to treat their developing trading partner countries (which are mainly exporters) as if they had no right to participate in their transport.[9]

Resolution 120(V), acknowledging the "complexity" of bulk markets, instructed the secretariat to carry out studies of the repercussions of phasing out flags of convenience and to identify legal mechanisms that could facilitate this process.

The resulting studies were discussed by the Ad Hoc Group in 1980, when opposition from the OECD Group B, except for France, began to crystallize. The secretariat noted that beneficial or "real" ownership of open registry tonnage was limited to a handful of states. It argued that phasing out open registries would not involve repatriation of ships to

7. Ibid., p. 117.

8. Quoted in Anna Bredimas and John G. Tzoannis, "In Search of a Common Shipping Policy for the European Community," *Journal of Common Market Studies* 20 (December 1981), p. 111.

9. UNCTAD, *Merchant Fleet Development*, TD/222 (Manila: United Nations, 1979), p. 15.

countries of ownership, because of the wide discrepancies in labor costs (or, in Greece, shortage of labor). Thus, it could be claimed that flags of convenience impeded the functioning of the law of comparative advantage. If they were abolished, vessel ownership would eventually devolve on less developed countries: "More than any other single measure in international shipping, phasing out of open registries would contribute to the implementation of the New International Economic Order."[10]

The Working Group recommended a number of measures to achieve an "orderly transfer" of tonnage during the "phasing out" period.[11] First, *host* governments should close their open registries over a ten-year period by insisting on equity participation in all registered vessels; they should gradually seek employment of their nationals; and they should remove substandard vessels and improve safety inspection procedures. Second, *home* governments should gather information on ownership of flag-of-convenience tonnage and should restrain nationals from utilizing open registries unless they complied with the actions of host states, and shipowners from home governments should help less developed countries to own and operate tonnage. Third, *labor-supplying* countries should seek to attract external investment in national fleets, including joint venture capital. In addition, they should seek technical assistance to train officers, while gradually withdrawing labor from open registry vessels.

Finally, the Working Group noted the desirability of establishing an international convention on flags of registry. Such a convention would confront the same issues as had the ILC and Law of the Sea Convention of 1958. It would establish the degree of ownership necessary for a host flag, the identification of beneficial owners, and the extent of national employment under a national flag, and it would attempt to create an international consensus. The Working Group noted the difficulties inherent in such a task: the process would be time-consuming, and "even more serious is the question of whether it would be realistic to expect countries to reach agreement on a standard set of rules for registration at this stage of developments."[12]

10. UNCTAD, *The Repercussions of Phasing Out Open Registries,* TD/B/C.4/AC.1/5 (Geneva: United Nations, 1979), p. 15.
11. UNCTAD, *Legal Mechanisms for Regulating the Operation of Open-Registry Fleets During the Phasing Out Period,* TD/B/C.4/AC.1/6 (Geneva: United Nations, 1979), pp. 4–5.
12. Ibid., p. 10.

Since 1980, UNCTAD has been paralyzed by bloc conflict on the question of phasing out open registries. In general, divisions have not penetrated the traditional blocs, as they have in liner shipping. With French dissent, the OECD countries have sought refuge in the formally free characteristics of bulk shipping. Their spokesmen have challenged the assumption that if flags of convenience were phased out, tonnage would gravitate to the Third World. Far from contributing to instability, as the OEEC once asserted and UNCTAD now claims: "Open registry is responsive to free-market requirements and enforces the balance of supply over demand. . . . Phasing out open registries will destroy the inherent efficiency of the industry and rob developing countries of the many advantages readily available to their profitable participation."[13] The OECD has recommended that the developing countries report on specific barriers to entry. At the same time it reiterates its support for greater vigilance in safety standards and pollution prevention.

The UNCTAD secretariat identifies open registries as a major cause of the related sectoral crises in shipping and shipbuilding. The fiscal policies of Western countries, especially the United States, encourage owners to plow back profits into new buildings to maintain tax shelters. Thus, flag-of-convenience registries outpace traditional flags during expansionary periods, and this process actually accelerates during recession as owners seek to increase the size of open registry operations.[14] According to the secretariat, "The surplus of shipping and shipbuilding capacity represents one of the most serious world-wide misallocations of capital investment in recent history."[15]

Despite the considerable exertions of the Group of 77 and the UNCTAD Shipping Division, progress in the bulk sector has not been comparable to that in the liner sector. Political and economic factors impede change. First, the OECD has united against the Third World. Second, the United States has been vehemently opposed to modifications of the flag-of-convenience system. No indirect support for the Third World has emanated from U.S. quarters; U.S. opponents of flags of convenience have had no impact on policy. Third, LDCs have recognized that concrete legal measures are not

13. Frank Chao, "Politics and Practical Reality," *Seatrade* (November 1981), p. 168.
14. UNCTAD, *Action on the Question of Open Registries,* p. 11.
15. Ibid., p. 9. Ironically, the secretariat now arrives at the conclusions its bitterest enemies once drew.

possible in this climate. Individual LDCs have been less successful in implementing significant cargo-sharing policies in the bulk trades. Political impediments to change are reinforced by the structure of ownership and control of ships and raw materials; the marketplace itself represents an obstacle to extensive Third World participation in bulk shipping.

Opposition to flags of convenience has increased in the United States. United States flag bulk shipping owners, supported by maritime unions, have pushed for greater protection. Citing the virtual disintegration of the U.S. bulk fleet in particular, these interests have attacked open registries and promoted legislation to reserve a portion of imports and exports to the United States flag fleet. At the same time they have sought to increase subsidies so as to enable such tonnage to be offered competitively. These measures have attracted widespread support in Congress. In 1977 an oil preference bill was passed in Congress but was vetoed by President Carter. In 1982, members of Congress unsuccessfully sought to reserve 40 percent of U.S. dry bulk exports to U.S. vessels. In 1983 Congresswoman Lindy Boggs introduced a bill to reserve 5 percent of American dry and liquid bulk exports and imports to United States flag vessels, gradually increasing the share to 20 percent. At congressional hearings the Seafarers International Union supported the bill, while opponents included the American Farm Bureau Federation, the National Council of Farmers Cooperatives, the American Petroleum Institute, the U.S. Council for International Business, the Chemical Manufacturers Association, the Coal Exporters Association, CENSA, and FACS (the Federation of American Controlled Shipping).[16]

Multinational corporations continue to defend open registries, however, and their views prevail in governmental circles. In UNCTAD, the United States response has generally been low key, based on skepticism about the viability of phasing out as well as on satisfaction with the unity of OECD countries. Underlying this skeptical attitude is intense hostility to the idea of a genuine link, as the following congressional exchange illustrates:

> Chairman: "Mr. Loree, UNCTAD has announced that it is working for the abolition of flags of convenience by the year 1991. How do you assess this effort?"

16. See Peter Goldman, "What Price U.S. Fleet Expansion?" *Seatrade* (June 1982), pp. 3–5. See also *FACS Forum* (May 1983), pp. 1–4.

> *Mr. Loree [chairman of FACS]:* "I would say offhandedly that there is a greater chance that the UNCTAD Shipping Division will be phased out by 1991 than the Liberian and Panamanian fleets, Mr. Chairman."[17]

In June 1981, a U.N. resolution recommending the phasing out of open registries was adopted by a vote of 49 to 16. The resolution won Soviet bloc support. On behalf of the Eastern bloc, Soviet spokesmen reiterated the views of LDCs that limiting open registries was "the only sound way to prevent a crisis in world shipping."[18] OECD countries, with the exception of France, Belgium, and Turkey, continue to resist UNCTAD efforts. France abstained on the U.N. resolution, carefully placing its opposition to open registries in the context of labor and safety considerations rather than general principles. Prior to 1983 the United States boycotted talks in Geneva on the subject of open registries, arguing that the tradition of consensus in UNCTAD deliberations was being violated. Since 1983, the United States has agreed to participate in Geneva discussions provided they are limited to consideration of "problems" of flag-of-convenience operations.

UNCTAD shipping experts viewed the extension of cargo-sharing to the bulk trades and the phasing out of open registries as inevitable and consistent with general shifts in the international division of labor and the comparative cost elements involved, especially labor. They also assumed an evolutionist or reformist outlook according to which global economic reform is to proceed gradually. Although the secretariat has energetically pressed its theoretical critique, it has been less bold in practice, having been willing to accept a less comprehensive settlement than the one achieved in the liner trades. Such a settlement calls for a link between vessel and flag in principle but contains loopholes designed to permit the continuation of open registry shipping. It emphasizes enhanced international regulation of flag-of-convenience vessels, and joint ventures between developing and developed countries as a means of encouraging Third World fleet develop-

---

17. U.S. Congress, House, Committee on Merchant Marine and Fisheries, *Omnibus Maritime Bill: Hearings Before the Subcommittee of the House Committee on Merchant Marine and Fisheries,* 96th Cong., 1980, pt. 3, p. 158. Mr. Loree further testified, "I assess this effort as basically a Russian-COMECON state-controlled left-wing, if you will, inspired effort to take some very damaging shots at the free enterprise shipping in the world." Nevertheless, Loree acknowledged that "certain provisions of the [UNCTAD] Liner Code have some appeal."

18. U.N. *Chronicle* 18 (December 1982), pp. 39–41; *Wall Street Journal,* 15 April 1982, p. 30.

ment in the bulk sector. The terms of the debate over open registries thus appear to be shifting from the question of abolition to the reform of specific deleterious effects.

The United Nations Conference for Registration of Ships began in Geneva in the summer of 1984, with 109 countries participating. The conference ended with a plenary session in February 1986 in which a draft convention was accepted. Contrary to the early hopes of the secretariat, the convention ultimately proved to be a victory for flags of convenience. This was foreshadowed by an agreement in mid-1985 in which language on three key issues—ownership, manning, and management—was changed. On manning, a "satisfactory part" of the vessel's crew are supposed to be citizens of the flag state. However, owners are able to take account of "sound and economically viable operation" of vessels, allowing shipowners to continue current practices.

The immediate causes of the secretariat's moderation and the resulting parallel between the U.N. conference and the Law of the Sea Convention of 1958 included the departure of Dr. Al Jadir from the UNCTAD secretariat; the fact that some Latin American states, themselves possessing FOC tonnage, were unwilling to take a firm stand; and the efforts of the Soviet Union and some leading Third World maritime nations to produce a compromise.[19] The structural basis for this decision, however, was the role played, despite the official "neutrality" of the Reagan administration, by the U.S. delegation at Geneva, which included the chairman of the FACS, the chief lobbyist for flags of convenience, and which adopted a hard-line stance against any meaningful change. Thus, a decade of work in the United Nations led not to a "phasing out" of open registries but, rather, to ratification of the status quo.

The Basis of American Power

Flags of convenience remain the dominant force in bulk shipping. Their presence influences national policies and the international labor market. Although the bulk sector has been hit hard by the recession, it has experi-

19. *Seatrade* (March 1986), p. 19; Bruce Vail, "UNCTAD Salutes the Status Quo," *American Shipper* (September 1985), p. 64; S. Farrell, "The Use of Flags of Convenience by Latin American Shipping," *Journal of Maritime Policy and Management* 11 (January–March 1984).

enced much less political turbulence than the liner sector. If the advanced states have not united perfectly against the Third World challenge, neither have they engaged in a significant degree of internal conflict. The formally free market survives, bolstered by the structure of bulk commodity markets. The United States remains the principal shipping power on the basis of its dominant position within these markets. The collapse of the United States flag bulk fleet, far from being a sign of weakness, as most commentators argue, is actually an index of American strength and ability to sustain its "godsons," Liberia and Panama.

As noted in Chapter 3, power in bulk shipping stems largely from the strategies of multinational corporations; controlling transportation is an important aspect of their operation. U.S. multinationals retain their grip over raw materials either through outright ownership or through direct control based on interconnected marketing and distribution chains.

The structure of ownership and control of the major oil and bulk commodities corresponds to the ownership and control of transportation. Taken out of geopolitical context, nationalization does not in itself represent an insurmountable challenge to multinationals. As Burton Kaufman concludes in his study of oil cartels:

> What had developed by 1973 was not so much the breakup of the old oil cartel and its replacement by OPEC as the interlocking of an oligopoly and a cartel. . . . By their control of world oil, the oil majors (and some of the larger independents, like Occidental) provided the OPEC countries with assured outlets for their oil without the type of competition that could drive prices down. At the same time, the OPEC nations afforded the oil majors a preferred status insofar as supplies of oil were concerned.[20]

An emphasis on the contextual or nondecisional structure of the bulk trades, as opposed to a bargaining focus, reveals the considerable degree of control exerted by the major multinational companies. In oil, for example, the Seven Sisters account for 52 percent of world crude oil production, either through ownership or agreements with national oil firms. An additional twenty-two companies, most of which are American, account for 12 percent of supplies.[21] Nationalization has not extended significantly

20. Burton I. Kaufman, *The Oil Cartel Case: A Documentary Study of Anti-Trust Activity in the Cold War Era* (Westport: Greenwood, 1978), p. 10.

21. UNCTAD, *The Maritime Transport of Hydrocarbons*, TD/222/Supp. 3 (Manila: United Nations, 1979), p. 12.

into phases other than extraction. As a recent U.N. study noted, "Many of the national oil-exporting companies maintain close connections with their former concession holders through production participation agreements or long-term purchase agreements (3 to 5 years) which stipulate minimum and maximum volumes."[22] Thus, the Seven Sisters continue to control distribution and marketing. Through ownership or long-term charter, the major oil companies control 74 percent of world tanker tonnage.[23] The Seven Sisters have relatively greater involvement in tankers than the independents have.

OPEC states have been unwilling or unable to establish substantial tanker fleets and, despite the eagerness of some Western independent shipowners to establish joint ventures, Arab fleets represent less than 3 percent of world bulk tonnage.[24] In the mid-1970s, many observers assumed that the wealthier OPEC nations would expand into shipping. Capital-intensive investment in supertankers would be appropriate for many Middle Eastern countries and could also help to recycle petro-dollars to Western or Third World shipyards. However, efforts in this direction initiated by the United Arab Shipping Company and the Arab Maritime Petroleum Transport Company coincided with the collapse of the tanker market; oil companies refused to charter OPEC tonnage, and some Arab states suffered heavy losses.[25] As a result, expansion of Arab shipping has been modest. Between 1978 and 1983, the Arab merchant fleet had increased from 6.7 million grt to 13 million grt, led by Kuwait (2.3 million grt) and Saudi Arabia (9.2 million grt). In 1982, the LDCs as a whole owned 10.7 percent of the world tanker fleet.[26]

Seventy-eight percent of dry bulk carryings consist of five major commodities: iron ore, coal, grain, phosphates, and bauxite/alumina.[27] Multinational control of the shipping of these commodities is no less overwhelm-

22. Ibid., p. 13.
23. Ibid., p. 21.
24. "Survey on Arab Shipping," *Norwegian Shipping News* 36 (10 April 1980); Salman D. Salman Al Hashim, "Formation of a Strong Arab Shipping Policy," in Seatrade, *Arab Shipping 1983: A Seatrade Guide* (Colchester: Seatrade, 1983).
25. William Hall, "Home Fleets Build Up," *Financial Times*, 5 June 1980; UNCTAD, *Merchant Fleet Development*, p. 5.
26. Seatrade, *Arab Shipping 1983*, p. 11; UNCTAD, *Review of Maritime Transport, 1982* (Geneva: United Nations, 1983), Appendix 1.
27. UNCTAD, *Control by Transnational Corporations over Dry Bulk Cargo Movements—Report by the UNCTAD Secretariat*, TD/B/C.4/203 (Geneva: United Nations, 1980), p. 3.

ing than over oil. Domination of the transportation network is reinforced not only by control or ownership of the mines or fields, but also, in many cases, by the strong position of developed countries with respect to flow of trade: exports from many less developed countries are delivered only to a handful of advanced countries. These two factors define the limits of fleet expansion both in terms of the North-South division and among advanced countries.

In iron ore, the United States owns 32 percent of world mining production, followed by Brazil and Australia (17 percent), Sweden (8 percent), and West Germany (2.5 percent). Ten steel companies receive 56 percent of iron ore imports, with Japanese and American firms predominating.[28] In many cases, the steel companies have equity links in iron ore mines; these arrangements now often take the form of joint ventures. Marketing agreements usually stipulate f.o.b. purchases, thus allowing the steel mills to designate the ship. In 1979, less developed countries owned 7 percent of the world ore/bulk fleet. The six major importing countries—Japan, West Germany, the United States, the United Kingdom, Italy, and Belgium— owned 48 percent, including open registry tonnage.[29] In most countries "specialized trading firms" centralize purchasing on a national basis. In West Germany, for example, two firms handle all iron ore imports. In France, Usinor owns all purchasing rights. These central purchasing agencies establish favorable conditions for a higher degree of cartelization in bulk shipping—the "bulk pools." Thus the French, through a central government purchasing agency, have been able to build up the French bulk pool Cetragpa on the basis of increasing coal imports and French flag preference.[30]

The international grain trade is even more highly centralized than iron ore. The United States, Canada, Australia, Argentina, France, and Brazil collectively account for 92 percent of world grain exports. Ten countries account for two-thirds of imports. The U.S.S.R. and Japan together import 30 percent of world grain exports. Five family-owned firms dominate the international grain trade: Bunge (Europe-Bahamas), Cargill (U.S.), Continental (French), Louis Dreyfus (French), and Garnac (U.S.-Swiss). From

28. Ibid., p. 8. These figures are for 1976, excluding the PRC and the Soviet bloc.
29. Ibid.
30. "Joint Ventures Aid Dry Bulk Operators," *Seatrade* (October 1981), pp. 111–13. See also Bernard J. Abrahamsson, *International Ocean Shipping: Current Concepts and Principles* (Boulder: Westview, 1980), p. 137.

1970 to 1975 they accounted for over 90 percent of exports of grain from both the United States and the EC. These firms also engage in related activities such as grain purchasing, marketing, distribution, and transportation. Between 1970 and 1975, between one-third and one-half of Cargill's grain exports from the United States were sold to foreign subsidiaries.[31]

Coal, bauxite/alumina, and phosphates reveal a similar pattern of centralized ownership and control. The United States accounts for 31 percent of world coal exports.[32] Jamaica, Australia, and Guinea account for two-thirds of world bauxite exports; the United States imports 41 percent of the world total. Four U.S. firms possess 44 percent of world alumina capacity. Alcoa's aluminum plant absorbs all of the Dominican Republic's bauxite exports; Reynolds's plant in Texas accounts for all of Haiti's exports.[33] A high percentage of world bulk trade thus involves intra-firm transactions.

The open bulk shipping market operates in the context of vertically integrated multinational corporations. It also functions within a general structure of dependency involving not only multinational corporations but also financial, technological, and political relations. Although the Baltic Exchange and the spot market continue to play a role in international shipping, many contracts are negotiated privately or involve affiliates. One UNCTAD study estimated that less than 10 percent of world tonnage is chartered on the open market; the rest is provided by industrial carriers or independent owners directly or indirectly tied to multinationals.[34]

A number of studies of commercial practices in the bulk trades have been undertaken. Detailed analyses of commodity movements and case studies of particular trades have been made in order to identify barriers to the entry of Third World fleets into these trades.[35] From the point of view of the UNCTAD secretariat, the existence of such barriers justifies phasing

31. UNCTAD, *Control by Transnational Corporations,* p. 13.

32. Ibid., Annex 2.

33. Ibid., p. 18; and U.N. Economic and Social Council, Commission on Transnational Corporations, *Transnational Corporations in the Shipping Industry: The Case of Bauxite/Alumina,* E/C.10/1982/14 (Manila: United Nations, 1982), p. 15.

34. UNCTAD, *Merchant Fleet Development: Guidelines for Developing Countries—Report by the UNCTAD Secretariat,* TD/B/C.4/186 (Geneva: United Nations, 1979), p. 11.

35. See esp. UNCTAD, *Report of the Group of Experts on Problems Faced by the Developing Countries in the Carriage of Bulk Cargoes in Its Second Session,* TD/B/C.4/234 (Geneva: United Nations, 1981); and UNCTAD, *Report of the Group of Experts on International Sea Transport of Liquid Hydrocarbons in Bulk in Its Second Session,* TD/B/C.4/263/5 (Geneva: United Nations, 1984).

out open registries and implementing cargo-reservation schemes. The OECD bloc, in contrast, has sought to show that the market is largely competitive and therefore offers opportunities for fleet development within the rules and procedures of the existing regime.

Despite substantial efforts by researchers in the UNCTAD Shipping Division, the results are not wholly conclusive. Replies to questionnaires are often ambiguous or incomplete. Moreover, by definition the concept of "barriers to entry" is loaded. From the point of view of developed states, the market does not in itself establish barriers. Only specific and readily identifiable monopolistic practices constitute barriers to entry. However, the complex of open registries, financial dependency, and general dependency relations operates, *in addition to* specific monopolistic practices, as a barrier to the establishment of Third World bulk fleets.

In general, UNCTAD studies underline the extremely high degree of concentration and integration in global raw-materials industries. In this context, obvious barriers to Third World participation in shipping do exist. The effectiveness of such barriers differs depending on the commodity and the countries involved. It is also a function of, inter alia, the supply-and-demand structure of various commodities. Under conditions of recession, "pure" market forces and the increased leverage of importers will militate against LDC entrants. Third World countries will lack the capital to diversify; the bargaining advantage will shift decisively to importers.

Peru's iron ore trade provides an example of the difficulties LDCs have in establishing bulk fleets. As noted in Chapter 2, 50 percent of Peruvian iron ore is exported to Japan. Yet only 3 percent of Japan's iron ore imports are purchased from Peru. This alone gives Japan a great deal of leverage over the terms of shipment. Although Peru negotiates directly with the six large Japanese steel companies, Japanese shipowners and steel companies coordinate their activities. Until 1977, sales of iron ore were made on a c.i.f. basis, permitting the seller to arrange for shipment. Even then, however, a provision in the contract specified the use of Japanese ships. After 1977, when the iron ore market collapsed, Japanese steel companies pressed to convert c.i.f. contracts to f.o.b. In 1979, all tonnage operating in the Peru-Japan iron ore trade was either owned or chartered by Japan.[36]

The situation in bauxite/alumina seems to confirm the general conclu-

36. UNCTAD, *Iron Ore Trade from Latin America to Japan—A Study by the UNCTAD Secretariat*, TD/B/C.4/AC.2/2 (Geneva: United Nations, 1981), p. 5.

sions of the UNCTAD secretariat concerning "captive" cargoes. Research on this commodity reveals an industry dominated by a few vertically integrated firms who view shipping as a key link in overall operations. For the six largest firms, shipping is considered an "internal operation" even if tonnage is chartered or independent shipowners are used. Only 13 percent of bauxite cargo and 23 percent of alumina is *not* sold to affiliates as part of such internal operations.[37]

The case of international oil trades is highly complex. Here the proponents of the closed market perspective point to the percentage of oil traded between affiliates. Importers purchase 47 percent of crude oil and 27 percent of petroleum products from subsidiaries. Between 25 and 33 percent of tonnage is either owned or on short-term charter to major oil companies, with additional tonnage on long-term charter. Again, contracts tend to be made on f.o.b. terms, permitting the developed countries to nominate the vessel.[38]

Oil presents a less clear-cut case than most other bulk commodities, however. The fragmentation of OPEC and the loosening grip of the Seven Sisters have led to a greater use of the spot market for oil. This, in turn, has strengthened the market position of independent shipowners, who compete for cargoes in theoretically open markets.

Undoubtedly, then, some characteristics of the bulk regime block new entrants. These include:

1. Purchase of commodities on f.o.b. terms.
2. Formal or informal links between importers and shipowners.
3. Long-term contracts.
4. Fixtures not made through brokers.
5. Sales between affiliates.[39]

In addition, the existence of open registries certainly does endow the shipowners of the North with overwhelming market power that is especially difficult to oppose as commodity prices fall.

In Chapter 4 it was noted that the entry of LDCs into liner shipping did not necessarily represent the optimal deployment of their scarce resources.

37. U.N. Economic and Social Council, Commission on Transnational Corporations, *Transnational Corporations in the Shipping Industry*, p. 5.
38. Ibid., p. 7.
39. UNCTAD, *Report of the Group of Experts on International Sea Transport of Liquid Hydrocarbons*, p. 9 and Annex II, p. 1.

Moreover, it was asserted that the terms on which Third World countries have sought to enter liner markets did not change the fundamental bases of dependency and underdevelopment in any obvious way. A similar logic applies, with equal or greater force, to bulk shipping, which is also relatively capital-intensive. Even if open registries were phased out, it is not clear that ships would automatically migrate to LDC flags; even if they did so, they would undoubtedly seek a regulatory climate similar to that of Liberia and Panama.[40] The modest changes that do appear possible (for example, joint ventures) are outcomes of the current dependency relationship and serve to perpetuate it. Significant gains for LDCs in bulk shipping appear to depend on fundamental changes in the relationship between the developed and the developing world. Yet fundamental change would almost certainly mean a long-term reduction in world shipping tonnage as internal markets in the Third World expand and the international division of labor wherein Third World countries export primary products in return for manufactured commodities is superseded.

Change and Continuity in the Regime

If flags of convenience serve to reinforce an international divison of labor dominated by the North, they also, as was shown in Chapter 3, are key elements in the distribution of power in the North. Liberia and Panama helped the United States to establish primacy in the bulk sector during the 1950s and 1960s. The shipping strategy complemented the drive for world power and the concomitant control over raw materials. The traditional maritime countries were compelled to adapt national shipping policies to the activities of open registries or permit national shipowners to join the rush to these flags themselves. Both these mutually reinforcing options have been taken by European countries and Japan to varying degrees. Because control over significant cargo is a prerequisite to real maritime power, it follows that Britain and Japan, the countries that, second to the United States, play leading roles as consumers or owners of bulk commodities, should prove most capable of consolidating their position in the U.S.-dominated regime.

Tables 26 and 27, on the control of oil and bulk shipping registered

40. Stanley G. Sturmey, *The Open Registry Controversy and the Development Issue* (Bremen: Institute of Shipping Economics and Logistics, 1983).

Table 26.   Employment, by Beneficial Owner, of Open Registry Tanker Fleets over 5,000 dwt, 1979 (thousands dwt)

	Number of Ships	National Trade	Cross-Trade	Laid Up/ Indeterminate	Total
United States	375	15,127	32,251	3,261	50,639
Greece	263	2,813	18,651	3,871	25,335
Hong Kong	112	267	17,136	375	17,778
Japan	91	2,638	5,080	329	8,047
All countries	977	24,095	78,836	8,186	111,117
Leading four as percentage of total	86	86	93	96	92

SOURCE: Adapted from UNCTAD, *Trade Routes of Open Registry Vessels*, TD/222/Supp. 5 (Geneva: United Nations, 1979).

Table 27.   Employment, by Beneficial Owner, of Open Registry Bulk and Combined Fleets over 5,000 dwt, 1979 (thousands dwt)

	Number of Ships	National Trade	Cross-Trade	Laid Up/ Indeterminate	Total
United States	195	5,767	2,897	1,093	9,757
Greece	238	1,130	8,300	1,161	10,591
Hong Kong	324	434	10,324	335	11,093
Japan	141	3,429	449	128	5,290
All countries	1,175	6,312	31,288	2,953	47,979
Leading four as percentage of total	76	80	70	92	77

SOURCE: Adapted from UNCTAD, *Trade Routes of Open Registry Vessels*, TD/222/Supp. 5 (Geneva: United Nations, 1979).

under flags of convenience, show that the United States has acquired two allies in flags of convenience—Japan and Britain–Hong Kong. Because the tables distinguish between national and cross-trades, they also give the basis of fleet expansion in each country. Japan is either the primary or leading consumer of iron ore (40 percent of world production), grain (17 percent), and coal (48 percent), and is a leading importer of bauxite/alumina. It consumes 11 percent of oil production.[41] Although it is interesting to note that, especially in oil, Japan has become a significant cross-trader, in

41. UNCTAD, *The Maritime Transport of Hydrocarbons*, p. 9.

general its bulk fleet is deployed to transport raw materials to Japan. Privileged access to shipbuilding has also contributed to Japan's overall maritime effort.

The Hong Kong Shipowners Association controls approximately 60 million dwt of shipping, most of which is bulk tonnage. In terms of beneficial ownership, Hong Kong is second in world shipping tonnage only to the United States. Approximately 90 percent of Hong Kong–owned tonnage is registered in Liberia or Panama.[42] Hong Kong plays a central role in Japanese maritime policy. Through the *shikumisen* system, Japanese shipowners and banks make an agreement with a foreign owner, usually in Hong Kong, to order and purchase a ship built and financed in Japan. The ship is then chartered back to the Japanese shipowner, allowing Japanese shipping to tap foreign capital sources while simultaneously reducing labor costs by operating under an open registry.[43] Although the system has been used less often since the late 1970s, it was a key element of Japan's foreign trade strategy.

If Japan's status in Hong Kong has been established as primarily that of a consumer, Britain's presence is sustained by ownership and control over raw materials, especially oil, and by the standing of Hong Kong in international finance. Information on ownership and control of shipping is closely held, especially when it involves flags of convenience. However, a detailed examination of the trade literature suggests that British capital plays a dominant role in Hong Kong shipping. The contraction of certain segments of the British flag fleet—especially bulk—throughout the 1970s should be viewed in the context of rapid Hong Kong expansion. In addition to the substantial tonnage transferred to the Hong Kong flag by British owners, two groups, Y. K. Pao's Worldwide and C. Y. Tung's Island Navigation Corporation, control roughly half of the 60 million dwt. Eastern Asia Navigation Company, Jardine Matheson, John Swire and Sons, and Wheelock Marden are also important Hong Kong shipowners. The extent of corporate linkages between these groups and the centrality of the Hong Kong and Shanghai Bank, a British Overseas Bank, in this network suggest the strong indirect presence of the British in flag-of-convenience shipping. The Hong Kong and Shanghai Bank owns one half of Y. K. Pao's Worldwide Shipping Company. Not surprisingly, the growing relationship of Hong Kong owners to British Shipbuilders appears to fit the pattern of developing shipbuilding nationalism. In 1981, Hong Kong owners had 380,000 dwt on order in U.K. yards.[44]

The heavy involvement of British capital in world shipping is also demonstrated by the continuing role played by U.K. banks in the Norwegian economy. According to the *Norwegian Shipping News*, "The Norwegian shipping industries' finances are to a great degree bound to external financing, especially to foreign credit institutions."[45] British banks have predominated, at least through the 1970s. Much of this capital is directed to bulk shipping, where Norway's presence is greatest. For example, Hambros Bank (U.K.) was a major creditor of Reksten's tanker empire. When this collapsed in the wake of the oil crisis of 1973–74, the Norwegian government was induced by creditors to guarantee the loans. In the final carving up of Reksten holdings, Hambros received seven large tankers, which it operates under the Norwegian flag.[46]

American strength in bulk shipping is based on both consumption and control of resources. The United States is obviously strongest in tankers; in dry bulk shipping it is somewhat less dominant. Table 28 presents the basic pattern of control over transportation by the three major shipping nations, Japan, the United States, and the United Kingdom. Hong Kong tonnage can be assumed to be shared between Japan and Britain; Greek owners have a longstanding relationship with the United States. Although Norway is clearly a major actor, much ship financing is external, and Norway is not an important consumer of bulk commodities. The table undoubtedly understates the role of the three major countries, especially the United States, for much American-owned tonnage is registered in Western Europe.

In contrast to these nations, West Germany and France are relatively weak in this sector. West Germany has begun to expand into flags of convenience, but the size of its beneficially owned tanker fleet is small. In 1984, West German–controlled flag-of-convenience tonnage represented almost

44. "British Yards Tap More Hong Kong Business," *Fairplay International Shipping Weekly* 280 (16 July 1981), p. 8. See also "British Yards Corner a Piece of the Hong Kong Action," *Fairplay International Shipping Weekly* 280 (18 June 1981), p. 12.

45. *Norwegian Shipping News* 31 (30 May 1975), p. 9.

46. *Norwegian Shipping News* 38 (19 March 1982), p. 5.

Table 28.   Beneficial Ownership of World Bulk Fleet, 1984 (dwt)

	Flag of Convenience[a]	Home	Total	% of Total World Bulk Fleet
United States	49.7	16.1	65.8	13
United Kingdom	5.6	18.3	23.9	5
Japan	22.9	51.8	74.7	15
Hong Kong	37.3	8.7	46.0	9
Greece	36.4	51.4	87.8	17.
Norway	8.0	26.1	34.1	7
Total (six countries)	159.9	172.4	332.3	66

SOURCE: UNCTAD, *Review of Maritime Transport, 1984* (Geneva: United Nations, 1985).

[a]Tonnage includes some general cargo and container vessels.

two-thirds of the beneficially owned West German fleet.[47] West Germany and France reacted to the oil crisis by creating government-sponsored tanker expansion programs. French law stipulates that two-thirds of oil imports must be shipped under the French flag. In practice a system of waivers is used and much French flag tonnage is U.S.-owned. Neither France nor West Germany possesses the resources to challenge the major sponsors of these flags. Japan's resource vulnerability might induce it to consider bilateralism and joint ventures with trading partners as the basis of phasing out open registries. Japanese shipping power is ultimately based on consumption of raw materials in a sector grounded in ultimate Anglo-American control.

The Soviet Union has supported Third World condemnation of flags of convenience. Its activity in bulk shipping is comparatively low, reflecting its own lack of involvement in Third World resource markets. Moreover, the Soviet challenge to America's control of energy is not immediately economic but, rather, geopolitical. The Siberian gas pipeline complements the TSCL and offers Western Europe a means of reducing dependence on the United States. Thus, Soviet activity in the sphere of transportation emphasizes the geographical base of Soviet power and the long-run comparative advantages that location bestows. U.S. policymakers perceive the pipeline to be a far greater threat than the TSCL. However, aside from its rhetorical support for the Third World in UNCTAD, the U.S.S.R. has not played a

47. UNCTAD, *Review of Maritime Transport, 1984* (Geneva: United Nations, 1985).

significant role in the politics of the regime. Indeed, contrary to the fears of America's flag-of-convenience lobby, the U.S.S.R. has not made such flags an important issue, and it was instrumental in convincing Third World states to compromise during the Convention on Ship Registration.

Safety and Pollution

As mentioned in Chapter 3, flags of convenience represent a competitive national shipping policy and also an indirect form of government aid. Thus, Western European reaction to use of flags of convenience as a competitive policy of the United States was muted by the recognition of absolute benefits accruing to all shipowners. Open registries have held wages in check and limited national and intergovernmental attempts to impose safety regulation. Since the late 1960s, increasing governmental, public, and scholarly interest in the ocean environment has been generated, primarily in response to catastrophic accidents at sea such as the sinking of the *Torrey Canyon* in 1967 and of the *Amoco Cadiz* in 1978.[48] The principle of privatization, buttressed by U.S. support for flags of convenience, has persisted in the bulk sector. The weak regulatory thrust has entered not through abolition of flags of convenience but, rather, through the limited extent to which ships registered under such flags have been induced to abide by international safety and pollution controls.

The IMO has been able to sponsor a series of conventions on pollution. Since the late 1960s the ratification record has improved somewhat. However, many states accede to conventions for public-relations reasons; the conventions are cosmetic measures that help to conceal the indifference of shipowners and governments. As Michael M'Gonigle and Mark Zacher noted in their study of tanker pollution, "Most commentators have treated this problem [implementation of conventions] far too cursorily in their concern for the formulation of the rules themselves."[49] It is impossible to compile accurate statistics on breaches of regulations, but the more or less stable rate of accidents at sea suggests that standards have not improved significantly over the last decade.

Oil companies and large independent tanker owners appear at times to

48. See esp. R. Michael M'Gonigle and Mark W. Zacher, *Pollution, Politics, and International Law: Tankers at Sea* (Berkeley and Los Angeles: University of California Press, 1979).
49. Ibid., p. 327.

have utilized the environmental lobby as a competitive weapon against smaller, less highly capitalized firms. Since the collapse of the tanker market, the leading firms have attempted to organize cooperative schemes to reduce tonnage. These have been proposed in Intertanko (Independent Tanker Owners Association), and in the International Maritime Industries Forum, which is made up of European shipowners, shipbuilding firms, banks, and oil companies. At various times lay-up plans and scrap-and-build policies have been recommended. They have been opposed on antitrust grounds by smaller shipowners and the U.S. Department of Justice. According to some observers, the large shipowners sought to capitalize on the *Argo Merchant* disaster by establishing technical requirements designed to drive out smaller owners. These motives may underlie Liberia's recent decision to increase its inspection requirements. The loss ratio of ships registered under the Liberian flag is now below the world average.[50]

A similar situation exists for safety and working conditions. Here the stark differences between sea and air transport remain and are illuminating. As the UNCTAD secretariat recently observed, "Even in market economy countries with normal registries the machinery for enforcing standards in merchant shipping can only be described as extremely lax when compared with the machinery for enforcing standards in civil aviation."[51] Although the state has penetrated most spheres of shipping, safety and labor sectors continue to be characterized by extreme privatization. Thus, classification societies, not governments, bear responsibility for surveying ships and certifying standards. Beholden ultimately to shipowners, their ability to sponsor change is tempered by economic recession and national competition among classification societies themselves. Where enforcement is mandated by law, inspection is a low priority for most governments.[52] As with attempts to control pollution, inspection rules are meaningless when there is no system for enforcing them. The European Community's Memorandum of Understanding on Port State Control, brought into effect in 1982, has

50. Erling D. Naess, *My Life: Autobiography of a Shipping Man* (Colchester: Seatrade, 1977), pp. 237–39. See also Rodney P. Carlisle, *Sovereignty for Sale: The Origins and Evolution of the Panamanian and Liberian Flags of Convenience* (Annapolis: Naval Institute Press, 1981), pp. 183–86. For loss ratios between 1980 and 1984, see "Casualty Statistics," *Fairplay* 292 (25 October 1985), p. 38.

51. UNCTAD, *Action on the Question of Open Registries*, p. 13.

52. Ibid., p. 14; M'Gonigle and Zacher, *Pollution, Politics, and International Law*, pp. 362–63.

enabled member governments to inspect and detain ships that do not conform to international standards. This is a significant area of EC maritime transport policy, and this initiative may be expected to strengthen the movement to regulate flags of convenience.

The anomalous position of shipping regarding pollution and safety is consistent with the view of flags of convenience as a manifestation of the competitive strategies of oil and mining multinationals not only against foreign shipowners but also against international maritime labor. Trade unions have been the staunchest advocates of safety and social standards. However, their power to secure lasting changes is undermined by open registries and the insecurity created by "de-manning." Hence, regulatory policies focus primarily on the technical standards of individual ships and crew competency rather than on the core of management practices and the financial pressures on shipowners.[53]

The generally poor safety and environmental standards thus stem only partly from the physical problems in ocean transportation. The condition of ships and the working environment are greatly affected by the nature of the regime and the limitations this regime imposes, directly or indirectly, on both international organizations and maritime unions. IMO is the smallest and poorest agency in the United Nations. Highly dependent on scientific personnel, it operates on the margins of international shipping politics. Even its highly technical conventions have not fared well in national policy; its ratification record is low, and compliance has been lower still.[54] According to government sources, even in ships flying the British flag the seaman's occupation is thirty-five times more dangerous than ordinary manufacturing work and four times more dangerous than coalmining.[55] Recent pressure on Liberia and other open registry countries has

53. For a critical approach to safety and regulatory standards, see Noel Mostert, *Supership* (New York: Alfred A. Knopf, 1974). The insurance industry indirectly reinforces the lack of regulatory pressure by failing to provide adequate incentives regarding safety. M'Gonigle and Zacher concluded that "the effect of the insurance structure on state policy is to restrict the scope of state activity to the existing commercial framework" (*Pollution, Politics, and International Law*, p. 381). See also Chris Cragg, "Fifteen-Year Disaster Figures as U.K. Loses Thousands at Sea," *Seatrade* (February 1981).

54. M'Gonigle and Zacher, *Pollution, Politics, and International Law*, pp. 336–38.

55. *Seatrade* (December 1983), p. 15; see also United Kingdom, Department of Trade, *Casualties to Vessels and Accidents to Men, 1976* (London: HMSO, 1978). For a general critique of flags of convenience, see R. S. Doganis and B. N. Metaxas, *The Impact of Flags of Convenience* (London: Polytechnic of Central London Transport Studies, 1976).

had some effect on safety and environmental standards. However, the mere existence of open registries serves as a deterrent to fundamental change.

Conclusion

Power in the regime for bulk shipping ultimately stems from control, either as consumer or provider, over its cargoes: oil and the major bulk commodities. Of course, the ability to control transportation also serves to reinforce control over raw materials. Chapter 4 showed how flags of convenience enabled the United States to overcome domestic problems arising from relatively high wages and to establish a regime that served its immediate transportation needs. Flags of convenience, operating beyond the immediate sway of governments, represented, at one level, an instance of "sovereignty at bay." Yet their existence was also an expression of power relations between North and South; between the United States and Western Europe; and between capital and labor on a global scale.

The theory of hegemonic stability adopted in this study did not anticipate that as U.S. hegemony eroded, the distribution of power in specific regimes would become more plural. Rather, the theory expected that, given America's underlying power, as American hegemony declined the United States would seek a closer correspondence between outcomes and more narrowly conceived interests. Therefore, it predicted that in those regimes in which America continued to have a vested interest in the status quo, very little change would occur. The situation in bulk shipping conforms to this logic. In contrast to the liner sector, in the bulk sector the United States did not make concessions following World War II. At the present time, the regime is less obviously and instrumentally dominated by American firms than it was two decades ago; Japan and Britain have established a major presence in flags of convenience, and other countries, such as West Germany, have begun to "flag out" to open registries. There has also been some weakening of the control of the Seven Sisters and other major extractive companies over transportation. Yet these developments do not portend a major change in the nature of the regime or its balance of power. In contrast to the liner sector, where the fragmentation of the OECD and U.S. revisionist attitudes provided a crucial context for a successful Third World challenge, in the bulk sector there has been no comparable break-up of the North. The United States has vigorously defended the status quo, and the Third World challenge in this sector has foundered.

Privatization continues to be the key organizing principle in bulk shipping. Although regulation has had some impact, particularly in the areas of safety and environmental protection, it has not impinged on major political issues. Freight rates and the allocation of shipping by flag and firm continue to be determined by the workings of an oligopoly, although this oligopoly has certainly been weakened in recent years. Government-sponsored cargo-sharing measures are very limited, although some Third World countries have established programs. Finally, the existence of flags of convenience continues to inhibit governments in attempting promotional schemes. Realizing that no amount of promotion can match what the flags of convenience have to offer, governments are inclined to allow their shipowners to use such flags.

For LDCs, the issue of flags of convenience does not, strictly speaking, hinge on the replacement of market principles with those of authoritative allocation. The UNCTAD secretariat views flags of convenience as a serious restraint on the operation of a truly competitive market, contending that in the absence of such flags tonnage would gravitate to the Third World according to the law of comparative advantage. Ironically, the UNCTAD secretariat resurrected failed OEEC arguments and turned them, with an equal lack of success, on their former adherents.

CONCLUSION

This study has used the concept of regime as a means of organizing data in an extremely complex industry. Since the rise of the Netherlands in the early seventeenth century, the leading power in the international political economy has tried to construct an international shipping regime to support its bid for global hegemony. In the cases of the Netherlands and Britain, a definite relationship can be seen between the principles and practices of freedom of the seas and hegemonic ascendancy. In contrast, the Navigation Acts, the key legal expression of mercantilist foreign policy, enabled Britain to supplant the Netherlands and to achieve maritime supremacy. Once Britain ruled the waves, it reinstated a freedom-of-the-seas regime in which economic and political power were once again formally distinct. The nineteenth-century freedom-of-the-seas regime, however, allowed rival maritime powers to appear. As the distribution of power became more equal, neither the challengers nor the hegemonic leader was willing or able to abide by regime rules.

After defining *regime change* as involving a transformation of basic principles and practices, I have contended that in 1945 a postwar or Atlantic regime was established which survived, in its essential features, until the mid-1960s, when a new regime began to emerge. To be sure, change in the nature and purpose of American power does not, in itself, provide a comprehensive explanation for regime change. Domestic structures constitute an important variable that must be included in a causal model of change. However, the politics of hegemonic decline provide the starting point for the explanation of change; the extent to which domestic structures affect change is itself conditioned by the distribution of international power.

In contrast to historical regimes, which may be described as either free-trade or mercantilist, the new regime resists simple characterization: some essential elements remain subject to intense bloc politics; the regime displays contradictory aspects; and principles do not always correspond to practices. It is perhaps more accurate to term the new regime *incipient*, or a *quasi-regime*.[1] Moreover, it seems doubtful that a more coherent set of principles and practices is likely to emerge in the late 1980s and early 1990s.

At the end of World War II, the United States faced the challenge of organizing an international shipping regime that would realize three at least partially contradictory goals: a relatively open regime, no longer fragmented by the intense nationalism characterizing the interwar period; a regime that would buttress America's claim to global commercial ascendancy; and a regime that contributed to the goals of economic reconstruction and political stability in Western Europe. I have used the term *privatization* to describe the constitutive principle of the postwar regime. In the liner trades, the Eurocentric system of privately controlled liner conferences was retained, and government regulation was minimized. As a result, shipowners from the traditional maritime powers retained their role as key decisionmakers. The market mechanism, in the framework of liner cartels, determined the size of national flag fleets and freight rates. It minimized, although never eliminated, governmental promotion. American shipowners participated in this system, but they played a subordinate role. The Third World was largely excluded. On the whole, the system facilitated the expansion of world trade. Politically, however, it created resentment not only in the Third World and the Soviet bloc but also in the United States.

In bulk shipping, privatization served the long-range or hegemonic interests of the United States as well as the immediate goal of asserting American control over global transportation of bulk commodities. Flags of convenience enabled American shipowners to avoid the chronic problems associated with the United States flag merchant fleet, especially that of relatively high labor costs. Flags of convenience undoubtedly contributed to lowering the final price of bulk commodities, although not, perhaps, as much as their supporters contended. As in liner shipping, privatization generated public resentment. In contrast to liner shipping, however, in bulk shipping American multinationals and the government have successfully opposed attempts to revise the system.

Change in international shipping has resulted from the growing assertiveness of forces seeking to introduce the principle of regulation. The practical effects of change have been much greater in the liner sector than

---

1. The term *quasi-regime* is borrowed from Oran Young, "International Regimes: Problems of Concept Formation," *World Politics* 32 (April 1980).

in the bulk sector. In liner shipping, both the Third World and the United States have become dissatisfied with the role played by strong or closed conferences. The Third World has sought a largely protectionist regime in which closed conferences are retained under the wing of the state. The United States, in contrast, has decided to regulate conferences in order to establish a more competitive system of ocean transportation. A greater degree of competition is favored by the large U.S. liner operators as well as by U.S. shippers, who believe it will enhance their export potential. In bulk shipping the principle of regulation has made some headway, resulting in modest improvements in safety and environmental standards. This is most evident in the recent record of vessels flying the Liberian flag. However, the essence of the regime, that is, freedom from taxation and the creation of a global labor market, remains.

The New International Maritime Order?

The Third World has identified shipping as an integral component of the strategy for a new international economic order, and most analyses of the industry have focused on the key role played by the Third World in fomenting international change. It is certainly true that the Third World has established the intellectual foundations for a new nationalist or neo-mercantilist order. The Third World's vision of a new regime is expressed in the UNCTAD Code of Conduct for Liner Conferences, in which the national interest replaces the market as the constitutive principle. The sphere of private decision-making is greatly reduced: decisions to expand (or contract) shipping are to be made on the basis of political and general commercial objectives, not simply according to market forces or the preferences of individual firms or conferences.

Yet the passage of the UNCTAD Code of Conduct has not resolved the crisis of international shipping, nor has the Third World provided a set of principles and practices upon which a new order might be constructed. Rather, it has provoked increasing national and international conflict. This study has argued that the key protagonists are the United States and the traditional maritime powers of Western Europe, who have organized their maritime strategies through the common shipping policy. Ultimately, the nature of the new regime, including its intellectual basis, will be determined by the resolution of Atlantic conflict.

It is possible to argue, in very broad terms, that the decline of U.S. hegemony has resulted in a trend toward protection in shipping, consistent with the principles of the UNCTAD Code and reminiscent of the 1930s. It is conceivable, although doubtful, that protectionist forces, centered on some liner firms and the U.S. Congress, will predominate in the making of future shipping policy. U.S. policy certainly does reflect a strong nationalist tradition, and some of the weaker Western European countries, such as Belgium and France, are flirting with protectionist solutions. Moreover, as the conference system becomes increasingly disorganized and competitive, many Third World nations threaten even stronger protectionist measures. Nevertheless, as Chapter 8 indicated, U.S. policy mixes protectionism with attempts to forge a more competitive regime conducive to the worldwide expansion of American (and other) cross-traders. Moreover, U.S. policy now appears willing to tolerate the virtual elimination of the American merchant shipbuilding industry in order to encourage this trend. European Community policy, similarly, combines contradictory tendencies. The crisis of international shipping is not unfolding in a straightforward protectionist direction.

In essence, U.S. maritime policy is neither protectionist nor "free," and this seems to explain the contradictory, patchwork character of the present regime. The orientation of the United States does, however, continue to be *global* in scope. In rejecting the Third World's code and Europe's Brussels Package, the United States has, thus far, opposed the concept of maritime blocs and the possibility of coexisting regimes, in favor of a unified international freight market, albeit one that incorporates systematic violations of market principles. The emerging regime, which appears to be based on regulation American-style, may be termed one of *unilateral globalism,* which differs from the multilateralism of the hegemonic phase and the very weak trend toward pluralism.[2]

Theory and Regime Change

The theory of hegemonic stability is a conflict model of international relations. It assumes that stable regimes are made possible by a distribution of power in which tendencies toward conflict are suppressed and that regimes themselves institutionalize power relations. Yet many scholars have asserted

2. The phrase is borrowed from Antonio Gambino, "Atlantic vs. Pacific?" *L'Espresso,* 6 November 1983.

that analyses based on the structure of power and interest fail to provide a sufficiently descriptive and explanatory account of developments in regimes. They view regimes as at least partially autonomous of international power politics or assume that individual regimes are more or less discrete politicoeconomic structures, each containing a separate balance of power and political logic.

Moreover, observers of international shipping have tended to celebrate the potential of the international shipping industry to produce international harmony. They have discerned signs of international community in the workings of the industry and have emphasized the expanded role of international maritime organizations. Indeed, even the most ardent advocates of the New International Economic Order for shipping have, at least implicitly, assumed a high level of cooperation among Western powers even while claiming that these powers exploit the Third World. A model of the international shipping regime that emphasizes the cooperative tendencies of the industry does yield important insights. However, it fails to explain or predict the most important changes in shipping since World War II, and it does not offer concepts that help to explain how or why change has benefited some states and groups at the expense of others.

Ultra-Imperialism?

By virtue of its unique cosmopolitan features, international shipping offers an appropriate case for evaluating approaches to international relations that stress the cooperative tendencies of international business or hold that socially and politically significant aspects of international regimes are distinct from structures of power and interest. Samuel Lawrence, in pointing to the internationalist consequences of shipping cartels, has restated a classic theme of international political economy:

> The conference system, because it tends to mute conflicts of interest between national flag carriers, helps to lessen the abrasions of international politics. It is quite possible for serious competitive struggles to develop within conferences. In numerous instances bloc voting by national flag lines has followed a national policy pattern. However, while each line and each national flag group is interested in enhancing its own profit and advancing its own national interest, it also has an important stake in maintaining the integrity of the conference, which may require that both individual and national interests be set aside in favor of the common good. Experience since World War II [to 1965] suggests that when

a choice must be made, conference carriers are more likely to identify their interests with the conference system than with the government which has registered their ships.[3]

This formulation acknowledges that national strategies influence conference decision-making but argues that the conference system reduces international conflict. Since 1965 important changes have occurred that could be expected to strengthen the transnational element. The conference system reached a new evolutionary phase in the late 1960s. The new ultra-conferences combine not single firms, but international consortia seeking to pool capital and profits and allocate cargoes.

From the point of view of the individual firm, conference loyalties will often, but not always, override national factors. To this extent, then, conferences mitigate rivalry. However, from the perspective of the regime as a whole, conferences have served to intensify international conflict. This is especially true of the closed conference.

Shipping cartels display the defensive reaction of established firms to outside competition, regardless of their efficiency or the putative uniqueness of shipping economics. Arguments for the greater efficiency of conferences, mentioned in Chapter 2, undoubtedly have merit. Nevertheless, established in the context of the age of imperialism, conferences were originally the functional equivalents of formal colonialism: they represented an attempt (initially, mainly by British shipowners) to maintain existing market shares. Thus they engendered hostility from excluded shipowners and non-European shippers, first in the United States, then in the Third World. For this reason conferences are prone to instability. As economic development proceeds, conference practices are resented by at least some regions or groups of shipowners. Trades have to be restructured. Conflict is more

3. Samuel A. Lawrence, *U.S. Merchant Shipping Policies and Politics* (Washington, D.C.: Brookings Institution, 1966), p. 30. The potential of transnational firms to overwhelm state power was cited by Karl Kautsky, among others, who called this phenomenon "ultra-imperialism." It was, of course, criticized by Lenin, in *Imperialism* and other works. For recent versions of the theory, see Stephen Hymer and Robert Rowthorn, "Multinational Corporations and International Oligopoly: The Non-American Challenge," in Charles P. Kindleberger, ed., *The International Corporation: The Non-American Challenge* (Cambridge, Mass.: MIT Press, 1970); and Martin Nicolaus, "The Universal Contradiction," *New Left Review* 57 (January–February 1970). For more traditional perspectives, see Ernest Mandel, *Europe vs. America* (New York: Monthly Review Press, 1970); Riccardo Parboni, *The Dollar and Its Rivals: Recession, Inflation, and International Finance* (London: New Left Books / Verso, 1981).

acute; although conferences artificially distort the law of comparative advantage they do not eliminate competition but, rather, raise the stakes of commercial rivalry.

The higher degree of collusion in ultra-conferences and consortia since the late 1960s was a response to growing competition between two incipient trade blocs, Western Europe and the United States. International consortia were Europe's response to the "American challenge," which had technological, political, and geopolitical dimensions. Shipping firms retain their autonomy; shares of trade are allocated on the basis of existing market share. The serious disputes among OECD states and the tensions and policy differences arising in the EC over the UNCTAD Code of Conduct for Liner Conferences highlight the national economic conflict, which conferences do not resolve. Even where conferences overcome the contradictions between shipping firms, agreements are often overridden by the needs of overall foreign economic policies.

The higher degree of interdependence that ultra-conferences promote does, to be sure, make the articulation of a coherent national maritime strategy more difficult. Disarticulation at the national level gives rise to the proliferation and increased significance of transnational coalitions, both governmental and private. This is most evident in U.S. shipping policy, as described in Chapter 7. Although the fragmentation of the bureaucracy is most severe in the United States, most Western European countries are also experiencing internal conflicts; the maritime sector as a whole is pitted against industrial interests, or elements of the maritime sector are in conflict; these rifts are reproduced at government level, giving policy a tentative and fragmentary character.

Increasing bureaucratic conflict does not, however, diminish the analytical utility of the concept of state power. Conflicts in the bureaucracy play out the domestic repercussions of international rivalry; they are signs of increasing tension in world politics. The energetic application of antitrust law by the Department of Justice has antagonized not only European and Japanese lines but also those subsidized American lines that seek greater stability and guaranteed market shares. Yet, despite the difficulty of defining *national interest,* and the widespread view that the United States lacks a coherent maritime policy (which is true in an important sense), the *effect* of U.S. actions has been remarkably consistent with overall trade objectives.

The analysis presented here thus affirms the analytical concepts of state power, anarchy, and uneven development. It also concurs with the conclusions of the Alexander Report of 1914 that conferences represent a truce between shipping firms. International shipping transactions do not, in the long run, mute international economic conflict. Rather, they express it by institutionalizing a temporary and unstable balance of market power. Conferences do not signify ultra-imperialism, just imperialism.

In the bulk sector, flags of convenience have been portrayed by some observers as representing the extreme case of "sovereignty at bay." Shipowners have largely been successful in transcending state controls. Some sources suggest that a minimum of 15 percent of FOC tonnage is "adrift" or of unidentified ownership. This study has documented the numerous ways that flags of convenience have contributed to the privatization of the shipping industry. At a level of analysis that does not differentiate between the interests of national capitals or include geopolitical considerations, flags of convenience do provide a "bonus to big capital."[4]

Yet the existence of open registries is deeply and inexorably dependent on the fulfillment of American economic and strategic interests. Flags of convenience have been the joint project of the U.S. government and the multinationals. As Robert Blackwell, a former assistant secretary of state for maritime affairs, observed, Liberia is "a phantom maritime power that was created by American businessmen."[5] Behind the oil and other extractive and agribusiness corporations stands sovereignty: the departments of State and Defense. Flags of convenience are a manifestation of American hegemony and power.

International Organizations

The role played by international shipping organizations supports the foregoing interpretation and conclusions. Activities of international maritime organizations correspond to the balance of power in shipping and the international political economy as a whole. As the balance of power shifted and existing organizations became obsolete, new ones that more faithfully reflected political and economic divisions sprang up. IMCO and IMO,

4. Esko Antola, "The Flag of Convenience System: Bonus for Big Capital," *Instant Research on Peace and Violence* 4 (1974).
5. *New York Times*, 13 February 1977, p. 1.

the shipping activities of the OEEC and OECD, and developments within UNCTAD all serve to illustrate this point.

Even after ratification, the clauses mandating that IMCO should examine "economic" questions of substance were effectively eliminated, casualties of the privatized regime that was established after World War II. Opponents of a strong IMCO simply carried out their attacks from within rather than from without. The struggle to ratify IMCO and the marginal role it eventually played in the determination of basic rules and procedures are evidence of deep underlying divisions in shipping. Multilateralism and the possibility of effective international organization succumbed to the interests of the advanced capitalist countries and particularistic interpretations of free trade.

Established under United States patronage, the OEEC was the organizational expression of the Marshall Plan, European reconstruction, and American cold war strategy. Its charter called for liberalization of trade, finance, and invisible transactions. Progress in shipping was much greater than in most other areas. In seeking to generalize liberalism, the OEEC furthered the interests of most Western European shipowners. An instrument of the traditional maritime countries, the Maritime Transport Committee of the OEEC, in contrast to IMCO, was able to take up highly political concerns such as open registries, flag discrimination, and subsidies, and its decisions were legally binding for member nations. On issues involving protectionism among member states, the work of the OEEC was effective. The maze of prewar and wartime restrictions was eliminated, and relatively free access to cargoes and ships was guaranteed. In the late 1950s the OEEC unsuccessfully fought the proliferation of flags of convenience.

The OECD incorporated the United States into the expanded twenty-four-member body of advanced Western capitalist states and Japan. The Maritime Transport Committee remained and continued to coordinate shipping affairs. The OECD Code of Liberalization was the first legally binding international convention on commercial shipping rules and the first code specifically calling for free competition. However, the entry of the United States destroyed the relative homogeneity of the OEEC on shipping matters. The United States carefully qualified its support for free trade, and many other countries simply refused to sign the convention. The failure of the OECD to expand the system of open markets highlights the disintegrative tendencies in European-American maritime affairs and, to a lesser extent, the nationalist agitation emanating from the Third World. As an organization seeking to coordinate U.S. and European shipping, the Maritime Transport Committee of the OECD spanned two blocs but failed to give adequate organizational expression to either. These limitations gave rise to the formation of CENSA and CSG.

Whereas the OECD became little more than a forum for negotiations and a useful source of research, CENSA and CSG operated on a broader scale and, to a limited degree, still function as potent political groupings. In effect, they represent the regional arm of Western European and Japanese shipping in its opposition to American regulatory and cargo-reservation policies and to Third World nationalism. However, as the rejection of the CENSA Code by less developed countries in 1971 demonstrated, the CENSA/CSG formation lacks a universal mandate. It is gradually being superseded by EC shipping policy.

During the postwar period, disintegrative tendencies in the regime precluded the establishment of autonomous international organizations with plausible claims to universality. IMCO quickly retreated to the periphery of world shipping politics, while the Maritime Transport Committee reflected the strains of European-American relations and, eventually, the dissatisfaction of the Third World with the conference system. The establishment of UNCTAD in 1964 marked the Third World as a force in shipping and heralded the rise of shipping nationalism. UNCTAD represents a return to the ideal of multilateralism, but only because it incorporates in its negotiating structure, albeit imperfectly, all the various blocs.

UNCTAD's Committee on Shipping evolved partially as a response to the emasculation of IMCO, and it reflected the Third World's dissatisfaction with privatization as the basis of international shipping. UNCTAD's initial document stressed "sound economic criteria" as the basis of national shipping policies, but this orientation changed as the balance of power in UNCTAD shifted to the bloc of Third World countries known as the Group of 77, after the traditional maritime powers refused to make meaningful concessions. In UNCTAD, less developed countries control the secretariat and all other positions of power through the principle of "one country, one vote." Thus, throughout its history, the secretariat and the Committee on Shipping have taken up Third World concerns. They have depended on divisions within and among other blocs in order to pass legislation such as the UNCTAD Code of Conduct for Liner Conferences.

Third World countries have perceived that expansion of the functions and mandate of international organizations is an effective means toward establishing a regulatory regime.

Dominated by less developed countries, UNCTAD gives expression to Third World maritime nationalism. It reflects and illustrates the limitations and illusions of the NIEO. Contrary to the perceptions of Western shipping spokesmen, who view the secretariat as the main enemy, UNCTAD articulates but does not create political and economic initiatives. The simplest illustration of the subordinate role played by the Committee on Shipping and the secretariat is the tendency for Third World protectionism to overstep the bounds of the UNCTAD Code of Conduct. Increasingly, Western shipowners are coming to regret their opposition to the code and the delay over its ratification. Ironically, it is becoming a conservative instrument in the hands of its former enemies.

UNCTAD imperfectly incorporates the main politicoeconomic blocs in international relations. As such, it is usually afflicted by paralysis. This weak role is evident in the lack of movement on the issue of flags of convenience. But when it can engage tangible interests UNCTAD can score some successes. The limited progress in liner shipping derives largely from the splitting of the OECD (Group B) and the particular interests that UNCTAD could activate in the United States. However, the divisions between Europe and America remain central to world shipping developments. Because the UNCTAD Code of Conduct does not synchronize these diverging traditions, it does not serve as the basis for a stable new order.

International organizations are key elements of international shipping not because they play an important independent role in the regime but, rather, because they institutionalize conflict. The increasing prominence of international maritime organizations is an indication of the greater intensity of interstate and interfirm competition in the regime. Since 1945, international organizations have served as avenues for the pursuit of national maritime policies. At the same time, international organizations have helped to partially resolve conflicts of the regime, thus making possible higher levels of interdependence.

To identify power as the strategic determinant of the regime is not to deny either the reality or the salience of international shipping cooperation. Regimes may be said to institutionalize power relations, but regimes are relatively autonomous of power and interest. In important respects cooperation among states is increasing. But the collusive or cooperative tendency can only be adequate described and explained with reference to the framework of international power relations.

Of course, it would be implausible and narrowly reductionist to claim that there is a perfect correspondence between regimes and structures, or that there are no chronological lags between regimes and the determinant structures of power and interest.[6] All institutions produce unintended consequences and facilitate behavior and ideas that follow an independent course; ideas cannot be reduced to interests; politics is more than a reflection of economics. For example, much of the work of IMO dealing with technical questions can be described as nonpolitical. Nevertheless, as a rule, if international maritime organizations do not conform to the structure of interests but, rather, seek to steer a course against the prevailing powers, they are either destroyed or ignored.

Shipping and the Politics of Hegemonic Decline

The analysis of shipping has a number of important implications for theory in international political economy. At the outset I assumed that the theory of hegemonic stability might yield important explanatory concepts. It has provoked a great deal of discussion in the literature on international political economy, and it is useful in helping to understand basic historical changes in shipping. Before the twentieth century, international shipping regimes oscillated between free trade and mercantilism, as was shown in Chapter 2. Hegemonic leaders established freedom-of-the-seas regimes in shipping. However, the attempt to demonstrate a correlation between hegemony and free trade in post-1880 shipping regimes was rejected here. Instead, a correlation between hegemony and stability was hypothesized, and evidence in support of this hypothesis has been presented. The postwar regime was never strictly a free-trade regime. Despite the attempts of the Third World and other protectionists, the emerging order is not nationalist or statist.

In general, there is a strong correlation between stability in shipping and American hegemony. As hegemony has eroded, conflict in shipping

---

6. The question of lags is addressed by Stephen Krasner in "Regimes and the Limits of Realism: Regimes as Autonomous Variables," *International Organization* 36 (Spring 1982).

has increased. This study has detailed the specific ways that America's post-war maritime policies contributed to global stability by making concessions to allied powers. However, by the mid-1960s the United States was no longer willing or able to tolerate a regime in which the costs to trading and shipping interests were substantial. Therefore, the United States sought to bring about a closer identity between its interests and the practices of the regime. The regulation of liner conferences, together with technological innovations originating in the United States, has constituted a serious challenge to the traditional maritime powers.

The interpretation of hegemonic stability adopted in this study makes it necessary to consider the role played by domestic structures as a key variable in the explanation of regime change: stable international regimes knit together the domestic structures of the strongest actors in the system; leaders seek to establish and sustain regimes that are compatible with the domestic politics of the major powers. This study has attempted to show that under conditions of hegemony, the domestic structure of the United States was relatively insulated from the regime. However, as hegemony declined, the domestic structure began to have a greater impact on the nature of the regime, generating conflict. America's post-hegemonic residue of power encourages Washington to impose preferences on trading partners, either as a result of preoccupation with domestic politics or as a result of nationalistic convictions stressing the preservation of autonomy or the idea that "what's good for America is good for the world." The incentive to overcome domestic conflicts and constraints diminishes considerably as hegemony wanes and the international environment becomes less malleable and predictable.

Of course, change in America's maritime sector has contributed to America's determination to establish a regulatory regime for liner conferences. In the United States, not surprisingly, the smaller firms favor protectionist measures. The emerging large lines, aspiring to a greater role in cross-trades and "round the world" services, were crucial to the passage of the U.S. Shipping Act of 1984. Together with the large shippers they represent a new, dominant coalition in shipping policy, although there are important differences among the members of this coalition. Their size and global ambitions make them wary of bloc solutions. In the bulk sector, however, the dominant coalition of multinationals and the executive branch of government has survived largely intact.

The analysis of domestic structures provides a more comprehensive explanation for events in shipping. Whereas declining hegemony as a variable simply predicted instability and conflict, without specifying the forms that conflict and change would assume, the examination of domestic structures makes it possible to extend and deepen the analysis: it helps in understanding the origins and in explaining and predicting the nature of specific changes in the regime, and in showing how and why such changes help or hurt various states. In arguing for the importance of domestic structures, this study has developed an analysis of the politics of the maritime sectors of the leading shipping nations. National shipping policies are influenced by the role and power of shipping in the economy as a whole and the relations of production that influence the decisions of shipping firms. Maritime structures have evolved in different states in response to the pressures of industrialization and a given state's economic, geographical, and chronological point of entry into international trade. Once established, domestic structures appear to be relatively immune to the pressures of the regime. The postwar regime imposed limitations on the maritime ambitions of France and West Germany. It reinforced the power of shipping firms in British society. As hegemonic leader, the United States supported a regime that did not enhance the short-term interests of its maritime sector or exporters. However, as hegemony declined, the domestic structure becomes a crucial variable in explaining conflict and change in international regimes.

My emphasis on the politics of declining hegemony differs from standard empirical applications of the theory of hegemonic stability. As noted in Chapter 1, the standard approach does not generally make a distinction between *hegemony* and *power*. It assumes a strong tendency toward international pluralism, expressed either in the emergence of a variegated, complex system in which states have different degrees of power in different regimes, or in a balance of economic power in which Western Europe and Japan have become rivals or partners of the United States and not simply "middle powers." The standard approach has been weakest in the investigation of the structural basis of American politicoeconomic power, which, this study contends, continues to be very great.

The assumption that the international distribution of power is diffuse, coupled with the general agreement that American leadership underwrote international economic stability during the 1950s and 1960s, has suggested to many that the central problem for the study of the contemporary international political economy is that of cooperation among equals. A great deal of theorizing has sought to show how and why such cooperation is problematic, exploring either hypothetically or empirically the conditions under which cooperation is possible. Yet the assumption of international pluralism makes it difficult to appreciate the strong and often destabilizing impact of American actions and policies on trading partners. In shipping, an approach that fails to distinguish conceptually between hegemony and the great power the United States possesses in its post-hegemonic phase cannot explain or predict the continuation (in bulk shipping) and increase (in liner shipping) of American power.

This study does not provide evidence that states cannot, in principle, cooperate in the absence of a hegemonic leader. Such evidence would require the existence of a roughly equal distribution of power among states, which does not exist at the present time. Nor does this study provide a brief for the old regime in shipping or argue that American preferences are inherently less desirable than the old order. Rather, it argues that the problem of cooperation in the world political economy should be analyzed in the context of America's continuing predominance. Of course, one should be wary of making generalizations on the basis of a single case study. Yet the case of shipping does appear to conform to America's general approach to the international economy in the late 1980s. Recognizing that America's great underlying economic power compensates for its inability to realize its aspirations in international organizations, policymakers have pressed for market-oriented regimes while practicing benign neglect in international organizations.[7] A similar logic seems to apply in such diverse regimes as agriculture and services. In each of these cases, American policies and actions are creating great pressure to reshape international regimes in ways that, although they accord with new national objectives, would create national and international turbulence. In shipping, the preferred instrument of American influence has not been international organizations but, rather, the marketplace. The crucial regime document appears to be not an international code but national law, the U.S. Shipping Act of 1984, which itself serves to restructure national and international relations. No longer shackled by the responsibilities of hegemony, the United States has become, in important respects, a revisionist power, capable of maintaining its superiority if not of restoring hegemony.

7. Henry Nau, "Where Reaganomics Works," *Foreign Policy* 57 (Winter 1984–85).

SELECTED BIBLIOGRAPHY

I. Official Reports and Documents

EUROPEAN COMMUNITY

European Commission. *Progress Towards a Common Transport Policy: Maritime Transport*. Brussels: European Community, March 1985.
———. "Report of the Commission to the Council—State Aid to Shipbuilding." Brussels: European Community, 1979.
———. *Report on the State of the Shipbuilding Industry in the Community*. Brussels: European Community. Annual.
European Parliament. *Working Documents on the Community Shipping Industry: An Interim Report Drawn Up on Behalf of the Committee on Economic and Monetary Affairs*. Doc. 479/76. Brussels: European Community, December 1976.
———, Ad Hoc Merchant Shipping Committee. *EEC Shipping Policy—Flags of Convenience*. Brussels: European Community, 1979.

JAPAN

Ministry of Transport. *The Current Situation of Japanese Shipping, 1985*. Tokyo: Japan Maritime Development Association, 1985.

ORGANIZATION FOR ECONOMIC COOPERATION AND DEVELOPMENT

Maritime Transport Committee. *Maritime Transport*. Paris: OECD. Annual.

ORGANIZATION FOR EUROPEAN ECONOMIC COOPERATION

Maritime Transport Committee. *Maritime Transport*. Paris: OEEC. Annual (to 1960).
———. *Study on the Expansion of the Flag of Convenience Fleets and on Various Aspects Thereof*. Paris: OEEC, 1958.

UNITED KINGDOM

Booth Committee Report. *See* Departmental Committee on Shipping and Shipbuilding.

287

British Shipbuilders, Corporate Planning Division. "Shipbuilding in Recession."
    1980. (Mimeographed.)
Committee of Inquiry into Shipping. *Report* (Rochdale Report). Cmnd. 4337.
    London: HMSO, 1970.
Court of Inquiry into Certain Matters Concerning the Shipping Industry. *Final
    Report* (Pearson Report). Cmnd. 3211. London: HMSO, 1967.
Departmental Committee on Shipping and Shipbuilding. *First Report* (Booth
    Committee Report). Cmnd. 9092. London: HMSO, 1918.
Department of Industry and Trade. *General Trends in Shipping: A Report on the
    U.K. Merchant Fleet, World Shipping and Seaborne Trade.* Series 2, No. 6. Lon-
    don: Dept. of Industry and Trade, November 1979.
Department of Trade. *Casualties to Vessels and Accidents to Men, 1976.* London:
    HMSO, 1978.
———. *Implementation of the United Nations Convention on a Code of Conduct for
    Liner Conferences.* London: HMSO, 1982.
Department of Trade and Industry. *British Shipbuilding, 1972: A Report to the De-
    partment of Trade and Industry* (Booz-Allen Report). London: HMSO, 1973.
House of Lords. *Official Report, Parliamentary Debates: Protection of Trading Inter-
    ests Bill.* Hansard, Vol. 404, No. 70. London: HMSO, 24 January 1980.
———, Select Committee on the European Communities. *Liner Conferences.* Ses-
    sion 1977–78, 25th Report. R/3245/77. London: HMSO, 1978.
———. *Shipbuilding.* Session 1977–78, 32nd Report. R/3216/77. London:
    HMSO, 1978.
Imperial Shipping Committee. *British Shipping in the Orient.* London: HMSO,
    1939.
Rochdale Report. *See* Committee of Inquiry into Shipping.
Royal Commission on Shipping Rings. *Report.* Cmnd. 4668. London: HMSO,
    1909.
Shipbuilding Inquiry Committee. *1965–1966 Report* (Geddes Report). Cmnd.
    2937. London: HMSO, 1966.

UNITED NATIONS

Department of Public Information. "UNCTAD Shipping Committee Calls for
    Phasing Out of Flags of Convenience." *U.N. Chronicle* 18 (August 1981).
Economic and Social Council. *U.N. Maritime Conference, Geneva 1948—Docu-
    ments.* London: IMCO, 1948.
———, Commission on Transnational Corporations. "Studies on the Effects of the
    Operations and Practices of Transnational Corporations: Other Studies." *Trans-
    national Corporations in the Shipping Industry: The Case of Bauxite/Alumina.*
    E/C.10/1982/14. Manila: United Nations, 1982.
International Labor Organization. "Conditions in Ships Flying the Panama Flag:
    Report of the Committee of Inquiry of the I.L.O." Geneva: I.L.O., 1950.
International Law Commission. *Yearbook.* Annual.
United Nations Conference on Trade and Development. *Action on the Question of*

Open Registries. TD/B/C.4/220. Geneva: United Nations, 1981.

———. *Basic Economics of Containerization and Unitization in Ocean Shipping: Note by the UNCTAD Secretariat.* TD/B/C.4/34. Geneva: United Nations, 1967.

———. *Beneficial Ownership of Open-Registry Fleets.* TD/222/Supp. 1. Geneva: United Nations, 1979.

———. *Beneficial Ownership of Open-Registry Fleets—1980—Report by the UNCTAD Secretariat.* TD/B/C.4/218. Geneva: United Nations, 1980.

———. *Comparative Labour Costs.* TD/222/Supp. 4. Geneva: United Nations, 1979.

———. *Consultation in Shipping: Report by the Secretary General.* TD/B/C.4/20 Rev. 1. Geneva: United Nations, 1967.

———. *Control by Transnational Corporations over Dry Bulk Cargo Movements— Report by the UNCTAD Secretariat.* TD/B/C.4/203. Geneva: United Nations, 1980.

———. *The Effectiveness of Shippers' Organizations: A Report by the UNCTAD Secretariat.* TD/B/C.4/154. Geneva: United Nations, 1976.

———. *Establishment or Expansion of Merchant Marines in Developing Countries.* TD/26/Supp. 1. Geneva: United Nations, 1967.

———. *Final Act and Report, 1st Session.* Geneva: United Nations, 1964.

———. *Formation and Strengthening of Shippers' Commodity Groups.* TD/B/C.4/ 188. Geneva: United Nations, 1979.

———. *International Legislation on Shipping.* TD/32/Rev. 1. Geneva: United Nations, 1968.

———. *Iron Ore Trade from Latin America to Japan: A Study by the UNCTAD Secretariat.* TD/B/C.4/AC.2/2. Geneva: United Nations, 1981.

———. *Legal Mechanisms for Regulating the Operation of Open-Registry Fleets During the Phasing Out Period.* TD/B/C.4/AC.1/6. Geneva: United Nations, 1979.

———. *Level and Structure of Freight Rates, Conference Practices and Adequacy of Shipping Services.* TD/B/C.4/38/Rev. 1. Geneva: United Nations, 1969.

———. *The Liner Conference System.* TD/B/C.4/62/Rev. 1. New York: United Nations, 1970.

———. *The Maritime Transport of Hydrocarbons.* TD/222/Supp. 3. Manila: United Nations, 1979.

———. *Merchant Fleet Development.* TD/222. Manila: United Nations, 1979.

———. *Merchant Fleet Development: Guidelines for Developing Countries Report by the UNCTAD Secretariat.* TD/B/C.4/186. Geneva: United Nations, 1979.

———. *Multimodal Transport and Containerization: Guidelines on the Introduction of Containerization and Multimodal Transport and the Modernization and Improvement of the Infrastructure of Developing Countries.* TD/B/C.4/238. Geneva: United Nations, 1982.

———. *Multinational Shipping Enterprises.* TD/108/Supp. 1/Rev. 1. Geneva: United Nations, 1972.

———. *The Nature and Extent of Cargo Reservation.* TD/B/C.4/63. Geneva: United Nations, 1970.

———. *Programme of Action for Cooperation Among Developing Countries: Draft Pro-

gramme of Action for Co-operation Among Developing Countries in the Area of Shipping, Ports and Multimodal Transport. Report by the UNCTAD Secretariat. TD/B/C.4/273. Geneva: United Nations, 1984.

―――. *The Regulation of Liner Conferences: A Code of Conduct for the Liner Conference System.* TD/104/Rev. 1. Geneva: United Nations, 1972.

―――. *The Repercussions of Phasing Out Open Registries.* TD/B/C.4/AC.1/5. Geneva: United Nations, 1979.

―――. *Report of the Committee on Shipping on Its Fourth Session, 20 April–4 May, 1970.* TD/B/C.4/73. Geneva: United Nations, 1970.

―――. *Report of the Group of Experts on International Sea Transport of Liquid Hydrocarbons in Bulk in Its Second Session.* TD/B/C.4/263/5. Geneva: United Nations, 1984.

―――. *Report of the Group of Experts on Problems Faced by the Developing Countries in the Carriage of Bulk Cargoes in Its Second Session.* TD/B/C.4/234. Geneva: United Nations, 1981.

―――. *Report of the Preparatory Committee for the United Nations Conference on Conditions for Registration of Ships.* TD/RS/CONF/PC/14. Geneva: United Nations, 1984.

―――. *Review of Maritime Transport.* Geneva: United Nations. Annual.

―――. *A Set of Basic Principles Concerning the Conditions upon Which Vessels Should Be Accepted on National Shipping Registers—Report by the UNCTAD Secretariat.* TD/RS.CONF/PC/2. Geneva: United Nations, 1983.

―――. *Shipping in the 1970s.* TD/177. Geneva: United Nations, 1972.

―――. *Status of the Convention on a Code of Conduct for Liner Conferences—Note by the UNCTAD Secretariat.* TD/B/C.4/206. Geneva: United Nations, 1980.

―――. *Status of the Convention on a Code of Conduct for Liner Conferences: Note by the UNCTAD Secretariat.* TD/B/C.4/281. Geneva: United Nations, 1984.

―――. *Terms of Shipment: Report by the UNCTAD Secretariat.* TD/B/C.4/36/Rev. Geneva: United Nations, 1969.

―――. *Trade Routes of Open Registry Vessels.* TD/222/Supp. 5. Geneva: United Nations, 1979.

―――. *United Nations Conference of Plenipotentiaries on a Code of Conduct for Liner Conferences: Reports and Other Documents.* TD/Code/13. Geneva: United Nations, 1974.

―――. *U.N. Conference of Plenipotentiaries on a Code of Conduct for Liner Conferences—Final Act and Annexes.* TD/Code/11 Rev. 1. Geneva: United Nations, 1974.

―――. *Unitization of Cargo.* TD/B/C.4/75. Geneva: United Nations, 1970.

UNITED STATES

Alexander Report. *See* Congress. House. Committee on Merchant Marine and Fisheries. *Report on Steamship Agreements.*

Congress. House. *Ocean Shipping Act of 1979 Hearings: Omnibus Maritime Bill.* 96th Cong., 1979.

——. *Shipping Act of 1984—Conference Report 98–600.* 98th Cong., 2d sess., 23 February 1984.

——. Committee on the Judiciary (Celler Committee). Report of the Anti-Trust Committee. *The Ocean Freight Industry.* 87th Cong., 1962.

——. Committee on Merchant Marine and Fisheries. *Closed Conferences and Shippers' Councils in U.S. Liner Trades: Hearings Before a Subcommittee of the House Committee on Merchant Marine and Fisheries.* 95th Cong., 1978.

——. *Omnibus Maritime Bill: Hearings Before the Subcommittee of the House Committee on Merchant Marine and Fisheries.* 96th Cong., 1980.

——. *Regulatory Reform: Hearings Before the Subcommittee on Merchant Marine on H.R. 4374.* 97th Cong., 1982.

——. *Report on Steamship Agreements and Affiliations in the American Foreign and Domestic Trades* (Alexander Report). 63rd Cong., 1914.

——. *Steamship Conference Study.* 86th Cong., 1959.

——. *Third Flag Hearings Before the Subcommittee on Merchant Marine on H.R. 7940 and H.R. 14564.* 94th Cong., 1975, 1976.

——. *United Nations Conference on Trade and Development Oversight: Hearings Before the Subcommittee on Merchant Marine.* 97th Cong., 1981.

——. Subcommittee on Merchant Marine and Fisheries. *Study of Vessel Transfer, Trade-In and Reserve Fleet Policies.* 85th Cong., 1957.

Congress. Joint Economic Committee. *Discriminatory Ocean Freight Rates and the Balance of Payments.* 88th Cong., 1965.

Congress. Senate. Committee on Commerce, Science, and Transportation. *Ocean Shipping Act of 1978: Hearings before the Senate Subcommittee on Merchant Marine and Tourism of the Senate Committee on Commerce, Science, and Transportation.* 95th Cong., 1978.

——. *Ocean Shipping Act of 1979.* 96th Cong., 1979.

——. *Ocean Shipping Act of 1980.* S. Rept. No. 96–659. 96th Cong., 1980.

——. *Shipping Act of 1981: Hearings Before the Subcommittee on Merchant Marine on S. 1593.* 97th Cong., 1981.

Congress. Senate. Committee on Interstate and Foreign Commerce. *Ship Transfers to Foreign Flags: Hearings Before the Merchant Marine and Fisheries Subcommittee of the Committee on Interstate and Foreign Commerce.* 85th Cong., 1957.

Department of Commerce. Maritime Administration (MARAD). *Annual Report.* Washington, D.C.: G.P.O. Annual.

——. *Expansion of the Soviet Merchant Marine into U.S. Maritime Trades.* Washington, D.C.: G.P.O., 1977.

——. "The Impact of Bilateral Shipping Agreements in the U.S. Trades." Washington, D.C.: G.P.O., 1979.

——. Office of International Activities. *Maritime Subsidies.* Washington, D.C.: G.P.O. Biannual.

——. Office of Policy and Planning. *The Maritime Aids of the Six Major Maritime Nations.* Washington, D.C.: G.P.O., 1977.

——. *The U.S. Merchant Marine and the International Conference System* (Harbridge House Study). Washington, D.C.: G.P.O., 1978.

Department of Commerce. Maritime Administration and Under-Secretary of State for Commerce and Transportation. *Maritime Subsidy Policy.* Washington, D.C.: G.P.O., 1954.

Department of Justice. Anti-Trust Division. *The Regulated Ocean Shipping Industry.* Washington, D.C.: G.P.O., 1977.

Federal Maritime Commission. *Annual Report.* Washington, D.C.: G.P.O. Annual.

Government Accounting Office. *Changes in Federal Maritime Regulation Can Increase Efficiency and Reduce Costs in the Ocean Liner Shipping Industry.* GAO/ PAD–82–11. Washington, D.C.: G.P.O., 1982.

National Academy of Sciences. National Council. *Maritime Transportation of Unitized Cargo—A Comparative Analysis of Breakbulk and Unitized Services.* Maritime Cargo Transportation Conference. Washington, D.C.: National Academy of Sciences, 1959.

II. Books, Articles, and Pamphlets

Abrahamsson, Bernard J. *International Ocean Shipping: Current Concepts and Principles.* Boulder: Westview, 1980.

————. "The Marine Environment and Ocean Shipping: Some Implications for the New Law of the Sea." *International Organization* 31 (Spring 1977).

Adelman, M. A. *The World Petroleum Market.* Baltimore: Johns Hopkins University Press, 1972.

Ademuni-Odeke. *Protectionism and the Future of International Shipping: The Nature, Development and Role of Flag Discriminations and Preferences, Cargo Reservation and Cabotage Restrictions, State Intervention and Maritime Subsidies.* Dordrecht: Martinus Nijhoff, 1984.

Adler, J. Hans. "British and American Shipping Policies: A Problem and a Proposal." *Political Science Quarterly* 59 (June 1944).

Agman, Robert S. "Competition, Rationalization, and U.S. Shipping Policy." *Journal of Maritime Law and Commerce* 8 (October 1976).

Akaha, Tsuneo. "Japan: Energy, Sea Lanes, and Security." *Marine Policy Reports.* University of Delaware, Center for the Study of Marine Policy, Vol. 7, No. 3. December 1984.

Aldcroft, Derek H. *British Transport Since 1914: An Economic History.* Devon: David and Charles, 1975.

————. "Reflections on the Rochdale Inquiry into Shipping: A Review Article." *Maritime History* 1 (September 1971).

American Merchant Marine Conference. *Proceedings—Volume 10.* New York: Propeller Club of the United States, 1944.

Amin, Samir, Giovanni Arrighi, André Gunder Frank, and Immanuel Wallerstein. *Dynamics of Global Crisis.* New York: Monthly Review Press, 1982.

Antola, Esko. "The Flag of Convenience System: Bonus for Big Capital." *Instant Research on Peace and Violence* 4 (1974).

Arkes, Hadley. *Bureaucracy, the Marshall Plan, and the National Interest.* Princeton, N.J.: Princeton University Press, 1972.

Astin, Trevor, ed. *Crisis in Europe, 1560–1660.* Garden City: Anchor, 1967.

Athay, Robert. *Economics of Soviet Merchant Shipping Policy.* Chapel Hill: University of North Carolina Press, 1971.

Atlantic Council of the United States. *The Soviet Merchant Marine: Economic and Strategic Challenge to the West.* Washington, D.C.: Atlantic Council, 1978.

Aubrey, Henry C. *Atlantic Economic Cooperation: The Case of the OECD.* New York: Council on Foreign Relations, 1967.

Avery, William P., and David P. Rapkin, eds. *America in a Changing World Political Economy.* New York: Longman, 1982.

Baily, Michael. "British Shipowners Beware the Greeks." *Times* (London), 2 December 1980.

———. "The Shipping Industry and the Bureaucrats of Brussels." *Times* (London), 30 June 1976.

Ball, Joseph H. *The Government-Subsidized Union Monopoly: A Study of Labor Practices in the Shipping Industry.* Washington, D.C.: Labor Policy Association, 1966.

Banberger, Werner. "U.N. Shipping Body Is Set Back Anew." *New York Times,* 15 April 1956.

Barker, James C., and Robert Brandwein. *The U.S. Merchant Marine in National Perspective.* Lexington, Mass.: D.C. Heath, 1970.

Barston, R. P., and Patricia Birnie, eds. *The Maritime Dimension.* London: Allen and Unwin, 1980.

Barthy-King, Hugh. *The Baltic Exchange: The History of a Unique Market.* London: Hutchinson, 1977.

Beargie, Tony. "Maritime Lobbyists Battle for Tax Dollars." *American Shipper* 26 (February 1984).

Behrens, C. B. A. *Merchant Shipping and the Demands of War.* London: Longman, Green, 1959.

Bekiashev, Kamil A., and Vitali A. Serebrakov. *International Marine Organization: Essays on Structure and Activities.* The Hague: Martinus Nijhoff, 1981.

Bell, Richard. "European Shipowners Demand Action Against Trans-Siberian Box Line." *Container News* 11 (April 1981).

Benwell Community Project. *The Making of a Ruling Class: Two Centuries of Capitalist Development on the Tyneside.* Final Report, Series No. 6. Newcastle-upon-Tyne: Benwell Community Project, 1978.

Berg, Eivinn. "United States/Norway—Partners or Opponents in International Shipping?" *Norwegian Shipping News* 32 (10 December 1976).

Berglund, Abraham. *Ocean Transportation.* New York: Longman, 1931.

Bess, H. David, and Martin T. Farris. *U.S. Maritime Policy: History and Prospects.* New York: Praeger, 1981.

Beth, Hans Ludwig, Arnulf Hader, and Robert Kappel. *Twenty-Five Years of World Shipping.* London: Fairplay, 1984.

Block, Fred L. *Origins of International Economic Disorder: A Study of U.S. Inter-*

national Monetary Policy from World War II to the Present. Berkeley and Los Angeles: University of California Press, 1977.

Boczek, Boleslaw Adam. *Flags of Convenience: An International Legal Study*. Cambridge, Mass.: Harvard University Press, 1962.

Böhme, Hans. "Current Issues and Progress in European Shipping Policy." *World Economy* 6, no. 3 (September 1983).

———. "Eastern Bloc Competition and Freedom of the Seas." *Fairplay International Shipping Weekly* 258 (9 September 1976).

———. *Restraints on Competition in World Shipping*. Thames Essay No. 15. London: Trade Policy Research Centre, 1978.

Bousquet, Nicole. "From Hegemony to Competition: Cycles of the Core?" In Terence K. Hopkins and Immanuel Wallerstein, eds., *Processes of the World System*, Vol. 3: *Political Economy of the World System Annuals*. Beverly Hills: Sage, 1980.

Bredimas, Anna, and John G. Tzoannis. "In Search of a Common Shipping Policy for the European Community." *Journal of Common Market Studies* 20 (December 1981).

British Shippers' Council. *Annual Report*. Annual.

Bromley, J. S., and E. H. Kossmann, eds. *Britain and the Netherlands in Europe and Asia*. London: Macmillan, 1968.

Brown, R. T. *Transport and the Economic Integration of Latin America*. Washington, D.C.: Brookings Institution, 1966.

Brown, Ronald G., and Akinori Uesugi. "Japanese Regulation of Ocean Freight Shipments." *Journal of Maritime Law and Commerce* 11, no. 3 (April 1980).

Brown, Seyom, et al. *Regimes for the Ocean Space and Weather*. Washington, D.C.: Brookings Institution, 1977.

Burley, Kevin. *British Shipping and Australia*. London: Cambridge University Press, 1968.

Cafruny, Alan W. "The Political Economy of International Shipping: Europe vs. America." *International Organization* 39 (Winter 1985).

Calleo, David P. "American Foreign Policy and American European Studies: An Imperial Bias?" In Wolfram Hanreider, ed., *The United States and Western Europe*. Cambridge, Mass.: Winthrop, 1974.

———. *The Imperious Economy*. Cambridge, Mass.: Harvard University Press, 1982.

Calleo, David P., and Benjamin N. Rowland. *America and the World Political Economy: Atlantic Dreams and National Realities*. Bloomington: Indiana University Press, 1973.

Callinoupolos, Gregory. "In Search of Freedom." *Seatrade* (December 1982).

Carlisle, Rodney P. "The American Century Implemented: Stettinius and the Liberian Flag of Convenience." *Business History Review* 54 (Summer 1980).

———. *Sovereignty for Sale: The Origins and Evolution of the Panamanian and Liberian Flags of Convenience*. Annapolis: Naval Institute Press, 1981.

Cates, John M., Jr. "United Nations Maritime Conference, Geneva, 1948." Department of State Publication 3196, International Organization and Conference Series IV. Washington, D.C.: G.P.O., 1948.

CENSA. *See under* Council of European and Japanese National Shipowners Associations.

Chamber of Shipping of the United Kingdom. *Annual Report*. London. Annual.

————. *The Coming Crisis for British Shipping*. London: Chamber of Shipping of the United Kingdom, 1959.

Chao, Frank. "Politics and Practical Reality." *Seatrade* (November 1981).

Christianson, Uwe. "Questions of Shipping Policy." *Intereconomics* 14 (March–April 1979).

Chrzanowski, Ignacy. *Concentration and Centralization of Capital in Shipping*. Westmead: Saxon House, 1975.

Chrzanowski, Ignacy, Maciej Krzyanowski, and Krzystof Luks. *Shipping Economics and Policy—A Socialist View*. London: Fairplay, 1979.

Cipolla, Carlo. *Guns, Sails, and Empires*. New York: Pantheon, 1965.

Clapham, J. H. "The Last Years of the Navigation Acts." In E. M. Carus-Wilson, ed., *Essays in Economic History*, Vol. 3. London: Edward Arnold, 1962.

Colombos, C. John. *The International Law of the Sea*. 6th rev. ed. New York: David McKay, 1967.

Conybeare, John. "Public Goods, Prisoner's Dilemmas, and the International Political Economy." *International Studies Quarterly* 28 (March 1984).

Cornford, Andrew J., and Raymond B. Glasgow. "The Process of Structural Change in the World Economy: Some Aspects of the Rise of Shipbuilding Industry in Developing Countries." *Trade and Development* 1 (Winter 1981).

Council of European and Japanese National Shipowners Associations. "Sailing in Harmony: Self-Regulation in Shipping Works—and Works Well." London: CENSA, 1968.

————. "Why Does the Anti-Trust Philosophy of the U.S. Hurt the Overseas Trade in U.S. Shipping? American Shippers International Forum." London: CENSA, 1977.

Council of European and Japanese National Shipowners Associations and European Shippers Councils. *Code of Practice for Conferences*. London: CENSA, 1971.

Cowhey, Peter, and Edward Long. "Testing Theories of Regime Change: Hegemonic Decline or Surplus Capacity?" *International Organization* 37 (Spring 1983).

Cragg, Chris. "Fifteen-Year Disaster Figures as United Kingdom Loses Thousands at Sea." *Seatrade* (February 1981).

Curzon, Gerald. *Multi-Lateral Commercial Diplomacy: The General Agreement on Tariffs and Trade and Its Impact on National Commercial Policies and Technique*. London: Michael Joseph, 1965.

Davis, Ralph. *English Merchant Shipping and Anglo-Dutch Rivalry in the Seventeenth Century*. London: HMSO, 1975.

————. *The Rise of the English Shipping Industry in the Seventeenth and Eighteenth Centuries*. London: Macmillan, 1962.

Deakin, B. M. *Shipping Conferences: A Study of Their Origin, Development, and Economic Practices*. Cambridge: Cambridge University Press, 1973.

Dell, Edmund. "Reflections on International Civil Aviation and Shipping Policy." *Journal of the Chartered Institute of Transport* (January 1979).

Dell, Sidney. *A Latin American Common Market?* Oxford: Oxford University Press, 1966.

Denton, Geoffrey, and Sean O'Cleireacain. *Subsidy Issues in International Commerce.* Thames Essay No. 5. London: Trade Policy Research Centre, 1972.

Despicht, Nigel. *Policies for Transport in the Common Market.* Sidcup, Kent: Lambarde Press, 1964.

Deutsch, Karl. *Analysis of International Politics.* Englewood Cliffs, N.J.: Prentice-Hall, 1968.

Deutsch, Karl, et al. *Political Community and the North Atlantic Area: International Organization in the Light of Historical Experience.* Princeton: N.J.: Princeton University Press, 1957.

Dick, H. W. "Containerisation and Liner Conferences: A Polemic." *Maritime Policy and Management* 10 (July–September 1983).

Doganis, R. S., and B. N. Metaxas. *The Impact of Flags of Convenience.* London: Polytechnic of Central London Transport Studies, 1976.

Douglas, Peter. "Let's Focus on Freight Rates!" *Seatrade* (February 1984).

Drugg, Hans Dieter. *Why We Consider Consultation the Superior System to Regulation in United States Liner Shipping.* Hamburg: Hapag-Lloyd, November 1978.

Economist Intelligence Unit. *Ocean Shipping and Freight Rates and Developing Countries.* Geneva: United Nations, 1964.

Ellsworth, Robert A. "Liner Conferences: Evolution of United States Policy." *Marine Policy* 7 (October 1983).

Engler, Robert. *The Politics of Oil: A Study of Private Power and Democratic Decision.* New York: Macmillan, 1961.

Escarpenter, Claudio. *The Economics of Ocean Transport: The Cuban Case Before 1958.* Madison: University of Wisconsin Press, 1965.

Evans, A. A. *Technical and Social Changes in the World's Ports.* Geneva: I.L.O., 1969.

Exxon Public Affairs Department. *Tankers and the Flags They Fly.* New York: Exxon, 1979.

Fair, Marvin, and Howard Reese, eds. *Merchant Marine Policy.* Cambridge, Md.: Cornell Maritime Press, 1963.

Farid, Abdel Majid, ed. *Oil and Security in the Persian Gulf.* New York: St. Martin's Press, 1981.

Farrant, Stephen. "Full Steam into Europe." *Times* (London), 15 December 1980.

Farrell, S. "The Use of Flags of Convenience by Latin American Shipping." *Journal of Maritime Policy and Management* 11 (January–March 1984).

Fasbender, Karl, and Wolfgang Wagner. *Shipping Conferences, Rate Policy, and Developing Countries: The Argument of Rate Discrimination.* Hamburg: Weltarchiv GMBH, 1973.

Fayle, C. Ernest. *A Short History of the World's Shipping Industry.* London: Allen and Unwin, 1933.

Feis, Herbert. *The Sinews of Peace.* New York: Harper and Row, 1944.

Finlayson, Jock A., and Mark W. Zacher. "The GATT and the Regulation of Trade Barriers: Regime Dynamics and Functions." *International Organization* 35 (Autumn 1981).

Fleming, Douglas. "Safe Harbors." *Journal of Maritime Policy and Management* 13 (January–March 1986).

Frank, André Gunder. "Services Rendered." *Monthly Review* 13 (June 1965).

Frankel, Ernest. *Ocean Transportation*. Cambridge, Mass.: MIT Press, 1973.

——. *Regulation and Policies of American Shipping*. Boston: Auburn House, 1982.

Fraser, Nicholas, Phillip Jacobson, Mark Ottaway, and Lewis Chester. *Aristotle Onassis*. New York: J. B. Lippincott, 1977.

Fulton, T. W. *The Sovereignty of the Sea*. London: Blackwood, 1911.

Furuta, R., and Y. Hirai. *A Short History of Japanese Shipping*. Tokyo: Tokyo News Service, 1967.

Gambino, Antonio. "Atlantic vs. Pacific?" *L'Espresso* 6 (November 1983).

Gardner, Bernard. "The Container Revolution and Its Effects on the Structure of Traditional U.K. Liner Shipping Companies." *Journal of Maritime Policy and Management* 12 (July–September 1985).

General Council of British Shipping. *British Shipping Review*. London. Annual.

——. *Red Ensign vs. the Red Flag*. London: GCBS, 1975.

German Transport Interests. *Competition from the Trans-Siberian Container Link and Its Overall Implications for the Federal Republic of Germany*. Hamburg: Hapag-Lloyd, September 1978.

Gilman, Sidney. *The Competitive Dynamics of Container Shipping*. London: Gower, 1983.

Gilpin, Robert. *U.S. Power and the Multinational Corporation*. New York: Basic Books, 1975.

——. *War and Change in International Politics*. Cambridge: Cambridge University Press, 1981.

Goldman, Peter. "National Policies Recognized as United States and China Enter Sea Trade Pact." *Seatrade* (October 1980).

——. "What Price U.S. Fleet Expansion?" *Seatrade* (June 1982).

Gorshkov, S. G. *The Sea Power of the State*. Annapolis: Naval Institute Press, 1979.

Gorter, Wytze. *United States Shipping Policy*. New York: Harper and Row, 1955.

Goss, R. O., ed. *Studies in Maritime Economics*. London: Cambridge University Press, 1968.

——, ed. *Advances in Maritime Economics*. London: Cambridge University Press, 1977.

Gramsci, Antonio. *Selections from the Prison Notebooks*. London: Lawrence and Wishart, 1971.

Grant, Wyn, and David Marsh. *The Confederation of British Industry*. London: Hodden and Stoughton, 1977.

Grey, Michael. "The United States: The Building of a Maritime Policy." *Fairplay International Shipping Weekly* 11 (October 1979).

Guimaraes, Macedo Soares. "Obsolete Regulations in Maritime Transport." *Inter-economics* 4 (March–April 1969).

Guzhenko, Timofei. "Soviet Merchant Marine and World Shipping." *Marine Policy* 1 (April 1977).

Haas, Ernst. "Why Collaborate? Issue Linkage and International Regimes." *World Politics* 32 (April 1980).

Haas, Ernst, and John Gerard Ruggie, eds. *International Responses to Technology. International Organization* (special issue) 29 (Summer 1975).

Hapag-Lloyd. *The Organization of Liner Shipping in the Container Age Illustrated by the North Atlantic Trade.* Hamburg: Hapag-Lloyd, 1975.

Harbron, J. D. "Argentina's State Merchant Shipping." *Shipping World,* 24 May 1961.

Harper, Lawrence A. *The English Navigation Laws: A Seventeenth Century Experiment in Social Engineering.* New York: Columbia University Press, 1939.

Harvard University Graduate School of Business Administration. *The Use and Disposition of Ships and Shipyards at the End of WW II.* Washington, D.C.: G.P.O., June 1945.

Heine, Irwin. *U.S. Merchant Marine: A National Asset.* Washington, D.C.: National Maritime Council, 1976 (addendum, 1978).

Herman, Amos. *Shipping Conferences.* Deventer: Kluer, 1983.

Hill, Peter. "Shipbuilding Output at Lowest in Fifty Years." *Times* (London), 31 December 1980.

Hinz, Christoph. "Protectionism in Shipping: Some Current and Future Trends." *Marius* (Oslo) 42 (May 1979).

Hobsbawm, Eric J. *Industry and Empire.* London: Penguin, 1968.

———. "The Crisis of the Seventeenth Century." In Trevor Astin, ed., *Crisis in Europe, 1560–1660.* Garden City: Anchor, 1967.

Hobson, John H. *The Evolution of Modern Capitalism.* New York: Scribners, 1916.

Hodgins, Charlie, and John Prescott. *Not Wanted on Voyage: The Seamen's Report to the Labour Movement on the Shipping Strike.* London: National Union of Seamen, 1966.

Hogwood, Brian. *Government and Shipbuilding: The Politics of Industrial Change.* Westmead: Saxon House, 1979.

Institute of Shipping Economics and Logistics. *Shipping Statistics* 29, no. 12. Bremen: Institute of Shipping Economics and Logistics, December 1985.

International Transport Workers Federation. *PanLibHonCo.: The Modern Shipping Problem.* New York: International Transport Workers Federation, 1958.

Jacoby, Neil H. *Multinational Oil: A Study in Industrial Dynamics.* New York: Macmillan, 1974.

Jantscher, Gerald R. *Bread upon the Waters: Federal Aids to the Maritime Industries.* Washington, D.C.: Brookings Institution, 1975.

Jönsson, Christer. "Sphere of Flying: The Politics of International Aviation." *International Organization* 35 (Spring 1981).

Joeston, Joachim. *Onassis: A Biography*. New York: Abelard-Schuman, 1963.

Jones, J. R. *Britain and Europe in the Seventeenth Century*. New York: W. W. Norton, 1963.

Juda, Lawrence. *The UNCTAD Liner Code: United States Maritime Policy at the Crossroads*. Boulder: Westview, 1984.

———. "World Shipping, UNCTAD, and the NIEO." *International Organization* 35 (Summer 1981).

Kappel, Robert. "Liberia's International Shipping Strategy—The Role of Flags of Convenience and the Repercussions for National Development." Bremen: Institute of Shipping Economics and Logistics, 1985. (Mimeographed.)

Katzenstein, Peter J. "International Relations and Domestic Structures: Foreign Economic Policies of Advanced Industrial States." *International Organization* 30 (Winter 1976).

———, ed. *Between Power and Plenty: Foreign Economic Policies of Advanced Industrial States*. Madison: University of Wisconsin Press, 1978.

Kaufman, Burton I. *The Oil Cartel Case: A Documentary Study of Anti-Trust Activity in the Cold War Era*. Westport: Greenwood, 1978.

Keohane, Robert O. *After Hegemony: Cooperation and Discord in the World Political Economy*. Princeton, N.J.: Princeton University Press, 1984.

———. "The Theory of Hegemonic Stability and Changes in International Economic Regimes, 1967–1977." In Ole Holsti, Randolph Siverson, and Alexander L. George, eds., *Change in the International System*. Boulder: Westview, 1980.

Keohane, Robert O., and Joseph S. Nye. *Power and Interdependence: World Politics in Transition*. Boston: Little, Brown, 1977.

Kifner, John. "Liberia: A Phantom Maritime Power Whose Fleet Is Steered by Big Business." *New York Times*, 14 February 1977.

Kilgour, John. "Effective U.S. Control?" *Journal of Maritime Law and Commerce* 8 (April 1977).

———. *The U.S. Merchant Marine: National Maritime Policy and Industrial Relations*. New York: Praeger, 1975.

Kilmarx, Robert A., ed. *America's Maritime Legacy: A History of the U.S. Merchant Marine and Shipbuilding Industry Since Colonial Times*. Boulder: Westview, 1979.

Kindleberger, Charles P. "Dominance and Leadership in the International Economy: Exploitation, Public Goods, and Free Rides." *International Studies Quarterly* 25 (June 1981).

———. *Foreign Trade and the National Economy*. New Haven: Yale University Press, 1962.

———. *The World in Depression, 1929–1939*. Berkeley and Los Angeles: University of California Press, 1973.

———, ed. *The International Corporation: The Non-American Challenge*. Cambridge, Mass.: MIT Press, 1970.

King, Ralph. "National Industrial Traffic League Forms Maritime Advisory Group." *American Shipper* 26 (February 1984).

————. "Paul O'Leary Opens an Old Wound." *American Shipper* 25 (July 1983).

Knudsen, Olav. *The Politics of International Shipping.* Lexington, Mass.: D. C. Heath, 1973.

Krasner, Stephen. *Defending the National Interest: Raw Materials Investments and U.S. Foreign Policy.* Princeton, N.J.: Princeton University Press, 1978.

————. "State Power and the Structure of International Trade." *World Politics* 28 (April 1976).

————. *Structural Conflict: The Third World Against Global Liberalism.* Berkeley and Los Angeles: University of California Press, 1985.

————. "Transforming International Regimes: What the Third World Wants and Why." *International Studies Quarterly* 25 (March 1981).

————, ed. *International Regimes. International Organization* (special issue) 36 (Spring 1982).

Krippendorff, Ekehart, and Volker Rittberger, eds. *The Foreign Policy of West Germany: Formation and Contents.* Beverly Hills: Sage, 1980.

Kwasniewski, Klaus. "Shipping Policy of the Comecon Countries." *Marine Policy* 1 (April 1977).

Larsen, Paul, and Valerie Vetterick. "The EC and the UNCTAD Liner Code." *Law and Policy in International Business* (March 1979).

Lauriat, George. "Self-Interest Becalms ASEAN Maritime Plan." *Far Eastern Economic Review,* 15 July 1977.

————. "Slow Speed Ahead for ASEAN." *Far Eastern Economic Review,* 16 June 1978.

Lauterpacht, Sir Hersh. "Codification and Development of International Law." *American Journal of International Law* 49 (January 1955).

Lawrence, Samuel A. *International Sea Transport: The Years Ahead.* Lexington, Mass.: D. C. Heath, 1972.

————. *U.S. Merchant Shipping Policies and Politics.* Washington, D.C.: Brookings Institution, 1966.

Lenin, V. I. *Imperialism—The Highest Stage of Capitalism: A Popular Outline.* New York: International Publishers, 1939.

Levikov, G., and M. Khanin. "Some Problems of International Shipping." *International Affairs* (Moscow) (December 1972).

Levine, Daniel, and Sara Ann Platt. "The Contribution of United States Shipbuilding and the Merchant Marine to the Second World War." In Robert A. Kilmarx, ed., *America's Maritime Legacy: A History of the U.S. Merchant Marine and Shipbuilding Since Colonial Times.* Boulder: Westview, 1979.

"The Link Between Ship and Flag." *Shipping World and World Shipbuilding,* 12 February 1958.

Longstreth, Frank. "The City, Industry and the State." In Colin Crouch, ed., *State and Economy in Contemporary Capitalism.* London: St. Martin's Press, 1979.

Lotta, Raymond. *America in Decline,* Vol. 1. Chicago: Banner, 1984.

Lucas, N. J. D. *Energy and the European Communities.* London: Europa, 1977.

————. *Energy in France: Planning, Politics, and Policy.* London: Europa, 1979.

M'Gonigle, R. Michael, and Mark W. Zacher. *Pollution, Politics, and International Law: Tankers at Sea.* Berkeley and Los Angeles: University of California Press, 1979.

McKeown, Timothy J. "Hegemonic Stability Theory and Nineteenth Century Tariff Levels in Europe." *International Organization* 37 (Winter 1983).

Maclay, John S. "The General Shipping Situation." *International Affairs* 22 (October 1946).

Malinowski, Wladyslaw R. "Towards a Change in the International Distribution of Shipping Activity." In L. M. S. Rajwar et al., *Shipping and Developing Countries.* New York: Carnegie Endowment for International Peace, 1971.

Mance, Osborne, and J. E. Wheeler. *International Sea Transport.* London: Oxford University Press, 1945.

Mandel, Ernest. *Europe vs. America.* New York: Monthly Review Press, 1970.

Marder, Arthur. *Anatomy of British Seapower.* New York: Alfred A. Knopf, 1940.

Marine News. *America's Postwar Merchant Marine Forecast.* New York: Marine News, 1944.

Marx, Daniel. *International Shipping Cartels—A Study of Industrial Self-Regulation by Shipping Conferences.* Princeton, N.J.: Princeton University Press, 1953.

Metaxas, Basil N. *Economics of Tramp Shipping.* London: Athlone, 1971.

Meyer, Herbert F. "The Communist Internationale Has a Capitalist Accent." *Fortune* 45 (February 1977).

Middleton, Ian. "Back from the Brink." *Seatrade* (November 1978).

————. "EEC Competition Rules Proposals— A Stab in the Back?" *Seatrade* (September 1980).

————. "Le Nouvel Age?" *Seatrade* (October 1981).

Modelski, George. "Long Cycles of Global Politics and the Nation-State." *Comparative Studies in Society and History* 20 (April 1978).

Moon, Parker T. *Imperialism and World Politics.* New York: Macmillan, 1926.

Moore, K. A. *The Early History of Freight Conferences: Background and Main Developments Until Around 1900.* National Maritime Museum, Maritime Monographs and Reports 51. London: Yale Press Ltd., 1981.

Morris, Michael. "Brazilian Ocean Policy in Historical Perspective." *Journal of Maritime Law and Commerce* 3 (April 1979).

————. "The Domestic Context of Brazilian Maritime Policy." *Ocean Development and International Law: The Journal of Maritime Affairs* 2, no. 4 (April 1977).

————. *International Politics and the Sea: The Case of Brazil.* Boulder: Westview, 1979.

————. "The NIEO and the New Law of the Sea." In Karl P. Souvant and Hajo Hasenpflug, eds., *The NIEO: Confrontation or Cooperation Between North and South?* Boulder: Westview, 1977.

Morrison, Colin. "FMC Rings a Bell on Soviet Bus Shipment." *Seatrade* (May 1978).

Mostert, Noel. *Supership*. New York: Alfred A. Knopf, 1974.

Naess, Erling D. *The Great PanLibHon Controversy: The Fight over Flags of Convenience*. London: Exeter Press, 1972.

———. *My Life: Autobiography of a Shipping Man*. Colchester: Seatrade, 1977.

———. *Tanker Industry: Problems and Prospects*. Bergen: Institute for Shipping Research, 1965.

Nicolaus, Martin. "The Universal Contradiction." *New Left Review* 57 (January–February 1970).

Norman, V. D. *Norwegian Shipping in the National Economy*. Bergen: Institute for Shipping Research, 1971.

North, Douglas. "Ocean Freight Rates and Economic Development." *Journal of Economic History* 18 (December 1958).

Northrup, Herbert, and Richard L. Rowan. *The International Transport Workers Federation*. Philadelphia: The Wharton School, University of Pennsylvania, 1983.

O'Laughlin, Carleen. *The Economics of Sea Transport*. Harmondsworth: Penguin, 1967.

Otterson, J. E. *Foreign Trade and Shipping*. New York: McGraw-Hill, 1945.

Padwa, David J. "The Curriculum of IMCO." *International Organization* 14 (Autumn 1960).

Pantelides, Evangelos T. "Greek Shipping and the Accession of Greece to the EEC." *Marine Policy* 3 (January 1979).

Parboni, Riccardo. *The Dollar and Its Rivals: Recession, Inflation, and International Finance*. London: New Left Books/Verso, 1981.

Perroux, François. "An Outline of the Theory of the Dominant Economy." In George Modelski, ed., *Transnational Corporations and World Order: Readings in International Political Economy*. San Francisco: W. H. Freeman, 1979.

Platt, D. C. M. *Finance, Trade and Politics in British Foreign Policy*. Oxford: Clarendon Press, 1968.

Political and Economic Planning. "The British Shipping Industry." *Planning*, no. 25 (November 1959).

Potter, Pittman. *The Freedom of the Seas in History, Law, and Politics*. New York: Longman, Green, 1924.

President's Materials Policy Commission (Paley Commission). *Resources for Freedom*. Washington, D.C.: G.P.O., 1952.

Puchala, Donald, ed. *Issues Before the 35th General Assembly of the United Nations, 1980–1981*. New York: U.N. Association of the United States, 1980.

Ramsay, R. A. "UNCTAD's Failures." *International Organization* 38 (Spring 1984).

———. "World Trade vs. the Supply of Shipping and Ships." *Marine Policy* 4 (January 1980).

Ranken, M. B. F., ed. *Greenwich Forum VI: World Shipping in the 1980's*. Guildford: Wertbury House, 1981.

Renouf, Anthony. "Loss of Autonomy But Not of Ships." *Seatrade* (January 1981).

———. "The OECD's Herman Janssen: The Role of Government in Shipping." *Seatrade* (August 1976).

———. "The UNCTAD Liner Code: A Critical Dissent." *Bulletin* (Institute of Development Studies, Sussex), Vol. 11 (1980).

Reuben, Edwin P., ed. *The Challenge of the New International Economic Order.* Boulder: Westview, 1981.

Rinman, Thorsten, and Rigmer Linden. *Shipping: How It Works.* Gothenburg, Sweden: Rinman and Linden, 1979.

Robinson, Ross. "Containerization in Ports of Third World Asia: An Overview of Present Patterns and the Direction of Future Growth." *Journal of Maritime Policy and Management* 12 (October–December 1985).

Rochester, Anna. *American Capitalism, 1607–1800.* New York: International Publishers, 1949.

Röhreke, Hans. *The Formal and Material Concept of Flag Equality.* Göteborg: Gumperts, 1961.

Rosenberg, Felix, Jr. *Sea War: The Story of the U.S. Merchant Marine in World War II.* New York: Rinehart, 1956.

Roullier, J. "IMCO: Its Activities and Achievements." *Baltic and International Maritime Conference Monthly Circular.* June 1965.

Rowland, Benjamin, ed. *Balance of Power or Hegemony: The Interwar Monetary System.* New York: New York University Press, 1976.

Russett, Bruce. "The Mysterious Case of Vanishing Hegemony, Or, Is Mark Twain Really Dead?" *International Organization* 39 (Spring 1985).

Safford, Jeffrey J. "Anglo-American Maritime Relations During the Two World Wars: A Comparative Analysis." *American Neptune* 41 (October 1981).

Sager, Karl-Heinz. "Russia Has Signed UNCTAD Code But Will She Ratify?" *Norwegian Shipping News* 34 (March 1978).

———. *Shipping Conferences: A Form of Maritime Cooperation to Which There Is No Alternative.* Hamburg: Hapag-Lloyd, 1979.

———. *A West European Shipowner's Reply to Mr. Averin and to His Involuntary Aides in the United States.* London: Hapag-Lloyd, 1979.

Saraiwa, Carlos Oswaldo. "Brazilian International Shipping Policy." *Lawyer for the Americas* 4 (February 1972).

Sasaki, H. *The Shipping Industry in Japan.* Geneva: I.L.O., 1972.

Saugstad, Jesse. *Shipping and Shipbuilding Subsidies.* Washington, D.C.: G.P.O., 1934.

Saxner, Howard. "On Troubled Waters: Subsidies, Cartels, and the Maritime Commission." In Mark J. Green, ed., *The Monopoly Makers.* New York: Grossman, 1973.

Schiering, Wulf-Pieter. "UNCTAD Liner Code Convention and EC Shipping Policy." *Aussenpolitik: German Foreign Affairs Review* 30 (Second Quarter 1979).

Schmidt, Lienhard. "The International Shipping Policy Issues at UNCTAD V, Manila, May 1979." Hamburg: Hapag-Lloyd, 1979. (Mimeographed.)

Schmidt, Lienhard, and Otto Seiler. "The UNCTAD Code of Conduct for Liner

Conferences—An Analysis and Evaluation of Its Applicability in the U.S. Foreign Trade Lines." Hamburg: Hapag-Lloyd, 1979.

Seatrade. *Arab Shipping 1980: A Seatrade Guide.* Colchester: Seatrade, 1980.

———. *Arab Shipping 1983: A Seatrade Guide.* Colchester: Seatrade, 1983.

———. *EEC Shipping 1979: A Seatrade Guide.* Colchester: Seatrade, 1979.

———. *Far East Shipping 1980/81: A Seatrade Guide.* Colchester: Seatrade, 1981.

———. *Latin American Shipping 1981: A Seatrade Guide.* Colchester: Seatrade, 1981.

———. *Latin American Shipping 1983: A Seatrade Guide.* Colchester: Seatrade, 1983.

———. *United States Yearbook 1983* (5th edition). Colchester: Seatrade, 1983.

Seaward, Nick. "Genuine Link—A Bridge Too Far?" *Seatrade* (September 1980).

———. "Liner Code Battleground for East/West Protagonists." *Seatrade* (August 1980).

Seaward, Nick, et al. "The Eternal Debate—Independents Gain Ground." *Seatrade* (October 1980).

———. "Shipper Report—Introduction: The Changing Balance." *Seatrade* (October 1980).

Serafetinidis, M., et al. "The Development of Greek Shipping Capital and Its Implications for the Political Economy of Greece." *Cambridge Journal of Economics* 5 (September 1981).

Shah, M. J. "The Implementation of the United Nations Convention for Liner Conferences 1974." *Journal of Maritime Law and Commerce* 4 (October 1977).

Shonfield, Andrew. *British Economic Policy Since the War.* London: Penguin, 1958.

Sigma Services. "The U.N. Liner Code." Farnham, Surrey: Sigma Services, 1979.

Silverstein, Harvey. *Superships and Nation States—The Transnational Policies of IMCO.* Boulder: Westview, 1978.

Singh, Nagendra. *Achievements of UNCTAD I and UNCTAD II in the Field of Shipping and Invisibles.* New Delhi: S. Chand, 1969.

Sletmo, Gunnar K., and Ernest W. William. *Liner Conferences in the Container Age.* New York: Macmillan, 1981.

Smith, J. Russell. *Influence of the Great War upon Shipping.* New York: Macmillan, 1919.

Stevens, W. O., and A. Westcott. *A History of Seapower.* New York: Doubleday, 1944.

Stork, Joe. *Middle East Oil and the Energy Crisis.* New York: Monthly Review Press, 1975.

Strange, Susan. "Europe and the United States: The Transatlantic Aspects of Inflation." In Richard Medley, ed., *The Politics of Inflation: A Comparative Analysis.* New York: Pergamon, 1981.

———. "The Management of Surplus Capacity, Or, How Does Theory Stand Up to Protectionism 1970s Style?" *International Organization* 33 (Summer 1979).

———. *Sterling and British Policy.* Oxford: Oxford University Press, 1971.

———. "Still an Extraordinary Power." In Ray Lombra and Bill Witte, eds., *The*

Political Economy of International and Domestic Monetary Relations. Ames: Iowa State University Press, 1982.

———. "Who Runs World Shipping?" *International Affairs* (London) 52, no. 3 (1976).

———. "Who Runs World Shipping? An Experimental Study in International Political Economy." *International Studies Notes* 3 (Fall 1976).

Strange, Susan, and Richard Holland. "International Shipping and the Developing Countries." *World Development* 4 (March 1976).

Sturmey, Stanley G. *British Shipping and World Competition.* London: Athlone, 1962.

———. *The Code—The Next Five Years.* Bremen: Institute of Shipping Economics and Logistics, 1980.

———. "The UNCTAD Code of Conduct for Liner Conferences: A 1985 View." *Journal of Maritime Policy and Management* 13 (October–December 1985).

———. *The Open Registry Controversy and the Development Issue.* Bremen: Institute of Shipping Economics and Logistics, 1983.

———. *Shipping Economics: Collected Papers.* London: Macmillan, 1975.

Todd, Daniel. *The World Shipbuilding Industry.* New York: St. Martin's Press, 1985.

Tresselt, Dag. *The Controversy over the Division of Labor in International Seaborne Transport.* Bergen: Institute for Shipping Research, 1970.

Turner, Louis. *Oil Companies in the International System.* London: Allen and Unwin, 1979.

University of Wales, Department of Maritime Studies. *Liner Shipping in the U.S. Trades: A UWIST Study for CENSA.* London: University of Wales, Department of Maritime Studies, 1978.

Valkenier, Elizabeth K. "Development Issues in Recent Soviet Scholarship." *World Politics* 32 (July 1980).

———. *The Soviet Union and the Third World: An Economic Bind.* Boulder: Westview, 1983.

von Geusau, F. A. M. Alting, ed. *Energy in the European Communities.* Leiden: A. W. Sijthoff, 1975.

Walker-Leigh, Vanya. "Will French Shipping's Brave New World Ever Be Built?" *Seatrade* (February 1982).

Wallerstein, Immanuel. *The Modern World System,* Vol. 2. New York: Academic Press, 1980.

Waltz, Kenneth. *Theory of International Politics.* Reading, Mass.: Addison-Wesley, 1979.

Whitehurst, Clifton, Jr. *The U.S. Merchant Marine: In Search of an Enduring Maritime Policy.* Annapolis: Naval Institute Press, 1983.

Williams, Judith Blow. *British Commercial Policy and Trade Expansion, 1750–1850.* Oxford: Clarendon Press, 1972.

Williamson, J. A. *The Ocean in English History.* Oxford: Clarendon Press, 1941.

Wioncek, Miguel, ed. *Latin American Economic Integration: Experiences and Prospects.* New York: Praeger, 1966.

World Bank. *The Developing Countries and International Shipping*. Washington, D.C.: World Bank, November 1981.

Yeats, Alexander J. *Trade Barriers Facing Developing Countries*. New York: St. Martin's Press, 1979.

Young, Oran. "International Regimes: Problems of Concept Formation." *World Politics* 32 (April 1980).

Zeis, Paul M. *American Shipping Policy*. Princeton, N.J.: Princeton University Press, 1938.

Zimmerman, Erich W. *Ocean Shipping*. New York: Prentice-Hall, 1923.

III. Trade Publications

American Shipper. Jacksonville, Florida.
Containerization International. London.
Container News. New York.
EEC Shipping: Facts and Figures. Brussels: CAACE.
FACS Forum. New York.
Fairplay International Shipping Weekly. London.
General Council of British Shipping, *Annual Reports*. London.
German Shipowners Association, *Annual Reports*. Hamburg.
Journal of Commerce. New York.
Lloyds List. London: Lloyds of London Press.
Norwegian Shipping News. Oslo.
Polish Maritime News. Gdynia.
Seatrade Magazine. Colchester, U.K.
Soviet Shipping. Moscow: Association of Soviet Shipowners.

INDEX

Compositor: G&S Typesetters, Inc.
Printer: Edwards Brothers, Inc.
Binder: Edwards Brothers, Inc.
Text: 10/13 Galliard
Display: Friz Quadrata